CAMBRIDGE GREE

Slingers from Nineveh (Xenophon's Mespila), *c.* 700 BC

XENOPHON

ANABASIS

BOOK III

LUUK HUITINK
Ruprecht-Karls-Universität Heidelberg

TIM ROOD
University of Oxford

CAMBRIDGE
UNIVERSITY PRESS

University Printing House, Cambridge CB2 8BS, United Kingdom

One Liberty Plaza, 20th Floor, New York, NY 10006, USA

477 Williamstown Road, Port Melbourne, VIC 3207, Australia

314–321, 3rd Floor, Plot 3, Splendor Forum, Jasola District Centre, New Delhi – 110025, India

79 Anson Road, #06–04/06, Singapore 079906

Cambridge University Press is part of the University of Cambridge.

It furthers the University's mission by disseminating knowledge in the pursuit of education, learning, and research at the highest international levels of excellence.

www.cambridge.org
Information on this title: www.cambridge.org/9781107079236
DOI: 10.1017/9781139941457

First published 2019

Printed and bound in Great Britain by Clays Ltd, Elcograf S.p.A.

A catalogue record for this publication is available from the British Library.

Library of Congress Cataloging-in-Publication Data
NAMES: Xenophon, author. | Huitink, Luuk, 1981– editor. | Rood, Tim, editor.
TITLE: Xenophon, Anabasis book III / Luuk Huitink, Tim Rood.
OTHER TITLES: Anabasis. Book III | Cambridge Greek and Latin classics.
DESCRIPTION: Cambridge : Cambridge University Press, 2019. | Series: Cambridge Greek and Latin classics
IDENTIFIERS: LCCN 2018027195 | ISBN 9781107079236
SUBJECTS: LCSH: Xenophon. Anabasis.
CLASSIFICATION: LCC PA4494 .A63 2019 | DDC 935/.05092–dc23
LC record available at https://lccn.loc.gov/2018027195

ISBN 978-1-107-07923-6 Hardback
ISBN 978-1-107-43743-2 Paperback

CONTENTS

MAPS AND FIGURES

MAPS

FIGURES

PREFACE

The 'Xenophon factory' (Albert Rijksbaron's term) is ripe for reopening. Scholarship on both Xenophon and the Greek language has progressed considerably since the profusion of editions of *Anabasis* (aimed mainly at schools) in the nineteenth and early twentieth centuries. The aims of this volume are to offer up-to-date guidance on literary, historical and cultural aspects of *Anabasis* and to help students read Greek better. To achieve these goals, the volume draws on the pragmatic approach to the Greek language that provides the methodology for the *Cambridge Grammar of Classical Greek* (of which LH is one of the authors) and devotes specific attention to Xenophon's lexical innovations. In the conviction that Xenophon is just as important (if not more so) to the development of Greek historiography, and of Greek prose in general, as Herodotus and Thucydides, we have made Xenophon's narrative strategies another focal point of this commentary, and we frequently home in on the reception of episodes from *Anabasis* III in antiquity.

This commentary could not have been completed without help from many quarters. We are extremely grateful to the series editors Pat Easterling, Neil Hopkinson and Richard Hunter for their comments and guidance; to Michael Sharp, Marianne Nield and Mary Bongiovi for overseeing the production at Cambridge University Press; and to Iveta Adams for her wonderfully clear and rigorous copy-editing. Rhiannon Ash, Emily Baragwanath, Michel Buijs, John Dillery, Marco Dorati, Michael Flower, William Furley, Simon Hornblower, Christopher Pelling, Albert Rijksbaron, Nick Stylianou and Athanassios Vergados all provided comments on sections of the commentary, while Andreas Willi read part of the Introduction. Chris Pelling and Andreas Willi also answered specific queries, as did John Ma, Christopher Tuplin and the late Martin West. Stephen Duncan, Antoine Jérusalem and Chris Stevens, the Engineering tutors at St Hugh's College, offered advice on 3.5.8–11. Our interpretation of 3.4.21 has been helped by extensive discussion with Chris Pelling, Scott Scullion and David Thomas (all of whom still disagree with us, and with each other). David Thomas further deserves especial thanks for his detailed comments on the entire volume and further email exchanges about particular ἀπορίαι. We also received valuable feedback on drafts from participants in a number of graduate seminars on Xenophon (TR's at UCLA in spring 2015, LH's at Leiden University in winter 2016 and Emily Baragwanath's at UNC Chapel Hill in spring 2016) as well as from participants in workshops on commentaries held in Heidelberg and Amsterdam. More practical assistance was offered by Lucy Gwynn of Eton College Library, who supplied photographs of MS E; Emily Robotham, who provided bibliographical help at an early stage; Jonathan Griffiths, who did most of the work on the indexes; and Lionel Scott, who sent a CD-ROM with images from Google Earth for each stage of the route.

For LH, work on the commentary began at Merton College, Oxford, and he wishes to express a debt of gratitude to the Warden and Fellows of that institution. Soon after, however, the commentary became integral to his work in the Heidelberg ERC group *Experience and Teleology in Ancient Narrative* (ERC Grant Agreement n. 312321 (AncNar)); he wishes in particular to acknowledge the support of Jonas Grethlein. Finally LH would like to thank Rhiannon Ash for her hospitality in Oxford at various times. TR would like to thank Andrea Capovilla and his son Simon for putting up with Xenophon with such good humour, and the Principal and Fellows of St Hugh's College, Oxford, for providing an ideal setting in which to work as well as a year's sabbatical leave in 2014–15.

K. W. Krüger's 1826 commentary on *Anabasis* starts with a dedication ΤΟΙΣ ΤΩΝ ΜΥΡΙΩΝ ΜΙΜΗΤΑΙΣ ΤΟΙΣ ΠΡΟΣ ΤΗΝ ΤΩΝ ΒΑΡΒΑΡΩΝ ΚΑΙ ΚΡΥΠΤΟΒΑΡΒΑΡΩΝ ΩΜΟΤΗΤΑ ΚΑΙ ΑΠΙΣΤΙΑΝ ΚΑΙ ΑΣΕΒΕΙΑΝ ΚΑΙ ΛΟΓΩΙ ΚΑΙ ΕΡΓΩΙ ΑΓΩΝΙΣΑΜΕΝΟΙΣ ΤΕ ΚΑΙ ΑΓΩΝΙΖΟΜΕΝΟΙΣ ('to the imitators of the Ten Thousand, who have contended and contend in word and deed against the savagery, faithlessness and impiety of the barbarians and crypto-barbarians'). The surprising thing about this dedication is that it purports to come from Xenophon himself, relayed to the commentator from the underworld by the god Hermes. Hermes' accompanying letter suggests that the 'imitators' Xenophon had in mind were not just those fighting at that time for Greek independence but also liberals struggling against reactionary political and educational measures in Prussia following the defeat of Napoleon. We have no message from Xenophon to report, and the strong racial overtones in the reception history of *Anabasis* are one reason why we are reluctant to invoke the language of 'crypto-barbarism' ourselves. But we hope at least that this collaboration may stand as a testimonial to the benefits of co-operation between European nations.

As for the dedication of our own work: LH would like to dedicate it to his teacher, Roel Groenink, who introduced him to *Anabasis* at school and turned that first encounter with Greek literature into a transformative experience; TR would like to express his deep gratitude to Robert Parker and Simon Hornblower, his tutors while he was an undergraduate at Oriel and a constant source of inspiration since.

ABBREVIATIONS

GENERAL PRINCIPLES

Abbreviations of ancient authors and works generally follow *OCD* and LSJ.

'X.' refers to the narrator and the historical figure, while 'Xenophon' refers to the character in *Anabasis*, and 'X(enophon)' is used when it is impossible to distinguish the historical figure from the character.

T followed by a numeral refers to the outline in the Appendix on topography (pp. 42–4).

EDITIONS AND COMMENTARIES CITED BY THE EDITOR'S NAME

Bandini, M., and L.-A. Dorion, *Xénophon: Mémorables*, 3 vols., Paris, 2000–11

Barrett, W. S., *Euripides: Hippolytos*, Oxford, 1964

Bowie, A. M., *Herodotus: Histories Book VIII*, Cambridge, 2007

Brennan, S. G., and D. Thomas, *The landmark Xenophon's Anabasis*, New York, forthcoming

Dindorf, L., *Xenophontis Expeditio Cyri*, Leipzig, 1825; 2nd edn Oxford, 1852

Dover, K. J., *Aristophanes: Clouds*, Oxford, 1968

Dover, K. J., *Aristophanes: Frogs*, Oxford, 1993

Dover, K. J., *Plato: Symposium*, Cambridge, 1980

Flower, M. A., and J. Marincola, *Herodotus: Book IX*, Cambridge, 2002

Fraenkel, E., *Aeschylus: Agamemnon*, 3 vols., Oxford, 1950

Hainsworth, B., *The Iliad: a commentary*, vol. III: *Books 9–12*, Cambridge, 1993

Hornblower, S., *Herodotus: Book V*, Cambridge, 2013

Hude, C., *Xenophontis expeditio Cyri*, rev. J. Peters, Leipzig, 1972

Hunter, L. W., *Aeneas on siegecraft: a critical edition*, Oxford, 1927

Hutchinson, G. O., *Aeschylus: Seven against Thebes*, Oxford, 1985

Jebb, R. C., *Sophocles: the plays and fragments*, Part V: *The Trachiniae*, Cambridge, 1892

Kraus, C. S., *Livy: Ab urbe condita Book VI*, Cambridge, 1994

Krüger, K. W., *Ξενοφῶντος Κύρου Ἀνάβασις*, Halle, 1826

Lendle, O., *Kommentar zu Xenophons Anabasis (Bücher 1–7)*, Darmstadt, 1995

Lenfant, D., *Ctésias de Cnide: La Perse; L'Inde; autres fragments*, Paris, 2004

Lipka, M., *Xenophon's Spartan constitution: introduction, text, commentary*, Berlin, 2002

MacDowell, D. M., *Andocides: On the mysteries*, Oxford, 1962

MacDowell, D. M., *Gorgias: Encomium of Helen*, Bristol, 1982
Marchant, E. C., *Xenophontis opera omnia*, vol. III: *Expeditio Cyri*, Oxford, 1904
Masqueray, P., *Xénophon: Anabase*, 2 vols., Paris, 1930–1
Mather, M. W., and J. W. Hewitt, *Xenophon's Anabasis: Books I–IV*, New York, 1910
Mayor, J. E. B., *Thirteen satires of Juvenal*, 2 vols., London, 1886–8
Mülke, C., *Solons politische Elegien und Iamben (Fr. 1–13; 32–37 West)*, Munich, 2002
Nisbet, R. G. M., and N. Rudd, *A commentary on Horace, Odes, Book III*, Oxford, 2004
Oakley, S. P., *A commentary on Livy: Books VI–X*, 4 vols., Oxford, 1997–2005
Patillon, M., *Pseudo-Aelius Aristide: Arts rhétoriques, Livre II*, Paris, 2002
Pelling, C. B. R., *Plutarch: Life of Antony*, Cambridge, 1998
Pendrick, G. J., *Antiphon the Sophist: the fragments*, Cambridge, 2002
Pomeroy, S. B., *Xenophon: Oeconomicus: a social and historical commentary*, Oxford, 1994
Rehdantz, C., *Xenophons Anabasis*, 2nd edn, 2 vols., Berlin, 1867–9
Rhodes, P. J., *A commentary on the Aristotelian Athenaion politeia*, 2nd edn, Oxford, 1993
Rijksbaron, A., *Plato: Ion, or On the Iliad*, Leiden, 2007
Russell, D. A., *Longinus: On the sublime*, Oxford, 1964
Rusten, J. S., *Thucydides: The Peloponnesian war, Book II*, Cambridge, 1989
Stronk, J. P., *The Ten Thousand in Thrace: an archaeological and historical commentary on Xenophon's Anabasis, Books VI.iii–vi – VII*, Amsterdam, 1995
Stylianou, P. J., *A historical commentary on Diodorus Siculus Book 15*, Oxford, 1998
Todd, S. C., *A commentary on Lysias, Speeches 1–11*, Oxford, 2007
Walbank, F. W., *A historical commentary on Polybius*, 3 vols., Oxford, 1957–9
Wankel, H., *Demosthenes: Rede für Ktesiphon über den Kranz*, 2 vols., Heidelberg, 1976
Whitehead, D., *Aineias the Tactician: How to survive under siege*, Oxford, 1990
Wilamowitz-Moellendorff, U. von, *Euripides: Herakles*, 2 vols., Berlin, 1889

OTHER ABBREVIATIONS

Barr. R. Talbert, ed., *Barrington atlas of the Greek and Roman world*, Princeton, 2000
BNJ I. Worthington, ed., *Brill's new Jacoby* (www.brillonline.com), 2007–
CCX M. A. Flower, ed., *The Cambridge companion to Xenophon*, Cambridge, 2017

CGCG E. van Emde Boas, A. Rijksbaron, L. Huitink and M. de Bakker, *Cambridge grammar of classical Greek*, Cambridge, 2019

Chantraine P. Chantraine, *Dictionnaire étymologique de la langue grecque*, Paris, 1968–80

CT S. Hornblower, *A commentary on Thucydides*, 3 vols., Oxford, 1991–2008

FGE D. L. Page, ed., *Further Greek epigrams*, Cambridge, 1981

FGrH F. Jacoby, ed., *Die Fragmente der griechischen Historiker*, 15 vols., Berlin and Leiden, 1923–58

FHG C. Müller, ed., *Fragmenta historicorum Graecorum*, Berlin, 1841–70

FRHist T. J. Cornell, ed., *The fragments of the Roman historians*, 3 vols., Oxford, 2013

Gautier L. Gautier, *La langue de Xénophon*, Geneva, 1911

GP J. D. Denniston, *The Greek particles*, 2nd edn, Oxford, 1954

GSW W. K. Pritchett, *The Greek state at war*, 5 vols., Berkeley, 1971–91

HCT A. W. Gomme, A. Andrewes and K. J. Dover, *A historical commentary on Thucydides*, 5 vols., Oxford, 1945–81

K–A R. Kassel and C. Austin, eds., *Poetae comici Graeci*, Berlin, 1983–

K–G R. Kühner and B. Gerth, *Ausführliche Grammatik der griechischen Sprache*. Part II: *Satzlehre*, 2 vols., Hanover, 1898–1904

LGPN *A lexicon of Greek personal names*, 8 vols. published to date, Oxford, 1987–

LSJ H. D. Liddell, R. Scott and H. Stuart Jones, *A Greek–English Lexicon*, with revised supplement edited by P. G. W. Glare and A. A. Thomson, Oxford, 1996

ML R. Meiggs and D. M. Lewis, *A selection of Greek historical inscriptions to the end of the fifth century* BC, rev. edn, Oxford, 1988

OCD[4] S. Hornblower, A. J. S. Spawforth and E. Eidinow, eds., *The Oxford classical dictionary*, 4th edn, Oxford, 2012

OGIS W. Dittenberger, *Orientis Graecae inscriptiones selectae*, 2 vols., Leipzig, 1903–5

RLA *Reallexikon der Assyriologie und vorderasiatischen Archäologie*, 14 vols. published to date, Berlin, 1928–

SAGN I. J. F. de Jong *et al.*, eds., *Studies in ancient Greek narrative*, Leiden and Boston, 4 vols. published to date, 2004–

Smyth H. W. Smyth, *Greek grammar*, revised by G. M. Messing, Cambridge, MA, 1956

Sturz F. W. Sturz, *Lexicon Xenophonteum*, 4 vols., Leipzig, 1801–4

Threatte L. Threatte, *The grammar of Attic inscriptions*, 2 vols., Berlin, 1980–96

TrGF B. Snell, R. Kannicht and S. Radt, eds., *Tragicorum Graecorum fragmenta*, 5 vols., Göttingen, 1971–2004

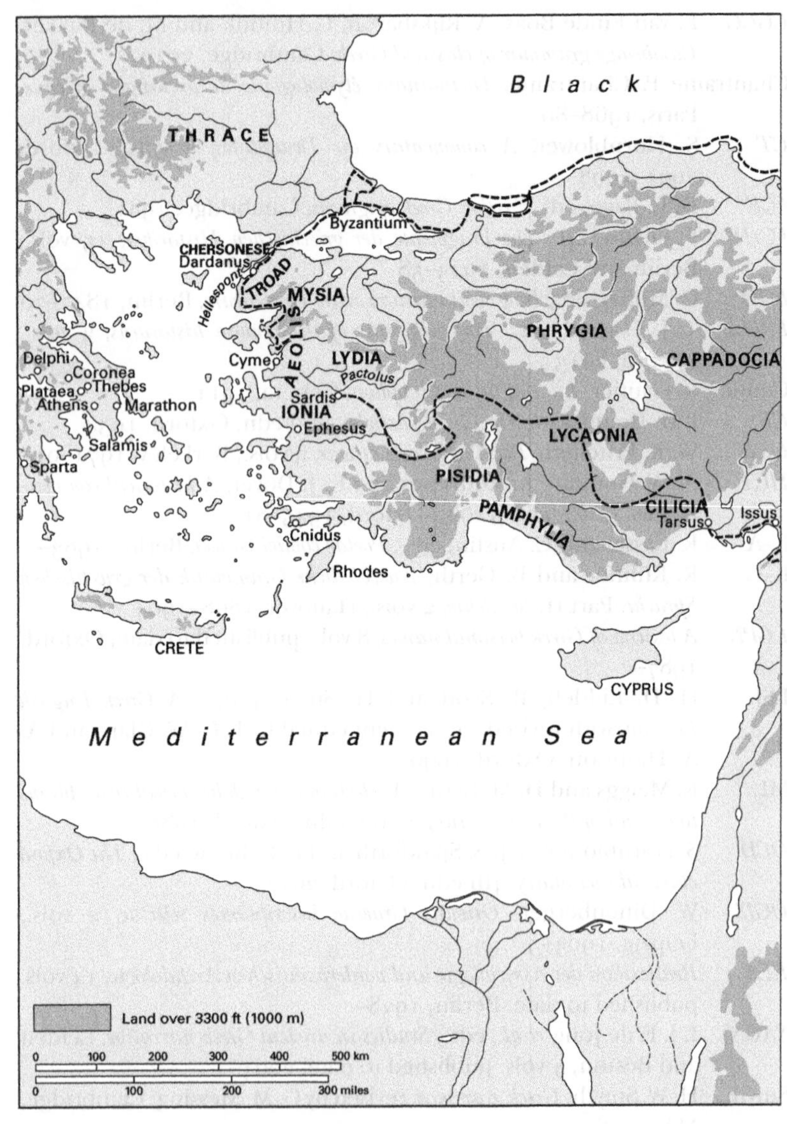

Map 1. The route of the Ten Thousand

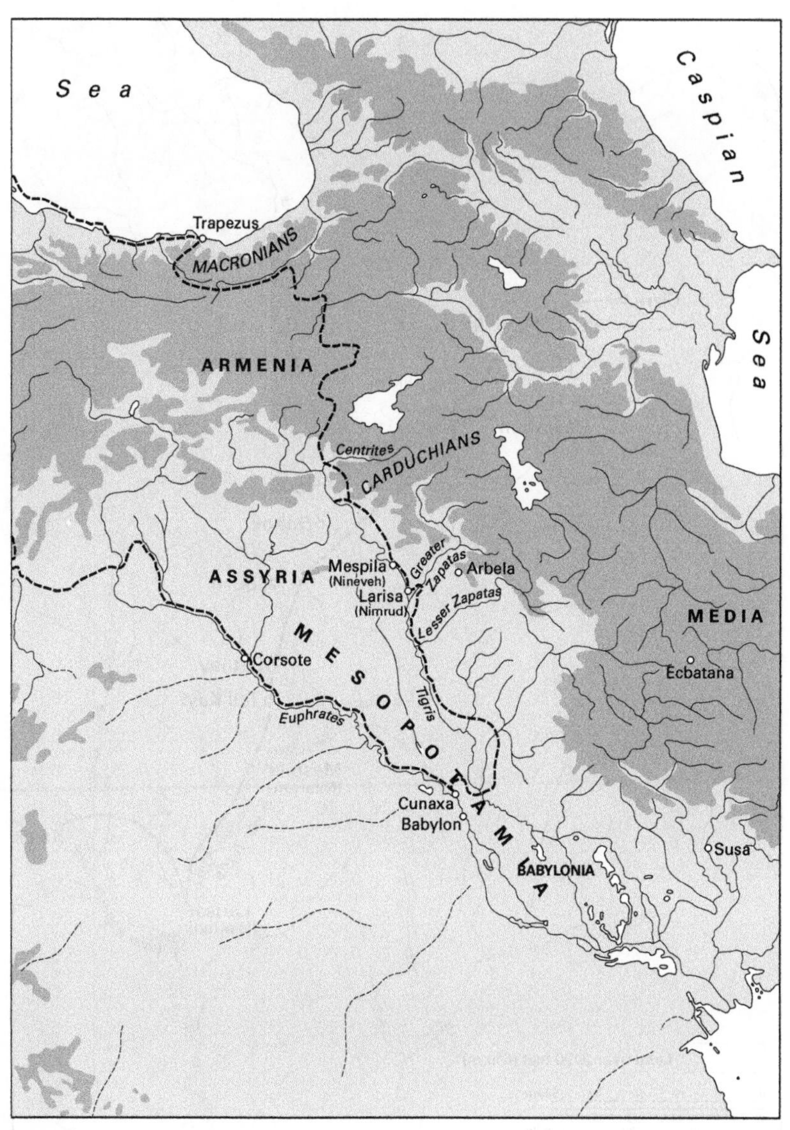
Sea
Caspian Sea
Trapezus
MACRONIANS
ARMENIA
Centrites
CARDUCHIANS
ASSYRIA
Mespila
(Nineveh)
Larisa
(Nimrud)
Greater Zapatas
Arbela
Lesser Zapatas
MEDIA
Ecbatana
MESOPOTAMIA
Corsote
Tigris
Euphrates
Cunaxa
Babylon
Susa
BABYLONIA

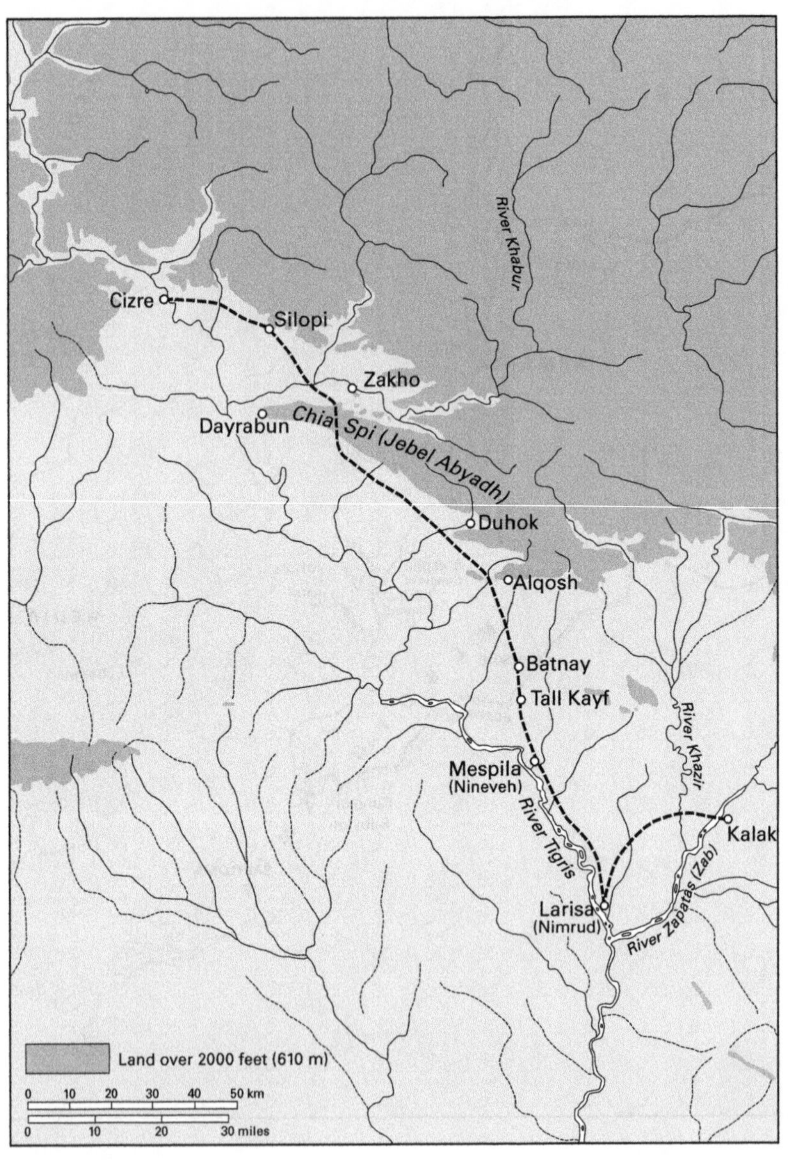

Map 2. The route in Book 3

INTRODUCTION

1 CYRUS AND THE PERSIAN EMPIRE

The events X. describes in *Anabasis* 3[1] were an unexpected consequence of the ambitions of a Persian prince, Cyrus. In 407[2] Cyrus had been appointed by his father, Darius II, to a special command in western Asia Minor. Previously the Persian satrap (3.4.31n.) Tissaphernes had played off the two protagonists of the Peloponnesian War (431–404), Athens and Sparta, against each other. But now Cyrus' arrival marked the start of concerted Persian support for Sparta – the ultimate cause of Spartan victory in the war. In return, Cyrus received Spartan support (700 hoplite troops under a Spartan general Chirisophus) for his attempt to overthrow his brother Artaxerxes, who had succeeded to the Persian throne on the death of Darius in 405. Despite a bold march into the heart of the Persian empire, the attempt failed, and it was this failure and the subsequent breakdown of negotiations with the Persians that left the surviving Greek soldiers in the desperate position on the banks of the Greater Zab described at the start of Book 3.

What had been at stake in Cyrus' rebellion was rule over the vast Persian empire, which stretched from the shores of Asia Minor to Afghanistan and India.[3] At around the start of the first millennium, the Persians, who spoke a language from the Iranian branch of Indo-European, had moved (probably from central Asia) to what is now the region of Fars (Greek *Persis*) in south-west Iran. They appear as tribute-payers in Assyrian inscriptions from the ninth century, and seem to have fallen under the control of the Medes (also speakers of an Iranian language) in the latter part of the seventh century, after the overthrow of the Assyrians (3.4.7–12n.). The Persian empire itself was founded by Cyrus II (known as 'the elder Cyrus' or 'Cyrus the Great'; Old Persian *Kūrush*), who ruled 559–530. Cyrus defeated the Medes, conquered the wealthy Lydian empire in western Asia Minor, thereby bringing under his sway the Greek cities in that region which had been subjected by the Lydian king Croesus, and then seized control in Babylonia. He also expanded Persian rule eastwards. Cyrus' son Cambyses extended the empire further by conquering

[1] The title *Anabasis* ('March upcountry') applies properly only to the first of its seven books; similarly *Cyropaedia* applies only to the first stages of that work. It is not certain that the titles of X.'s works are original.

[2] Dates in sections 1–6 of the Introduction are BC unless indicated otherwise.

[3] Briant 2002 is the fundamental study of the Persian empire. See also Waters 2014 for an accessible shorter account and Kuhrt 2007 for a valuable collection of sources. For X.'s presentation of Persia, see *CCX* 360–75; Hirsch 1985; Tuplin 2004a.

Egypt in 525. Cambyses' death was followed by political disorder which was resolved when Darius seized power and founded the Achaemenid dynasty (Darius sought to connect his own family with Cyrus' by claiming a common ancestor, Achaemenes). It was during Darius' reign that the first major clashes between Greeks and Persians occurred: the Greek cities in Ionia revolted from Persian rule in 499 and received help from Athens, which led to the burning of part of the satrapal capital Sardis. Some years later, in 490, Darius sought revenge by sending an expedition against mainland Greece, but his army was defeated by the Athenians at Marathon (3.2.11n.). His son Xerxes sent a larger expedition in 480, but this too was defeated (3.2.13n.), though it did succeed in burning the Athenian acropolis. From that point the Persians made no further attempts on mainland Greece; when opportunity arose towards the end of the century, however, they sought to strengthen their hold on Asia Minor (their claim to which they had never abandoned) by supporting Sparta against Athens, which after the victory over Xerxes had established a position of hegemony over many of the coastal cities and offshore islands (a peace treaty between Persia and Athens may have been agreed in the early 440s).

The account offered in *Anabasis* of the background to Cyrus' revolt is sketchy. X. mentions the official Spartan support only allusively (1.2.21, 4.2; contrast the much more explicit treatment at *Hell.* 3.1.1).[4] He says nothing about the state of the Persian empire (Cyrus may have been encouraged to strike when he did by a revolt against Persian rule in Egypt (cf. 2.1.14, 5.13)) and little about the attachments of the Persian nobility.[5] As for Cyrus' motives, it is Plutarch (*Artax.* 2.4) who mentions that his claim to the throne was based on his having been the first son born after Darius became king – though this version may be influenced by Herodotus' possibly unreliable account of the succession of Xerxes (7.2–3). X. suggests instead that Cyrus' revolt was an escalation of the suspicion between the brothers that had been fostered by Tissaphernes, who felt himself overshadowed by Cyrus' appointment in Asia Minor. This account might seem to prepare a bit too well for the stress on the mutual suspicion between Greeks and Persians that features strongly in *Anabasis* 2–3. That it is at least plausible may nonetheless be seen from other examples of fraternal hostility in the Achaemenid court: thus Darius II had seized power by overthrowing a half-brother who had himself killed his brother.

[4] Similarly sketchy is X.'s account of relations after the army's arrival at the Black Sea coast between Spartan officials and the Spartiate Neon, who takes over (unelected) from Chirisophus when the latter is absent seeking ships from the Spartans and then after his death (see Huitink and Rood 2016: 217–18).

[5] Against recent Achaemenid historians who stress loyalty to the king, Lee 2016 argues that many elite Persians hedged their bets.

A clearer picture emerges in *Anabasis* of the way Cyrus presented his plans to the Greek mercenaries. When he was gathering the different contingents, he used a variety of pretexts, including the suggestion that he was preparing a punitive expedition against the Pisidians (1.1.11, 3.1.9), who occupied a mountainous region north of Lycia and Pamphylia and were perceived as troublesome (3.2.23n.). This suggestion was later used as a pretext for the whole army (1.2.1). Later still, when the army mutinied at Tarsus, after bypassing the Pisidians in its march through Asia Minor, Cyrus responded by claiming that he was leading them against a personal enemy on the Euphrates (1.3.20) rather than against the king, as they suspected (1.3.1). It was only when the Greeks reached the Euphrates that he finally revealed that he was actually leading them against the king (1.4.11).

X.'s detailed picture of Cyrus' subterfuge is complicated by his claim that the object of the expedition was known all along to one of the Greek generals – the Spartan exile Clearchus (3.1.10).[6] The first-century universal historian Diodorus, by contrast, claims that all the generals knew that Cyrus was marching against the king (14.19.9). In view of the controversy generated by Cyrus' expedition, X. might be thought to be defending the other generals and the army as a whole from the charge that they knowingly sought to overthrow the king (for an Athenian, even following Cyrus was controversial, given his role in the Peloponnesian War, 3.1.5n.). Diodorus' statement, however, may not accurately reflect his likely source, the fourth-century historian Ephorus, or else Ephorus may have extrapolated this claim from X.[7] In any case, X.'s claim that Clearchus alone knew of Cyrus' plans is restricted to those Greeks who were with Cyrus from the start; Cyrus' aim must have been known to Chirisophus, but he joined the expedition only at a later date.[8] X.'s main concern, then, is to build up a picture of close collaboration between Cyrus and Clearchus: on his first mention, Clearchus is said to be admired by Cyrus (1.1.9); he is shown manipulating the soldiers into following Cyrus when they mutiny at Tarsus (1.3); he is the only Greek admitted into Cyrus' tent for the trial of an errant Persian officer (1.6); and he holds a position on the right wing in the decisive battle against the king at Cunaxa (1.8.4).[9]

The march through Asia Minor and down the Euphrates is described by X. in *Anabasis* 1. That book ends with Cyrus' death at Cunaxa and his

[6] Earlier X. states that the soldiers suspected all the generals of having had prior knowledge (1.4.12); at 1.3.21 ('no one had been told even then that he was leading them against the king, at least not openly (ἐν τῶι γε φανερῶι)') he hints at secret information.

[7] Stylianou 2004: 87.

[8] Bassett 2001: 12 wrongly impugns X.'s reliability on this account.

[9] Cunaxa is named as the location of the battle at Plut. *Artax.* 8.2 (but not by X.).

Greek mercenaries stranded in the heart of the Persian empire. The rest of *Anabasis* tells the story of their unexpected survival – their return to the sea up the Tigris valley (Book 3), through Kurdistan and Armenia (Book 4), their march along the Black Sea coast, and finally, on their approach to the Hellespont and after they have crossed over into Europe, their dealings with the Spartans (now the dominant power in Greece) and Seuthes, a Thracian dynast (Books 5–7). It is an exciting tale in its own right and a useful source for the Persian empire (e.g. 3.4.17, 31nn.; Tuplin 2004a) – even if modern Achaemenid historians have been frustrated that it does not do more to supplement the knowledge gained in the past century from the discovery of clay tablets from Persepolis and other archival material. But the fame of the account has above all lain in its depiction of the army with which Xenophon was serving.

2 THE TEN THOUSAND

The Ten Thousand has been the term used since antiquity to describe the mercenaries recruited by Cyrus' Greek generals;[10] in *Anabasis* X. most often calls them 'the Greeks' (for his other works, see 3.2.17n.). His careful delineation of the different contingents reveals that their total number was in fact 12,900 – that is, 10,600 heavy-armed troops (hoplites) and 2,300 light-armed (peltasts). It was presumably the largest unit of Greek mercenaries ever assembled, foreshadowing the increasing importance of mercenaries and the growing specialization of the art of war in the Greek world in the fourth century.[11]

The Ten Thousand have often been seen as a model political unit. Thus Edward Gibbon contrasted the lassitude of a Roman army stranded in Mesopotamia after the death of the emperor Julian with the vigorous response of the Ten Thousand at the start of *Anabasis* 3, following the loss of their generals: 'Instead of tamely resigning themselves to the secret deliberations and private views of a single person, the united councils of the Greeks were inspired by the generous enthusiasm of a popular assembly: where the mind of each citizen is filled with the love of glory, the pride of freedom, and the contempt of death.'[12] From the nineteenth century onwards, the qualities displayed by the Ten Thousand have been

[10] Plut. *Ant.* 45.12; Arr. *Anab.* 1.12.3, 2.7.8; Justin 5.11.10; *Suda* ξ 48 Adler; note also the interpolation ἐκ τῶν ἀμφὶ τοὺς μυρίους in the **f** MSS at *An.* 5.3.3. The term could have been partly inspired by *An.* 3.2.31, 5.7.9, 6.4.3 (cf. Schaefer 1961 on 10,000 as a desirable size for a city). Bonner 1910 points out that they were roughly 10,000 when they reached the Black Sea.

[11] On Greek mercenaries, see Parke 1933; Trundle 2004. On the influence of this increasing specialization on X.'s language, see section 5 below.

[12] Gibbon 1994: I.951. Cf. Gillies 1790: II.317 n. 2.

particularly associated with democratic Athens: the French historian Hippolyte Taine called them 'a sort of Athens wandering in the middle of Asia' (though only a handful of the soldiers are known to have come from that city).[13]

However they have been viewed subsequently, the Ten Thousand did not start out as a '*polis* on the march'. They were originally part of a much larger army that included many non-Greeks. While the Greek component of this larger army always seems to have marched together, it was itself a collection of smaller units, ranging from 500 to 2,000 in size, enlisted by Cyrus' Greek generals (στρατηγοί) in Asia Minor, the Chersonese and the Greek mainland. These units were divided into companies (λόχοι) of about a hundred men, each led by a captain (λοχαγός) and itself divided into still smaller units (3.4.21n.); there were also strong bonds between tent-mates (σύσκηνοι).[14] Besides this, the contingents were at times caught up in the rivalries among the Greek generals who were competing for Cyrus' favour: during the mutiny at Tarsus, Clearchus attracted to his contingent more than 2,000 of the troops with Xenias and Pasion (1.3.7) – both of whom soon thereafter abandoned the expedition (1.4.7); later, the troops of the main rivals, Clearchus and Meno, almost came to blows (1.5.12–17).

In X.'s account, it is after the arrest of the generals – in the dramatic scene at the start of Book 3 that was picked out by Gibbon – that the Ten Thousand first function as a unified political community. It is true that, after Cyrus' death, there are no further hints of different contingents within the Greek army (though rivalries among the generals continue). But decisions are taken by the generals without consultation of the troops (e.g. 2.1.2–5, 8–23, 2.3–5, 8–12), though the troops do sometimes make

[13] See Rood 2004b: 99–100.

[14] These subdivisions do not in themselves weaken the parallel with the *polis*, given that the *polis* too had numerous other types of social bond; the stimulating study by Lee 2007 argues nonetheless for the priority of these small-scale ties over the *polis* model (articulated in the classic sociological analysis of Nussbaum 1967) – though part of Lee's evidence is the experience of modern soldiers. Cf. also Dalby 1992; Dillery 1995: 63–95. Hornblower 2004a sees the democratic pattern in other Greek armies too. For analogies of city and army, see e.g. Soph. *Aj.* 1073–6, *Phil.* 386–8; Isoc. 6 (proposal that the Spartans should abandon their city and live like an army off the land); cf. Hdt. 8.61 and the Thucydidean image of the Athenian army in Sicily as like a city (Avery 1973: 8–13). The political language of the city was applied to symposia (Dover on Pl. *Symp.* 176a1–178a5) and to festivals (the women's assembly in Ar. *Thesm.*). Within *Anabasis,* note the accusation that Xenophon is a 'demagogue' (7.6.4); the terms for voting at 1.4.15, 3.2.9 (with qualifications in n.), 38(n.), 5.1.4, 14, 6.11, 35, 7.3.14; the judicial language at 4.4.14, 5.7.34, 6.6.18; the formal dealings with Greek cities (e.g. the offer of ξένια at 6.1.15); also 3.1.37, 3.20nn.

their views heard (e.g. 2.4.2–4, 5.29), and among the generals Clearchus assumes a leading role owing to his personal authority (2.2.5; cf. 2.2.21, 4.5, 18). At the start of Book 3, by contrast, new generals (Xenophon among them) are elected to replace the ones who have been lost, and the whole army meets and votes by hand on a range of proposals. But it is only a democratic community in a limited sense: no further such meetings take place in the course of the retreat to the sea, and even at the first assembly speakers resort to voting only because they are sure of the outcome (the votes are unanimous), to give the troops the feeling that their destiny is in their own hands. It is still the generals (sometimes with the captains) who make all the strategic and tactical decisions (3.3.11–19, 4.21, 5.7–12, 14–17, 4.1.12–13, 26–8, 3.14–15, 6.7–19).

X. presents the army as most similar to a '*polis* on the march' after its arrival at the Black Sea: it now holds frequent meetings,[15] votes on some measures (albeit still with no opposition indicated), and negotiates as a body with the Greek and non-Greek inhabitants (e.g. 5.5.7–25, 6.2–14, 6.1.15). Even so, the soldiers are hostile to the possibility of establishing a permanent new *polis* on the Black Sea coast (5.6.19, 7.1, 6.4.7). The army's unity also succumbs to the renewed prominence of its ethnic divisions: an Arcadian group splits off for a time, with disastrous results (6.3; cf. 5.5.5). Even when the army is united, moreover, the presentation is not consistently positive: the soldiers increasingly succumb to greed, at one point even electing a single leader for the sake of greater efficiency and profit in plundering expeditions (6.1.17–18); and their violence alienates the Greek cities along the coast (e.g. 5.7.17–26).

For Cyrus the initial attraction of the Greek troops had lain in their military rather than political qualities. Greek hoplites were experienced at fighting as a cohesive force. This type of fighting was made possible by their heavy armour – though just how heavy their armour was and just how cohesively they fought are both matters of controversy. The traditional view of hoplites charging and pushing close together may reflect an ideal rather than reality.[16] In practice there was probably considerable variation among the hoplites: while they would all presumably have been equipped with shields of wood faced with bronze and with a long spear for thrusting and a short sword, their breastplates would have been of either bronze or folded linen (perhaps with bronze plates), and some would have worn heavy enclosed bronze helmets, others lighter conical ones.[17] Whatever the differences of armour, the power of a hoplite phalanx is

[15] For a list (fifteen or sixteen in all), see Ferrario 2014: 196 n. 74.

[16] The essays in Kagan and Viggiano 2013 offer an overview of different positions.

[17] See Snodgrass 1999; Lee 2007: 111–17; also 3.3.20n.

suggested by two scenes in the opening book of *Anabasis*: a parade early in the march where a charge by the hoplites frightens the non-Greek spectators (1.2.15–18), and the battle against the king, which is presented as an easy victory for the Greek hoplites against the troops stationed opposite them (3.1.23n.). During their retreat, by contrast, it was the hoplites' ability to adapt to changes in terrain that was vital: mobile companies were instituted to prevent disorder as the line contracted and expanded (3.4.19–23n.), and the troops fought in columns spaced out to outflank the enemy (4.8.10–19).

Even more vital for the success of the retreat was close co-ordination with the light-armed troops (3.2.36n.). The peltasts mainly came from mountainous areas on the fringes of the Greek world; there were many non-Greeks among them (e.g. 800 Thracians recruited by Clearchus, 1.2.9). With their equipment of light crescent-shaped wicker shields, long javelins and short swords, they were far more mobile than hoplites in mountainous terrain. The diversity of the army was further boosted by 200 Cretan archers (3.3.7n.) and by a volunteer force of slingers constituted from Rhodians in the course of the retreat (3.3.16n.).

There were also non-combatants accompanying the army, including market-traders and personal attendants (3.2.36, 3.16, 4.49nn.).[18] In addition, there were women companions and slaves, though they appear only infrequently in X.'s account – for instance as dancers or as spectators of athletic games.[19] And as the army progressed it took prisoners, some of whom acted as guides (3.1.2n.), others as additional sexual partners (4.1.14, 6.3, 7.4.7).

Why did so many Greeks enlist with Cyrus?[20] A broad overview of their motives is offered when X. explains why the soldiers are opposed to the idea of founding a city on the shores of the Black Sea: most of them wanted to return home because they 'had sailed out not owing to a lack of livelihood but hearing of Cyrus' excellence' (6.4.8; cf. 3.1.3n.). If applied to the whole army, this comment is belied by X.'s own narrative: there were some – like the seer Silanus, a particular beneficiary of Cyrus' generosity (1.7.18) – who had good reason to return home (5.6.17–18, 6.4.13; cf. 5.7.15), but most of the survivors joined the Spartans at the end of the expedition, resuming a career of mercenary service in Asia Minor. X.'s comment at 6.4.8 can still be defended if it is taken to exclude those members of the Ten Thousand who, even if they came originally from

[18] For the suppression of slave attendants in ancient historical narratives, see Hunt 1998; Lee 2007: 256–9 argues that there were in fact relatively few accompanying the Ten Thousand.

[19] Lane Fox 2004c; Lee 2004.

[20] Roy 1967, with some modification in Roy 2004, is the fundamental study.

mainland Greece, were already serving as mercenaries in Asia Minor, following a long tradition of such service (in 440, for instance, the Samians were provided with 700 Greek mercenaries by the satrap Pissuthnes (Thuc. 1.115.4)); those thus excluded would probably include many of the hoplites (almost two thirds of the total) who came from the relatively poor regions of Arcadia and Achaea in the Peloponnese.[21] In his obituary notice for Clearchus, moreover, X. refers to the authority he exercised over those who were serving with him 'owing to want or constrained by some other necessity' (2.6.13). This claim refers to Clearchus' whole career rather than exclusively to the Ten Thousand, but it must capture the circumstances of some of the troops.

That the majority of the mercenaries were not driven by extreme poverty is nonetheless suggested by their conditions of service. The hoplites probably supplied their own equipment; as noted above, some were even wealthy enough to bring servants with them. The rate of pay (3.5.8n.) was not particularly high by comparison with the known rates for other types of employment, though pay was at least given for each day of service. While serving under Cyrus, they also had to buy food at quite high prices from local villages or from the merchants who accompanied the expedition, though they were sometimes allowed to plunder once they were outside the districts that Cyrus himself ruled (3.1.2n.).

Overall, while X. is probably right in disclaiming extreme poverty as a motive, a considerable variety of motives must be allowed. The army included the Spartan general Clearchus, who after an adventurous career was now an exile (3.1.10n.). Another Spartan exile was Dracontius (probably a captain), who had accidentally killed a boy in his youth (4.8.25). And the variety of motives is further expanded if we turn to the man whose circumstances are explored most elaborately, Xenophon himself.

3 XENOPHON'S LIFE

The sources for our knowledge of X.'s life are *Anabasis* itself; the short anecdotal biography by Diogenes Laertius (2.48–59) written in the third century AD and drawing on a range of earlier authors; and a few anecdotes preserved by other writers. Besides this, a certain amount may be inferred from X.'s other works. All the various sources must be treated with some scepticism:[22] X.'s own treatments because he may have been

[21] Roy 2004: 276. Roy persuasively argues that the overall proportion of Arcadians and Achaeans does not reflect a sudden crisis at the end of the Peloponnesian War, but an Arcadian tradition of raising sons in the expectation that some of them would go abroad to serve as mercenaries.

[22] Against the common practice of judging from X.'s narrative style in particular passages whether he was an eyewitness, see Anderson 1986: 37.

concerned to defend himself or to exaggerate his own influence, other sources because they reflect later fabrication.[23]

X. was probably born in the early 420s. The best evidence for this date comes from the scene in *Anabasis* 3 where Xenophon insists that his youth is no reason for him not to take a lead in stirring the troops (3.1.25): that his ξένος Proxenus was already a general at the age of 30 (2.6.20) suggests that X. was, if anything, somewhat younger (the ξενία itself need not imply that they were the same age, especially if it was inherited, 3.1.4n.).[24] At any rate, there is no reason to trust the *akme* dates (i.e. the date at which X. reached the age of 40) given by ancient sources: 'the fourth year of the ninety-fourth Olympiad' (401/400: Diog. Laert. 2.55) and 'the ninety-fifth Olympiad' (400/399–397/396: *Suda* ξ 47 Adler) are both evidently based on Xenophon's overall role in *Anabasis*, while 'the eighty-ninth Olympiad' (424/423–421/420: cited from another source by Diog. Laert. 2.59) seems to be based either on Xenophon's presence at the dinner described in X.'s *Symposium* (dramatic date 422, but his presence is probably an authenticating fiction) or on the story that he was saved by Socrates at the battle of Delium (424).[25]

Diogenes offers the information that X. came from the inland Attic deme of Erchia and that his father's name was Gryllus (2.48). Nothing further is known of the father, but he was presumably wealthy, to judge from his son's pursuits – horses (3.3.19, 4.47–9nn.), hunting (cf. *Cynegeticus*) and Socrates (3.1.5n.). As for the origin of the Socratic connection, Diogenes tells the story that Socrates prevented X. moving forward in an alley and reduced him to ἀπορία by asking first where food was sold, then where men become noble and good (2.48) – a story that seems to anticipate X.'s later ability to extract the Greeks from tight spots (3.1.2n.). The extent of X.'s acquaintance with Socrates has sometimes been doubted, particularly by Platonic scholars, but this scepticism (which reflects the

[23] See 3.1.4n. for one example; other examples include his being enamoured of Clinias (Diog. Laert. 2.49 – clearly based on Critobulus' expression of love for Clinias at X. *Symp.* 4.12); and the very popular story of his response while sacrificing to news of his son's death (Tuplin 1993: 32 n. 76 gives the sources; add Jerome, *Epistles* 60.5.2). Fictional letters sent by or to X. can be found in Hercher, *Epistolog. Graec.* For modern treatments of X.'s life, see *CCX* 15–36; Breitenbach 1967: 1571–8; Anderson 1974; Badian 2004; the most detailed treatment, Delebecque 1957, is unfortunately marked by circularity, in that it infers the dates of (different parts of) X.'s various works from their supposed political leanings.

[24] At Athens 30 was the age-limit for holding some offices and for jury service ([Arist.] *Ath. Pol.* 30.2, 63.3), but Xenophon is not thinking of formal offices at 3.1.25(n.). Falappone 1979 supports an early date for X.'s birth, but her attempt to dismiss the evidence of 3.1.14 (as relating to age in comparison with the other soldiers rather than the appropriate age for generalship) is not convincing.

[25] Str. 9.2.7; Diog. Laert. 2.22–3; the story was perhaps in turn inspired by the story that Socrates saved Alcibiades at Potidaea (Pl. *Symp.* 220d5–e7).

general lowering of X.'s reputation as both philosopher and historian in the course of the nineteenth century) has been rebutted by recent work on *Memorabilia*.[26]

It is generally assumed that X. served in the Athenian cavalry in the final stages of the Peloponnesian War and that he stayed on in Athens during the reign of the Thirty Tyrants (404–403), the junta imposed by the Spartans after Athens' defeat. It is also possible that he was among the small cavalry contingent that supported the exiled Athenian democrats (*Hell.* 2.4.25). He certainly offers a negative image of the Thirty in both *Hellenica* and *Memorabilia* and a positive image of the lasting reconciliation achieved after their overthrow (*Hell.* 2.4.43); his presentation of the civil war could equally reflect disillusion with the direction taken by the Thirty, gratitude to the democracy for the amnesty, and a consistent commitment to the democracy.

Xenophon's decision to sail to Asia is presented in *Anabasis* as a response to a promise that he will become a φίλος of Cyrus. It was not his aim to leave Athens for good: he asks the Delphic oracle about how he can return safe and successful (3.1.6); Cyrus promises to send him back home after the supposed Pisidian expedition (3.1.9(n.)); and he is still planning to return home during the later stages of the expedition.[27] Attempts to uncover X.'s actual motivations must bear in mind the possible ideological and apologetic undercurrents of his self-presentation. An aristocratic ethos underlies the insistence that Xenophon wants a relationship with Cyrus defined by reciprocity rather than by service for cash (X. insists that he was not serving as a general, company commander or soldier, 3.1.4n.). And Xenophon's professed desire to return to Athens after joining Cyrus may reflect X.'s later desire to show his civic commitment to Athens.

Modern scholars often suggest instead that X. left Athens because he was disenchanted with the Athenian democracy or even (assuming he served in the cavalry under the Thirty) because he feared for his own safety despite the amnesty.[28] Like many attempts to reconstruct X.'s life, however, these suggestions run the risk of circularity: X.'s decision to leave

[26] In particular the edition by Bandini and Dorion, the introduction to which offers a valuable overview of the reception of X. as a Socratic; see also Dorion 2013.

[27] 7.7.57; cf. 6.4.8, discussed above. At 6.2.15, 7.1.4, 8, 38 Xenophon wants to sail off, but where is not specified; in speeches at 7.6.11, 33, however, he specifies home as his destination. Even at 7.2.37–8, where he is at least tempted by Seuthes' offer of some strongholds on the Thracian coast, his thoughts are largely on a place of refuge from the Spartans at a time when returning to Athens would have been difficult.

[28] See *CCX* 338–59 for a general account of X.'s relationship with Athens.

Athens is regarded as evidence for his having fought against the democracy. Whatever his attitude to the democracy, a further motivation may well have been (as Mary Renault suggested in her 1956 novel *The Last of the Wine*)[29] a desire to study the leadership of Cyrus, a figure of interest for Socrates (to judge from *Oec.* 4.18–25) and the Socratics.[30] It is not unfeasible in turn that Cyrus' motive for accepting X. in an unorthodox position may have been his Socratic connection and his potential as propagandist.[31]

Xenophon plays a small role in *Anabasis* 1–2. His few appearances do nonetheless suggest that he was a person of some prominence: he rides up to Cyrus to ask for orders before Cunaxa (1.8.15–17); is walking with Proxenus outside the camp when Persian envoys arrive (2.4.15); and even has a speaking role in a scene where he goes with two surviving generals to find out news about the generals who had gone to visit Tissaphernes (2.5.37–42; see 3.1n.).[32]

It is at the start of Book 3, after the seizure of the generals, that Xenophon's role becomes central. He inspires the downcast officers and soldiers; is elected a general and positioned in the rear; and then provides the moral and strategic leadership that ensures the army's successful retreat to the sea (Books 3–4). He continues as one of the generals in the march along the Black Sea coast, while coming under fire for some of his earlier behaviour (Books 5–6). After the Greeks' arrival in Byzantium, he leads the remaining troops during a winter's campaigning for the Thracian dynast Seuthes and then into service with the Spartans (Book 7). It is not impossible that at this point he returned to Athens and sailed back to Asia later, but it is usually thought that he stayed with the Spartans. He himself states that he accompanied the Spartan king Agesilaus on his return to Greece in 394, when Sparta was faced by war against a coalition of four cities including Athens (5.3.6).

At some point after the end of the expedition a vote of exile was passed against X. (7.7.57; for the procedure see 3.1.5n.). X.'s exile seems to be foreshadowed in Socrates' warnings against serving with Cyrus (3.1.5), but it is by no means clear that X.'s service with Cyrus was the cause of his exile.[33] Conceivably, that service was just a pretext and the real cause was X.'s political association with the Thirty; if so, his condemnation would be in line with the politically motivated actions against Socrates

[29] Renault 2015: 397. [30] Gera 1993: 7–10. [31] Gray 2010b: 11.

[32] The **f** MSS attribute to Xenophon a dramatic speaking role in the scene immediately after Cunaxa when Persian envoys come demanding that the Greeks hand over their weapons (2.1.12–13), but the **c** MSS read Θεόπομπος; it is more likely that the latter was corrupted into the former than vice versa.

[33] As assumed by Paus. 5.6.5; Erbse 2010: 483–6.

and Andocides at around the same time.[34] Another possibility is that X.'s involvement in an expedition against the Persian king got him into trouble when the Athenians were seeking or receiving Persian help against Sparta (that is, in the run-up to or in the early stages of the Corinthian War (395–387)).[35] A further possibility is that X. was exiled for supporting Sparta, either soon after he and the remnants of the Ten Thousand joined up with the Spartans (Diog. Laert. 2.51) or some years later, after he was present on the Spartan side at the battle of Coronea.[36]

At some point after he was exiled, X. was settled by the Spartans at Scillus, not far from Olympia (5.3.7). With his portion of the tithe from the sale of some captives taken during the retreat, he bought a piece of land for Artemis, built a temple, and founded a festival in her honour (5.3.7–13). Little is known of his subsequent life other than the brief description he gives of the festival. He must have left Scillus when the Spartans' power in the Peloponnese declined after their defeat at Leuctra (371). Our sources differ about where he went next: Diogenes reports that he lived and died in Corinth (2.53, 56), Pausanias that he was later pardoned by the Eleans and died back in Scillus, where his grave was shown (5.6.6). He seems to have had renewed dealings with Athens: his exile was revoked (Diog. Laert. 2.59); a close concern with Athenian interests is revealed by two of his works, *Hipparchicus* (*De equitum magistro*) and *Poroi*; and his son Gryllus died fighting in the Athenian cavalry at Mantinea in 362 and received tributes, including an encomium by Isocrates and a dialogue on rhetoric by Aristotle which was named after him (Diog. Laert. 2.54–5; Arist. frr. 1–3 Ross). It cannot be shown, however, that X. himself ever lived in Athens again. As for the date of his death, all that can be said is that the last datable allusion in any of his works (*Por.* 5.9) is to 355/354.[37]

4 *ANABASIS*

Anabasis is now widely regarded as X.'s masterpiece. This has not always been the case: in earlier centuries *Cyropaedia* or the Socratic works were

[34] Brennan 2011: 60–4. Green 1994 links the exile with fears that X. might aid the oligarchic outpost at Eleusis, but this outpost had probably already fallen by 399. *Hell.* 3.1.4 refers to the restored democracy sending in that year 300 cavalry to join the Spartans in Asia Minor – in the hope that they would be killed.

[35] Tuplin 1987a.

[36] E.g. Rahn 1981. For Coronea, see *An.* 5.3.6; the evidence that X. fought at the battle (Plut. *Ages.* 18.1) is probably an inference from this passage.

[37] Diog. Laert. 2.56 is evidently mistaken in putting his death in the archonship of Ctesiclides (360/359). X.'s inclusion in the canon of long-lived men (Lucian, *Macrob.* 21; cf. Diod. 15.76.4; Diog. Laert. 2.56) is probably based on one of the wrong assumptions of his date of birth noted above.

more respected, and X. himself was regarded more as a philosopher than as a historian; and in the nineteenth and twentieth centuries *Anabasis* suffered from its use as a school text (even if that use contributed greatly to X.'s fame). But while some of his other works have at times been more famous, it is clear that *Anabasis* has enjoyed a wide readership from antiquity into the modern era: it was much imitated by later historians and cited by literary critics in antiquity, as both the Commentary and the treatment of X.'s language below will show, and there have been numerous editions and translations since the fifteenth century.[38]

Book 3 has played an important role in the afterlife of *Anabasis*. No single moment in this book has achieved the fame of the cry θάλαττα θάλαττα uttered when the army sees the Black Sea (4.7.24), but its opening description of the Greeks' despair after the seizure of the generals (which offers the necessary contrast to that moment of joy) and of the subsequent assemblies (which set the recovery in motion) has been much admired. One tribute to the power of this scene comes in the excerpts from Xenophon's soliloquy (3.1.13–14) which form the epigraph to an early chapter in Richard Adams' 1972 children's classic *Watership Down* – suggesting a parallel between Xenophon in Mesopotamia and the rabbit who leads his group to safety through the dangers of the South Downs (the chapter is entitled 'Hazel's decision').[39] In the nineteenth century the geographer James Rennell hailed X. as 'the soul that re-animated this body of Greeks', suggesting that 'eloquence was never employed with more effect',[40] while Henry Layard, excavator of Nimrud and Nineveh, proclaimed that 'the world has rarely seen a more glorious sight than was witnessed on the banks of the Zab on that memorable morning'.[41] Layard himself was one of many travellers in the Ottoman empire who tried to follow in X.'s footsteps, noting as they went the survival of many of the customs X. described, including the hobbling of horses at night, rafts of inflated skins on the Tigris, and regional governors' palaces surrounded by villages with provisions.[42]

[38] For the ancient reception of X., see pp. 23–4, 33 and Index s.v. 'Xenophon, *Anabasis*, reception'; further Münscher 1920; Tuplin 1993: 20–8; Chiron 2014; Pernot 2014; for the modern reception of *Anabasis*, see Marsh 1992 (early editions and translations); Rijksbaron 2002 (school editions); Rood 2004b, 2010a (American reception, including p. 19 with n. 24 for Hanson and Emerson on 3.2.18, p. 30 for a neo-Nazi appropriation of 3.1.42, and p. 57 for Thoreau on 3.5.8–12), 2013a, 2013b, 2015a; Roche 2016 (Nazi education); Lacave 2017 (French military). For X.'s reception in general, see *CCX* Part v.

[39] Adams 1972: 10. [40] Rennell 1816: 137. [41] Layard 1853: 227.

[42] Hobbling (3.4.35n.): Kinneir 1818: 481n.; Porter 1821–2: II.537. Rafts (cf. 3.5.8–12n.): Kinneir 1818: 482n.; Southgate 1840: II.215; Layard 1853: 53n.; Millingen 1870: 76–9. Provisions (3.4.24, 31): Morier 1818: 272.

Chapter introductions in the Commentary will offer a progressive analysis of how X. tells the story of the army's recovery from its despair in Book 3. Here, a number of preliminary questions about the work as a whole will be addressed: how is it to be classified, and when, how and why was it written?

Genre

Anabasis has often invited comparison with modern genres such as travel writing and the war memoir – 'the time-honoured tradition of retired generals'.[43] Formally, however, it is not a memoir at all: X. conceals the identity of the author and of the main character Xenophon by using third-person forms to refer to his own actions.[44] Determining how X. himself viewed *Anabasis* is complicated by the fact that he dispenses with a formal prologue and conclusion.[45] The lack of a prologue is one feature it shares with *Hellenica*, but in that work X. is continuing Thucydides, and he does in any case later state principles of inclusion which conform to or modify conventional historiographical claims. *Anabasis*, by contrast, offers no statement of its aims in the course of the narrative.

While it may lack overt generic signals, *Anabasis* does at least position itself implicitly in relation to a number of existing genres. It evokes Greek epic, in particular the *Odyssey* (3.2.25n.), as well as geographical writings, including (in parts of the Black Sea section) the genre of the *periplus*.[46] It also includes speeches that hint at the conventional aims of other Greek prose genres. Like epideictic orators and some historians, speakers are concerned with questions of praise and blame (e.g. 3.1.45(n.), 7.6.15, 7.52). In some instances, the concern with praise overlaps with the historiographical aim of preserving the memory of the past: thus Xenophon closes a battle exhortation with the thought that 'it is pleasant that whoever says or does something brave and gallant now is making himself remembered among the people whom he would want to remember him' (6.5.24; cf. e.g. 5.8.25–6). Xenophon's appeal to the joy of being remembered is itself one of the noble speeches that will give him the joy of being remembered.[47]

43 Usher 1969: 83. Lee 2005 and Humble 2011 offer comparisons with these modern genres.

44 The work may have been published pseudonymously: see below.

45 Even the interpolated summary at 7.8.25–6 is only a summary of the length of the expedition and of the rulers of the lands through which the army passed.

46 See *SAGN* II.158.

47 Cf. Flower 2012: 54–8; also 2.6.17, 5.6.17, 7.3.19 for characters' (desire for) fame. See also Baragwanath 2016 on projected futures in *Anabasis*.

Taken as a whole, *Anabasis* can be described as 'a narrative history of recent events, focalized around an individual group'.[48] Seen in these terms, it is comparable with Herodotus' account of Xerxes' march into Greece and of Thucydides' account of the Athenians' invasion of Sicily (the former possibly, the latter certainly a significant intertext[49]). It is indeed Thucydidean historiography that supplies the closest antecedent to *Anabasis* as a whole. The particular similarities are threefold: in both works the author presents his own actions in the third person; adopts a relatively covert narratorial style and a broadly linear temporal structure; and foregrounds the relationship between speech, thought and action. At the same time, *Anabasis* departs from the Thucydidean mode of historiography in some important ways: it gives a far more extensive role to religion and the gods; it is much more diverse in its subject matter; it includes more marked shifts of narratorial style (see section 6 below); and taken as a whole it shifts generically, in Bradley's terms, from 'history' (Books 1–2) to 'novelesque autobiography' (Books 3–7).[50]

In its diversity *Anabasis* encompasses many of the main themes of X.'s other works.[51] The style of the detailed character descriptions recalls *Agesilaus.* Like *Memorabilia,* it includes Socratic conversation – indeed, a scene where Socrates advises a rash young man whose loyalty to Athens is open to suspicion – and offers defence of unfairly victimized people. Like *Symposium,* it offers accounts of banquets, with conversation, dancing and laughter (6.1.3–13, 7.3.16–34). But it is *Cyropaedia* with which it has the closest similarities. Like that work, *Anabasis* has a Persian setting and deals with the education of a Cyrus (1.9), with hunting (1.5.2–3, 5.3.10), with anecdotes of homosexual love (4.6.3, 7.4.7) and with military strategy (see 3.3.12–19, 4.19–23nn.) (some of these topics recur in the technical works on hunting and horsemanship). It resembles *Cyropaedia,* too, in its inclusion of speeches in which leaders are advised on how to command obedience (7.7.20–47; cf. *Hipparchicus,* which is framed as an address). It is no coincidence that *Cyropaedia* is the work with which *Anabasis* shares most of its linguistic peculiarities (see section 5 below).

The generic innovation of *Anabasis* would be lessened if there were earlier accounts of the march of the Ten Thousand. The Byzantine lexicographer Stephanus offers four very short citations from an *Anabasis* supposedly written by Sophaenetus of Stymphalus, one of the oldest generals (3.2.37n.). The fragments themselves are merely toponyms and ethnics and so reveal nothing about the style or date of the work:

[48] Marincola 1999: 316 (cf. his broader treatment at *CCX* 103–18). For ancient views of *Anabasis* as historiographical, see Tuplin 1993: 21.

[49] Rood 2004a: 310; 3.2.36n. [50] Bradley 2010: 539–40.

[51] *CCX* Part II offers a good overview of X.'s individual works.

it could have been a straightforward narrative with none of X.'s generic range. But it is quite likely that Sophaenetus did not write an *Anabasis* at all. It is not that a prose work by an Arcadian is inconceivable in the fourth century: the technical manual on siegecraft by Aeneas Tacticus (who was probably also from Stymphalus) would provide a parallel of sorts. But it is odd that the work left no trace until so late a date (there is no compelling reason to think that it was used by Diodorus or Diodorus' likely source, Ephorus).[52] It may, then, have been a later rhetorical exercise in history-writing, composed when Xenophon was an established classic.[53]

Evidence of an earlier account has also been seen in X.'s summary of Cyrus' expedition and the Greeks' retreat in *Hellenica*: 'How Cyrus collected an army and marched upcountry against his brother, and how the battle happened, and how he died, and how afterwards the Greeks came through in safety to the sea – this has been written by Themistogenes of Syracuse' (3.1.2). This passage is odd because it refers to Themistogenes rather than to X.'s own *Anabasis* and because it closes the expedition with the arrival at the sea, ignoring the Ten Thousand's march along the Black Sea coast and their subsequent adventures in Thrace. In response to these problems, some scholars have thought that X. was alluding to an earlier account which did indeed end with the arrival at the sea.[54] But it is more likely that X. was referring to his own *Anabasis* – a suggestion already made by Plutarch (*Mor.* 345e).[55]

Publication

For Plutarch, the reason X. mentioned a version by Themistogenes was that he had published *Anabasis* under a pseudonym in order to make his self-praise more palatable. Whether this explanation should be accepted

[52] Stylianou 2004.

[53] Westlake 1987. One inspiration could have been 6.5.13–22, where the cautious warner Sophaenetus is opposed to the dynamic young Xenophon. Sophaenetus' authorship is dismissed by Stylianou 2004: 73–4 (as based on misunderstanding of a military handbook) and Almagor 2012: 29 n. 147 (assuming textual corruption in Stephanus).

[54] E.g. Cousin 1905: xix. If so, it would still be uncertain whether Themistogenes himself was a participant in the expedition. It is in theory possible that X. was referring to an earlier, shorter draft of his own work, but this is probably to lay too much stress on the details of the bare summary.

[55] Similarly Maclaren 1934. See *FGrH* 108, with Pitcher in *BNJ* for a full discussion (which slightly favours accepting that there was a separate work) and further bibliography. Themistogenes is otherwise unknown except for a short *Suda* entry (θ 123 Adler) which also attributes to him some works about his fatherland – presumably a later fiction (like the story that Themistogenes was X.'s lover (*FGrH* 108 T 4)).

is hard to say.[56] For one thing, it is unclear how pseudonymous publication would have worked in the fourth century. And if X. was trying to conceal his own authorship, he did not make a good job of it: the narrator shows much greater knowledge of the mind of Xenophon than that of any other character, including two dreams (3.1.11–14n.) and at one point a direct reporting of thoughts (3.1.13n.); and all later references to the account in antiquity identify it as X.'s. Plutarch's explanation is nonetheless still as plausible as any: already in X.'s time the book trade (cf. 7.5.14) may have been sufficiently established for this to have been possible.[57]

The date of *Anabasis* is even more uncertain than the name under which it was published. The same uncertainty holds true for most of X.'s works: the most that can be confidently stated on internal evidence is that *Hellenica* and *Poroi* were finished in the 350s and *Cyropaedia* and *Agesilaus* at some point after the late 360s.[58] As for *Anabasis*, there have been attempts to propose dates in the 390s or 380s, for part of the work at least. These claims rest partly on assumptions about X.'s method (the detail of the work is supposed to show that it was written soon after the events) and partly on assumptions about his aims in writing the account. The following sections of this Introduction will argue that these proposals cannot be sustained. At most, it can be said that the account of Xenophon's life at Scillus (5.3.7–13) was certainly written after his exile and at a time when he had children old enough to hunt on horseback (probably the late 380s),[59] and that the imperfect tenses employed in the description of the festival Xenophon established at Scillus may indicate a date of composition after he was expelled in the aftermath of Leuctra.[60] If so, the inclusion of the text of an inscription Xenophon set up, which includes an implied warning to future holders of the estate (5.3.13), would have added point. But, as we have seen, it is in any case possible that X. returned to Scillus. The imperfect tenses could then have been used because the festival was recurrent or because X. was writing in

[56] See Pelling 2013, a valuable comparison of the narratorial voices of X. and Caesar (with pp. 39–42 on pseudonymity), and his broader treatment at *CCX* 241–62.

[57] Further evidence might be seen in the lack of self-naming at the start of X.'s work (by contrast with prose predecessors such as Hecataeus, Herodotus, Thucydides and Antiochus of Syracuse); this seems to presuppose that the author's name was attached in some way to the papyrus roll.

[58] Gray 2010b: 7 n. 32. The list of suggested dates of X.'s works in Huss 1999: 17 n. 15 shows an increasing tendency to concentrate X.'s literary activity in the years after 370.

[59] 7.6.34 shows that Xenophon did not have children at the time of the expedition (though Seuthes at 7.2.38 imagines that he might at least have a daughter of marriageable age).

[60] The description is often said to be nostalgic, but this may be a projection of modern feelings (cf. Rood 2012 on the reception of X.'s 'delightful retreat').

anticipation of a future audience (though some present tenses are used in the account of the estate and temple).[61]

Methods

How X. wrote *Anabasis* is as hard to determine as its date. The wealth of detail about the relative chronology of the expedition and the distances covered (the stages and parasangs) has encouraged speculation that X. took information from an earlier writer such as Ctesias of Cnidus, a Greek doctor who served in Artaxerxes' court and who is said to have given an account of 'the number of stages, days and parasangs from Ephesus to Bactria and India' (F33 Lenfant). While this possibility cannot be wholly discounted, it seems unlikely that Ctesias (or any other written parasang list) provided all the information required for X.'s account, given the fact that during the marches upcountry and to the sea the army was rarely on one of the main routes or 'royal roads' (existing *periplus* literature would have made distances along the Black Sea coast easier to gather, but X. no longer adopts the same style for the later sections of the expedition). It is more likely that X. or another participant kept notes of some sort during the expedition; such notes could have been a useful way of quantifying the length of service under Cyrus and keeping track of the route.[62]

The question of X.'s methods in writing up the events of the expedition is distinct from that of his geographical source. For the most part, he relates without qualification events that could have been known to an eyewitness. When he relates events that he could not have seen himself, he at times makes clear that the detail is based on eyewitness report (e.g. 1.6.5) or on inference (e.g. 2.2.17–18, 3.1, 6), but there are times when he adopts a more 'omniscient' style (see section 6 below). He also refers, particularly in the Cunaxa narrative, to what (anonymous) people 'said' (1.8.20) or 'say' (1.8.18, 24, 28, 29) (cf. 3.4.11, 5.15nn.).[63] On one occasion he even specifies a written source – Ctesias (1.8.26, 27, for two details of the battle of Cunaxa);[64] there is, however, no evidence that Ctesias wrote a narrative either of the march upcountry or of the retreat.

Views of the method employed in the writing of *Anabasis* are bound up with the question whether the account was intended to be an accurate representation of what happened. Gibbon memorably contrasted the 'vague and languid' *Cyropaedia* with the 'circumstantial and animated'

[61] Attempts to date the works on linguistic grounds have not been successful: X.'s linguistic choices differ between works by genre rather than date (see p. 30 below).

[62] For fuller discussion, see Rood 2010b.

[63] See Gray 2010c.

[64] Almagor 2012: 28–36 revives the view of Dürrbach that the Ctesias citations are interpolated.

Anabasis: 'Such is the eternal difference between fiction and truth.'[65] As Roberto Nicolai has argued, however, it may be better to conceive an opposition between truth and exemplarity.[66] Nicolai himself suggests that X. was more concerned with didactic goals than with accuracy – but that suggestion is based above all on *Cyropaedia* and may still underestimate the extent to which X. thought he was presenting an accurate account. In the case of *Anabasis*, the wealth of plausible detail creates the much stronger impression of truth that Gibbon admired, but it is still likely that X. was prepared to give some weight to exemplarity – and in particular to the exemplary leadership of Xenophon. And whatever the degree of conscious invention, it must be remembered that, whenever the account was written down, the final telling would have been moulded by X.'s frequent replaying of the events in both thought and speech, and, like all historical narratives, would have shaped events in accordance with pre-existing story patterns and conventions.

Purpose

It is often assumed that X. wrote *Anabasis* to promote a particular cause – though there has been some disagreement over the audience he was trying to influence. Two such causes could have been the reputation of X. himself and of the rest of the Ten Thousand. A very negative picture of the Greek mercenaries was given by Isocrates in the *Panegyricus*, a speech composed in 380, which referred to them as '6,000 Greeks who were not picked troops, but men who, owing to circumstances, were unable to live in their own countries' (4.146). Given that Isocrates' aim was to expose the supposed weakness of Persia, it was rhetorically apt for him to lower both the number and the status of the troops who accompanied Cyrus. While it is conceivable that X.'s upbeat portrayal of the motives of those who sailed out (6.4.8, discussed above) was responding to Isocrates (which would confirm a post-380 date for the work), the possibility of a precise link between these two passages should not blind us to the numerous other stories about the expedition that must have circulated throughout Greece. And however the mercenaries were portrayed in these retellings, there is a decisive obstacle to the view that X. wrote the work to defend them *en masse* – namely the increasingly negative way in which they are presented as the account progresses (see above).

As for X.'s own reputation, it has been suggested that he was responding to retellings of the march (whether oral or in written works such as

[65] Gibbon 1994: I.952 n. 115. Grote 1903–6: VII.176 similarly contrasts 'the romance of the Cyropaedia' with 'the history of the Anabasis'.

[66] Nicolai 2014: 83.

Sophaenetus') by participants who either criticized his leadership or downplayed his role.[67] These two versions of X.'s pursuit of self-interest are in tension: if he did not play a prominent role in the retreat he would not have needed to defend himself. In favour of the first suggestion there is at least the fact that X. mentions that charges were brought against his leadership during the retreat.[68] But it should be stressed that Xenophon's response to these charges is foregrounded in the course of the account (particularly in Books 5 and 7). Even the goal of self-defence, then, takes on an exemplary aspect: *Anabasis* shows a skilled apologist in action.

The second charge (that X. was moved by vanity rather than self-defence) is often supported by X.'s absence from Diodorus' account of the Ten Thousand's retreat (which is therefore assumed to be based on a rival version).[69] But Diodorus does not present any other figure playing the role of saviour during the retreat, and in a later section he does credit X. with leadership of the army in Thrace (14.37.1; cf. 3.2.37n.). Detailed analysis of Diodorus' account in any case suggests that *Anabasis* itself was his ultimate source.[70] Rather than reading X.'s account against a specific earlier version, it is more reasonable to conclude that X. did play an important role, but that the version of that role in *Anabasis* may reflect concerns (such as ideals of leadership) other than a strict adherence to the truth.

Another suggested motivation for X.'s account is that he was trying to win favour with the Athenians following his exile. This suggestion, however, seems to be undermined by the account of Xenophon's motives for joining Cyrus: he does not conceal the fact that he was invited by someone who finds Cyrus more valuable than his own fatherland (3.1.5n.) and that he was present with Agesilaus on his return to Greece (5.3.6) – to fight against a coalition that included Athens. If, then, X. was trying to gain popularity at Athens, it was by the overall presentation of his contribution as an Athenian to the success of the retreat rather than by a specific attempt to meet the grievances that had led to his exile.

A fourth common assumption is that *Anabasis* was written as an anti-Persian tract. Delebecque proposed that the first part (with its stress on Persian treachery) was written as a protest against the King's Peace

[67] E.g. Gwynn 1929; Cawkwell 2004. [68] E.g. Dürrbach 1893.

[69] X. is also not named in the short summary at Justin 5.11.10–11. Other summaries (e.g. Polyb. 3.6.10; Arr. *Anab.* 1.12.3; Frontin. *Str.* 4.2.8) attribute sole responsibility for the army's return to X.; these assessments are either directly or indirectly based on X.'s account.

[70] Stylianou 2004.

of 387/386.[71] More often, it is thought that X. was encouraging a Greek attack on the Persian empire, perhaps in the early 360s, a time when Athens and Sparta were co-operating against Thebes and keen to dissociate the new Arcadian confederacy from Thebes, and when Thebes was looking to Persia for help.[72] As it happens, there is clear contemporary evidence in both X. (*Hell.* 3.4.2, 6.1.12) and Isocrates (4.145–9, 5.90) that the expedition was used to advocate an attack on Persia (for Isocrates, a possible solution to Greece's internal problems). In addition, in his speeches to the officers and soldiers at the start of Book 3 Xenophon himself seems to indulge in thoughts of such an attack and to encourage seeing the Greeks' performances both at Cunaxa and during the retreat as military triumphs that bear comparison with the great Greek victories in 490 and 480/479. But neither X.'s awareness of such readings nor the Panhellenic 'big talk' in Book 3 proves that he wrote with that aim in mind (see further 3.2.26n.). Nor does the description of the army's disintegration in the later stages of the expedition lend credence to the idea that X. was actively pushing an expansionist policy.[73]

Rather than being reduced to a propaganda piece for a particular political cause, *Anabasis* demands to be read against the broader interests that pervade X.'s corpus – in particular, the concern with leadership noted in the discussion of genre above.[74] This concern is shown in different ways in different works: *Hellenica* includes overt judgements on different leaders;[75] in *Hiero*, the poet Simonides lectures the Sicilian tyrant Hiero on how he can not only be happy himself but can also make his subjects happy; in *Poroi*, X. offers Athenian leaders advice on how to save the Athenians from poverty without wronging their allies, while in *Agesilaus* he makes the case that the Spartan king was an exemplary leader because of the benefits he bestowed on his followers (7.1). Leadership is also a theme in the Socratic works: in *Memorabilia*, Socrates discusses Homeric models of leadership (3.2) and offers advice to cavalry commanders (3.3, cf. *Hipparchicus*), while *Oeconomicus* suggests how husband and wife can command obedience outside and within the house, with elaborate parallels with the military and political officers and with royal gift-giving within the Persian empire (4.4–25). It is in *Cyropaedia*, however, that this theme is most dominant. The work starts from an observation about the

[71] Delebecque 1946–7. He further suggested that the second part was meant to bolster Sparta (though it scarcely presents an attractive image of the way Spartan leaders exercise power abroad).

[72] E.g. Morr 1926–7; Cawkwell 2004: 64–6. Robert 1950 argues that X. was seeking to advertise his own credentials as leader of a Persian expedition.

[73] See further 3.2.7–32n.; Rood 2004a.

[74] *CCX* 323–37; Wood 1964; Azoulay 2004b; Gray 2011; Buxton 2016.

[75] Gray 2011: 79–117.

problems of instability and disobedience in the city and in the household, and proceeds to hold up the elder Cyrus as a paradigm to show that humans can be ruled on the basis of knowledge, just like animals (1.1); Cyrus is then instructed in the arts of command in conversations with his father (1.6); and he proceeds to offer a lesson in how to win friends and influence people. Running through these various works is a common set of assumptions: good leaders will secure the willing obedience of their followers, notably by their accessibility, by setting an example themselves, and by the use of rewards and punishments; the techniques of leadership can be transferred from one realm to another; and the mark of successful leadership is the imposition of order and an increase of prosperity.

In *Anabasis* the theme of leadership is foregrounded in a number of ways. The opening two books present contrasting models of leadership both in the narrative and in the obituaries of Cyrus and Clearchus: Cyrus' more distanced wielding of power through gift-distribution and honours is opposed to the hands-on style of Clearchus. From Book 3 onwards, Xenophon's skills are brought out implicitly. As Dio Chrysostom (18.14–17) noted, he displays rhetorical virtuosity in response to many different audiences and situations. Refuting the charge that Socrates corrupted the young, he is conspicuously pious in his religious observances.[76] He is equally effective in action. In one scene, he is rebuked by a soldier for riding on horseback while others toil uphill carrying heavy shields; at once he dismounts and grabs the soldier's shield (3.4.47–9). In another, set in the harsh Armenian winter, he starts chopping firewood and thereby inspires others to follow his example (4.4.11–12). He demonstrates through these and other actions the principle of reciprocity on which X.'s thinking about leadership is centred: the commander's willingness to endure hardship (cf. e.g. *Cyr.* 1.6.25; *Ages.* 5.3) will inspire willing obedience in the troops, especially if he is *seen* toiling.[77]

While leadership is a pervasive theme in X.'s works, the variety of ways in which the theme is treated suggests that he was not just offering variations on a single theme but probing from different perspectives the relations of leaders and led. His works raise questions about how much the good of the many is a cloak for the ambition of the few; and the frequently observed difficulty of maintaining order points up the limitations (and desirability) of exemplarity. In keeping with these wider interests, *Anabasis* can be read as an analytical work that instructs the reader not

[76] See 3.1.5, 2.10nn.; also his condemnation of perjury at 3.1.22. Danzig 2007 probably underplays X.'s piety in suggesting that he disapproved of perjury (as opposed to other forms of deceit) purely on prudential grounds; cf. the stress on perjury in X.'s hostile obituary of Meno (2.6.22, 25).

[77] See e.g. 2.3.12 Κλέαρχον ἑώρων σπουδάζοντα; Gray 2011: 40–1, 182–5; Ferrario 2012: 365.

by repeating dogmas but by explaining how events unfold and by the unobtrusive way in which it does so – by presenting a series of snapshots of human decisions, by weighing calculations, words and actions against the often unexpected results.

5 XENOPHON'S DICTION

Attic or Non-Attic?

If the study of X.'s language is 'a final frontier for Xenophontic studies',[78] then that is above all because of the riddles posed by his lexical choices. Close study reveals that X.'s vocabulary contains, especially in *Anabasis* and *Cyropaedia*, a great many words and forms which are entirely or almost entirely alien to the rest of classical Attic prose.[79] Some of these words are unique to X. (e.g. 3.4.36 διαγγέλλομαι), while others are used first by X. and then recur in the Hellenistic *koine* (e.g. 3.4.37 ὑπερδέξιος). Yet other words are shared between X. and non-Attic writing in Ionic (e.g. 3.4.16 σίνομαι for Attic βλάπτω), Doric (e.g. 3.1.2 κατακαίνω for Attic ἀποκτείνω) or both (e.g. X.'s extensive use of σύν instead of μετά (3.3.2n.)). Other usages again are shared between X. and high poetry (e.g. 3.1.29 τλήμων, a word otherwise virtually confined to epic and tragedy). In addition, there are many familiar lexical items which occur first in X. in a novel sense (e.g. 3.2.36 πλευραί 'flanks' and 3.4.42 στόμα 'mouth', first in X. as metaphors for the sides and front of an army).

The classification of unusual items in X.'s vocabulary into dialectisms (Ionicisms and Doricisms), poeticisms and Hellenistic (*koine*) words goes back to ancient critics associated with the Atticist revival of the Roman imperial period, who tried to show that X. fell short of writing 'pure' Attic prose.[80] Thus the strict Atticist second-century AD grammarian Phrynichus (*Eclog.* 62 Fischer) states that 'X. offends against his native dialect' (παρανομεῖ . . . Ξενοφῶν εἰς τὴν πάτριον διάλεκτον) by using Ionic ὀδμή ('smell') for Attic ὀσμή.[81] The Byzantine scholar Photius (*Lex.* ε

[78] *CCX* 223.

[79] The fundamental study remains that of Gautier, dating from 1911; much useful information is gathered in the lexicon of Sturz and in Sauppe 1869. Brief overviews are Rutherford 1881: 160–74; Hoffmann and Debrunner 1969: 137–9; Hiersche 1970: 216–21; Pomeroy 9–15.

[80] For an overview of ancient debates about X.'s style, see Münscher 1920: 163–82. For Atticism, which reached its peak in the Second Sophistic, see Kim 2010. Ancient lexica and commentaries contain numerous glosses on words in X.; see e.g. 3.3.18, 4.24, 4.36, 4.42nn.

[81] The truth of this and similar statements about phonological features is difficult to verify, owing to the possibility that the medieval MSS on which our text of X. is based were Atticized by scribes. All MSS in any case read ὀσμή everywhere (× 17). See also next note.

2535), whose lexicon preserves much older material, records that X. used ἠώς ('dawn') instead of ἕως at *Cyr.* 1.1.5 'in an immoderately poetic fashion' (ποιητικῶς κατακόρως).[82] Phrynichus' contemporary, the Atticizing lexicographer Moeris, objects to X.'s use (4.3.26) of ἀκμήν ('still') on the grounds that, while the word was in common usage in Moeris' own time, the proper old Attic word was ἔτι (α 149 Hansen; cf. Phryn. *Eclog.* 93 Fischer). The fourth-century AD grammarian Helladius (*apud* Phot. *Bibl.* 533b25–8) thought that he knew why X. wrote the way he did: arguing that X. should not be regarded as a 'lawgiver of Attic usage' (νομοθέτην . . . ἀττικισμοῦ), he stated that 'it is not at all surprising if a man who spent time on campaigns and mixing with foreigners debases some aspects of his native dialect' (οὐδὲν θαυμαστόν, ἀνὴρ ἐν στρατείαις σχολάζων καὶ ξένων συνουσίαις εἴ τινα παρακόπτει τῆς πατρίου φωνῆς).

Modern scholars have generally followed these ancient assessments and painted a picture of X. as 'eccentric and unreliable as a guide to Attic prose usage, whether from artistic incapacity or the variety of his linguistic experience as an exile'.[83] Wackernagel, for instance, dismissed X. as a *Halbattiker* ('half-Attic'),[84] while other scholars asserted that X. 'must be regarded as outside the limits of Attic law' and 'is past praying for',[85] or that reading X. was a bewildering experience: 'Now Attic, now Ionic, now poetry, now prose, it is a bizarre diction peculiar to X.'[86] In the most systematic study of X.'s lexical choices, Gautier argued that the facts are best accounted for by the assumption that during the long time X. spent away from Athens he lost his sense of what was proper Attic and what was not. Gautier supposed that X. soaked up many non-Attic words and used these more or less subconsciously and usually without stylistic motivation alongside their Attic equivalents. Finally, he argued that X.'s diverse linguistic contacts foreshadowed the large-scale societal processes which would soon lead to the demise of the individual dialects and the rise of the Hellenistic *koine*, which X. therefore anticipated in certain respects, again more or less by accident.

It is one of the chief aims of this commentary to offer an alternative view of X.'s lexical choices. The assumption that X. would have written 'pure' Attic prose if only he had been able to do so is untenable for various reasons. First, there is little to recommend the view that X. had forgotten

[82] Again, all MSS read πρὸς ἕω. Intriguingly, however, at 3.5.15, where the same phrase occurs, **c** has πρὸς ἠῶ. If ἠῶ is the correct reading, it is probably a dialectism rather than a poeticism.
[83] Bers 1984: 13. [84] Wackernagel 1907: 5. [85] Rutherford 1881: 115, 203.
[86] Richards 1907: 159.

what 'proper' Attic was (and not only because he undoubtedly had access to works of Athenian authors like Plato and Isocrates) and was incapable of distinguishing between the various Greek dialects. As Kenneth Dover, a dissenting voice, has observed, 'acquaintance with many varieties of a language is as likely to sharpen the ear for differences as to blunt it, especially in so articulate a writer',[87] and allowance must be made for X.'s creativity.[88] Secondly, it is unrealistic to suppose that either X. or the 'pure' Attic authors to whom he is unfavourably compared (notably the orators) wrote more or less the way they spoke. Indeed, that supposition rests on an outdated view of the nature and the sources of 'pure' Attic. Once it is understood that 'pure' Attic is a deliberate literary construct which cannot be equated with the Attic vernacular, it becomes plausible that the variety of registers and dialects X. employs marks a conscious departure from this artificial norm.

The following sections will develop this view, while the Commentary contains further notes on individual lexical items and expressions.

'Pure' Attic

The first Greek prose was written in the Ionic dialect, but the closing decades of the fifth century saw the rise of Attic as a feasible alternative, as evidenced, for instance, by the speeches of Antiphon and the *History* of Thucydides.[89] However, these early practitioners to varying degrees avoided key Attic phonological markers which could be perceived as parochial, writing, for example, Ionic (and generally Greek) -σσ- and -ρσ- instead of Attic -ττ- and -ρρ-. Their morphology and vocabulary, too, were influenced by their Ionic predecessors. Antiphon, for example, uses ψαύειν (3.3.5), the common verb for 'touch' in Ionic (it often occurs in Herodotus and the Hippocratic corpus), which is entirely replaced by ἅπτεσθαι in later classical Attic prose (except for a single instance in X. (*Mem.* 1.4.12)). At the same time, many Ionicisms may have been felt as 'poeticisms', since many current Ionic words occurred in epic, the basis of which is Ionic, and continued to be used in high poetry, such as tragedy (ψαύειν occurs in both); or as 'archaisms', since Ionic and Attic spring

87 Dover 1997: 110.

88 Thus, while the heavy use of prepositional prefixes is a widespread development in fourth-century Attic (see Willi 2003b: 62, and for X. in general Balode 2011), X. appears to have actively coined quite a few, in particular with the prefixes ἀντι- (3.1.16n.), δυσ- (3.5.16n.) and ὑπερ- (3.5.7n.); they serve to underline some of his ethical and practical preoccupations. He also seems to have coined compounds of different kinds (e.g. with ἀξιο-, 3.1.24n.).

89 On the crystallization of Attic as a literary language for prose, see Adrados 2005: 142–60; Horrocks 2010: 67–78; Colvin 2014: 163–8.

from the same source (Ionic–Attic), so that we can hardly exclude the possibility that ψαύειν, for instance, was used in early Attic and was primarily felt to be old-fashioned rather than Ionic.

After this beginning, Attic rapidly became the main vehicle for Greek literary prose, not only for the 'homespun' Athenian genres of forensic and political oratory and Socratic dialogue, but also for historiography; here Thucydides was the model, so that in the first half of the fourth century not only X. but also non-Athenian historians like Philistus of Syracuse and Ephorus of Cyme wrote Attic (although Ctesias of Cnidus appears to have followed Herodotus in writing Ionic). Along with the rapid rise in the prestige of Attic came a decline in the influence of the established conventions of prose writing in Ionic: fourth-century authors such as Lysias and Plato always have -ττ-, and X. records the famous cry of the soldiers upon seeing the sea as θάλαττα θάλαττα (4.7.24), even though most of them would have shouted θάλασσα θάλασσα. These stylistic developments have led in turn to the assumption that the gap between the language of literary prose and conversational Attic narrowed over the course of the fifth and fourth centuries, particularly in the case of oratory: orators such as Lysias and Demosthenes wrote speeches for delivery in the courts and the Assembly and manage to give the impression of capturing vernacular speech.[90]

It is this fourth-century oratorical prose which has usually (if often implicitly) been taken as the benchmark of 'pure' Attic by ancient and modern scholars alike. 'Pure' comes to mean 'close to the real thing' and to have normative overtones, implying that it was (or should have been) the goal to write an Attic 'close to the real thing'. In actual fact, both uses of the word are highly problematic.

The Nature of 'Pure' Attic Prose and X.'s Dialectisms

If 'pure' implies 'close to the real thing', then the question arises what 'the real thing' is supposed to be. Even if we leave aside the differences which must have existed between the speech of, say, city and country dwellers or young and old, the period under consideration was one of increasing linguistic diversity.[91] Owing to Athenian imperialism and trading, non-Attic

[90] Cf. Richards 1907: 157: the orators 'use, we are safe in saying, the actual Attic speech of their time, not indeed in all its colloquial idiom and ease, but in its serious and slightly formal shape'. Cf. Colvin 2014: 166, who argues that if the orators share a word or grammatical form with Athenian prose inscriptions and/or with the spoken parts of Aristophanic comedy, it may be assumed that it was current in Attic.

[91] Niehoff-Panagiotidis 1994: 201–18; Crespo 2010: 126–30; Colvin 2014: 109–11.

Greeks converged on Athens and Athenians spent more time abroad, and both sorts of interaction must have affected speech habits. Indeed, already in the final decades of the fifth century, the 'Old Oligarch' ([X.] *Ath. Pol.* 2.8) observed that the Athenians, 'hearing every kind of dialect (φωνή), have taken something from each' and use a 'mixed' (κεκραμένῃ) form of speech made of all sorts of Greek and even foreign elements. A specific development was that the Athenian administration of much Ionic-speaking territory in the empire produced a convergence of Ionic and Attic, which remained the language of diplomacy and international commerce after the loss of the empire and which can be traced in official inscriptions from the fourth century. This so-called 'Great Attic', which might more accurately be described as a 'modern Ionicized Attic', would evolve into the Hellenistic *koine*.[92]

Since we can trace little of this variation and development in the formal prose of the orators – in fact, notwithstanding the differences between various authors and speeches, it is the uniformity of their language which is most striking – their diction appears to be 'pure' mostly in the sense that it is quite standardized and considerably removed from conversational language. In fact, the orators even use a 'purified' language, in that it appears to be the result of a conscious effort to select from co-existing forms. Among the words and forms which fourth-century orators began to eschew were items which were felt to be vulgar (that is, spoken by the lower strata of Athenian society), poetic, archaic and Ionic (the latter three often amounting to the same thing).[93] The orators thereby created a distinctive prose style which was distinguished from other types of Attic literature (such as tragedy) and was in part an ideological construct, formed in reaction to the convergence of Ionic and Attic; in any case, the possibility should not be excluded that certain words were targeted for elimination precisely because they could be perceived as belonging to a different dialect.[94]

These considerations throw a new light on perceived 'dialectisms' (especially Ionicisms) in X. Some of them may in fact have been part of the spoken language for a long time, but then avoided by most fourth-century Attic prose authors.[95] If ψαύειν is best interpreted as an archaism, it may

[92] Horrocks 2010: 74. The classic account is Thumb 1974: 202–53.

[93] Adrados 2005: 156–60.

[94] So Hunter xlvi; cf. Niehoff-Panagiotidis 1994: 219–20.

[95] Adrados 2005: 160. Niehoff-Panagiotidis 1994: 204–5 gives the example of ἀκμήν (4.3.26) used in the sense of ἔτι, which we have seen was regarded by some ancient grammarians as 'newfangled' (and it is common in the *koine*). It was, however, used by Aeschylus (fr. 339a Radt), possibly as a colloquialism; perhaps we should conclude that the word remained in use in Attic but was shunned as a vulgarism by other fourth-century authors.

be a case in point, and another example may be ἀσινέστατα (3.3.3): ἀσινής is commonly regarded as an Ionic word,[96] but in Ionic texts it means both 'doing no harm' and 'suffering no harm', while X. (cf. 2.3.27; *Cyr.* 1.4.7; *Eq.* 5.1) and the 'late' Plato (*Leg.* 649d8, 670d7), the only classical Attic prose authors who adopt the word before it shows up again in the *koine*, use it only in the former, active, sense. This pattern may indicate that the word had a career in the Attic vernacular independent from its use in Ionic, but that it was rejected by the orators, perhaps precisely because it could be perceived as Ionic. This impression is reinforced by the fact that the cognate verb σίνομαι is also found in X. (× 5, e.g. 3.4.16) and Plato (*Leg.* 936e4), while Isocrates (*Ep.* 4.11) uses the cognate noun σίνος in a letter, which 'may show that it belonged to the colloquial sphere'.[97] Another example may be πέπανται (3.3.18). πέπαμαι (from *πάομαι) is commonly regarded as a Doricism (for Attic) κέκτημαι,[98] but its attestation in Solon (F13.7 West) and occasionally in Aeschylus and Euripides has led some scholars to suppose that the word was adopted into Attic early on from neighbouring Boeotians (whose Aeolic dialect may also have had the word).[99] While πέπαμαι does not become part of the *koine*, there is no telling how long it survived in spoken Attic, and it is difficult to say with confidence that from a fourth-century Athenian perspective X.'s use of the word is a Doricism rather than, say, an archaism or colloquialism.

Since Attic was in the process of incorporating Ionic influences, some 'Ionicisms' in X. were probably experienced as *innovative* Attic. This holds, for instance, for X.'s use of ἐδώκαμεν (3.2.5n.) instead of ἔδομεν; official inscriptions from the middle of the fourth century start to show up the aorist marker -κ- of the reduplicated athematic verbs in the plural (and this becomes much more regular after *c.* 300), but since the official language of inscriptions is conservative, such forms may well have been entrenched in the spoken language of many Athenians from the end of the fifth century.[100] The same may hold for X.'s slight preference for originally Ionic ἤν (e.g. 3.1.23) over older Attic ἐάν (3.1.14n.) in *Anabasis*,[101] or for his use of originally Ionic ἔστε (3.1.19n.) alongside ἕως (e.g. 3.1.43), and of two neuters in -μα (3.2.19 ὄχημα, 5.2 βόσκημα), as many examples of this type of

[96] Gautier 56.

[97] Lipka 51. Adrados 2005: 146, 195 speaks in this connection of a 'subterranean' Attic vocabulary, which comes into view in X. and the late works of Plato.

[98] Gautier 34.

[99] Wilamowitz-Moellendorff on Eur. *HF* 1426; Mülke on Solon F13.7 West.

[100] Willi 2010: 105; for the inscriptional evidence, see Threatte II.600–19.

[101] Cf. Willi 2003a: 235. If the manuscripts and editions can be trusted, the distribution between ἤν and ἐάν is 83 : 50 in *Anabasis* and even 200 : 43 in *Cyropaedia*, but 0 : 57 in *Hellenica* and 2 : 78 in *Memorabilia*. X. also uses the form ἄν (with long ᾱ) in *Anabasis* 3 at 3.2.25, 4.2, 5.8. Cf. the distribution of κατακαίνω and ἀποκτείνω discussed on p. 30 below.

noun spread from Ionic into the *koine*.[102] Other 'dialectisms' may belong to this category: if X. occasionally uses ἐξαπίνης (× 8, e.g. 3.3.7) next to ἐξαίφνης (× 17), while the orators do not, this may well tell us something about Attic purism, because the attestation of ἐξαπίνης in Aristophanes (all in *Wealth*, from the 380s) and later in Menander suggests that the word was not alien to Attica from the beginning of the fourth century.[103]

Generic Norms and their Extensions

When one considers the various genres which together make up 'Attic literature' (tragedy, comedy, oratory, Socratic dialogue and historiography), it immediately becomes clear that there are significant linguistic differences between them.[104] This lack of a single normative 'literary Attic' raises the question whether it is legitimate to compare X. with the orators and find him wanting. To be sure, it is often supposed that historiography evolved in a way similar to oratory: Thucydides' language was still characterized by Ionicisms (which in some cases amount to the same thing as poeticisms or archaisms), but the same no longer held for fourth-century practitioners of the genre. However, while this may be true in some respects (as with the shift from -σσ- to -ττ-), the loss of virtually all fourth-century historiography *except* X. makes it difficult to assess just how similar things were and to reconstruct the expectations of X.'s first audiences.[105] For instance, while the orators may have shied away from clear poeticisms in order to avoid sounding pompous, there is no obvious reason why historiographers should have followed suit, and X. uses several words in 3.1 (n.) which are shared only with (high) poetry and can be taken as adding poetic 'colouring' to scenes of high drama (3.1.3n. πόθος, 1.11n. σκηπτός, 1.23n. τρωτός, 1.29n. τλήμων).[106] His awareness of the genre-specific propriety of different kinds of words is further shown by the fact that παν- compounds, which are associated with an elevated register (3.3.13n. παγχαλέπως, as opposed to colloquial Attic πάνυ χαλεπῶς) and appear to be employed by X. at moments of heightened *pathos*, occur frequently in his historiographical narratives (*Hell.* × 30, *An.* × 9, *Cyr.* × 25) but are entirely absent from the Socratic works.

In general, it is important to keep in mind that historiography was less tied to Athenian localities and institutions than oratory and Socratic

[102] Thumb 1974: 216. [103] See Willi 2003b: 61. [104] Cf. Willi 2010: 106–7.

[105] The comments on X.'s language by grammarians from the Roman imperial period are not a good guide, because they operated with a strongly normative concept of what constitutes 'good' Attic, mostly determined by the orators. It should also be remembered that X. attracted such scrutiny precisely because he could be considered an *Attic* classic (a status which, say, Ephorus did not achieve).

[106] For poeticisms in X. and their identification, see Tsagalis 2002.

literature, and that its generic conventions were not yet strictly defined. One nascent motif in Thucydides which X. took further in *Anabasis*, *Hellenica* and *Agesilaus* is the occasional placement of Laconian Doric expressions in the mouths of Spartan speakers.[107] The lexical items in question are common words and oaths, which almost all readers must have instantly recognized as typically Spartan: *(a)* τελέθω for γίγνομαι (6.6.36 and, in a formulaic phrase, 3.2.3 δεῖ ... ἄνδρας ἀγαθοὺς τελέθειν); *(b)* ἐξέρπει for ἐξέρχεται (7.1.8); *(c)* (ναὶ) τὼ σιώ (i.e. Castor and Pollux; 6.6.34, 7.6.39; *Hell.* 4.4.10; *Ages.* 5.5) for (μὰ) τὼ θεώ (i.e. Demeter and Persephone). X. renders short speeches more or less entirely in Doric at *Hell.* 1.1.23 (a letter), 3.3.2, 4.4.10. The state of our knowledge of fourth-century historiography does not permit us to say whether X. was alone in exploiting this opportunity for added realism and characterization, but it does strongly suggest that X. was aware of, and could artfully exploit, dialectal variation.

A number of other Doricisms and general dialectisms which do not make it into the *koine* can be interpreted as a different kind of expression of X.'s 'international' aspirations. An example is Doric κατακαίνω (3.1.2(n.) νικῶντες μὲν οὐδένα ἂν κατακάνοιεν), which occurs alongside Attic ἀποκτείνω (e.g. 2.4.6, a speech by a Spartan (!), νικῶντες μὲν τίνα ἂν ἀποκτείναιμεν;). Examples such as these seem random, but they may in fact be consciously employed from time to time to signal to the reader that this is not a parochial Attic work: the employment of such words at certain intervals is enough to give the work a non-Attic patina.[108] It is significant in this respect that the distribution of this type of dialectal word over X.'s various works is uneven: they are much rarer in *Hellenica* and the Socratic works than in *Agesilaus*, *Anabasis* and especially *Cyropaedia*. Thus the distribution between κατακαίνω and ἀποκτείνω is 3 : 3 in *Agesilaus*, 16 : 24 in *Anabasis* and 25 : 6 in *Cyropaedia*, but κατακαίνω is absent altogether from *Hellenica* (× 99 ἀποκτείνω) and the Socratic works (× 14 ἀποκτείνω). It is impossible to draw conclusions from these data about the chronology of X.'s works.[109] Rather, it appears that most dialectisms show up in works which do not deal with Athenian affairs, which are generically adventurous and which may well represent attempts to appeal to an audience

[107] Cf. Thuc. 1.81.6 (τάμωμεν, with the MSS), 4.40.2, 5.63.3, with Colvin 1999: 63. For X.'s use of the device, see Hiersche 1970: 217–18; Colvin 1999: 70–3; Gray 2014: 327–8; *CCX* 224. Cf. also the presumably Syracusan Doric future παιξοῦνται (from παίζω) at *Symp.* 9.2 in a speech of a Syracusan. In *Cyropaedia* there are, of course, no Greek characters.

[108] See Thomas in Brennan/Thomas for a similar suggestion; cf. Willi 2012 on the inconsistent Doric of Theocritus.

[109] As shown by Tuplin 1993: 193–7 (on the basis of statistics for a wider range of examples).

across the Greek-speaking world.[110] In the case of these works, then, rather than expecting 'proper' Attic, it is better to regard X.'s style as one possible development of the 'international' and 'expanded' version of Attic adopted by Thucydides.[111]

Military Jargon

Some items in the list of rare or previously unattested words and senses in X. with which this section opens do not easily fit the categorizations proposed here; these are διαγγέλλομαι 'pass an order to one another' (3.4.36), ὑπερδέξιος 'higher ground' (3.4.37) and πλευραί (3.2.36) and στόμα (3.4.42) used for the 'sides' and 'front' of an army. These words have in common that they appear only or first in X. (some, like ὑπερδέξιος and στόμα, are common in Polybius and other writers of the *koine*) and that they cannot be assigned to an obvious source in a dialect or literary genre. The fact that the first two are compounds (though of familiar types) and the latter two have a metaphorical quality may at first sight suggest that X.'s own creativity is the source. That many of the relevant words pass into the *koine* speaks against this explanation, however, since there is no reason to assume that X.'s creative coinages would find such widespread acceptance.

It is more likely that these and other lexical items reflect a specialized, technical military jargon. X.'s use of technical terms is well documented, including his precise terms for military ranks and other offices associated with Spartan institutions.[112] It may be surmised that the increasing professionalization and specialization of warfare in fourth-century Greece went hand in hand with the development of a technical vocabulary designed to give expression to changes in organization and tactics and, given the increasing role of mercenaries in Greek armies, to facilitate communication between officers and soldiers from different parts of Greece (there is no need to look for a single regional provenance of the relevant terms).

The items in question give themselves away as belonging to a specific technical military register (rather than being poetic or creative) because they possess one or usually more of the following characteristics. *(a)* They

[110] In the case of *Agesilaus* a specifically Spartan audience may also be targeted. Suggestive in this respect is the fact that *Agesilaus* displays a number of non-Attic words for which the corresponding passages in *Hellenica* employ 'properly' Attic synonyms: Gautier 134; Tuplin 1993: 194–5.

[111] To follow Colvin's (2014: 163–4) characterization of Thucydides.

[112] Gautier 150–3; Lipka 46–7; Dillery 2016: 249–50. See, however, Huitink and Rood 2016 for some qualifications to X.'s precision.

are metaphorical. It is well known that metaphor plays an important part in the formation of technical languages,[113] and specialized military vocabulary is no exception: cf. Latin *aries* ('ram' > 'battering ram') and *testudo* ('tortoise' > 'shield' and 'battle formation wherein the soldiers hold their shields above their heads'),[114] or the British and American ranks 'corporal' for the leader of a 'body' of troops (cf. Latin *corpus*), 'captain' for the 'head' of such a body (cf. *caput*) and 'colonel' from *columna* 'column/pillar'. As we shall see, the Greek terms in question partake of similar metaphors, which are usually based on simple physical resemblances: e.g. πλαίσιον (3.2.36n.), ἀκρωνυχία (3.4.37n.). *(b)* The word formations are productive and easy to parallel: e.g. διαγγέλλομαι (3.4.36n.), ἀκρωνυχία (3.4.37n.). *(c)* A number of items are shared between X. and his close contemporary Aeneas Tacticus, a general (probably) and the writer of a technical manual on siegecraft; e.g. ὑπερδέξιος (3.4.37n.).[115] While there may have been (now lost) written works which served as their communal source, it is more likely that both availed themselves of living military language. *(d)* Quite a few of these words enter the *koine*, recurring especially in Polybius; e.g. οὐρά (3.4.38n.), ὑπερβολή (3.5.18n.). It is more plausible that Polybius and X. tapped into the same source material (actual military language) than that X. influenced Polybius in these instances. *(e)* They often fulfil a number of criteria thought to be characteristic of technical vocabulary: for instance, they have a clear technical reference and are not likely to have been used outside the military sphere for which they were designed, and they seem standardized (for example by being expressively neutral, i.e. not carrying positive or negative connotations).[116]

In availing himself of recognizably technical military terms, X. opens up a new avenue in narrative historiography. Whereas Herodotus and Thucydides wrote about warfare in a high literary register, X. adds a realistic touch to his report. Some of the words (such as φάλαγξ 3.3.11n.) are regularly used by X., but he uses others only occasionally, to special effect. Thus, in *Anabasis* 3, a book very much concerned with evolving tactics, διαγγέλλομαι appears in a context in which various ways of giving orders are thematized, and ὑπερδέξιος and ἀκρωνυχία occur in a context in which Xenophon finds new ways of dealing with a tactical problem.

[113] See e.g. Lloyd 1987: 172–214; Langslow 2000: 178–201.

[114] For the military vocabulary of the Romans, see De Meo 1986: 171–207.

[115] Hunter lvi–lviii lists many overlaps in the vocabulary of X. and Aeneas Tacticus and concludes (p. lviii) that the majority of them concern 'new technical terms and new compounds, necessitated by the growth both of the art of war and of other sciences, and the need for an extended vocabulary to keep pace with it'.

[116] For such criteria, see Willi 2003a: 56–70.

6 STYLE: SPEECH AND NARRATIVE

Repetition and Variety

Pomeroy's 1994 claim that 'modern analysis of Xenophon's prose has not essentially progressed beyond the observations of the ancient critics' remains a fair assessment, not only in relation to his vocabulary, but also in relation to his style.[117] In this case, part of the reason for this lack of progress lies in the fact that the treatment of style by X.'s ancient critics was more complex – as well as more positive – than that of diction.[118] There were, it is true, short soundbites hailing X. as 'the Attic Muse' (Diog. Laert. 2.57 Ἀττικὴ Μοῦσα) or 'the Attic bee' (*Suda* ξ 47 Adler Ἀττικὴ μέλιττα) – as well as grand claims that 'the Muses spoke with Xenophon's voice' (Cic. *Orat.* 62 *Xenophontis voce Musas quasi locutas ferunt*) – all tributes to 'the sweetness of his style' (γλυκύτητι τῆς ἑρμηνείας), in Diogenes' terms. Apart from 'sweetness', several other descriptive terms were routinely used to characterize X.'s style: 'grace' or 'charm' (χάρις),[119] 'clarity' (σαφήνεια),[120] and 'simplicity' (ἀφέλεια).[121] But these same qualities could be invoked in more careful and nuanced analyses, such as are found in late second-century handbooks of style like Hermogenes' Περὶ ἰδεῶν (404–6 Rabe) and in Ps.-Aristides' Περὶ ἀφελοῦς λόγου.[122] And there were some mixed assessments. Ps.-Longinus felt that even the 'demi-gods' (ἥρωες) X. and Plato occasionally went too far in seeking 'paltry pleasantries' (μικροχαρῆ) which detracted from the general dignity of their style (*Subl.* 4.4). More damning is the unfavourable comparison drawn by Dionysius of Halicarnassus between X. and Herodotus. Dionysius acknowledged that X. 'puts words together with no less marked attractiveness and charm than Herodotus' (συντίθησιν αὐτὰ ἡδέως πάνυ καὶ κεχαρισμένως οὐχ ἧττον Ἡροδότου), but thought that he lacked Herodotus' 'sublimity, beauty and impressiveness' (ὕψος . . . καὶ κάλλος καὶ μεγαλοπρέπειαν): 'when, on occasion, he wishes to enliven his style, like an offshore breeze he blows for a short time, but is soon stilled' (κἄν ποτε διεγεῖραι βουληθῆι τὴν φράσιν, ὀλίγον ἐμπνεύσας ὥσπερ ἀπόγειος αὔρα ταχέως σβέννυται) (*Pomp.* 4; cf. *De imitatione* fr. 31 Rademacher–Usener).

[117] Pomeroy 14.

[118] For discussions of ancient criticism, see also nn. 38 and 122. There were several books devoted to X. alone that are no longer extant; see Russell on Ps.-Longin. *Subl.* 8.1.

[119] E.g. Ath. 10.421b; Quint. *Inst.* 10.1.82 (*Xenophontis illam iucunditatem inadfectatam, sed quam nulla consequi adfectatio possit,* 'Xenophon's charm – effortless, but such as no effort could achieve'); Tac. *Dial.* 31.6 (*iucunditatem*).

[120] E.g. Dio Chrys. 18.14. [121] E.g. Men. Rhet. 390.1 Spengel.

[122] For Hermogenes, see Wooten 1987 (introduction and annotated translation); for Ps.-Aristides, see the edition of Patillon, and Rutherford 1998: 64–79 (discussion), 124–53 (annotated translation).

The limitations of modern criticism are seen in a tendency to patronize X. at the same time as praising him. Representative of numerous sweeping assessments are the comments of Norden in *Die antike Kunstprosa*. Norden spoke of X. as 'the unadorned child of Nature' while relating his development to the environment in which he grew up: thus X. was 'an authentic Athenian with his instinctive feeling for moderation', whose name evokes 'the idea of a simple grace – the specifically Attic quality'.[123] Racial assumptions of Athenian superiority underlie many instances of this sort of broad-brush characterization: strikingly, they fail to attend to some of the warnings in ancient critics that X.'s apparent simplicity conceals its own art (e.g. Ps.-Aristid. *Rh.* 2.31, 42, 82 Patillon).

Much more promising are the approaches to X.'s narrative technique that have developed in recent decades. Vivienne Gray in particular has sought to redeem X. by demonstrating his literary artistry – his use of narrative patterns marked by repetition and variation, often playing off similar episodes in Homer and Herodotus – and even by reading X. as a narrative theorist: one of his typical patterns involves highlighting 'second wave' responses to the exemplary actions of leaders, and this pattern is in turn expressive of X.'s understanding of his own didacticism.[124]

If one turns from these assessments to *Anabasis* 3 itself, the picture that emerges of X.'s style is above all one of variety. There are lengthy formal speeches which mirror the style of civic assemblies (3.2.7–32n.), short exchanges marked by the language of formal diplomacy (e.g. 3.3.2-4), and in addition a few short and vivid snatches of conversation (e.g. 3.4.38–43, 47–9, 5.5, 6nn.). There is much action-packed narrative where the turn of events is rapidly conveyed through short paratactic clauses (3.4.38–43n.). But X. also mimics the language of inventories (3.4.31n.), formal decrees (3.2.38n.) or scientific discourse (3.4.19–23n.), and there are hints of other specialized discourses (for instance, geographical and military writing). A particularly important source of variation in X.'s style is to be found in the differences between the speeches and the narrative. Some of these differences may be seen as attempts to capture the rhythms and tone of spoken discourse: thus the speeches contain instances of anacoluthon (3.1.17, 2.11, 12), colloquialisms (3.1.13) and proverbial expressions (3.1.27). On the other hand, the speeches are

[123] Norden 1974: 101–2 ('das schmucklos schreibende Naturkind; ein echter Athener mit seinem instinktiven Gefühl für das Maßvolle; die Vorstellung einfacher Grazie, also der spezifisch attischen Eigenschaft'). Norden was paraphrasing Blass, who called X. 'kein Kunstredner, sondern ein Naturredner', 'a speaker not by art but by nature' (1892: 479).

[124] See esp. Gray 2011. Important contributions in the modern rehabilitation of X. include Higgins 1977; Gray 1989; Tuplin 1993; Dillery 1995; Tamiolaki 2010; and the essays in Tuplin 2004b, Gray 2010a, Hobden and Tuplin 2012, and *CCX*.

understandably more likely to contain 'high' rhetorical features such as negative–positive antithesis (e.g. 3.2.21), anaphora (e.g. 3.2.24, 30nn.) and near-synonyms (3.2.4, 4.25), though all these features are found to a lesser extent in the narrative too.

While the difference between speech and narrative is a strong feature of historiographical predecessors such as Thucydides, X. departs from the Thucydidean precedent in his increased use of dialogue and in his greater concern for the stylistic characterization of different speakers. Chirisophus employs a typically Spartan brevity (3.2.1n.); Cleanor is consistently a vigorous and forceful, but relatively unnuanced, speaker (3.2.4n.); the most frequent speaker, Xenophon, is given scope for more elaborate and subtle rhetorical manoeuvres, building on the intensity and force of the other speakers. The following excerpts from the exhortatory speeches made before the whole army following the loss of the generals can serve as illustrations of these contrasts:

- Chirisophus (3.2.2–3): χαλεπὰ μὲν τὰ παρόντα . . . ὅμως δὲ δεῖ . . . μὴ ὑφίεσθαι, ἀλλὰ πειρᾶσθαι ὅπως ἢν μὲν δυνώμεθα καλῶς νικῶντες σωιζώμεθα· εἰ δὲ μή, ἀλλὰ καλῶς γε ἀποθνήισκωμεν. The Spartan general is not without rhetorical effectiveness: he develops his argument first through a μέν/δέ contrast, and then through a short negative–positive antithesis. The ὅπως-clause offers a forceful expansion by means of another μέν/δέ contrast and particularly by the 'apodotic' ἀλλά – a marked feature of an impromptu spoken style – with the following γε capping the repetition of καλῶς. Presumably a slight pause is to be imagined after εἰ δὲ μή: 'if not – at all events let us die nobly'.
- Cleanor (3.2.4): ὁρᾶτε μέν, ὦ ἄνδρες, τὴν βασιλέως ἐπιορκίαν καὶ ἀσέβειαν, ὁρᾶτε δὲ τὴν Τισσαφέρνους ἀπιστίαν. Cleanor makes more open use of rhetorical figures, building up emphasis through the anaphora of ὁρᾶτε and the μέν/δέ balance so as to mask the emptiness of the contrived opposition of 'the king' and 'Tissaphernes'. Whereas Chirisophus makes heavy use of verbs, Cleanor employs a series of abstract nouns with a strong moral colouring but with little regard for their difference in meaning (as in Thucydides, the greater use of moral vocabulary is itself a more general feature of the speeches as opposed to the narrative).
- Xenophon (3.2.15): καὶ τότε μὲν δὴ περὶ τῆς Κύρου βασιλείας ἄνδρες ἦτε ἀγαθοί· νῦν δ' ὁπότε περὶ τῆς ὑμετέρας σωτηρίας ὁ ἀγών ἐστι, πολὺ δήπου ὑμᾶς προσήκει καὶ ἀμείνονας καὶ προθυμοτέρους εἶναι. This sentence illustrates Xenophon's greater use of variety and elaboration in the build-up of his arguments. The past–present contrast is drawn out with considerable expansion in the second limb: rather than modifying the main verb, like the antithetical περὶ τῆς Κύρου βασιλείας, the

phrase περὶ τῆς ὑμετέρας σωτηρίας stands in a subordinate clause; ἀγαθοί in the first limb (itself emphasized by hyperbaton) is then picked up by the more elaborate πολὺ . . . καὶ ἀμείνονας καὶ προθυμοτέρους (two comparative adjectives for a single positive, again with hyperbaton). Further emphasis is provided by particles: δή in the first limb asserts that the message of the past is clear to all; δήπου (× 6 in *Anabasis*, all in long speeches by Xenophon himself) in the second adds a touch of tentativeness to the *a fortiori* argument.

Besides these pointed differences between speakers, there is stylistic differentiation in the speeches made by Xenophon himself, in part owing to his sensitivity to his different audiences (3.1.15–25n.). One sign of this differentiation is his use of rhetorical questions, which are grouped in his self-address (× 4 in 3.1.13–14) and in speeches addressed to Proxenus' captains (× 3 in 3.1.17–18, × 3 in 3.1.28–9). The use of rhetorical questions conveys the urgency of the situation when no steps have yet been made in response to the seizure of the generals; it may also suggest a close relationship between speaker and addressee. The longer speech Xenophon makes to the surviving generals and captains, by contrast, does not have a single rhetorical question, while the even longer speech through which he attempts to instil courage in the whole army has only one (3.2.16).[125] The almost complete absence of rhetorical questions in this last speech may itself be explained by its distinctive rhetorical timbre: of all Xenophon's speeches it is most rich in the stylistic features familiar from the formal rhetoric developed in Athens in the fifth century, including overt signposting and the 'apagogic' style argument associated with Gorgias, and it is only in this speech that Xenophon borrows from the style of epideictic rhetoric (3.2.7–32n.).

The variety that can be observed in the narrative and speeches testifies to the artfulness of X.'s writing. His artistry can be grasped still more clearly by paying attention to narratological categories such as the narratorial voice, time, and perspective.[126]

Narrative Technique

Variety can also be seen as a hallmark of X.'s narrative technique in *Anabasis*. Throughout *Anabasis* 3, the narrative voice is generally covert: there are no first-person forms for the narrator. This narratorial stance contrasts with the more overt interventions found in the extensive

[125] See also 3.2.19n.

[126] See *CCX* 263–78 for a general treatment of X.'s narrative style; for narratological treatments of *Anabasis* see *SAGN* I.129–46 (narrator), II.147–63 (time), III.161–78 (space), IV.172–90 (character).

obituary notices in Books 1 and 2 (1.9, 2.6), as well as with the frequent references to what 'is' or 'was' said that cluster in the narrative of the battle of Cunaxa (p. 18). The move to a more covert narrator coincides with Xenophon's increasing centrality in the story. The perspectives of the narrator X. and the character Xenophon become closely linked: how the narrator knows about events in the past such as Xenophon's consultation of the Delphic oracle, or about events in the narrative present such as Xenophon's dream, is not explained.[127] The closer linking of narrator and character is confirmed by a number of generalizing comments that are included in one section of the book: X. moves from the immediate 'now' of the story to illustrate the sort of general military truths that underlie the tactical innovations introduced in the course of the retreat (3.4, 3.4.16–18, 19–23nn., cf. 3.4.34–6n.).

Both the account of Xenophon's visit to Delphi and the various passages where generalizations are introduced illustrate another source of *Anabasis*' variety – the handling of narrative order. Though for the most part *Anabasis* does follow a linear order, there are a number of notable flashbacks or anticipations of later events (in narratological terms, analepses and prolepses), and these departures from a simple chronological order are important for understanding X.'s overall purpose. Small-scale flashbacks are used to introduce information as it has an impact on the generals' decision-making (3.3.5, 4.2nn.), while the uneven distribution of background information about the places through which the army travels makes a thematic contribution even as it provides a valuable historical insight into the limitations of the Greeks' knowledge of Persia (3.4.7–12n.).

X.'s treatment of narrative speed is equally varied. Book 3 starts with three meetings including speeches represented in direct discourse – an effective way of slowing down the narrative pace and creating suspense. The slow rhythm is intensified by the preceding obituary notices (2.6) and by the flashback to how Xenophon came to join the expedition: all told, events that last fewer than twenty-four hours cover just under 10 per cent of the whole text. Similar changes of rhythm are achieved by speeches elsewhere in *Anabasis*: speeches in direct discourse comprise a third of the whole text but they are distributed unevenly (other strong concentrations are the end of Book 5, where Xenophon issues a warning against the growth of disorder, and Book 7, where Xenophon makes long defensive and didactic speeches (7.6.11–38, 7.20–47)).[128]

[127] Cf. Bradley 2010; Grethlein 2012.

[128] For analysis of speech representation in *Anabasis*, including a full list of speeches and comparative statistics, see Tuplin 2014.

The army's marches, too, are handled differently over the course of the work. The successive stages are described in detail, initially in list form (e.g. 1.4.1, 9–11), but in Book 3 with much greater flexibility, mapping the alternation between difficult fighting and more regular marches in the Greeks' retreat. Throughout, X.'s selectivity is apparent in the choices made as to which episodes to treat in brief (e.g. the crossing of the Greater Zab at 3.3.6) and which to treat in greater detail (e.g. the futile proposal to bridge the Tigris at 3.5.8–11).

X.'s artistry is particularly shown in his handling of narrative perspective. Plutarch praised the account of the battle of Cunaxa (1.8) for the way 'Xenophon brings it all but before our eyes and through his vividness (*enargeia*) all the time places the reader, much affected and sharing in the dangers, near to the action, as if it had not been concluded, but is going on' (*Artax.* 8.1: Ξενοφῶντος . . . μονονουχὶ δεικνύοντος ὄψει καὶ τοῖς πράγμασιν ὡς οὐ γεγενημένοις, ἀλλὰ γινομένοις ἐφιστάντος ἀεὶ τὸν ἀκροατὴν ἐμπαθῆ καὶ συγκινδυνεύοντα διὰ τὴν ἐνάργειαν). Two of the features of that battle narrative that Plutarch was probably picking up were the sudden appearance of a messenger riding on a sweat-covered horse (1.8.1 ἤδη τε ἦν ἀμφὶ ἀγορὰν πλήθουσαν . . . , ἡνίκα Πατηγύας . . . προφαίνεται ἐλαύνων ἀνὰ κράτος ἱδροῦντι τῶι ἵππωι) and the description of the Persian army gradually appearing in the distance and moving closer to the Greeks, until the ranks and flashing armour could be seen (1.8.8–10).[129] It is this type of spatial orientation that operates for most of Book 3. The narrator's focus on the Greeks is shown in the handling of arrivals at and departures from the camp (e.g. 3.3.1n.); this spatial focus is matched at a linguistic level, where different Greek perspectives are embodied in the use of tenses (3.4.7n.) and particles (3.4.4n.) and in the designations βάρβαροι and πολέμιοι (3.4.34n.). And yet this use of perspective is not consistently maintained. It is true that X. never shifts the spatial focus to the enemy camp, but he does include reports of Persian thoughts, partly to highlight how the Greeks outwit them (3.4, 3.4.2nn.), and at one point he describes how the Persians perceive the Greeks from a distance (3.5.13n.).

Underlying the changes in technique across *Anabasis* and within Book 3 is a consistent concern with *argument*. By means of his narrative and particularly by means of his construction of the character of Xenophon, X. offers – as the Commentary will show in detail – both an analysis of how events turned out as they did and an explanation of why they took that course.

[129] Cf. Huitink 2019; also Grethlein 2013: 54–6 (but see *CCX* 274–7 for some reservations).

7 THE TEXTUAL TRADITION

The MSS on which our knowledge of the text of *Anabasis* 3 depends divide into two main families, named **f** and **c** after their most important representatives.[130] The chief MSS belonging to **f** are:

F *Vaticanus* 1335, tenth/eleventh century
M *Marcianus* 590 (olim 511), twelfth/thirteenth century
D *Bodleianus* (canon. gr. 39), fourteenth/fifteenth century
V *Vindobonensis* 95, fifteenth century
Z *Laurentianus* LV 21, fifteenth century
H *Guelferbytanus* (Aug. 71, 19), fifteenth century
T *Phillipsianus* 1627 (olim *Leidensis (Meermannianus)*), fifteenth century

Of these **F** and **M** are the most important, but the relationship between them and the other MSS belonging to **f** remains unclear. In this edition the siglum **f** is used to denote agreement between **F**, **M** and at least some other MSS belonging to its family.

The chief MSS belonging to **c** are:

C *Parisinus* 1640, first hand from 1320
B *Parisinus* 1641, after 1462
A *Vaticanus* 987, somewhat younger than B
E *Etonensis*, fifteenth century

While **C** dates from 1320, the text of *Anabasis* is preceded by a poem dedicating the work to the Byzantine emperor Leo VI (886–912), which shows that the text goes back, directly or indirectly, to a Byzantine MS dating from the ninth/tenth century. At some point, however, many corrections were made in **C**, which often agree with the **f** tradition; in the first four books especially, these corrections have made the first hand of **C** (for which the present edition uses the siglum **C**[1]) almost illegible in various places (e.g. 3.1.21, 4.12). **B**, **A** and probably also **E** are apographs from **C**, made after **C** was corrected. In this edition the siglum **c** is used to denote agreement between all MSS belonging to this family.

In 1932, Castiglioni collated three more MSS from the fourteenth and fifteenth centuries which turn out to be of considerable value:[131]

g *Ambrosianus* G 92 sup., presumably after 1450
a *Ambrosianus* A 78 inf., dated 1374
b *Ambrosianus* A 157 sup., dated 1426

[130] No papyri of *Anabasis* 3 have so far come to light.
[131] Castiglioni 1932.

Of these, **g** most often sides with **c** (e.g. 3.1.3, 3.6), but also contains some good material in agreement with **f** (e.g. 3.4.24); **a** and **b** have many affinities with **DV** (e.g. 3.1.26, 2.37), but **b** preserves a number of uniquely good readings, some of which were anticipated by modern scholars in ignorance of **b**'s existence (e.g. 3.2.27, 4.16, 25).

* * *

Since the editions of Dindorf (1825, 1852), most editors, including Marchant (1904) and Masqueray (1930–1; 3rd edn 1952), have based their editions on **c**, and in particular **C**ⁱ, which on the whole gives a 'smoother' and also somewhat shorter text than **f**, which raised the suspicion that scribal mistakes and additions were responsible for the state of **f**. In many editions, the **c** MSS are actually called 'better' (*meliores*), the **f** MSS 'worse' (*deteriores*). However, over a century ago Persson showed not only that the division into two families is not observable in the papyri or quotations of *Anabasis* in the works of other ancient authors (the so-called 'indirect tradition'), but also that on balance these important additional sources for the text of *Anabasis* side with **f** more often than with **c**.[132] Persson therefore suggested that **C**ⁱ represents a Byzantine edition of the text which was deliberately 'cleaned up'.

Persson decisively undermined the perceived superiority of **c**, even if his conclusion about **C**ⁱ went too far, inasmuch as it undoubtedly preserves good readings in many places (e.g. 3.2.11, 3.4). The upshot is that the choice between variants in the MSS of *Anabasis* needs to be based exclusively on their merits, whether they occur in **c** or **f**. The only critical edition which has given **f** its due is that of Hude (1931; rev. edn by Peters 1972). This edition forms the basis of the present text of *Anabasis* 3. The selective critical apparatus marks *(a)* departures from the text of Hude/Peters; *(b)* readings which are the result of conjectures proposed by modern scholars; *(c)* especially problematic passages, many of which are discussed in the Commentary.

APPENDIX: CHRONOLOGY AND TOPOGRAPHY

The events of *Anabasis* 3 can easily be charted by time and space according to the indications given by X.:

Day	*Reference*	*Location*	*Distance*
1	2.5.27–3.1.2	At R. Zapatas	
1/2	3.1.3–47	At R. Zapatas	
2	3.2.1–3.20	To villages	25 stades

[132] Persson 1915.

3	3.3.20–4.1	At villages	
4	3.4.1–9	To Larisa	
5	3.4.10–12	To Mespila	6 parasangs
6	3.4.13–18	To villages	4 parasangs
7	3.4.18	At villages	
8	3.4.18–23	Through plain[133]	
9	3.4.18–23	Through plain	
10	3.4.18–23	Through plain	
11	3.4.18–23	Through plain	
12	3.4.24–30	To villages (on mountain)	
13	3.4.31	At villages	
14	3.4.31	At villages	
15	3.4.31	At villages	
16	3.4.32–6	To village (in plain)	
16/17	3.4.37	Night march	60 stades
17	3.4.37	Through plain	
18	3.4.37	Through plain	
19	3.4.37–5.12	To villages	
20	3.5.13–18	Back to unburned villages	

It is much harder to translate these textual indications into absolute chronology and topography. Calculations of the date at which *Anabasis* 3 starts range from late September 401 to mid January 400. The uncertainty derives from three circumstances. (*a*) X. nowhere gives dates for any of the events. The absence of such dates is not in itself surprising given that there was no calendrical scheme accepted throughout the Greek world at the time he was writing and that local calendars were not precisely calibrated to the solar year. (*b*) He plots changes of season only indirectly, through occasional climatic indications. (*c*) There are a number of indirect chronological hints, but their interpretation is controversial.

The main chronological hint within Book 3 is found when the Greeks test the depth of the Tigris (3.5.7). Comparison with modern data for the river suggests that the depth X. gives (spears do not reach the top of the water) fits winter rather than autumn (unless it had been a very wet autumn), i.e. the latter part of the chronological range noted above. This late chronology seems to fit some of the other chronological clues: (*a*) natural produce such as the dates of Mesopotamia (2.3.15–16) or the 'mad honey' of the Pontic mountains (4.8.20) – assuming in both cases that X. is referring to the produce of the current season; (*b*) agricultural seasons as revealed by the state of the irrigation channels; (*c*)

[133] Reade 2015: 195 suggests that τῆι . . . ὑστεραίαι at 3.4.18 may indicate an extra day, but see 3.4.23n.

weather conditions as suggested by muddy stretches in the march down the Euphrates (1.5.7) and in particular as experienced during the crossing of the Carduchian mountains and the Armenian highlands in Book 4 (the late chronology would mean that the troops passed through the Armenian highlands after the worst of the winter had passed). At the same time, it should be noted that some scholars have argued that the various clues scattered through *Anabasis* can fit an early chronology; and others have combined the two chronologies by arguing that a portion of the march in Book 4 is missing (whether because X. deliberately suppressed it or because it has dropped out of the MSS).[134]

To turn to topography, the general direction of the march in Book 3 is not in doubt (unlike in Book 2 and especially in Book 4). More precise mapping is made difficult by a number of factors: (*a*) the paucity of distance indications; (*b*) the lack of toponyms between Mespila (3.4.10) and the River Centrites (4.3.1); (*c*) the omission of some features, e.g. the River Khabur near the chain of hills crossed at 3.4.24–31; (*d*) the fact that X.'s descriptions of landscape (which may have been written up from memory) were designed not to help readers recreate the route, but to make the military situation comprehensible: thus he divides terrain into plains (πεδία) – where cavalry function well; ravines (χαράδραι) and hills (γήλοφοι or λόφοι: 3.4.24n.) – where hoplites are still of some use; and mountains (ὄρη: see 3.4.37n. for their subdivisions), where light-armed troops are particularly effective; (*e*) the political situation in Iraq since the First Gulf War, which has made scholarly investigation on the ground impossible.[135] (One positive development in recent years is that Google Earth makes it possible to survey the route in detail from the air, and to some extent from the ground, with the help of uploaded photographs.)[136] The main points are as follows:

T1. At the Zapatas: It is clear from the preceding and succeeding stages (despite problems in what precedes) that this is the Greater rather than the Lesser Zab (the crossing of which is not mentioned, probably

[134] For the late chronology, see especially Brennan 2008, 2012 and Brennan in Brennan/Thomas. For the early chronology, see Glombiowski 1994 (followed by the chart at Lee 2007: 283–9). For the proposed lacuna, see Manfredi 1986: 211–15; Lane Fox 2004b: 35–46.

[135] The most recent first-hand scholarly survey is Manfredi 1986. Brennan 2005 is an account of a walk along the whole route in the early 2000s; on foot, he could not carry the same sort of scholarly apparatus as Manfredi. Many nineteenth- and early twentieth-century travellers discuss the route (for a survey, see Rood 2004b: 134–61), but it is sometimes difficult to follow their identifications owing to changes in toponyms and the quality of their maps.

[136] For ease of reference, the orthography adopted here generally follows Google Earth.

owing to its low level).[137] As for where it was crossed (3.3.6n.), nineteenth-century travellers were generally ferried across at Kalak ('Raft'), *c.* 25 miles upstream from its confluence with the Tigris, but (as the name suggests) the river is too deep to cross there without a bridge. If there was no bridge, Layard 1853: 60 suggests a suitable location for fording 5 miles downstream. Its width in this section corresponds with X.'s description (Southgate 1840: II.215–16).

T2. Ravine: The ravine beyond the villages 25 stades from the Zab is probably the Khazir, a tributary of the Zab, with very low water levels owing to the time of year; it could also be a steep-banked irrigation canal (Reade 2015: 193). This identification suits the facts that the journey from the Zab to Larisa involved two days' marching (Days 2 and 4), with only a small distance covered on the first day; and that it was at Larisa that they arrived (back) at the Tigris – which implies that they had not been marching along it (3.4.6).

T3–4. The identifications of Larisa with Nimrud and of Mespila with Nineveh are guaranteed by the overall route, the distances between the sites, and their descriptions (3.4.7–12n.).

T5. Villages: The day's march would have taken the army to a position around Tall Kayf (Ainsworth 1844: 143) or Batnay (Layard 1853: 61).

T6. Disruption caused by higher ground: Probably in the region of Alqosh.

T7. Palace and villages: In this section the Tigris runs from north-west to south-east and parallel to it towards the east is a high range of hills (the Chia Spi or Jebel Abyadh) backed by a flatter descent towards the River Khabur (on the Iraq–Turkey border). The palace complex was probably on the western side of the Chia Spi between Dayrabun (at the western end of the range) and Zakho (across the range to the south-east) (Reade 2015: 197), or else further to the south-east, in the high ground to the east of Duhok (Brennan/Thomas); this location leaves the army further ground to cover in the following days, but (to judge from aerial images) may offer the best fit with the description at 3.4.24. Other suggestions are: (*a*) At or around Zakho (later the site of a castle), with the Greeks following the line of today's main road from the Tigris valley;[138] (*b*) Dayrabun (Reade's preferred location), with the Greeks keeping to a flatter, straighter path west of the range. These

[137] Herodotus (5.52.4) mentions homonymous rivers in this area (without naming them); Ammianus Marcellinus (23.6.21) calls them 'Diabas' and 'Adiabas'. X. follows what Southgate 1840: II.215 identified as the local usage of calling the Greater Zab simply the Zab.

[138] Rennell 1816: 149–59; Ainsworth 1844: 144; Layard 1853: 61; Lendle 181 (with Map 20); similarly Boucher 1913: 166 and Manfredi 1986: 171–2 (with Map 12), both of whom present the army entering the high ground sooner than X.'s account suggests and marching along a ridge. Against Zakho itself there is also the description of the army descending to the plain on leaving the villages: Zakho itself is not on a hill (Ainsworth has to assume that X.'s phrasing is careless).

locations probably leave them too much ground to cover during Days 8–12, when they were pressed by the Persians, and too little during Days 17 and 18, when the Persians did not appear (though the need to carry the wounded, as at 3.4.32, and to cross the River Khabur could have slowed them down).[139] A further objection to (*a*) is the height of the Chia Spi, which makes the proposed sight line impossible.[140] The possibility should also be raised that X.'s topographical descriptions at this point are schematic: at 3.4.24–8, the precise detail of three hills allows for a clear military pattern – enemy action, repeated enemy action, Greek response;[141] if so, it is not surprising that precise details of the route are difficult to recover.

T8. Village in plain: Though X. does not make it clear, the plain to which the army descended is probably on the north-east side of the Chia Spi; this plain would allow a reasonably level descent towards the River Khabur, and a shorter route than if the army had descended to the west of the Chia Spi and passed near Dayrabun.

T9. Spur occupied by the Persians: Probably near Silopi.

T10. Large plain with villages: From Silopi the army could have travelled across the plain to reach the Tigris opposite Cizre, south of the point where the Cudi Dağı range meets the river. They would then have retraced their route to the south-east the following day.

139 If the palace was at Zakho, they would also have had to cross a tributary, the Hazil.

140 Reade 2015: 195; similarly Ainsworth 1844: 142, but he seems to assume that X. has retrojected the sight of the palace.

141 Another sequence of three hills is used to different effect during the march through the Carduchian mountains (4.2.10–20).

ΞΕΝΟΦΩΝΤΟΣ ΚΥΡΟΥ ΑΝΑΒΑΣΕΩΣ
ΛΟΓΟΣ ΤΡΙΤΟΣ

ΞΕΝΟΦΩΝΤΟΣ ΚΥΡΟΥ ΑΝΑΒΑΣΕΩΣ
ΛΟΓΟΣ ΤΡΙΤΟΣ

[Ὅσα μὲν δὴ ἐν τῆι ἀναβάσει τῆι μετὰ Κύρου οἱ Ἕλληνες ἔπραξαν 1
μέχρι τῆς μάχης, καὶ ὅσα ἐπεὶ Κῦρος ἐτελεύτησεν ἐγένετο ἀπιόντων
τῶν Ἑλλήνων σὺν Τισσαφέρνει ἐν ταῖς σπονδαῖς, ἐν τῶι πρόσθεν λόγωι
δεδήλωται.]

Ἐπεὶ δὲ οἵ τε στρατηγοὶ συνειλημμένοι ἦσαν καὶ τῶν λοχαγῶν καὶ τῶν 2
στρατιωτῶν οἱ συνεπόμενοι ἀπωλώλεσαν, ἐν πολλῆι δὴ ἀπορίαι ἦσαν οἱ
Ἕλληνες, ἐννοούμενοι ὅτι ἐπὶ ταῖς βασιλέως θύραις ἦσαν, κύκλωι δὲ αὐτοῖς
πάντηι πολλὰ καὶ ἔθνη καὶ πόλεις πολέμιαι ἦσαν, ἀγορὰν δὲ οὐδεὶς ἔτι
παρέξειν ἔμελλεν, ἀπεῖχον δὲ τῆς Ἑλλάδος οὐ μεῖον ἢ μύρια στάδια,
ἡγεμὼν δ᾽ οὐδεὶς τῆς ὁδοῦ ἦν, ποταμοὶ δὲ διεῖργον ἀδιάβατοι ἐν μέσωι
τῆς οἴκαδε ὁδοῦ, προυδεδώκεσαν δὲ αὐτοὺς καὶ οἱ σὺν Κύρωι ἀναβάντες
βάρβαροι, μόνοι δὲ καταλελειμμένοι ἦσαν οὐδὲ ἱππέα οὐδένα σύμμαχον
ἔχοντες, ὥστε εὔδηλον ἦν ὅτι νικῶντες μὲν οὐδ᾽ ἂν ἕνα κατακάνοιεν,
ἡττηθέντων δὲ αὐτῶν οὐδεὶς ἂν λειφθείη. ταῦτα ἐννοούμενοι καὶ ἀθύμως 3
ἔχοντες ὀλίγοι μὲν αὐτῶν εἰς τὴν ἑσπέραν σίτου ἐγεύσαντο, ὀλίγοι δὲ
πῦρ ἀνέκαυσαν, ἐπὶ δὲ τὰ ὅπλα πολλοὶ οὐκ ἦλθον ταύτην τὴν νύκτα,
ἀνεπαύοντο δὲ ὅπου ἐτύγχανον ἕκαστος, οὐ δυνάμενοι καθεύδειν ὑπὸ
λύπης καὶ πόθου πατρίδων, γονέων, γυναικῶν, παίδων, οὓς οὔποτ᾽
ἐνόμιζον ἔτι ὄψεσθαι. οὕτω μὲν δὴ διακείμενοι πάντες ἀνεπαύοντο.

Ἦν δέ τις ἐν τῆι στρατιᾶι Ξενοφῶν Ἀθηναῖος, ὃς οὔτε στρατηγὸς 4
οὔτε λοχαγὸς οὔτε στρατιώτης ὢν συνηκολούθει, ἀλλὰ Πρόξενος αὐτὸν
μετεπέμψατο οἴκοθεν ξένος ὢν ἀρχαῖος· ὑπισχνεῖτο δέ, εἰ ἔλθοι, φίλον
αὐτὸν Κύρωι ποιήσειν, ὃν αὐτὸς ἔφη κρείττω ἑαυτῶι νομίζειν τῆς
πατρίδος. ὁ μέντοι Ξενοφῶν ἀναγνοὺς τὴν ἐπιστολὴν ἀνακοινοῦται 5
Σωκράτει τῶι Ἀθηναίωι περὶ τῆς πορείας. καὶ ὁ Σωκράτης ὑποπτεύσας
μή τι πρὸς τῆς πόλεως ὑπαίτιον εἴη Κύρωι φίλον γενέσθαι, ὅτι ἐδόκει
ὁ Κῦρος προθύμως τοῖς Λακεδαιμονίοις ἐπὶ τὰς Ἀθήνας συμπολεμῆσαι,
συμβουλεύει τῶι Ξενοφῶντι ἐλθόντα εἰς Δελφοὺς ἀνακοινῶσαι τῶι θεῶι

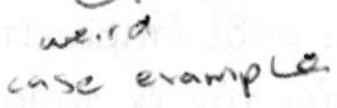

1.1 del. Bisschop et Dindorf
ἐν τῆι ἀναβάσει τῆι μετὰ Κύρου: τῆι Κύρου ἀναβάσει **c**
1.2 ἐννοούμενοι: ἐνθυμούμενοι **f**
ὅτι **C**[1]: μὲν ὅτι cett.
1.3 ἐτύγχανον **CBEg**: ἐτύγχανεν cett.
1.4 ὑπισχνεῖτο δέ **DF**: ὑπισχνεῖτο δὲ αὐτῶι cett.

6 περὶ τῆς πορείας. ἐλθὼν δ᾽ ὁ Ξενοφῶν ἐπήρετο τὸν Ἀπόλλω τίνι ἂν θεῶν
θύων καὶ εὐχόμενος κάλλιστα καὶ ἄριστα ἔλθοι τὴν ὁδὸν ἣν ἐπινοεῖ καὶ
καλῶς πράξας σωθείη. καὶ ἀνεῖλεν αὐτῶι ὁ Ἀπόλλων θεοῖς οἷς ἔδει θύειν.
7 ἐπεὶ δὲ πάλιν ἦλθε, λέγει τὴν μαντείαν τῶι Σωκράτει. ὁ δ᾽ ἀκούσας
ἠιτιᾶτο αὐτὸν ὅτι οὐ τοῦτο πρῶτον ἠρώτα πότερον λῶιον εἴη αὐτῶι
πορεύεσθαι ἢ μένειν, ἀλλ᾽ αὐτὸς κρίνας ἰτέον εἶναι τοῦτ᾽ ἐπυνθάνετο ὅπως
ἂν κάλλιστα πορευθείη. "ἐπεὶ μέντοι οὕτως ἤρου, ταῦτ᾽" ἔφη "χρὴ ποιεῖν
8 ὅσα ὁ θεὸς ἐκέλευσεν." ὁ μὲν δὴ Ξενοφῶν οὕτω θυσάμενος οἷς ἀνεῖλεν ὁ
θεὸς ἐξέπλει, καὶ καταλαμβάνει ἐν Σάρδεσι Πρόξενον καὶ Κῦρον μέλλοντας
9 ἤδη ὁρμᾶν τὴν ἄνω ὁδόν, καὶ συνεστάθη Κύρωι. προθυμουμένου δὲ
τοῦ Προξένου καὶ ὁ Κῦρος συμπρουθυμεῖτο μεῖναι αὐτόν· εἶπε δὲ ὅτι
ἐπειδὰν τάχιστα ἡ στρατεία λήξηι, εὐθὺς ἀποπέμψει αὐτόν. ἐλέγετο
10 δὲ ὁ στόλος εἶναι εἰς Πισίδας. ἐστρατεύετο μὲν δὴ οὕτως ἐξαπατηθείς,
οὐχ ὑπὸ Προξένου· οὐ γὰρ ἤιδει τὴν ἐπὶ βασιλέα ὁρμὴν οὐδὲ ἄλλος
οὐδεὶς τῶν Ἑλλήνων πλὴν Κλεάρχου· ἐπεὶ μέντοι εἰς Κιλικίαν ἦλθον,
σαφὲς πᾶσιν ἤδη ἐδόκει εἶναι ὅτι ὁ στόλος εἴη ἐπὶ βασιλέα. φοβούμενοι
δὲ τὴν ὁδὸν καὶ ἄκοντες ὅμως οἱ πολλοὶ δι᾽ αἰσχύνην καὶ ἀλλήλων καὶ
Κύρου συνηκολούθησαν· ὧν εἷς καὶ Ξενοφῶν ἦν.

11 Ἐπεὶ δὲ ἀπορία ἦν, ἐλυπεῖτο μὲν σὺν τοῖς ἄλλοις καὶ οὐκ ἐδύνατο
καθεύδειν· μικρὸν δ᾽ ὕπνου λαχὼν εἶδεν ὄναρ· ἔδοξεν αὐτῶι βροντῆς
γενομένης σκηπτὸς πεσεῖν εἰς τὴν πατρώιαν οἰκίαν, καὶ ἐκ τούτου
12 λάμπεσθαι πᾶσα. περίφοβος δ᾽ εὐθὺς ἀνηγέρθη, καὶ τὸ ὄναρ τῆι μὲν
ἔκρινεν ἀγαθόν, ὅτι ἐν πόνοις ὢν καὶ κινδύνοις φῶς μέγα ἐκ Διὸς ἰδεῖν
ἔδοξε· τῆι δὲ καὶ ἐφοβεῖτο, ὅτι ἀπὸ Διὸς μὲν βασιλέως τὸ ὄναρ ἐδόκει
αὐτῶι εἶναι, κύκλωι δὲ ἐδόκει λάμπεσθαι τὸ πῦρ, μὴ οὐ δύναιτο ἐκ
τῆς χώρας ἐξελθεῖν τῆς βασιλέως, ἀλλ᾽ εἴργοιτο πάντοθεν ὑπό τινων
13 ἀποριῶν. ὁποῖόν τι μὲν δή ἐστι τὸ τοιοῦτον ὄναρ ἰδεῖν ἔξεστι σκοπεῖν
ἐκ τῶν συμβάντων μετὰ τὸ ὄναρ. γίγνεται γὰρ τάδε· εὐθὺς ἐπειδὴ
ἀνηγέρθη πρῶτον μὲν ἔννοια αὐτῶι ἐμπίπτει· "τί κατάκειμαι; ἡ δὲ νὺξ
προβαίνει· ἅμα δὲ τῆι ἡμέραι εἰκὸς τοὺς πολεμίους ἥξειν. εἰ δὲ γενησόμεθα
ἐπὶ βασιλεῖ, τί ἐμποδὼν μὴ οὐχὶ πάντα μὲν τὰ χαλεπώτατα ἐπιδόντας,
14 πάντα δὲ τὰ δεινότατα παθόντας ὑβριζομένους ἀποθανεῖν; ὅπως δ᾽
ἀμυνούμεθα οὐδεὶς παρασκευάζεται οὐδὲ ἐπιμελεῖται, ἀλλὰ κατακείμεθα
ὥσπερ ἐξὸν ἡσυχίαν ἄγειν. ἐγὼ οὖν τὸν ἐκ ποίας πόλεως στρατηγὸν
προσδοκῶ ταῦτα πράξειν; ποίαν δ᾽ ἡλικίαν ἐμαυτῶι ἐλθεῖν ἀναμένω; οὐ
γὰρ ἔγωγ᾽ ἔτι πρεσβύτερος ἔσομαι, ἐὰν τήμερον προδῶ ἐμαυτὸν τοῖς
πολεμίοις."

1.6 θεοῖς: θεοὺς Buttmann

Ἐκ τούτου ἀνίσταται καὶ συγκαλεῖ τοὺς Προξένου πρῶτον λοχαγούς. 15
ἐπεὶ δὲ συνῆλθον, ἔλεξεν· "ἐγώ, ὦ ἄνδρες λοχαγοί, οὔτε καθεύδειν
δύναμαι, ὥσπερ οἶμαι οὐδ᾽ ὑμεῖς, οὔτε κατακεῖσθαι ἔτι, ὁρῶν ἐν οἵοις
ἐσμέν. οἱ μὲν γὰρ πολέμιοι δῆλον ὅτι οὐ πρότερον πρὸς ἡμᾶς τὸν 16
πόλεμον ἐξέφηναν πρὶν ἐνόμισαν καλῶς τὰ ἑαυτῶν παρεσκευάσθαι, ἡμῶν
δ᾽ οὐδεὶς οὐδὲν ἀντεπιμελεῖται ὅπως ὡς κάλλιστα ἀγωνιούμεθα. καὶ μὴν 17
εἰ ὑφησόμεθα καὶ ἐπὶ βασιλεῖ γενησόμεθα, τί οἰόμεθα πείσεσθαι; ὃς καὶ
τοῦ ὁμομητρίου καὶ ὁμοπατρίου ἀδελφοῦ καὶ τεθνηκότος ἤδη ἀποτεμὼν
τὴν κεφαλὴν καὶ τὴν χεῖρα ἀνεσταύρωσεν· ἡμᾶς δέ, οἷς κηδεμὼν μὲν
οὐδεὶς πάρεστιν, ἐστρατεύσαμεν δὲ ἐπ᾽ αὐτὸν ὡς δοῦλον ἀντὶ βασιλέως
ποιήσοντες καὶ ἀποκτενοῦντες εἰ δυναίμεθα, τί ἂν οἰόμεθα παθεῖν; ἆρ᾽ 18
οὐκ ἂν ἐπὶ πᾶν ἔλθοι ὡς ἡμᾶς τὰ ἔσχατα αἰκισάμενος πᾶσιν ἀνθρώποις
φόβον παράσχοι τοῦ στρατεῦσαί ποτε ἐπ᾽ αὐτόν; ἀλλ᾽ ὅπως τοι μὴ
ἐπ᾽ ἐκείνωι γενησόμεθα πάντα ποιητέον. ἐγὼ μὲν οὖν, ἔστε μὲν αἱ 19
σπονδαὶ ἦσαν, οὔποτε ἐπαυόμην ἡμᾶς μὲν οἰκτίρων, βασιλέα δὲ καὶ
τοὺς σὺν αὐτῶι μακαρίζων, διαθεώμενος αὐτῶν ὅσην μὲν χώραν καὶ οἵαν
ἔχοιεν, ὡς δὲ ἄφθονα τὰ ἐπιτήδεια, ὅσους δὲ θεράποντας, ὅσα δὲ κτήνη,
χρυσὸν δέ, ἐσθῆτα δέ· τὰ δ᾽ αὖ τῶν στρατιωτῶν ὁπότε ἐνθυμοίμην, 20
ὅτι τῶν μὲν ἀγαθῶν τούτων οὐδενὸς ἡμῖν μετείη, εἰ μὴ πριαίμεθα, ὅτου
δ᾽ ὠνησόμεθα ἤιδειν ἔτι ὀλίγους ἔχοντας, ἄλλως δέ πως πορίζεσθαι τὰ
ἐπιτήδεια ἢ ὠνουμένους ⟨τοὺς⟩ ὅρκους [ἤδη] κατέχοντας ἡμᾶς· ταῦτ᾽
οὖν λογιζόμενος ἐνίοτε τὰς σπονδὰς μᾶλλον ἐφοβούμην ἢ νῦν τὸν
πόλεμον. ἐπεὶ μέντοι ἐκεῖνοι ἔλυσαν τὰς σπονδάς, λελύσθαι μοι δοκεῖ καὶ 21
ἡ ἐκείνων ὕβρις καὶ ἡ ἡμετέρα ὑποψία. ἐν μέσωι γὰρ ἤδη κεῖται ταῦτα
τὰ ἀγαθὰ ἆθλα ὁπότεροι ἂν ἡμῶν ἄνδρες ἀμείνονες ὦσιν, ἀγωνοθέται
δ᾽ οἱ θεοί εἰσιν, οἳ σὺν ἡμῖν, ὡς τὸ εἰκός, ἔσονται. οὗτοι μὲν γὰρ 22
αὐτοὺς ἐπιωρκήκασιν· ἡμεῖς δὲ πολλὰ ὁρῶντες ἀγαθὰ στερρῶς αὐτῶν
ἀπειχόμεθα διὰ τοὺς τῶν θεῶν ὅρκους· ὥστε ἐξεῖναί μοι δοκεῖ ἰέναι ἐπὶ
τὸν ἀγῶνα πολὺ σὺν φρονήματι μείζονι ἢ τούτοις. ἔτι δ᾽ ἔχομεν σώματα 23
ἱκανώτερα τούτων καὶ ψύχη καὶ θάλπη καὶ πόνους φέρειν· ἔχομεν δὲ
καὶ ψυχὰς σὺν τοῖς θεοῖς ἀμείνονας· οἱ δὲ ἄνδρες καὶ τρωτοὶ καὶ θνητοὶ
μᾶλλον ἡμῶν, ἢν οἱ θεοὶ ὥσπερ τὸ πρόσθεν νίκην ἡμῖν διδῶσιν. ἀλλ᾽ 24
ἴσως γὰρ καὶ ἄλλοι ταὐτὰ ἐνθυμοῦνται, πρὸς τῶν θεῶν μὴ ἀναμένωμεν

1.17 καὶ ὁμοπατρίου om. **C**[1]
1.20 τούτων Cobet: πάντων codd. (παν in lit. **C**[1])
τοὺς add. Hude
ἤδη del. Damsté: ἤιδη Schneider
1.21 ὑποψία in lit. **C** praeter accentum et α: ἀπορία coni. Hude
1.24 ταὐτὰ Hug: ταῦτα vel ταῦτ᾽ codd.

ἄλλους ἐφ' ἡμᾶς ἐλθεῖν παρακαλοῦντας ἐπὶ τὰ κάλλιστα ἔργα, ἀλλ' ἡμεῖς
ἄρξωμεν τοῦ ἐξορμῆσαι καὶ τοὺς ἄλλους ἐπὶ τὴν ἀρετήν· φάνητε τῶν
25 λοχαγῶν ἄριστοι καὶ τῶν στρατηγῶν ἀξιοστρατηγότεροι. κἀγὼ δέ,
εἰ μὲν ὑμεῖς ἐθέλετε ἐξορμᾶν ἐπὶ ταῦτα, ἕπεσθαι ὑμῖν βούλομαι, εἰ δ'
ὑμεῖς τάττετ' ἐμὲ ἡγεῖσθαι, οὐδὲν προφασίζομαι τὴν ἡλικίαν, ἀλλὰ καὶ
ἀκμάζειν ἡγοῦμαι ἐρύκειν ἀπ' ἐμαυτοῦ τὰ κακά."
26 Ὁ μὲν ταῦτ' ἔλεξεν, οἱ δὲ λοχαγοὶ ἀκούσαντες ἡγεῖσθαι ἐκέλευον πάντες,
πλὴν Ἀπολλωνίδης τις ἦν βοιωτιάζων τῆι φωνῆι· οὗτος δ' εἶπεν ὅτι
φλυαροίη ὅστις λέγει ἄλλως πως σωτηρίας ἂν τυχεῖν ἢ βασιλέα πείσας,
27 εἰ δύναιτο, καὶ ἅμα ἤρχετο λέγειν τὰς ἀπορίας. ὁ μέντοι Ξενοφῶν μεταξὺ
ὑπολαβὼν ἔλεξεν ὧδε· "ὦ θαυμασιώτατε ἄνθρωπε, σύγε οὐδὲ ὁρῶν
γιγνώσκεις οὐδὲ ἀκούων μέμνησαι. ἐν ταὐτῶι γε μέντοι ἦσθα τούτοις ὅτε
βασιλεύς, ἐπεὶ Κῦρος ἀπέθανε, μέγα φρονήσας ἐπὶ τούτωι πέμπων ἐκέλευε
28 παραδιδόναι τὰ ὅπλα. ἐπεὶ δὲ ἡμεῖς οὐ παραδόντες, ἀλλ' ἐξωπλισμένοι
ἐλθόντες παρεσκηνήσαμεν αὐτῶι, τί οὐκ ἐποίησε πρέσβεις πέμπων καὶ
29 σπονδὰς αἰτῶν καὶ παρέχων τὰ ἐπιτήδεια, ἔστε σπονδῶν ἔτυχεν; ἐπεὶ δ'
αὖ οἱ στρατηγοὶ καὶ λοχαγοί, ὥσπερ δὴ σὺ κελεύεις, εἰς λόγους αὐτοῖς
ἄνευ ὅπλων ἦλθον πιστεύσαντες ταῖς σπονδαῖς, οὐ νῦν ἐκεῖνοι παιόμενοι,
κεντούμενοι, ὑβριζόμενοι οὐδὲ ἀποθανεῖν οἱ τλήμονες δύνανται, καὶ μάλ'
οἶμαι ἐρῶντες τούτου; ἃ σὺ πάντα εἰδὼς τοὺς μὲν ἀμύνεσθαι κελεύοντας
30 φλυαρεῖν φῄς, πείθειν δὲ πάλιν κελεύεις ἰόντας; ἐμοί, ὦ ἄνδρες, δοκεῖ τὸν
ἄνθρωπον τοῦτον μήτε προσίεσθαι εἰς ταὐτὸν ἡμῖν αὐτοῖς ἀφελομένους
τε τὴν λοχαγίαν σκεύη ἀναθέντας ὡς τοιούτωι χρῆσθαι. οὗτος γὰρ καὶ
τὴν πατρίδα καταισχύνει καὶ πᾶσαν τὴν Ἑλλάδα, ὅτι Ἕλλην ὢν τοιοῦτός
31 ἐστιν." ἐντεῦθεν ὑπολαβὼν Ἀγασίας Στυμφάλιος εἶπεν· "ἀλλὰ τούτωι γε
οὔτε τῆς Βοιωτίας προσήκει οὐδὲν οὔτε τῆς Ἑλλάδος παντάπασιν, ἐπεὶ
32 ἐγὼ αὐτὸν εἶδον ὥσπερ Λυδὸν ἀμφότερα τὰ ὦτα τετρυπημένον." καὶ
εἶχεν οὕτως. τοῦτον μὲν οὖν ἀπήλασαν· οἱ δὲ ἄλλοι παρὰ τὰς τάξεις
ἰόντες, ὅπου μὲν στρατηγὸς σῶς εἴη, τὸν στρατηγὸν παρεκάλουν (ὁπόθεν
δὲ οἴχοιτο, τὸν ὑποστράτηγον), ὅπου δὲ λοχαγὸς σῶς εἴη, τὸν λοχαγόν.
33 ἐπεὶ δὲ πάντες συνῆλθον, εἰς τὸ πρόσθεν τῶν ὅπλων ἐκαθέζοντο· καὶ
ἐγένοντο οἱ συνελθόντες στρατηγοὶ καὶ λοχαγοὶ ἀμφὶ τοὺς ἑκατόν.

1.26 λέγει **cDab**: λέγοι cett.
πείσας, εἰ δύναιτο: πείσαντες, εἰ δύναιντο Krüger
1.28 ἐξωπλισμένοι: ἐξοπλισάμενοι **c** (ἐξωπλ. **Ag**)
1.30 ἐμοί: ἐμοὶ δέ **f**
1.32 (ὁπόθεν . . . ὑποστράτηγον) sic interpunximus; an delendum?
ὅπου δὲ: ὅπου δ' αὖ **c**

ὅτε δὲ ταῦτα ἦν σχεδὸν μέσαι ἦσαν νύκτες. ἐνταῦθα Ἱερώνυμος Ἠλεῖος 34
πρεσβύτατος ὢν τῶν Προξένου λοχαγῶν ἤρχετο λέγειν ὧδε· "ἡμῖν, ὦ
ἄνδρες στρατηγοὶ καὶ λοχαγοί, ὁρῶσι τὰ παρόντα ἔδοξε καὶ αὐτοῖς
συνελθεῖν καὶ ὑμᾶς παρακαλέσαι, ὅπως βουλευσαίμεθα εἴ τι δυναίμεθα
ἀγαθόν. λέξον δ'" ἔφη "καὶ σύ, ὦ Ξενοφῶν, ἅπερ καὶ πρὸς ἡμᾶς."

Ἐκ τούτου λέγει τάδε Ξενοφῶν· "ἀλλὰ ταῦτα μὲν δὴ πάντες ἐπιστάμεθα, 35
ὅτι βασιλεὺς καὶ Τισσαφέρνης οὓς μὲν ἐδυνήθησαν συνειλήφασιν ἡμῶν,
τοῖς δ' ἄλλοις δῆλον ὅτι ἐπιβουλεύουσιν, ὡς ἢν δύνωνται ἀπολέσωσιν.
ἡμῖν δέ γε οἶμαι πάντα ποιητέα ὡς μήποτ' ἐπὶ τοῖς βαρβάροις γενώμεθα,
ἀλλὰ μᾶλλον, ἢν δυνώμεθα, ἐκεῖνοι ἐφ' ἡμῖν. εὖ τοίνυν ἐπίστασθε ὅτι ὑμεῖς 36
τοσοῦτοι ὄντες ὅσοι νῦν συνεληλύθατε μέγιστον ἔχετε καιρόν. οἱ γὰρ
στρατιῶται οὗτοι πάντες πρὸς ὑμᾶς ἀποβλέπουσι, κἂν μὲν ὑμᾶς ὁρῶσιν
ἀθυμοῦντας, πάντες κακοὶ ἔσονται, ἢν δὲ ὑμεῖς αὐτοί τε παρασκευαζόμενοι
φανεροὶ ἦτε ἐπὶ τοὺς πολεμίους καὶ τοὺς ἄλλους παρακαλῆτε, εὖ ἴστε ὅτι
ἕψονται ὑμῖν καὶ πειράσονται μιμεῖσθαι. ἴσως δέ τοι καὶ δίκαιόν ἐστιν 37
ὑμᾶς διαφέρειν τι τούτων. ὑμεῖς γάρ ἐστε στρατηγοί, ὑμεῖς ταξίαρχοι
καὶ λοχαγοί· καὶ ὅτε εἰρήνη ἦν, ὑμεῖς καὶ χρήμασι καὶ τιμαῖς τούτων
ἐπλεονεκτεῖτε· καὶ νῦν τοίνυν ἐπεὶ πόλεμός ἐστιν, ἀξιοῦν δεῖ ὑμᾶς αὐτοὺς
ἀμείνους τε τοῦ πλήθους εἶναι καὶ προβουλεύειν τούτων καὶ προπονεῖν,
ἤν που δέηι. καὶ νῦν πρῶτον μὲν οἶμαι ἂν ὑμᾶς μέγα ὠφελῆσαι τὸ 38
στράτευμα, εἰ ἐπιμεληθείητε ὅπως ἀντὶ τῶν ἀπολωλότων ὡς τάχιστα
στρατηγοὶ καὶ λοχαγοὶ ἀντικατασταθῶσιν. ἄνευ γὰρ ἀρχόντων οὐδὲν
ἂν οὔτε καλὸν οὔτε ἀγαθὸν γένοιτο ὡς μὲν συνελόντι εἰπεῖν οὐδαμοῦ,
ἐν δὲ δὴ τοῖς πολεμικοῖς παντάπασιν. ἡ μὲν γὰρ εὐταξία σώιζειν δοκεῖ,
ἡ δὲ ἀταξία πολλοὺς ἤδη ἀπολώλεκεν. ἐπειδὰν δὲ καταστήσησθε 39
τοὺς ἄρχοντας ὅσους δεῖ, ἢν καὶ τοὺς ἄλλους στρατιώτας συλλέγητε
καὶ παραθαρρύνητε, οἶμαι ἂν ὑμᾶς πάνυ ἐν καιρῶι ποιῆσαι. νῦν γὰρ 40
ἴσως καὶ ὑμεῖς αἰσθάνεσθε ὡς ἀθύμως μὲν ἦλθον ἐπὶ τὰ ὅπλα, ἀθύμως
δὲ πρὸς τὰς φυλακάς· ὥστε οὕτω γ' ἐχόντων οὐκ οἶδα ὅ τι ἄν τις
χρήσαιτο αὐτοῖς εἴτε νυκτὸς δέοι τι εἴτε καὶ ἡμέρας. ἢν δέ τις αὐτῶν 41
τρέψηι τὰς γνώμας, ὡς μὴ τοῦτο μόνον ἐννοῶνται τί πείσονται, ἀλλὰ
καὶ τί ποιήσουσι, πολὺ εὐθυμότεροι ἔσονται. ἐπίστασθε γὰρ δὴ ὅτι 42
οὔτε πλῆθός ἐστιν οὔτε ἰσχὺς ἡ ἐν τῶι πολέμωι τὰς νίκας ποιοῦσα,
ἀλλ' ὁπότεροι ἂν σὺν τοῖς θεοῖς ταῖς ψυχαῖς ἐρρωμενέστεροι ἴωσιν
ἐπὶ τοὺς πολεμίους, τούτους ὡς ἐπὶ τὸ πολὺ οἱ ἀντίοι οὐ δέχονται.

1.38 ὠφελῆσαι: ὀνῆσαι **f** (ὠν. **F**)

43 ἐντεθύμημαι δ' ἔγωγε, ὦ ἄνδρες, καὶ τοῦτο, ὅτι ὁπόσοι μὲν μαστεύουσι
ζῆν ἐκ παντὸς τρόπου ἐν τοῖς πολεμικοῖς, οὗτοι μὲν κακῶς τε καὶ
αἰσχρῶς ὡς ἐπὶ τὸ πολὺ ἀποθνήισκουσιν, ὁπόσοι δὲ τὸν μὲν θάνατον
ἐγνώκασι πᾶσι κοινὸν εἶναι καὶ ἀναγκαῖον ἀνθρώποις, περὶ δὲ τοῦ
καλῶς ἀποθνήισκειν ἀγωνίζονται, τούτους ὁρῶ μᾶλλόν πως εἰς τὸ
44 γῆρας ἀφικνουμένους καὶ ἕως ἂν ζῶσιν εὐδαιμονέστερον διάγοντας. ἃ
καὶ ἡμᾶς δεῖ νῦν καταμαθόντας (ἐν τοιούτωι γὰρ καιρῶι ἐσμεν) αὐτούς
45 τε ἄνδρας ἀγαθοὺς εἶναι καὶ τοὺς ἄλλους παρακαλεῖν." ὁ μὲν ταῦτα
εἰπὼν ἐπαύσατο.

Μετὰ δὲ τοῦτον εἶπε Χειρίσοφος· "ἀλλὰ πρόσθεν μέν, ὦ Ξενοφῶν,
τοσοῦτον μόνον σε ἐγίγνωσκον ὅσον ἤκουον Ἀθηναῖον εἶναι, νῦν δὲ καὶ
ἐπαινῶ σε ἐφ' οἷς λέγεις τε καὶ πράττεις καὶ βουλοίμην ἂν ὅτι πλείστους
46 εἶναι τοιούτους· κοινὸν γὰρ ἂν εἴη τὸ ἀγαθόν. καὶ νῦν" ἔφη "μὴ μέλλωμεν,
ὦ ἄνδρες, ἀλλ' ἀπελθόντες ἤδη αἱρεῖσθε οἱ δεόμενοι ἄρχοντας, καὶ
ἑλόμενοι ἥκετε εἰς τὸ μέσον τοῦ στρατοπέδου καὶ τοὺς αἱρεθέντας ἄγετε·
ἔπειτ' ἐκεῖ συγκαλοῦμεν τοὺς ἄλλους στρατιώτας. παρέστω δ' ἡμῖν" ἔφη
47 "καὶ Τολμίδης ὁ κῆρυξ." καὶ ἅμα ταῦτ' εἰπὼν ἀνέστη, ὡς μὴ μέλλοιτο
ἀλλὰ περαίνοιτο τὰ δέοντα. ἐκ τούτου ἡιρέθησαν ἄρχοντες ἀντὶ μὲν
Κλεάρχου Τιμασίων Δαρδανεύς, ἀντὶ δὲ Σωκράτους Ξανθικλῆς Ἀχαιός,
ἀντὶ δὲ Ἀγίου Κλεάνωρ Ἀρκάς, ἀντὶ δὲ Μένωνος Φιλήσιος Ἀχαιός, ἀντὶ
δὲ Προξένου Ξενοφῶν Ἀθηναῖος.

2 Ἐπεὶ δὲ ἥιρηντο, ἡμέρα τε σχεδὸν ὑπέφαινε καὶ εἰς τὸ μέσον ἧκον
οἱ ἄρχοντες, καὶ ἔδοξεν αὐτοῖς προφυλακὰς καταστήσαντας συγκαλεῖν
τοὺς στρατιώτας. ἐπεὶ δὲ καὶ οἱ ἄλλοι στρατιῶται συνῆλθον, ἀνέστη
2 πρῶτος μὲν Χειρίσοφος ὁ Λακεδαιμόνιος καὶ ἔλεξεν ὧδε· "ὦ ἄνδρες
στρατιῶται, χαλεπὰ μὲν τὰ παρόντα, ὁπότε ἀνδρῶν στρατηγῶν
τοιούτων στερόμεθα καὶ λοχαγῶν καὶ στρατιωτῶν, πρὸς δ' ἔτι καὶ οἱ
3 ἀμφὶ Ἀριαῖον οἱ πρόσθεν σύμμαχοι ὄντες προδεδώκασιν ἡμᾶς· ὅμως δὲ
δεῖ ἐκ τῶν παρόντων ἄνδρας ἀγαθοὺς τελέθειν καὶ μὴ ὑφίεσθαι, ἀλλὰ
πειρᾶσθαι ὅπως ἢν μὲν δυνώμεθα καλῶς νικῶντες σωιζώμεθα· εἰ δὲ μή,
ἀλλὰ καλῶς γε ἀποθνήισκωμεν, ὑποχείριοι δὲ μηδέποτε γενώμεθα ζῶντες
τοῖς πολεμίοις. οἶμαι γὰρ ἂν ἡμᾶς τοιαῦτα παθεῖν οἷα τοὺς ἐχθροὺς οἱ
θεοὶ ποιήσειαν."

1.43 πολεμικοῖς **c**: πολεμίοις **DF**: πολέμοις Dobree
1.44 ἡμᾶς: ὑμᾶς **c**
1.45 μετὰ δὲ τοῦτον: μετὰ τοῦτον δ' **f**
1.47 Ἀγίου: Ἀγίου Ἀρκάδος **c**: Ἀγίας **M**
Ἀρκάς: ὁ Ὀρχομένιος **c**
2.1 προφυλακάς: προφύλακας **f**
πρῶτος Bisschop et Cobet: πρῶτον codd.

Ἐπὶ τούτωι Κλεάνωρ ὁ Ὀρχομένιος ἀνέστη καὶ ἔλεξεν ὧδε· "ἀλλ' 4
ὁρᾶτε μέν, ὦ ἄνδρες, τὴν βασιλέως ἐπιορκίαν καὶ ἀσέβειαν, ὁρᾶτε δὲ τὴν
Τισσαφέρνους ἀπιστίαν, ὅστις λέγων ὡς γείτων τε εἴη τῆς Ἑλλάδος καὶ
περὶ πλείστου ἂν ποιήσαιτο σῶσαι ἡμᾶς, καὶ ἐπὶ τούτοις αὐτὸς ὀμόσας
ἡμῖν, αὐτὸς δεξιὰς δούς, αὐτὸς ἐξαπατήσας συνέλαβε τοὺς στρατηγούς,
καὶ οὐδὲ Δία ξένιον ᾐδέσθη, ἀλλὰ Κλεάρχωι <ξένος> τε καὶ ὁμοτράπεζος
γενόμενος αὐτοῖς τούτοις ἐξαπατήσας τοὺς ἄνδρας ἀπολώλεκεν. Ἀριαῖος 5
δέ, ὃν ἡμεῖς ἠθέλομεν βασιλέα καθιστάναι, καὶ ἐδώκαμεν καὶ ἐλάβομεν
πιστὰ μὴ προδώσειν ἀλλήλους, καὶ οὗτος οὔτε τοὺς θεοὺς δείσας οὔτε
Κῦρον τεθνηκότα αἰδεσθείς, τιμώμενος μάλιστα ὑπὸ Κύρου ζῶντος νῦν
πρὸς τοὺς ἐκείνου ἐχθίστους ἀποστὰς ἡμᾶς τοὺς Κύρου φίλους κακῶς
ποιεῖν πειρᾶται. ἀλλὰ τούτους μὲν οἱ θεοὶ ἀποτείσαιντο· ἡμᾶς δὲ δεῖ 6
ταῦτα ὁρῶντας μήποτε ἐξαπατηθῆναι ἔτι ὑπὸ τούτων, ἀλλὰ μαχομένους
ὡς ἂν δυνώμεθα κράτιστα τοῦτο ὅ τι ἂν δοκῆι τοῖς θεοῖς πάσχειν."
Ἐκ τούτου Ξενοφῶν ἀνίσταται ἐσταλμένος ἐπὶ πόλεμον ὡς ἐδύνατο 7
κάλλιστα, νομίζων, εἴτε νίκην διδοῖεν οἱ θεοί, τὸν κάλλιστον κόσμον τῶι
νικᾶν πρέπειν, εἴτε τελευτᾶν δέοι, ὀρθῶς ἔχειν τῶν καλλίστων ἑαυτὸν
ἀξιώσαντα ἐν τούτοις τῆς τελευτῆς τυγχάνειν· τοῦ λόγου δὲ ἤρχετο ὧδε·
"τὴν μὲν τῶν βαρβάρων ἐπιορκίαν τε καὶ ἀπιστίαν λέγει μὲν Κλεάνωρ, 8
ἐπίστασθε δὲ καὶ ὑμεῖς οἶμαι. εἰ μὲν οὖν βουλόμεθα πάλιν αὐτοῖς διὰ φιλίας
ἰέναι, ἀνάγκη ἡμᾶς πολλὴν ἀθυμίαν ἔχειν, ὁρῶντας καὶ τοὺς στρατηγούς,
οἳ διὰ πίστεως αὐτοῖς ἑαυτοὺς ἐνεχείρισαν, οἷα πεπόνθασιν· εἰ μέντοι
διανοούμεθα σὺν τοῖς ὅπλοις ὧν τε πεποιήκασι δίκην ἐπιθεῖναι αὐτοῖς
καὶ τὸ λοιπὸν διὰ παντὸς πολέμου αὐτοῖς ἰέναι, σὺν τοῖς θεοῖς πολλαὶ
ἡμῖν καὶ καλαὶ ἐλπίδες εἰσὶ σωτηρίας."
Τοῦτο δὲ λέγοντος αὐτοῦ πτάρνυταί τις· ἀκούσαντες δ' οἱ στρατιῶται 9
πάντες μιᾶι ὁρμῆι προσεκύνησαν τὸν θεόν, καὶ ὁ Ξενοφῶν εἶπε· "δοκεῖ
μοι, ὦ ἄνδρες, ἐπεὶ περὶ σωτηρίας ἡμῶν λεγόντων οἰωνὸς τοῦ Διὸς τοῦ
σωτῆρος ἐφάνη, εὔξασθαι τῶι θεῶι τούτωι θύσειν σωτήρια ὅπου ἂν
πρῶτον εἰς φιλίαν χώραν ἀφικώμεθα, συνεπεύξασθαι δὲ καὶ τοῖς ἄλλοις
θεοῖς θύσειν κατὰ δύναμιν. καὶ ὅτωι δοκεῖ ταῦτ'" ἔφη "ἀνατεινάτω τὴν
χεῖρα." καὶ ἀνέτειναν ἅπαντες. ἐκ τούτου ηὔξαντο καὶ ἐπαιάνισαν.
Ἐπεὶ δὲ τὰ τῶν θεῶν καλῶς εἶχεν, ἤρχετο πάλιν ὧδε· "ἐτύγχανον 10
λέγων ὅτι πολλαὶ καὶ καλαὶ ἐλπίδες ἡμῖν εἶεν σωτηρίας. πρῶτον
μὲν γὰρ ἡμεῖς μὲν ἐμπεδοῦμεν τοὺς τῶν θεῶν ὅρκους, οἱ δὲ πολέμιοι
ἐπιωρκήκασί τε καὶ τὰς σπονδὰς παρὰ τοὺς ὅρκους λελύκασιν. οὕτω
δ' ἐχόντων εἰκὸς τοῖς μὲν πολεμίοις ἐναντίους εἶναι τοὺς θεούς, ἡμῖν δὲ

2.4 ξένος: suppl. Castiglioni: γε pro τε coni. Bornemann

συμμάχους, οἵπερ ἱκανοί εἰσι καὶ τοὺς μεγάλους ταχὺ μικροὺς ποιεῖν
καὶ τοὺς μικροὺς κἂν ἐν δεινοῖς ὦσι σώιζειν εὐπετῶς, ὅταν βούλωνται.
11 ἔπειτα δέ, ἀναμνήσω γὰρ ὑμᾶς καὶ τοὺς τῶν προγόνων τῶν ἡμετέρων
κινδύνους, ἵνα εἰδῆτε ὡς ἀγαθοῖς τε ὑμῖν προσήκει εἶναι σώιζονταί
τε σὺν τοῖς θεοῖς καὶ ἐκ πάνυ δεινῶν οἱ ἀγαθοί. ἐλθόντων μὲν γὰρ
Περσῶν καὶ τῶν σὺν αὐτοῖς παμπληθεῖ στόλωι ὡς ἀφανιούντων τὰς
12 Ἀθήνας, ὑποστῆναι αὐτοὶ Ἀθηναῖοι τολμήσαντες ἐνίκησαν αὐτούς. καὶ
εὐξάμενοι τῆι Ἀρτέμιδι ὁπόσους κατακάνοιεν τῶν πολεμίων τοσαύτας
χιμαίρας καταθύσειν τῆι θεῶι, ἐπεὶ οὐκ εἶχον ἱκανὰς εὑρεῖν, ἔδοξεν
αὐτοῖς κατ' ἐνιαυτὸν πεντακοσίας θύειν, καὶ ἔτι καὶ νῦν ἀποθύουσιν.
13 ἔπειτα ὅτε Ξέρξης ὕστερον ἀγείρας τὴν ἀναρίθμητον στρατιὰν ἦλθεν
ἐπὶ τὴν Ἑλλάδα, καὶ τότε ἐνίκων οἱ ἡμέτεροι πρόγονοι τοὺς τούτων
προγόνους καὶ κατὰ γῆν καὶ κατὰ θάλατταν. ὧν ἔστι μὲν τεκμήρια
ὁρᾶν τὰ τρόπαια, μέγιστον δὲ μαρτύριον ἡ ἐλευθερία τῶν πόλεων ἐν
αἷς ὑμεῖς ἐγένεσθε καὶ ἐτράφητε· οὐδένα γὰρ ἄνθρωπον δεσπότην, ἀλλὰ
14 τοὺς θεοὺς προσκυνεῖτε. τοιούτων μέν ἐστε προγόνων. οὐ μὲν δὴ τοῦτό
γε ἐρῶ ὡς ὑμεῖς καταισχύνετε αὐτούς· ἀλλ' οὔπω πολλαὶ ἡμέραι ἀφ'
οὗ ἀντιταξάμενοι τούτοις τοῖς ἐκείνων ἐκγόνοις πολλαπλασίους ὑμῶν
15 αὐτῶν ἐνικᾶτε σὺν τοῖς θεοῖς. καὶ τότε μὲν δὴ περὶ τῆς Κύρου βασιλείας
ἄνδρες ἦτε ἀγαθοί· νῦν δ' ὁπότε περὶ τῆς ὑμετέρας σωτηρίας ὁ ἀγών
ἐστι, πολὺ δήπου ὑμᾶς προσήκει καὶ ἀμείνονας καὶ προθυμοτέρους εἶναι.
16 ἀλλὰ μὴν καὶ θαρραλεωτέρους νῦν πρέπει εἶναι πρὸς τοὺς πολεμίους.
τότε μὲν γὰρ ἄπειροι ὄντες αὐτῶν τό τε πλῆθος ἄμετρον ὁρῶντες, ὅμως
ἐτολμήσατε σὺν τῶι πατρίωι φρονήματι ἰέναι εἰς αὐτούς· νῦν δὲ ὁπότε
καὶ πεῖραν ἤδη ἔχετε αὐτῶν ὅτι οὐ θέλουσι καὶ πολλαπλάσιοι ὄντες
17 [μὴ] δέχεσθαι ὑμᾶς, τί ἔτι ὑμῖν προσήκει τούτους φοβεῖσθαι; μηδὲ μέντοι
τοῦτο μεῖον δόξητε ἔχειν, εἰ οἱ Κύρειοι πρόσθεν σὺν ἡμῖν ταττόμενοι
νῦν ἀφεστήκασιν. ἔτι γὰρ οὗτοι κακίονές εἰσι τῶν ὑφ' ἡμῶν ἡττημένων·
ἔφυγον γοῦν πρὸς ἐκείνους καταλιπόντες ἡμᾶς. τοὺς δ' ἐθέλοντας φυγῆς
ἄρχειν πολὺ κρεῖττον σὺν τοῖς πολεμίοις ταττομένους ἢ ἐν τῆι ἡμετέραι
18 τάξει ὁρᾶν. εἰ δέ τις ὑμῶν ἀθυμεῖ ὅτι ἡμῖν μὲν οὐκ εἰσὶν ἱππεῖς, τοῖς
δὲ πολεμίοις πολλοὶ πάρεισιν, ἐνθυμήθητε ὅτι οἱ μύριοι ἱππεῖς οὐδὲν
ἄλλο ἢ μύριοί εἰσιν ἄνθρωποι· ὑπὸ μὲν γὰρ ἵππου ἐν μάχηι οὐδεὶς
πώποτε οὔτε δηχθεὶς οὔτε λακτισθεὶς ἀπέθανεν, οἱ δὲ ἄνδρες εἰσὶν οἱ

2.11 αὐτοὶ **C**^{1}: αὐτοῖς cett.

2.16 μὴ del. Schenkl

2.17 Κύρ(ε)ιοι vel Κυρεῖοι codd. (**C**^{2} in lit.): del. Pantazides: Ἀριαίου Hug: βάρβαροι Sauppe: Πέρσαι οἱ Erbse

ἔφυγον Cobet: ἔφευγον codd.

ποιοῦντες ὅ τι ἂν ἐν ταῖς μάχαις γίγνηται. οὐκοῦν τῶν γε ἱππέων 19
πολὺ ἡμεῖς ἐπ' ἀσφαλεστέρου ὀχήματός ἐσμεν· οἱ μὲν γὰρ ἐφ' ἵππων
κρέμανται φοβούμενοι οὐχ ἡμᾶς μόνον, ἀλλὰ καὶ τὸ καταπεσεῖν· ἡμεῖς
δ' ἐπὶ γῆς βεβηκότες πολὺ μὲν ἰσχυρότερον παίσομεν, ἤν τις προσίῃ,
πολὺ δὲ μᾶλλον ὅτου ἂν βουλώμεθα τευξόμεθα. ἑνὶ μόνωι προέχουσιν
οἱ ἱππεῖς [ἡμᾶς]· φεύγειν αὐτοῖς ἀσφαλέστερόν ἐστιν ἢ ἡμῖν. εἰ δὲ δὴ 20
τὰς μὲν μάχας θαρρεῖτε, ὅτι δὲ οὐκέτι ὑμῖν Τισσαφέρνης ἡγήσεται οὐδὲ
βασιλεὺς ἀγορὰν παρέξει, τοῦτο ἄχθεσθε, σκέψασθε πότερον κρεῖττον
Τισσαφέρνην ἡγεμόνα ἔχειν, ὃς ἐπιβουλεύων ἡμῖν φανερός ἐστιν, ἢ οὓς
ἂν ἡμεῖς ἄνδρας λαβόντες ἡγεῖσθαι κελεύωμεν, οἳ εἴσονται ὅτι ἤν τι περὶ
ἡμᾶς ἁμαρτάνωσι, περὶ τὰς ἑαυτῶν ψυχὰς καὶ σώματα ἁμαρτάνουσι.
τὰ δὲ ἐπιτήδεια πότερον ὠνεῖσθαι κρεῖττον ἐκ τῆς ἀγορᾶς ἧς οὗτοι 21
παρεῖχον μικρὰ μέτρα πολλοῦ ἀργυρίου, μηδὲ τοῦτο ἔτι ἔχοντας, ἢ
αὐτοὺς λαμβάνειν, ἤνπερ κρατῶμεν, μέτρωι χρωμένους ὁπόσωι ἂν
ἕκαστος βούληται. εἰ δὲ ταῦτα μὲν γιγνώσκετε ὅτι κρείττονα, τοὺς δὲ 22
ποταμοὺς ἄπορον νομίζετε εἶναι καὶ μεγάλως ἡγεῖσθε ἐξαπατηθῆναι
διαβάντες, σκέψασθε εἰ ἄρα τοῦτο καὶ μωρότατον πεποιήκασιν οἱ
βάρβαροι. πάντες γὰρ οἱ ποταμοί, ἢν καὶ πρόσω τῶν πηγῶν ἄποροι ὦσι,
προσιοῦσι πρὸς τὰς πηγὰς διαβατοὶ γίγνονται οὐδὲ τὸ γόνυ βρέχοντες.
εἰ δὲ μήθ' οἱ ποταμοὶ διήσουσιν ἡγεμών τε μηδεὶς ἡμῖν φανεῖται, οὐδ' 23
ὧς ἡμῖν γε ἀθυμητέον. ἐπιστάμεθα γὰρ Μυσούς, οὓς οὐκ ἂν ἡμῶν
φαίημεν βελτίους εἶναι, ὅτι βασιλέως ἄκοντος ἐν τῆι βασιλέως χώραι
πολλάς τε καὶ εὐδαίμονας καὶ μεγάλας πόλεις οἰκοῦσιν, ἐπιστάμεθα δὲ
Πισίδας ὡσαύτως, Λυκάονας δὲ καὶ αὐτοὶ εἴδομεν ὅτι ἐν τοῖς πεδίοις
τὰ ἐρυμνὰ καταλαβόντες τὴν τούτων χώραν καρποῦνται· καὶ ἡμᾶς δ' 24
ἂν ἔφην ἔγωγε χρῆναι μήπω φανεροὺς εἶναι οἴκαδε ὡρμημένους, ἀλλὰ
κατασκευάζεσθαι ὡς αὐτοῦ που οἰκήσοντας. οἶδα γὰρ ὅτι καὶ Μυσοῖς
βασιλεὺς πολλοὺς μὲν ἡγεμόνας ἂν δοίη, πολλοὺς δ' ἂν ὁμήρους τοῦ
ἀδόλως ἐκπέμψειν, καὶ ὁδοποιήσειέ γ' ἂν αὐτοῖς καὶ εἰ σὺν τεθρίπποις
βούλοιντο ἀπιέναι. καὶ ἡμῖν γ' ἂν οἶδ' ὅτι τρισάσμενος ταῦτ' ἐποίει,

2.19 fors. οὔκουν . . . ἐσμεν;
ἑνὶ **C²f** Priscianus 2.352: ἑνὶ δὲ cett.
ἡμᾶς del. Rehdantz
2.20 ὑμῖν: ἡμῖν **VZ**
2.22 προσιοῦσι: προϊοῦσι **g**(**B**?)
2.23 ὅτι Cobet: οἳ codd.
βασιλέως ἄκοντος: ἄκοντος βασιλέως post χώραι **gE** (**E** om. βασ.): βασ. ἄκοντος in marg. add. **C¹**
τούτων: τούτου **f**
2.24 αὐτοῖς Morus: αὐτοὺς codd.

25 εἰ ἑώρα ἡμᾶς μένειν κατασκευαζομένους. ἀλλὰ γὰρ δέδοικα μὴ ἂν ἅπαξ
μάθωμεν ἀργοὶ ζῆν καὶ ἐν ἀφθόνοις βιοτεύειν, καὶ Μήδων δὲ καὶ Περσῶν
καλαῖς καὶ μεγάλαις γυναιξὶ καὶ παρθένοις ὁμιλεῖν, μὴ ὥσπερ οἱ λωτοφάγοι
26 ἐπιλαθώμεθα τῆς οἴκαδε ὁδοῦ. δοκεῖ οὖν μοι εἰκὸς καὶ δίκαιον εἶναι
πρῶτον εἰς τὴν Ἑλλάδα καὶ πρὸς τοὺς οἰκείους πειρᾶσθαι ἀφικνεῖσθαι
καὶ ἐπιδεῖξαι τοῖς Ἕλλησιν ὅτι ἑκόντες πένονται, ἐξὸν αὐτοῖς τοὺς νῦν
[οἴκοι] σκληρῶς ἐκεῖ πολιτεύοντας ἐνθάδε κομισαμένους πλουσίους ὁρᾶν.
ἀλλὰ γάρ, ὦ ἄνδρες, πάντα ταῦτα τἀγαθὰ δῆλον ὅτι τῶν κρατούντων
27 ἐστί. τοῦτο δὲ δεῖ λέγειν, πῶς ἂν πορευοίμεθά τε ὡς ἀσφαλέστατα καὶ
εἰ μάχεσθαι δέοι ὡς κράτιστα μαχοίμεθα. πρῶτον μὲν τοίνυν" ἔφη "δοκεῖ
μοι κατακαῦσαι τὰς ἁμάξας ἃς ἔχομεν, ἵνα μὴ τὰ ζεύγη ἡμῶν στρατηγῆι,
ἀλλὰ πορευώμεθα ὅπηι ἂν τῆι στρατιᾶι συμφέρηι· ἔπειτα καὶ τὰς
σκηνὰς συγκατακαῦσαι. αὗται γὰρ αὖ ὄχλον μὲν παρέχουσιν ἄγειν,
συνωφελοῦσι δ' οὐδὲν οὔτε εἰς τὸ μάχεσθαι οὔτ' εἰς τὸ τὰ ἐπιτήδεια
28 ἔχειν. ἔτι δὲ καὶ τῶν ἄλλων σκευῶν τὰ περιττὰ ἀπαλλάξωμεν πλὴν ὅσα
πολέμου ἕνεκεν ἢ σίτων ἢ ποτῶν ἔχομεν, ἵν' ὡς πλεῖστοι μὲν ἡμῶν ἐν
τοῖς ὅπλοις ὦσιν, ὡς ἐλάχιστοι δὲ σκευοφορῶσι. κρατουμένων μὲν γὰρ
ἐπίστασθε ὅτι πάντα ἀλλότρια· ἢν δὲ κρατῶμεν, καὶ τοὺς πολεμίους δεῖ
29 σκευοφόρους ἡμετέρους νομίζειν. λοιπόν μοι εἰπεῖν ὅπερ καὶ μέγιστον
νομίζω εἶναι. ὁρᾶτε γὰρ καὶ τοὺς πολεμίους ὅτι οὐ πρόσθεν ἐξενεγκεῖν
ἐτόλμησαν πρὸς ἡμᾶς πόλεμον πρὶν τοὺς στρατηγοὺς ἡμῶν συνέλαβον,
νομίζοντες ὄντων μὲν τῶν ἀρχόντων καὶ ἡμῶν πειθομένων ἱκανοὺς εἶναι
ἡμᾶς περιγενέσθαι τῶι πολέμωι, λαβόντες δὲ τοὺς ἄρχοντας ἀναρχίαι ἂν
30 καὶ ἀταξίαι ἐνόμιζον ἡμᾶς ἀπολέσθαι. δεῖ οὖν πολὺ μὲν τοὺς ἄρχοντας
ἐπιμελεστέρους γενέσθαι τοὺς νῦν τῶν πρόσθεν, πολὺ δὲ τοὺς ἀρχομένους
31 εὐτακτοτέρους καὶ πειθομένους μᾶλλον τοῖς ἄρχουσι νῦν ἢ πρόσθεν· ἢν
δέ τις ἀπειθῆι, ψηφίσασθαι τὸν ἀεὶ ὑμῶν ἐντυγχάνοντα σὺν τῶι ἄρχοντι
κολάζειν· οὕτως οἱ πολέμιοι πλεῖστον ἐψευσμένοι ἔσονται· τῆιδε γὰρ τῆι
ἡμέραι μυρίους ὄψονται ἀνθ' ἑνὸς Κλεάρχους τοὺς οὐδενὶ ἐπιτρέψοντας
32 κακῶι εἶναι. ἀλλὰ γὰρ καὶ περαίνειν ἤδη ὥρα· ἴσως γὰρ οἱ πολέμιοι
αὐτίκα παρέσονται. ὅτωι οὖν ταῦτα δοκεῖ καλῶς ἔχειν, ἐπικυρωσάτω ὡς
τάχιστα, ἵν' ἔργωι περαίνηται. εἰ δέ τι ἄλλο βέλτιον ἢ ταύτηι, τολμάτω
καὶ ὁ ἰδιώτης διδάσκειν· πάντες γὰρ κοινῆς σωτηρίας δεόμεθα."
33 Μετὰ ταῦτα Χειρίσοφος εἶπεν· "ἀλλ' εἰ μέν τινος ἄλλου δεῖ πρὸς
τούτοις οἷς λέγει Ξενοφῶν, καὶ αὐτίκα ἐξέσται ποιεῖν· ἃ δὲ νῦν εἴρηκε

2.26 οἴκοι del. Rehdantz

2.27 δὲ δεῖ Castalio (iam **b**): δεῖ **C'ADV**: δεῖ δὴ **E**: δὴ δεῖ cett.

δοκεῖ μοι ὡς τάχιστα ψηφίσασθαι ἄριστον εἶναι· καὶ ὅτωι δοκεῖ
ταῦτα, ἀνατεινάτω τὴν χεῖρα." ἀνέτειναν ἅπαντες. ἀναστὰς δὲ πάλιν 34
εἶπε Ξενοφῶν· "ὦ ἄνδρες, ἀκούσατε ὧν προσδεῖν δοκεῖ μοι. δῆλον ὅτι
πορεύεσθαι ἡμᾶς δεῖ ὅπου ἕξομεν τὰ ἐπιτήδεια· ἀκούω δὲ κώμας εἶναι
καλὰς οὐ πλέον εἴκοσι σταδίων ἀπεχούσας· οὐκ ἂν οὖν θαυμάζοιμι εἰ 35
οἱ πολέμιοι, ὥσπερ οἱ δειλοὶ κύνες τοὺς μὲν παριόντας διώκουσί τε καὶ
δάκνουσιν, ἢν δύνωνται, τοὺς δὲ διώκοντας φεύγουσιν, εἰ καὶ αὐτοὶ
ἡμῖν ἀπιοῦσιν ἐπακολουθοῖεν. ἴσως οὖν ἀσφαλέστερον ἡμῖν πορεύεσθαι 36
πλαίσιον ποιησαμένους τῶν ὅπλων, ἵνα τὰ σκευοφόρα καὶ ὁ πολὺς
ὄχλος ἐν ἀσφαλεστέρωι εἴη. εἰ οὖν νῦν ἀποδειχθείη τίνας χρὴ ἡγεῖσθαι
τοῦ πλαισίου καὶ τὰ πρόσθεν κοσμεῖν καὶ τίνας ἐπὶ τῶν πλευρῶν
ἑκατέρων εἶναι, τίνας δ' ὀπισθοφυλακεῖν, οὐκ ἂν ὁπότε οἱ πολέμιοι
ἔλθοιεν βουλεύεσθαι ἡμᾶς δέοι, ἀλλὰ χρώιμεθ' ἂν εὐθὺς τοῖς τεταγμένοις.
εἰ μὲν οὖν ἄλλο τις βέλτιον ὁρᾶι, ἄλλως ἐχέτω· εἰ δὲ μή, Χειρίσοφος μὲν 37
ἡγοῖτο, ἐπειδὴ καὶ Λακεδαιμόνιός ἐστι· τῶν δὲ πλευρῶν ἑκατέρων δύο
τῶν πρεσβυτάτων στρατηγῶν ἐπιμελοίσθην· ὀπισθοφυλακοῖμεν δ' ἡμεῖς
οἱ νεώτατοι ἐγὼ καὶ Τιμασίων τὸ νῦν εἶναι. τὸ δὲ λοιπὸν πειρώμενοι 38
ταύτης τῆς τάξεως βουλευσόμεθα ὅ τι ἂν ἀεὶ κράτιστον δοκῆι εἶναι.
εἰ δέ τις ἄλλο ὁρᾶι βέλτιον, λεξάτω." ἐπεὶ δ' οὐδεὶς ἀντέλεγεν, εἶπεν·
"ὅτωι δοκεῖ ταῦτα, ἀνατεινάτω τὴν χεῖρα." ἔδοξε ταῦτα. "νῦν τοίνυν" 39
ἔφη "ἀπιόντας ποιεῖν δεῖ τὰ δεδογμένα. καὶ ὅστις τε ὑμῶν τοὺς οἰκείους
ἐπιθυμεῖ ἰδεῖν, μεμνήσθω ἀνὴρ ἀγαθὸς εἶναι· οὐ γὰρ ἔστιν ἄλλως τούτου
τυχεῖν· ὅστις τε ζῆν ἐπιθυμεῖ, πειράσθω νικᾶν· τῶν μὲν γὰρ νικώντων
τὸ κατακαίνειν, τῶν δὲ ἡττωμένων τὸ ἀποθνήισκειν ἐστί· καὶ εἴ τις δὲ
χρημάτων ἐπιθυμεῖ, κρατεῖν πειράσθω· τῶν γὰρ νικώντων ἐστὶ καὶ τὰ
ἑαυτῶν σώιζειν καὶ τὰ τῶν ἡττωμένων λαμβάνειν."

Τούτων λεχθέντων ἀνέστησαν καὶ ἀπελθόντες κατέκαιον τὰς ἁμάξας **3**
καὶ τὰς σκηνάς, τῶν δὲ περιττῶν ὅτου μὲν δέοιτό τις μετεδίδοσαν
ἀλλήλοις, τὰ δὲ ἄλλα εἰς τὸ πῦρ ἐρρίπτουν. ταῦτα ποιήσαντες
ἠριστοποιοῦντο. ἀριστοποιουμένων δὲ αὐτῶν ἔρχεται Μιθραδάτης σὺν

2.34 προσδεῖν δοκεῖ Wyttenbach: προσδοκεῖ **C**[1]: προσδοκᾶν (-κεῖν **M**) δοκεῖ cett.
2.36 εἴη: ἦι **f**
τίνας χρὴ: τίνα χρὴ nonnulli edd.
2.37 ἄλλο Muret (et **M**?): ἄλλος codd.
ἡγοῖτο: ἡγείσθω **BM**[2]**bg**: ἡγεῖτο **CAM**[1]**E**
τῶν πρεσβυτάτων στρατηγῶν **DVab**: τῶν -ων -ω **B**[c]: τῶν -ων -οί cett.: τὼ -ω -ώ Cobet
ὀπισθοφυλακοῖμεν: ὀπισθοφυλακῶμεν **f**
2.38 δοκῆι Bornemann: δοκεῖ **c**: δοκοίει **F**: δοκοίη cett.
3.1 Μιθραδάτης **D**[1]: Μιθριδάτης codd. hic et alias

ἱππεῦσιν ὡς τριάκοντα, καὶ καλεσάμενος τοὺς στρατηγοὺς εἰς ἐπήκοον
2 λέγει ὧδε· "ἐγώ, ὦ ἄνδρες Ἕλληνες, καὶ Κύρωι πιστὸς ἦν, ὡς ὑμεῖς
ἐπίστασθε, καὶ νῦν ὑμῖν εὔνους· καὶ ἐνθάδε δ' εἰμὶ σὺν πολλῶι φόβωι
διάγων. εἰ οὖν ὁρώιην ὑμᾶς σωτήριόν τι βουλευομένους, ἔλθοιμι ἂν πρὸς
ὑμᾶς καὶ τοὺς θεράποντας πάντας ἔχων. λέξατε οὖν" ἔφη "πρός με τί
ἐν νῶι ἔχετε ὡς φίλον τε καὶ εὔνουν καὶ βουλόμενον κοινῆι σὺν ὑμῖν τὸν
3 στόλον ποιεῖσθαι." βουλευομένοις τοῖς στρατηγοῖς ἔδοξεν ἀποκρίνασθαι
τάδε· καὶ ἔλεγε Χειρίσοφος· "ἡμῖν δοκεῖ, εἰ μέν τις ἐᾶι ἡμᾶς ἀπιέναι
οἴκαδε, διαπορεύεσθαι τὴν χώραν ὡς ἂν δυνώμεθα ἀσινέστατα· ἢν δέ
τις ἡμᾶς τῆς ὁδοῦ ἀποκωλύηι, διαπολεμεῖν τούτωι ὡς ἂν δυνώμεθα
4 κράτιστα." ἐκ τούτου ἐπειρᾶτο Μιθραδάτης διδάσκειν ὡς ἄπορον εἴη
βασιλέως ἄκοντος σωθῆναι. ἔνθα δὴ ἐγιγνώσκετο ὅτι ὑπόπεμπτος εἴη·
καὶ γὰρ τῶν Τισσαφέρνους τις οἰκείων παρηκολούθει πίστεως ἕνεκα.
5 καὶ ἐκ τούτου ἐδόκει τοῖς στρατηγοῖς βέλτιον εἶναι δόγμα ποιήσασθαι
τὸν πόλεμον ἀκήρυκτον εἶναι ἔστ' ἐν τῆι πολεμίαι εἶεν· διέφθειρον γὰρ
προσιόντες τοὺς στρατιώτας, καὶ ἕνα γε λοχαγὸν διέφθειραν Νίκαρχον
Ἀρκάδα, καὶ ὤιχετο ἀπιὼν νυκτὸς σὺν ἀνθρώποις ὡς εἴκοσι.
6 Μετὰ δὲ ταῦτα ἀριστήσαντες καὶ διαβάντες τὸν Ζαπάταν ποταμὸν
ἐπορεύοντο τεταγμένοι τὰ ὑποζύγια καὶ τὸν ὄχλον ἐν μέσωι ἔχοντες. οὐ
πολὺ δὲ προεληλυθότων αὐτῶν ἐπιφαίνεται πάλιν ὁ Μιθραδάτης, ἱππέας
ἔχων ὡς διακοσίους καὶ τοξότας καὶ σφενδονήτας εἰς τετρακοσίους
7 μάλα ἐλαφροὺς καὶ εὐζώνους. καὶ προσήιει μὲν ὡς φίλος ὢν πρὸς τοὺς
Ἕλληνας· ἐπεὶ δ' ἐγγὺς ἐγένοντο, ἐξαπίνης οἱ μὲν αὐτῶν ἐτόξευον καὶ
ἱππεῖς καὶ πεζοί, οἱ δ' ἐσφενδόνων καὶ ἐτίτρωσκον. οἱ δὲ ὀπισθοφύλακες
τῶν Ἑλλήνων ἔπασχον μὲν κακῶς, ἀντεποίουν δ' οὐδέν· οἵ τε γὰρ
Κρῆτες βραχύτερα τῶν Περσῶν ἐτόξευον καὶ ἅμα ψιλοὶ ὄντες εἴσω
τῶν ὅπλων κατεκέκλειντο, οἱ δὲ ἀκοντισταὶ βραχύτερα ἠκόντιζον ἢ ὡς
8 ἐξικνεῖσθαι τῶν σφενδονητῶν. ἐκ τούτου Ξενοφῶντι ἐδόκει διωκτέον
εἶναι· καὶ ἐδίωκον τῶν τε ὁπλιτῶν καὶ τῶν πελταστῶν οἳ ἔτυχον σὺν
αὐτῶι ὀπισθοφυλακοῦντες· διώκοντες δὲ οὐδένα κατελάμβανον τῶν
9 πολεμίων. οὔτε γὰρ ἱππεῖς ἦσαν τοῖς Ἕλλησιν οὔτε οἱ πεζοὶ τοὺς
πεζοὺς ἐκ πολλοῦ φεύγοντας ἐδύναντο καταλαμβάνειν ἐν ὀλίγωι χωρίωι·

3.2 ἔφη om. **c**
3.3 εἰ: ἢν **f**
ἀποκωλύηι: ἐπικωλύηι **C[1]M**
3.4 ὑπόπεμπτος **C[1]E**: ὕποπτος cett.
3.6 μετὰ δὲ: δὲ om. **c**
Ζαπάταν Bochart (ex 2.5.1): ἐζότην (fors. ὀζότην) **C[1]**: ζάτην cett.
εἰς **CBg**: ὡς cett.
3.7 ἐγένοντο: ἐγένετο **f**
οἱ δὲ ἀκοντισταί: οἵ τε ἀκοντισταὶ f

πολὺ γὰρ οὐχ οἷόν τε ἦν ἀπὸ τοῦ ἄλλου στρατεύματος διώκειν· οἱ δὲ 10
βάρβαροι ἱππεῖς καὶ φεύγοντες ἅμα ἐτίτρωσκον εἰς τοὔπισθεν τοξεύοντες
ἀπὸ τῶν ἵππων, ὁπόσον δὲ προδιώξειαν οἱ Ἕλληνες, τοσοῦτον πάλιν
ἐπαναχωρεῖν μαχομένους ἔδει. ὥστε τῆς ἡμέρας ὅλης διῆλθον οὐ πλέον 11
πέντε καὶ εἴκοσι σταδίων, ἀλλὰ δείλης ἀφίκοντο εἰς τὰς κώμας.

Ἔνθα δὴ πάλιν ἀθυμία ἦν. καὶ Χειρίσοφος καὶ οἱ πρεσβύτατοι τῶν
στρατηγῶν Ξενοφῶντα ᾐτιῶντο ὅτι ἐδίωκεν ἀπὸ τῆς φάλαγγος καὶ
αὐτός τε ἐκινδύνευε καὶ τοὺς πολεμίους οὐδὲν μᾶλλον ἐδύνατο βλάπτειν.
ἀκούσας δὲ Ξενοφῶν ἔλεγεν ὅτι ὀρθῶς αἰτιῷντο καὶ αὐτὸ τὸ ἔργον 12
αὐτοῖς μαρτυροίη. "ἀλλ' ἐγώ" ἔφη "ἠναγκάσθην διώκειν, ἐπειδὴ
ἑώρων ἡμᾶς ἐν τῶι μένειν κακῶς μὲν πάσχοντας, ἀντιποιεῖν δὲ οὐδὲν
δυναμένους. ἐπειδὴ δὲ ἐδιώκομεν, ἀληθῆ" ἔφη "ὑμεῖς λέγετε· κακῶς μὲν 13
γὰρ ποιεῖν οὐδὲν μᾶλλον ἐδυνάμεθα τοὺς πολεμίους, ἀνεχωροῦμεν δὲ
παγχαλέπως. τοῖς οὖν θεοῖς χάρις ὅτι οὐ σὺν πολλῆι ῥώμηι, ἀλλὰ σὺν 14
ὀλίγοις ἤλθον, ὥστε βλάψαι μὲν μὴ μεγάλα, δηλῶσαι δὲ ὧν δεόμεθα.
νῦν γὰρ οἱ μὲν πολέμιοι τοξεύουσι καὶ σφενδονῶσιν ὅσον οὔτε οἱ 15
Κρῆτες ἀντιτοξεύειν δύνανται οὔτε οἱ ἐκ χειρὸς βάλλοντες ἐξικνεῖσθαι·
ὅταν δὲ αὐτοὺς διώκωμεν, πολὺ μὲν οὐχ οἷόν τε χωρίον ἀπὸ τοῦ
στρατεύματος διώκειν, ἐν ὀλίγωι δὲ οὐδ' εἰ ταχὺς εἴη πεζὸς πεζὸν ἂν
διώκων καταλαμβάνοι ἐκ τόξου ῥύματος. ἡμεῖς οὖν εἰ μέλλομεν τούτους 16
εἴργειν ὥστε μὴ δύνασθαι βλάπτειν ἡμᾶς πορευομένους, σφενδονητῶν
τε τὴν ταχίστην δεῖ καὶ ἱππέων. ἀκούω δ' εἶναι ἐν τῶι στρατεύματι
ἡμῶν Ῥοδίους, ὧν τοὺς πολλούς φασιν ἐπίστασθαι σφενδονᾶν, καὶ τὸ
βέλος αὐτῶν καὶ διπλάσιον φέρεσθαι τῶν Περσικῶν σφενδονῶν. ἐκεῖναι 17
γὰρ διὰ τὸ χειροπληθέσι τοῖς λίθοις σφενδονᾶν ἐπὶ βραχὺ ἐξικνοῦνται,
οἱ δέ γε Ῥόδιοι καὶ ταῖς μολυβδίσιν ἐπίστανται χρῆσθαι. ἢν οὖν αὐτῶν 18
ἐπισκεψώμεθα τίνες πέπανται σφενδόνας, καὶ τούτοις μὲν δῶμεν αὐτῶν
ἀργύριον, τῶι δὲ ἄλλας πλέκειν ἐθέλοντι ἄλλο ἀργύριον τελῶμεν, καὶ τῶι
σφενδονᾶν ἐν τῶι τεταγμένωι ἐθέλοντι ἄλλην τινὰ ἀτέλειαν εὑρίσκωμεν,
ἴσως τινὲς φανοῦνται ἱκανοὶ ἡμᾶς ὠφελεῖν. ὁρῶ δὲ ἵππους ὄντας ἐν 19
τῶι στρατεύματι, τοὺς μέν τινας παρ' ἐμοί, τοὺς δὲ τῶν Κλεάρχου
καταλελειμμένους, πολλοὺς δὲ καὶ ἄλλους αἰχμαλώτους σκευοφοροῦντας.
ἂν οὖν τούτους πάντας ἐκλέξαντες σκευοφόρα μὲν ἀντιδῶμεν, τοὺς δὲ
ἵππους εἰς ἱππέας κατασκευάσωμεν, ἴσως καὶ οὗτοί τι τοὺς φεύγοντας

3.10 προδιώξειαν: διώξειαν **c**
3.13 παγχαλέπως **C**[1]: πάνυ χαλεπῶς cett.
3.15 οἱ μὲν πολέμιοι: μὲν om. **C**[1]
3.18 τούτοις Cobet: τούτωι **c**: τούτων τῶι **f**
3.18 δῶμεν αὐτῶν ἀργύριον: ἀργύριον δῶμεν **E** om. αὐτῶν (αὐτῶ **H**[1])
ἐν τῶι τεταγμένωι **CBA** (cf. *Cyr.* 6.2.37): ἐντεταγμένωι **Ef**: ἐντεταλμένωι **M**
3.19 τῶν Κλεάρχου **C**[1]: παρὰ τῶ(ι) Κλεάρχω(ι) **E**: τῶ(ι) Κλεάρχω(ι) cett.

20 ἀνιάσουσιν." ἔδοξε ταῦτα. καὶ ταύτης τῆς νυκτὸς σφενδονῆται μὲν εἰς
διακοσίους ἐγένοντο, ἵπποι δὲ καὶ ἱππεῖς ἐδοκιμάσθησαν τῆι ὑστεραίαι
εἰς πεντήκοντα, καὶ σπολάδες καὶ θώρακες αὐτοῖς ἐπορίσθησαν, καὶ
ἵππαρχος ἐπεστάθη Λύκιος ὁ Πολυστράτου Ἀθηναῖος.

4 Μείναντες δὲ ταύτην τὴν ἡμέραν τῆι ἄλληι ἐπορεύοντο πρωϊαίτερον
ἀναστάντες· χαράδραν γὰρ ἔδει [αὐτοὺς] διαβῆναι ἐφ' ἧι ἐφοβοῦντο
2 μὴ ἐπιθοῖντο αὐτοῖς διαβαίνουσιν οἱ πολέμιοι. διαβεβηκόσι δὲ αὐτοῖς
πάλιν ἐπιφαίνεται ὁ Μιθραδάτης ἔχων ἱππέας χιλίους, τοξότας δὲ καὶ
σφενδονήτας εἰς τετρακισχιλίους· τοσούτους γὰρ ἤιτησε Τισσαφέρνην,
καὶ ἔλαβεν ὑποσχόμενος, ἂν τούτους λάβηι, παραδώσειν αὐτῶι τοὺς
Ἕλληνας, καταφρονήσας, ὅτι ἐν τῆι πρόσθεν προσβολῆι ὀλίγους ἔχων
3 ἔπαθε μὲν οὐδέν, πολλὰ δὲ κακὰ ἐνόμιζε ποιῆσαι. ἐπεὶ δὲ οἱ Ἕλληνες
διαβεβηκότες ἀπεῖχον τῆς χαράδρας ὅσον ὀκτὼ σταδίους, διέβαινε καὶ ὁ
Μιθραδάτης ἔχων τὴν δύναμιν. παρήγγελτο δὲ τῶν τε πελταστῶν οὓς
ἔδει διώκειν καὶ τῶν ὁπλιτῶν, καὶ τοῖς ἱππεῦσιν εἴρητο θαρροῦσι διώκειν
4 ὡς ἐφεψομένης ἱκανῆς δυνάμεως. ἐπεὶ δὲ ὁ Μιθραδάτης κατειλήφει, καὶ
ἤδη σφενδόναι καὶ τοξεύματα ἐξικνοῦντο, ἐσήμηνε τοῖς Ἕλλησι τῆι
σάλπιγγι, καὶ εὐθὺς ἔθεον ὁμόσε οἷς εἴρητο καὶ οἱ ἱππεῖς ἤλαυνον· οἱ
5 δὲ οὐκ ἐδέξαντο, ἀλλ' ἔφευγον ἐπὶ τὴν χαράδραν. ἐν ταύτηι τῆι διώξει
τοῖς βαρβάροις τῶν τε πεζῶν ἀπέθανον πολλοὶ καὶ τῶν ἱππέων ἐν
τῆι χαράδραι ζωοὶ ἐλήφθησαν εἰς ὀκτωκαίδεκα. τοὺς δὲ ἀποθανόντας
αὐτοκέλευστοι οἱ Ἕλληνες ἠικίσαντο, ὡς ὅτι φοβερώτατον τοῖς
6 πολεμίοις εἴη ὁρᾶν. καὶ οἱ μὲν πολέμιοι οὕτω πράξαντες ἀπῆλθον, οἱ
δὲ Ἕλληνες ἀσφαλῶς πορευόμενοι τὸ λοιπὸν τῆς ἡμέρας ἀφίκοντο ἐπὶ
7 τὸν Τίγρητα ποταμόν. ἐνταῦθα πόλις ἦν ἐρήμη μεγάλη, ὄνομα δ' αὐτῆι
ἦν Λάρισα· ὤικουν δ' αὐτὴν τὸ παλαιὸν Μῆδοι. τοῦ δὲ τείχους αὐτῆς
ἦν τὸ εὖρος πέντε καὶ εἴκοσι πόδες, ὕψος δ' ἑκατόν· τοῦ δὲ κύκλου ἡ
περίοδος δύο παρασάγγαι· ὠικοδόμητο δὲ πλίνθοις κεραμεαῖς· κρηπὶς
8 δ' ὑπῆν λιθίνη τὸ ὕψος εἴκοσι ποδῶν. ταύτην βασιλεὺς ὁ Περσῶν ὅτε
παρὰ Μήδων τὴν ἀρχὴν ἐλάμβανον Πέρσαι πολιορκῶν οὐδενὶ τρόπωι
ἐδύνατο ἑλεῖν· Ἥλιος δὲ νεφέλην προκαλύψας ἠφάνισε μέχρι ἐξέλιπον οἱ

3.20 ἔδοξε ταῦτα: ἔδοξε καὶ ταῦτα **c**
σπόλαδες **V** Pollux 7.70: στόλαδες cett.
καὶ θώρακες del. Lion

4.1 πρωϊαίτερον: πρωίτερον **cF**
αὐτοὺς om. **D**: ante ἔδει habet **f**

4.8 Ἥλιος δὲ νεφέλην προκαλύψας: Ζεὺς δὲ ἥλιον νεφέληι προκαλύψας Schenkl (maluerimus Ζεὺς δὲ νεφέλην προκαλύψας): ἥλιον δὲ νεφέλη προκαλύψασα Brodaeus, Amasaeo praemonente (*solem densa nubes obscurasset*)

ἄνθρωποι, καὶ οὕτως ἑάλω. παρὰ ταύτην τὴν πόλιν ἦν πυραμὶς λιθίνη, 9
τὸ μὲν εὖρος ἑνὸς πλέθρου, τὸ δὲ ὕψος δύο πλέθρων. ἐπὶ ταύτης πολλοὶ
τῶν βαρβάρων ἦσαν ἐκ τῶν πλησίον κωμῶν ἀποπεφευγότες. ἐντεῦθεν 10
δ' ἐπορεύθησαν σταθμὸν ἕνα παρασάγγας ἓξ πρὸς τεῖχος ἔρημον μέγα
πρὸς [τῆι] πόλει κείμενον· ὄνομα δὲ ἦν τῆι πόλει Μέσπιλα· Μῆδοι δ'
αὐτήν ποτε ὤικουν. ἦν δὲ ἡ μὲν κρηπὶς λίθου ξεστοῦ κογχυλιάτου,
τὸ εὖρος πεντήκοντα ποδῶν καὶ τὸ ὕψος πεντήκοντα. ἐπὶ δὲ ταύτηι 11
ἐπωικοδόμητο πλίνθινον τεῖχος, τὸ μὲν εὖρος πεντήκοντα ποδῶν, τὸ
δὲ ὕψος ἑκατόν· τοῦ δὲ κύκλου ἡ περίοδος ἓξ παρασάγγαι. ἐνταῦθα
λέγεται Μήδεια γυνὴ βασιλέως καταφυγεῖν ὅτε ἀπώλλυσαν τὴν ἀρχὴν
ὑπὸ Περσῶν Μῆδοι. ταύτην δὲ τὴν πόλιν πολιορκῶν ὁ Περσῶν βασιλεὺς 12
οὐκ ἐδύνατο οὔτε χρόνωι ἑλεῖν οὔτε βίαι· Ζεὺς δ' ἐμβροντήτους ποιεῖ
τοὺς ἐνοικοῦντας, καὶ οὕτως ἑάλω.

Ἐντεῦθεν δ' ἐπορεύθησαν σταθμὸν ἕνα παρασάγγας τέτταρας. εἰς 13
τοῦτον δὲ τὸν σταθμὸν Τισσαφέρνης ἐπεφάνη, οὕς τε αὐτὸς ἱππέας
ἦλθεν ἔχων καὶ τὴν Ὀρόντα δύναμιν τοῦ τὴν βασιλέως θυγατέρα
ἔχοντος καὶ οὓς Κῦρος ἔχων ἀνέβη βαρβάρους καὶ οὓς ὁ βασιλέως
ἀδελφὸς ἔχων βασιλεῖ ἐβοήθει, καὶ πρὸς τούτοις ὅσους βασιλεὺς ἔδωκεν
αὐτῶι, ὥστε τὸ στράτευμα πάμπολυ ἐφάνη. ἐπεὶ δ' ἐγγὺς ἐγένετο, 14
τὰς μὲν τῶν τάξεων εἶχεν ὄπισθεν καταστήσας, τὰς δὲ εἰς τὰ πλάγια
παραγαγὼν ἐμβαλεῖν μὲν οὐκ ἐτόλμησεν οὐδ' ἐβούλετο διακινδυνεύειν,
σφενδονᾶν δὲ παρήγγειλε καὶ τοξεύειν. ἐπεὶ δὲ διαταχθέντες οἱ Ῥόδιοι 15
ἐσφενδόνησαν καὶ οἱ [Σκύθαι] τοξόται ἐτόξευσαν καὶ οὐδεὶς ἡμάρτανεν
ἀνδρός (οὐδὲ γὰρ εἰ πάνυ προυθυμεῖτο ῥάιδιον ἦν), καὶ ὁ Τισσαφέρνης
μάλα ταχέως ἔξω βελῶν ἀπεχώρει καὶ <αἱ> ἄλλαι τάξεις ἀπεχώρησαν.
καὶ τὸ λοιπὸν τῆς ἡμέρας οἱ μὲν ἐπορεύοντο, οἱ δ' εἵποντο· καὶ οὐκέτι 16
ἐσίνοντο οἱ βάρβαροι τῆι τότε ἀκροβολίσει· μακρότερον γὰρ οἵ τε
Ῥόδιοι τῶν Περσῶν ἐσφενδόνων καὶ τῶν [πλείστων] τοξοτῶν <. . .>·

4.10 τῆι del. Krüger, πρὸς τῆι πόλει om. **C**[1]
4.11 λέγεται: ἐλέγετο **f**
4.12 δ' ἐμβροντήτους ποιεῖ: δὲ βροντῆι κατέπληξε Hug ex vestigiis **C**[1] (δ' ἐμ, τους, οιεῖ in ras.)
4.15 Σκύθαι del. Krüger
αἱ add. Larcher (iam **b**)
4.16 ἐσίνοντο: ἐπέκειντο **f**
τε del. Poppo (om. iam **b**): γε Matthiae
πλείστων om. **C**[1]
lac. longiorem indic. Hug: οἱ Κρῆτες ἐτόξευον suppl. Madvig

17 μεγάλα δὲ καὶ τὰ τόξα τὰ Περσικά ἐστιν· ὥστε χρήσιμα ἦν ὁπόσα
ἁλίσκοιτο τῶν τοξευμάτων τοῖς Κρησί, καὶ διετέλουν χρώμενοι τοῖς τῶν
πολεμίων τοξεύμασι, καὶ ἐμελέτων τοξεύειν ἄνω ἱέντες μακράν. ηὑρίσκετο
δὲ καὶ νεῦρα πολλὰ ἐν ταῖς κώμαις καὶ μόλυβδος, ὥστε χρῆσθαι εἰς
18 τὰς σφενδόνας. καὶ ταύτηι μὲν τῆι ἡμέραι, ἐπεὶ κατεστρατοπεδεύοντο
οἱ Ἕλληνες κώμαις ἐπιτυχόντες, ἀπῆλθον οἱ βάρβαροι μεῖον ἔχοντες
τῆι ἀκροβολίσει· τὴν δ' ἐπιοῦσαν ἡμέραν ἔμειναν οἱ Ἕλληνες καὶ
ἐπεσιτίσαντο· ἦν γὰρ πολὺς σῖτος ἐν ταῖς κώμαις. τῆι δὲ ὑστεραίαι
ἐπορεύοντο διὰ τοῦ πεδίου, καὶ Τισσαφέρνης εἵπετο ἀκροβολιζόμενος.
19 ἔνθα δὴ οἱ Ἕλληνες ἔγνωσαν πλαίσιον ἰσόπλευρον ὅτι πονηρὰ τάξις
εἴη πολεμίων ἑπομένων. ἀνάγκη γάρ ἐστιν, ἢν μὲν συγκύπτηι τὰ
κέρατα τοῦ πλαισίου ἢ ὁδοῦ στενοτέρας οὔσης ἢ ὀρέων ἀναγκαζόντων
ἢ γεφύρας, ἐκθλίβεσθαι τοὺς ὁπλίτας καὶ πορεύεσθαι πονήρως ἅμα
μὲν πιεζομένους, ἅμα δὲ καὶ ταραττομένους· ὥστε δυσχρήστους εἶναι
20 ἀνάγκη ἀτάκτους ὄντας. ὅταν δ' αὖ διάσχηι τὰ κέρατα, ἀνάγκη
διασπᾶσθαι τοὺς τότε ἐκθλιβομένους καὶ κενὸν γίγνεσθαι τὸ μέσον τῶν
κεράτων, καὶ ἀθυμεῖν τοὺς ταῦτα πάσχοντας πολεμίων ἑπομένων. καὶ
ὁπότε δέοι γέφυραν διαβαίνειν ἢ ἄλλην τινὰ διάβασιν, ἔσπευδεν ἕκαστος
βουλόμενος φθάσαι πρῶτος· καὶ εὐεπίθετον ἦν ἐνταῦθα τοῖς πολεμίοις.
21 ἐπεὶ δὲ ταῦτ' ἔγνωσαν οἱ στρατηγοί, ἐποίησαν ἓξ λόχους ἀνὰ ἑκατὸν
ἄνδρας, καὶ λοχαγοὺς ἐπέστησαν καὶ ἄλλους πεντηκοντῆρας καὶ ἄλλους
ἐνωμοτάρχους. οὗτοι δὲ πορευόμενοι, ὁπότε μὲν συγκύπτοι τὰ κέρατα,
ὑπέμενον ὕστεροι οἱ λοχαγοί ὥστε μὴ ἐνοχλεῖν τοῖς κέρασι, τοτὲ δὲ
22 παρῆγον ἔξωθεν τῶν κεράτων· ὁπότε δὲ διάσχοιεν αἱ πλευραὶ τοῦ
πλαισίου, τὸ μέσον ἀνεξεπίμπλασαν, εἰ μὲν στενότερον εἴη τὸ διέχον,
κατὰ λόχους, εἰ δὲ πλατύτερον, κατὰ πεντηκοστῦς, εἰ δὲ πάνυ πλατύ,
23 κατ' ἐνωμοτίας, ὥστε ἀεὶ ἔκπλεων εἶναι τὸ μέσον. εἰ δὲ καὶ διαβαίνειν
τινὰ δέοι διάβασιν ἢ γέφυραν, οὐκ ἐταράττοντο, ἀλλ' ἐν τῶι μέρει οἱ
λόχοι διέβαινον· καὶ εἴ που δέοι τι τῆς φάλαγγος, ἐπιπαρῆισαν οὗτοι.
τούτωι τῶι τρόπωι ἐπορεύθησαν σταθμοὺς τέτταρας.

4.17 ὁπόσα: ὁπόσα δ' **C**[1]**AE**
ηὑρίσκετο . . . σφενδόνας fors. post ἐν ταῖς κώμαις (18) transponendum
4.18 ἐν τῆι τότε: ἐν et τότε om. **C**[1]
4.21 οὗτοι: οὕτω Weiske
οἱ λοχαγοί (λόχοι Isaac Vossius) post πορευόμενοι **f**, del. Krüger
τοτὲ **D**: τότε **f**: τοὺς **c** (quo servato <οἱ μὲν> ὕστεροι Mangelsdorf)
4.22 ἀνεξεπίμπλασαν (ἀνεπίμπλασαν **E**) codd.: ἂν ἐξεπίμπλασαν Krüger (iam **b**)
4.23 λόχοι Valckenaer: λοχαγοὶ codd.

Ἡνίκα δὲ τὸν πέμπτον ἐπορεύοντο, εἶδον βασίλειόν τι καὶ περὶ αὐτὸ 24
κώμας πολλάς, τὴν δὲ ὁδὸν πρὸς τὸ χωρίον τοῦτο διὰ γηλόφων ὑψηλῶν
γιγνομένην, οἳ καθῆκον ἀπὸ τοῦ ὄρους ἐφ' ὧι ἦν [ἡ κώμη]. καὶ εἶδον μὲν
τοὺς λόφους ἄσμενοι οἱ Ἕλληνες, ὡς εἰκὸς τῶν πολεμίων ὄντων ἱππέων·
ἐπεὶ δὲ πορευόμενοι ἐκ τοῦ πεδίου ἀνέβησαν ἐπὶ τὸν πρῶτον γήλοφον 25
<καὶ> κατέβαινον, ὡς ἐπὶ τὸν ἕτερον ἀναβαίνειν, ἐνταῦθα ἐπιγίγνονται
οἱ βάρβαροι καὶ ἀπὸ τοῦ ὑψηλοῦ εἰς τὸ πρανὲς ἔβαλλον, ἐσφενδόνων,
ἐτόξευον ὑπὸ μαστίγων, καὶ πολλοὺς κατετίτρωσκον καὶ ἐκράτησαν 26
τῶν Ἑλλήνων γυμνήτων καὶ κατέκλεισαν αὐτοὺς εἴσω τῶν ὅπλων·
ὥστε παντάπασι ταύτην τὴν ἡμέραν ἄχρηστοι ἦσαν ἐν τῶι ὄχλωι
ὄντες καὶ οἱ σφενδονῆται καὶ οἱ τοξόται. ἐπεὶ δὲ πιεζόμενοι οἱ Ἕλληνες 27
ἐπεχείρησαν διώκειν, σχολῆι μὲν ἐπὶ τὸ ἄκρον ἀφικνοῦνται ὁπλῖται
ὄντες, οἱ δὲ πολέμιοι ταχὺ ἀπεπήδων. πάλιν δὲ ὁπότε ἀπίοιεν πρὸς 28
τὸ ἄλλο στράτευμα ταὐτὰ ἔπασχον, καὶ ἐπὶ τοῦ δευτέρου γηλόφου
ταὐτὰ ἐγίγνετο, ὥστε ἀπὸ τοῦ τρίτου γηλόφου ἔδοξεν αὐτοῖς μὴ κινεῖν
τοὺς στρατιώτας πρὶν ἀπὸ τῆς δεξιᾶς πλευρᾶς τοῦ πλαισίου ἀνήγαγον
πελταστὰς πρὸς τὸ ὄρος. ἐπεὶ δ' οὗτοι ἐγένοντο ὑπὲρ τῶν ἑπομένων 29
πολεμίων, οὐκέτι ἐπετίθεντο οἱ πολέμιοι τοῖς καταβαίνουσι, δεδοικότες
μὴ ἀποτμηθείησαν καὶ ἀμφοτέρωθεν αὐτῶν γένοιντο οἱ πολέμιοι. οὕτω 30
τὸ λοιπὸν τῆς ἡμέρας πορευόμενοι, οἱ μὲν <ἐν> τῆι ὁδῶι κατὰ τοὺς
γηλόφους, οἱ δὲ κατὰ τὸ ὄρος ἐπιπαριόντες, ἀφίκοντο εἰς τὰς κώμας καὶ
ἰατροὺς κατέστησαν ὀκτώ· πολλοὶ γὰρ ἦσαν οἱ τετρωμένοι. ἐνταῦθα 31
ἔμειναν ἡμέρας τρεῖς καὶ τῶν τετρωμένων ἕνεκα καὶ ἅμα ἐπιτήδεια πολλὰ
εἶχον, ἄλευρα, οἶνον, κριθὰς ἵπποις συμβεβλημένας πολλάς. ταῦτα δὲ
συνενηνεγμένα ἦν τῶι σατραπεύοντι τῆς χώρας. τετάρτηι δ' ἡμέραι
καταβαίνουσιν εἰς τὸ πεδίον. ἐπεὶ δὲ κατέλαβεν αὐτοὺς Τισσαφέρνης 32
σὺν τῆι δυνάμει, ἐδίδαξεν αὐτοὺς ἡ ἀνάγκη κατασκηνῆσαι οὗ πρῶτον
εἶδον κώμην καὶ μὴ πορεύεσθαι ἔτι μαχομένους· πολλοὶ γὰρ ἦσαν
οἱ ἀπόμαχοι, <οἵ τε> τετρωμένοι καὶ οἱ ἐκείνους φέροντες καὶ οἱ τῶν
φερόντων τὰ ὅπλα δεξάμενοι. ἐπεὶ δὲ κατεσκήνησαν καὶ ἐπεχείρησαν 33
αὐτοῖς ἀκροβολίζεσθαι οἱ βάρβαροι πρὸς τὴν κώμην προσιόντες, πολὺ

4.24 ἐφ' **MZg**: ὑφ' cett.
ἡ (om. **f**) κώμη del. Thomas
4.25 καὶ add. Stephanus (iam **b**)
ἀναβαίνειν: ἀναβαῖεν **f**
4.26 κατετίτρωσκον: ἐτίτρωσκον **c**
4.30 ἐν add. Bisschop
4.32 οἵ τε add. Zeune

περιῆσαν οἱ Ἕλληνες· πολὺ γὰρ διέφερεν ἐκ χώρας ὁρμῶντας ἀλέξασθαι
ἢ πορευομένους ἐπιοῦσι τοῖς πολεμίοις μάχεσθαι.
34 Ἡνίκα δ' ἦν ἤδη δείλη, ὥρα ἦν ἀπιέναι τοῖς πολεμίοις· οὔποτε γὰρ μεῖον
ἀπεστρατοπεδεύοντο οἱ βάρβαροι τοῦ Ἑλληνικοῦ ἑξήκοντα σταδίων,
35 φοβούμενοι μὴ τῆς νυκτὸς οἱ Ἕλληνες ἐπιθοῖντο αὐτοῖς. πονηρὸν γὰρ
νυκτός ἐστι στράτευμα Περσικόν. οἵ τε γὰρ ἵπποι αὐτοῖς δέδενται καὶ ὡς
ἐπὶ τὸ πολὺ πεποδισμένοι εἰσὶ τοῦ μὴ φεύγειν ἕνεκα εἰ λυθείησαν, ἐάν τέ
τις θόρυβος γίγνηται, δεῖ ἐπισάξαι τὸν ἵππον Πέρσηι ἀνδρὶ καὶ χαλινῶσαι,
δεῖ δὲ καὶ θωρακισθέντα ἀναβῆναι ἐπὶ τὸν ἵππον. ταῦτα δὲ πάντα χαλεπὰ
νύκτωρ καὶ θορύβου ὄντος ποιεῖν. τούτου ἕνεκα πόρρω ἀπεσκήνουν τῶν
36 Ἑλλήνων. ἐπεὶ δὲ ἐγίγνωσκον αὐτοὺς οἱ Ἕλληνες βουλομένους ἀπιέναι
καὶ διαγγελλομένους, ἐκήρυξε τοῖς Ἕλλησι συσκευάζεσθαι ἀκουόντων
τῶν πολεμίων. καὶ χρόνον μέν τινα ἐπέσχον τῆς πορείας οἱ βάρβαροι,
ἐπειδὴ δὲ ὀψὲ ἐγίγνετο, ἀπῆισαν· οὐδὲ γὰρ ἐδόκει λύειν αὐτοὺς νυκτὸς
37 πορεύεσθαι καὶ κατάγεσθαι ἐπὶ τὸ στρατόπεδον. ἐπειδὴ δὲ σαφῶς
ἀπιόντας ἤδη ἑώρων οἱ Ἕλληνες, ἐπορεύοντο καὶ αὐτοὶ ἀναζεύξαντες
καὶ διῆλθον ὅσον ἑξήκοντα σταδίους. καὶ γίγνεται τοσοῦτον μεταξὺ
τῶν στρατευμάτων ὥστε τῆι ὑστεραίαι οὐκ ἐφάνησαν οἱ πολέμιοι οὐδὲ
τῆι τρίτηι, τῆι δὲ τετάρτηι νυκτὸς προελθόντες καταλαμβάνουσι χωρίον
ὑπερδέξιον οἱ βάρβαροι, ἧι ἔμελλον οἱ Ἕλληνες παριέναι, ἀκρωνυχίαν
38 ὄρους, ὑφ' ἣν ἡ κατάβασις ἦν εἰς τὸ πεδίον. ἐπειδὴ δὲ ἑώρα Χειρίσοφος
προκατειλημμένην τὴν ἀκρωνυχίαν, καλεῖ Ξενοφῶντα ἀπὸ τῆς οὐρᾶς
39 καὶ κελεύει λαβόντα τοὺς πελταστὰς παραγενέσθαι εἰς τὸ πρόσθεν. ὁ
δὲ Ξενοφῶν τοὺς μὲν πελταστὰς οὐκ ἦγεν· ἐπιφαινόμενον γὰρ ἑώρα
Τισσαφέρνην καὶ τὸ στράτευμα πᾶν· αὐτὸς δὲ προσελάσας ἠρώτα· "τί
καλεῖς;" ὁ δὲ λέγει αὐτῶι· "ἔξεστιν ὁρᾶν· προκατείληπται γὰρ ἡμῖν ὁ
ὑπὲρ τῆς καταβάσεως λόφος, καὶ οὐκ ἔστι παρελθεῖν, εἰ μὴ τούτους
40 ἀποκόψομεν. ἀλλὰ τί οὐκ ἦγες τοὺς πελταστάς;" ὁ δὲ λέγει ὅτι οὐκ
ἐδόκει αὐτῶι ἔρημα καταλιπεῖν τὰ ὄπισθεν πολεμίων ἐπιφαινομένων.
"ἀλλὰ μὴν ὥρα γ'" ἔφη "βουλεύεσθαι πῶς τις τοὺς ἄνδρας ἀπελᾶι ἀπὸ
41 τοῦ λόφου." ἐνταῦθα Ξενοφῶν ὁρᾶι τοῦ ὄρους τὴν κορυφὴν ὑπὲρ αὐτοῦ
τοῦ ἑαυτῶν στρατεύματος οὖσαν, καὶ ἀπὸ ταύτης ἔφοδον ἐπὶ τὸν λόφον
ἔνθα ἦσαν οἱ πολέμιοι, καὶ λέγει· "κράτιστον, ὦ Χειρίσοφε, ἡμῖν ἵεσθαι
ὡς τάχιστα ἐπὶ τὸ ἄκρον· ἢν γὰρ τοῦτο λάβωμεν, οὐ δυνήσονται μένειν

4.34 οἱ Ἕλληνες om. **f**
4.35 δεῖ δὲ nos: δὴ **CE**: δὲ **A**: δεῖ cett.
4.36 οὐδὲ **V**: οὔτε **c**: οὐ **f**
λύειν αὐτοὺς: λυσιτελεῖν αὐτοῖς **f**: κωλύειν αὐτοὺς **B**

οἱ ὑπὲρ τῆς ὁδοῦ. ἀλλά, εἰ βούλει, μένε ἐπὶ τῶι στρατεύματι, ἐγὼ δ'
ἐθέλω πορεύεσθαι· εἰ δὲ χρήιζεις, πορεύου ἐπὶ τὸ ὄρος, ἐγὼ δὲ μενῶ
αὐτοῦ." "ἀλλὰ δίδωμί σοι" ἔφη ὁ Χειρίσοφος "ὁπότερον βούλει ἑλέσθαι." 42
εἰπὼν ὁ Ξενοφῶν ὅτι νεώτερός ἐστιν αἱρεῖται πορεύεσθαι, κελεύει δέ οἱ
συμπέμψαι ἀπὸ τοῦ στόματος ἄνδρας· μακρὸν γὰρ ἦν ἀπὸ τῆς οὐρᾶς
λαβεῖν. καὶ ὁ Χειρίσοφος συμπέμπει τοὺς ἀπὸ τοῦ στόματος πελταστάς, 43
ἔλαβε δὲ τοὺς κατὰ μέσον τοῦ πλαισίου. συνέπεσθαι δ' ἐκέλευσεν αὐτῶι
καὶ τοὺς τριακοσίους οὓς αὐτὸς εἶχε τῶν ἐπιλέκτων ἐπὶ τῶι στόματι
τοῦ πλαισίου. ἐντεῦθεν ἐπορεύοντο ὡς ἐδύναντο τάχιστα. οἱ δ' ἐπὶ τοῦ 44
λόφου πολέμιοι ὡς ἐνόησαν αὐτῶν τὴν πορείαν ἐπὶ τὸ ἄκρον, εὐθὺς
καὶ αὐτοὶ ὥρμησαν ἁμιλλᾶσθαι ἐπὶ τὸ ἄκρον. καὶ ἐνταῦθα πολλὴ μὲν 45
κραυγὴ ἦν τοῦ Ἑλληνικοῦ στρατεύματος διακελευομένων τοῖς ἑαυτῶν,
πολλὴ δὲ κραυγὴ τῶν ἀμφὶ Τισσαφέρνην τοῖς ἑαυτῶν διακελευομένων.
Ξενοφῶν δὲ παρελαύνων ἐπὶ τοῦ ἵππου παρεκελεύετο. "ἄνδρες, νῦν ἐπὶ 46
τὴν Ἑλλάδα νομίζετε ἁμιλλᾶσθαι, νῦν πρὸς παῖδας καὶ γυναῖκας, νῦν
ὀλίγον πονήσαντες ἀμαχεὶ τὴν λοιπὴν πορευσόμεθα." Σωτηρίδας δὲ ὁ 47
Σικυώνιος εἶπεν· "οὐκ ἐξ ἴσου, ὦ Ξενοφῶν, ἐσμέν· σὺ μὲν γὰρ ἐφ' ἵππου
ὀχῆι, ἐγὼ δὲ χαλεπῶς κάμνω τὴν ἀσπίδα φέρων." καὶ ὃς ἀκούσας ταῦτα 48
καταπηδήσας ἀπὸ τοῦ ἵππου ὠθεῖται αὐτὸν ἐκ τῆς τάξεως καὶ τὴν
ἀσπίδα ἀφελόμενος ὡς ἐδύνατο τάχιστα ἔχων ἐπορεύετο· ἐτύγχανε δὲ
καὶ θώρακα ἔχων τὸν ἱππικόν, ὥστε ἐπιέζετο. καὶ τοῖς μὲν ἔμπροσθεν
ὑπάγειν παρεκελεύετο, τοῖς δὲ ὄπισθεν παριέναι μόλις ἑπόμενος. οἱ δ' 49
ἄλλοι στρατιῶται παίουσι καὶ βάλλουσι καὶ λοιδοροῦσι τὸν Σωτηρίδαν,
ἔστε ἠνάγκασαν λαβόντα τὴν ἀσπίδα πορεύεσθαι. ὁ δὲ ἀναβάς, ἕως
μὲν βάσιμα ἦν, ἐπὶ τοῦ ἵππου ἦγεν, ἐπεὶ δὲ ἄβατα ἦν, καταλιπὼν τὸν
ἵππον ἔσπευδε πεζῆι. καὶ φθάνουσιν ἐπὶ τῶι ἄκρωι γενόμενοι τοὺς
πολεμίους. ἔνθα δὴ οἱ μὲν βάρβαροι στραφέντες ἔφευγον ἧι ἕκαστος **5**
ἐδύνατο, οἱ δὲ Ἕλληνες εἶχον τὸ ἄκρον. οἱ δὲ ἀμφὶ Τισσαφέρνην καὶ
Ἀριαῖον ἀποτραπόμενοι ἄλλην ὁδὸν ᾤχοντο. οἱ δὲ ἀμφὶ Χειρίσοφον
καταβάντες εἰς τὸ πεδίον ἐστρατοπεδεύσαντο ἐν κώμηι μεστῆι πολλῶν
ἀγαθῶν. ἦσαν δὲ καὶ ἄλλαι κῶμαι πολλαὶ πλήρεις πολλῶν ἀγαθῶν ἐν
τούτωι τῶι πεδίωι παρὰ τὸν Τίγρητα ποταμόν.

Ἡνίκα δ' ἦν δείλη, ἐξαπίνης οἱ πολέμιοι ἐπιφαίνονται ἐν τῶι πεδίωι, 2
καὶ τῶν Ἑλλήνων κατέκοψάν τινας τῶν ἐσκεδασμένων ἐν τῶι πεδίωι

4.43 αὐτῶι: αὐτοὺς **CBA**: αὐτοῖς Bornemann (iam **g**)
4.46 παῖδας καὶ γυναῖκας: τοὺς π. καὶ τὰς γ. **c**
4.48 τάχιστα ἔχων: ἔχων om. **f**
ἑπόμενος: ἑπομένοις **f**
4.49 βάσιμα: βάτα **CAg**

καθ' ἁρπαγήν· καὶ γὰρ νομαὶ πολλαὶ βοσκημάτων διαβιβαζόμεναι εἰς
3 τὸ πέραν τοῦ ποταμοῦ κατελήφθησαν. <. . .> ἐνταῦθα Τισσαφέρνης
καὶ οἱ σὺν αὐτῶι καίειν ἐπεχείρησαν τὰς κώμας, καὶ τῶν Ἑλλήνων
μάλα ἠθύμησάν τινες, ἐννοούμενοι μὴ τὰ ἐπιτήδεια, εἰ καύσοιεν, οὐκ
4 ἔχοιεν ὁπόθεν λαμβάνοιεν. καὶ οἱ μὲν ἀμφὶ Χειρίσοφον ἀπῆισαν ἐκ τῆς
βοηθείας· ὁ δὲ Ξενοφῶν ἐπεὶ κατέβη, παρελαύνων τὰς τάξεις ἡνίκα
5 ⟨τοῖς⟩ ἀπὸ τῆς βοηθείας ἀπήντησαν [οἱ Ἕλληνες] ἔλεγεν· "ὁρᾶτε,
ὦ ἄνδρες Ἕλληνες, ὑφιέντας τὴν χώραν ἤδη ὑμετέραν εἶναι; ἃ γὰρ
ὅτε ἐσπένδοντο διεπράττοντο, μὴ καίειν τὴν βασιλέως χώραν, νῦν
αὐτοὶ καίουσιν ὡς ἀλλοτρίαν. ἀλλ' ἐάν που καταλείπωσί γε αὑτοῖς τὰ
6 ἐπιτήδεια, ὄψονται καὶ ἡμᾶς ἐνταῦθα πορευομένους. ἀλλ' ὦ Χειρίσοφε"
ἔφη "δοκεῖ μοι βοηθεῖν ἐπὶ τοὺς καίοντας ὡς ὑπὲρ τῆς ἡμετέρας." ὁ δὲ
Χειρίσοφος εἶπεν· "οὔκουν ἔμοιγε δοκεῖ· ἀλλὰ καὶ ἡμεῖς" ἔφη "καίωμεν,
καὶ οὕτω θᾶττον παύσονται."
7 Ἐπεὶ δὲ ἐπὶ τὰς σκηνὰς ἦλθον, οἱ μὲν ἄλλοι περὶ τὰ ἐπιτήδεια ἦσαν,
στρατηγοὶ δὲ καὶ λοχαγοὶ συνῆλθον. καὶ ἐνταῦθα πολλὴ ἀπορία
ἦν. ἔνθεν μὲν γὰρ ὄρη ἦν ὑπερύψηλα, ἔνθεν δὲ ὁ ποταμὸς τοσοῦτος
τὸ βάθος ὡς μηδὲ τὰ δόρατα ὑπερέχειν πειρωμένοις τοῦ βάθους.
8 ἀπορουμένοις δ' αὐτοῖς προσελθών τις ἀνὴρ Ῥόδιος εἶπεν· "ἐγὼ θέλω,
ὦ ἄνδρες, διαβιβάσαι ὑμᾶς κατὰ τετρακισχιλίους ὁπλίτας, ἂν ἐμοὶ ὧν
9 δέομαι ὑπηρετήσητε καὶ τάλαντον μισθὸν πορίσητε." ἐρωτώμενος δὲ
ὅτου δέοιτο, "ἀσκῶν" ἔφη "δισχιλίων δεήσομαι· πολλὰ δ' ὁρῶ ταῦτα
πρόβατα καὶ αἶγας καὶ βοῦς καὶ ὄνους, ἃ ἀποδαρέντα καὶ φυσηθέντα
10 ῥαιδίως ἂν παρέχοι τὴν διάβασιν. δεήσομαι δὲ καὶ τῶν δεσμῶν οἷς
χρῆσθε περὶ τὰ ὑποζύγια· τούτοις ζεύξας τοὺς ἀσκοὺς πρὸς ἀλλήλους,
ὁρμίσας ἕκαστον ἀσκὸν λίθους ἀρτήσας καὶ ἀφεὶς ὥσπερ ἀγκύρας εἰς
τὸ ὕδωρ, διαγαγὼν καὶ ἀμφοτέρωθεν δήσας ἐπιβαλῶ ὕλην καὶ γῆν
11 ἐπιφορήσω· ὅτι μὲν οὖν οὐ καταδύσεσθε αὐτίκα μάλα εἴσεσθε· πᾶς γὰρ
ἀσκὸς δύο ἄνδρας ἕξει τοῦ μὴ καταδῦναι, ὥστε δὲ μὴ ὀλισθάνειν ἡ ὕλη

5.3 lac. stat. Krüger
5.4 βοηθείας **FMB**: βαθείας hic et infra **CAE**: βοηλασίας hic et infra Gemoll
τάς: ἐπὶ τὰς **f**
τοῖς supplevimus: οἱ suppl. Schenkl (et οἱ Ἕλληνες del.)
ἀπὸ: ἐκ **M**
ἀπήντησαν: ἀπή(ι)εσαν **f**
οἱ Ἕλληνες del. Bornemann
5.5 ὑμετέραν **CFMH**: ἡμετέραν alii
καταλείπωσί: καταλίπωσί **f**
5.7 ἦλθον: ἀπῆλθον **f**

καὶ ἡ γῆ σχήσει." ἀκούσασι ταῦτα τοῖς στρατηγοῖς τὸ μὲν ἐνθύμημα 12
χαρίεν ἐδόκει εἶναι, τὸ δ' ἔργον ἀδύνατον· ἦσαν γὰρ οἱ κωλύσοντες
πέραν πολλοὶ ἱππεῖς, οἳ εὐθὺς τοῖς πρώτοις οὐδὲν ἂν ἐπέτρεπον τούτων
ποιεῖν.

Ἐνταῦθα τὴν μὲν ὑστεραίαν ἐπανεχώρουν εἰς τοὔμπαλιν [ἢ πρὸς 13
Βαβυλῶνα] εἰς τὰς ἀκαύστους κώμας, κατακαύσαντες ἔνθεν ἐξῇσαν· ὥστε
οἱ πολέμιοι οὐ προσήλαυνον, ἀλλὰ ἐθεῶντο καὶ ὅμοιοι ἦσαν θαυμάζουσι
ὅποι ποτὲ τρέψονται οἱ Ἕλληνες καὶ τί ἐν νῶι ἔχοιεν. ἐνταῦθα οἱ μὲν 14
ἄλλοι στρατιῶται ἀμφὶ τὰ ἐπιτήδεια ἦσαν· οἱ δὲ στρατηγοὶ πάλιν
συνῆλθον, καὶ συναγαγόντες τοὺς αἰχμαλώτους ἤλεγχον τὴν κύκλωι
πᾶσαν χώραν τίς ἑκάστη εἴη. οἱ δὲ ἔλεγον ὅτι τὰ μὲν πρὸς μεσημβρίαν 15
τῆς ἐπὶ Βαβυλῶνα εἴη καὶ Μηδίαν, δι' ἧσπερ ἥκοιεν, ἡ δὲ πρὸς ἕω
ἐπὶ Σοῦσά τε καὶ Ἐκβάτανα φέροι, ἔνθα θερίζειν [καὶ ἐαρίζειν] λέγεται
βασιλεύς, ἡ δὲ διαβάντι τὸν ποταμὸν πρὸς ἑσπέραν ἐπὶ Λυδίαν καὶ
Ἰωνίαν φέροι, ἡ δὲ διὰ τῶν ὀρέων καὶ πρὸς ἄρκτον τετραμμένη ὅτι εἰς
Καρδούχους ἄγοι. τούτους δὲ ἔφασαν οἰκεῖν ἀνὰ τὰ ὄρη καὶ πολεμικοὺς 16
εἶναι, καὶ βασιλέως οὐκ ἀκούειν, ἀλλὰ καὶ ἐμβαλεῖν ποτε εἰς αὐτοὺς
βασιλικὴν στρατιὰν δώδεκα μυριάδας· τούτων δ' οὐδένα ἀπονοστῆσαι
διὰ τὴν δυσχωρίαν. ὁπότε μέντοι πρὸς τὸν σατράπην τὸν ἐν τῶι
πεδίωι σπείσαιντο, καὶ ἐπιμειγνύναι σφῶν τε πρὸς ἐκείνους καὶ ἐκείνων
πρὸς ἑαυτούς. ἀκούσαντες ταῦτα οἱ στρατηγοὶ ἐκάθισαν χωρὶς τοὺς 17
ἑκασταχόσε φάσκοντας εἰδέναι, οὐδὲν δῆλον ποιήσαντες ὅποι πορεύεσθαι
ἔμελλον. ἐδόκει δὲ τοῖς στρατηγοῖς ἀναγκαῖον εἶναι διὰ τῶν ὀρέων εἰς
Καρδούχους ἐμβάλλειν· τούτους γὰρ διελθόντας ἔφασαν εἰς Ἀρμενίαν
ἥξειν, ἧς Ὀρόντας ἦρχε πολλῆς καὶ εὐδαίμονος. ἐντεῦθεν δ' εὔπορον
ἔφασαν εἶναι ὅποι τις ἐθέλοι πορεύεσθαι. ἐπὶ τούτοις ἐθύσαντο, ὅπως 18
ὁπηνίκα καὶ δοκοίη τῆς ὥρας τὴν πορείαν ποιοῖντο· τὴν γὰρ ὑπερβολὴν
τῶν ὀρέων ἐδεδοίκεσαν μὴ προκαταληφθείη· καὶ παρήγγειλαν, ἐπειδὴ
δειπνήσειαν, συσκευασαμένους πάντας ἀναπαύεσθαι, καὶ ἕπεσθαι ἡνίκ'
ἂν τις παραγγείληι.

5.13 ἢ πρὸς Βαβυλῶνα del. Reiske: ὡς πρὸς Βαβυλῶνα **b**
ὅμοιοι ἦσαν θαυμάζουσι **T**[c]: ὅμοιοι ἦσαν θαυμάζοντες **f**: ὅμοιοι ἦσαν θαυμάζειν **c**: ὁμοῦ ἦσαν θαυμάζοντες Muretus: οἷοι ἦσαν θαυμάζειν Porson

5.14 καὶ οἱ λοχαγοὶ post στρατηγοὶ add. **f**
αἰχμαλώτους **f** Suid. s.v. ἤλεγχον (= η 197 Adler): ἑαλωκότας **c**

5.15 ἕω: ἠῶ (vel ἡῶ) **c**
ἔνθα . . . βασιλεύς fors. delendum
καὶ ἐαρίζειν om. **c**

COMMENTARY

3.1 XENOPHON'S RISE TO PROMINENCE

After the obituaries for the five generals seized and killed by the Persians (2.6), X. focuses again on the Greek army, now stationed on the south bank of the River Zapatas (T1). What follows is an emotive description of the army's despair during the night after the arrest of the generals and then the sudden intervention of their saviour, Xenophon. Such descriptions of 'nights of terror' are common in historians both ancient (Pelling on Plut. *Ant.* 48) and modern (e.g. Kaye 1857: II.357, describing the British retreat from Kabul in 1842). X.'s narrative art ('si Xénophon mérite le nom de poète, c'est ici', Gautier 105) is apparent from the frequency of rhetorical figures such as anaphora (3, 13, 37nn.) and expressive asyndeton (3, 29nn.); from the use of poeticisms (3, 11, 14, 23, 25, 29nn.); and from the way the narrator 'approaches Xenophon gradually, moving from the past to the present, from the outside to the inside, from indirect to direct rendering of his thoughts' (Grethlein 2013: 60). The artistry serves to highlight the decisive role of Xenophon. The preceding character sketches (2.6.1–29) of three of the dead generals – Clearchus (10n.), Proxenus (4n.) and Meno (47n.) – prepare by contrast for the way Xenophon's qualities are presented implicitly, through speech and action, rather than through overt narratorial comment, and also for the actual qualities that Xenophon as leader displays.

The scene has numerous links with X.'s account of the mutiny against Cyrus at Tarsus (1.3) (Introduction p. 3). In both scenes the Greeks are described as being in a state of ἀπορία. At Tarsus Clearchus claimed to be afraid to go in person to Cyrus: here the Greeks are facing the consequences of the fact that Clearchus did go in person to Tissaphernes, leader of the Persian army tailing the Greeks (Introduction pp. 1–2). There Clearchus told the Greeks it was no time to sleep: here Xenophon tells himself it is no time to sleep. Clearchus stressed that it would be hard for the Greeks to return home without a guide: now the lack of a guide is a real problem. There a soldier suggested they should choose new leaders: here they do choose new leaders. Through these links, X. suggests that the situation feared at that point has come to pass, and highlights Xenophon's response to the crisis. There are also frequent echoes of the uneasy negotiations between the Greeks and Persians in the aftermath of Cyrus' death (2–3, 2, 19, 21, 22, 26–32, 27, 28nn.), but the motifs are used with greater urgency now that relations with the Persians are openly hostile.

At the same time X. creates a sense of a clean narrative break by his treatment of the fate of the generals. Following their arrest (2.5.32), Ariaeus, one of Cyrus' Persian officers, tells the Greeks that Clearchus has been charged with perjury and killed, but that Proxenus and Meno are held in high esteem by the king for having given information against Clearchus (2.5.38). Xenophon's request that he hand over Proxenus and Meno (2.5.41) then receives no response. After this scene, X. mentions that the generals were decapitated (2.6.1), but without specifying when this happened except for the statement that Meno was kept alive for a year (29n.). After X. resumes his focus on the Greek army, the generals' fates are strangely not raised again in the encounters with the Persians in Book 3, as if the Greeks are aware of the information that X. has given at 2.6. Nor is the accusation of perjury against Clearchus clarified – even though Xenophon now accuses the Persians of perjury (22n.). X. in this way closes without resolution the question whether Proxenus and/or Meno collaborated with Tissaphernes against Clearchus (there had been hints in the narrative that Meno was scheming with the Persians (2.1.5, 2.1, 4.15; cf. Clearchus' suspicions at 2.5.15, 28), but not of Proxenus' involvement). He focuses instead on the role played by one of the new generals, Xenophon, in creating a new sense of community and purpose in the despondent Greek army.

3.1.1 [Ὅσα . . . δεδήλωται]: a summary covering Books 1–2. Similar summaries are prefixed to Books 2, 4, 5 and 7 and found in **f** at 6.3.1; though defended by some (e.g. Høeg 1950: 161), they were probably written by later editors. They are mentioned at Diog. Laert. 2.57 (second century AD), and are the model for Chariton 5.1.1–2, 8.1.1 (Perry 1967: 358 n. 16). **τῆς μάχης:** at Cunaxa (Introduction p. 3). **ἐν ταῖς σπονδαῖς:** 19n.

3.1.2–3 X. describes how the Greeks first reflect on, then respond to, their desperate situation. This passage is notable for the frequent use of negative formulations (οὐδείς, οὐ μεῖον, οὐδείς, ἀδιάβατοι, οὐδὲ ἱππέα οὐδένα σύμμαχον), implicitly contrasting the Greeks' actual and desired situations (for similar negative lists, cf. *Hell.* 2.2.10; Thuc. 8.1.2). Clearchus anticipated most of these perceived disadvantages when he argued that the Greeks should not separate from the Persians (2.4.5–6); Xenophon in his speech to the whole army will suggest that they are not as bad as they seem (3.2.7–32n.).

3.1.2 συνειλημμένοι ἦσαν: the pluperfect refers to a state resulting from the action described at 2.5.32 (*CGCG* 33.40), where five generals are arrested (συνελαμβάνοντο) in Tissaphernes' tent. **τῶν λοχαγῶν . . . οἱ συνεπόμενοι:** the twenty captains waiting at the doors of the tent

(2.5.30–1) and, presumably, the *c.* 200 soldiers who accompanied the officers to buy supplies (2.5.30); the deaths of the latter are only now made explicit. **ἐν πολλῆι δὴ ἀπορίαι:** δή indicates that the depth of their despair was an evident consequence of the loss of the army's leadership (3.3.11n.). The ἀπορία-motif structures the account of the retreat, which is marked by an alternation between obstacles overcome and the emergence of new difficulties (Rood 2014: 66–78). The language of ἀπορία is common in stories of early human development, where difficulties are overcome over time by trial and error (Rood 2015b), and in stories of questing heroes who are assisted by divine epiphanies (cf. *Mem.* 2.1.21; Davies 2013: 8–11) – two story-patterns against which can be read the sudden emergence here of Xenophon as saviour. A more ominous intertext is Thucydides' account (Books 6–7) of Athens' defeat in Sicily (415–413 BC), where ἀπορία-words are used with increasing frequency (cf. 3.2.36n.). **οἱ Ἕλληνες** is frequently used of the army as a whole, even though it included non-Greeks (3.2n.), and here highlights their Greek identity in an alien setting. **ἐννοούμενοι ὅτι** governs the following eight short clauses, each of which opens with a resonant word or phrase that defines the obstacle on which the Greeks reflect; the accumulation of clauses (which are capped by ταῦτα ἐννοούμενοι at 3) brings out the sense of mounting despair. The tenses in this elaborate report of indirect thought are, unusually, anchored to the temporal perspective of the narrator rather than to that of the Greeks (ἦσαν, προυδεδώκεσαν, παρέξειν ἔμελλεν instead of εἰσί, προδεδώκασιν, παρέξει, etc.: *CGCG* 41.15; Smyth 2624): the Greeks are seen to reflect on situations that actually exist. **ἐπὶ ταῖς βασιλέως θύραις:** a common expression (with antecedents in Near Eastern languages: Llewellyn-Jones 2013: 68–9) in Greek depictions of Persian royal courts (e.g. *Hell.* 1.6.7, *Cyr.* 6.1.1), figuring the king as inhabiting an internal space; the omission of the definite article is regular with βασιλεύς when it refers to the Persian king (LSJ s.v. III). The phrase is a 'sobering echo of their previous boast' (Higgins 1977: 164 n. 62) that they had defeated the king ἐπὶ ταῖς θύραις αὐτοῦ (2.4.4). **κύκλωι:** X. draws on an image of Greeks as surrounded and outnumbered by barbarians that is common especially in military contexts (e.g. Hdt. 8.10.1–2, 76–80, 9.18.1; see Rood 2014: 66–70). **πολλὰ . . . πολέμιαι,** while each agreeing with the nearest noun, are to be taken with both ἔθνη and πόλεις. **ἀγοράν:** the Greeks bought food from markets while Cyrus was alive (e.g. 1.3.14, 5.12), though they may have done some foraging once outside Cyrus' province (1.4.19, 5.4: cf. 3.4.18n.); after Cyrus' death they had no source of supplies (2.2.3, 11), and the provision of a market was one of the terms agreed with Tissaphernes (2.3.27, cf. 2.4.9, 5.30; 20n.). **τῆς Ἑλλάδος:** a vague expression, in *An.*, as often elsewhere, referring to 'the area of concentrated Greek settlement' (Roy 2004: 280) between Byzantium and the Ionian Sea (cf. 5.6.25, 6.1.17, 4.8, 7.1.29). Sometimes it is used of any lands inhabited by Greeks (Pind. *Pyth.* 1.75; Hdt. 2.182.1); in *An.* the army four times reaches πόλιν Ἑλληνίδα on the Pontic coast (4.8.22, 5.3.2, 5.3, 6.2.1). **οὐ μεῖον ἢ μύρια στάδια:** for μεῖον, see 3.4.34n. 10,000 was regularly used as a rough figure (Arist. *Poet.* 1457b11–13, cf. 1451a2). The figure (*c.* 1,250 miles) is in fact reasonably accurate as the crow flies (they were *c.* 1,000 miles from Byzantium and *c.* 1,200 from Athens), but Greeks would normally calculate distance by the length of routes. The use of stades rather than parasangs (3.4.10n.) marks a Greek perspective. **ἡγεμών:** the Greeks' earlier difficulties over the route (2.2.10) had been solved by Persian guides (2.3.6, 14, 4.10); from now on they will rely on prisoners as guides (3.5.15, 4.1.21, 2.23, 4.19, 5.1, 6.1–2, 17, 7.19–27; contrast 4.2.24 ἄνευ ἡγεμόνος) until they regain contact with fellow Greeks at Trapezus. **ποταμοὶ δὲ διεῖργον ἀδιάβατοι:** as the king's envoy Phalinus warned (2.1.11). ἀδιάβατος is first attested in X. (cf. *Hell.* 5.4.44, again in connection with ἀπορία); its use here is echoed by Arr. *Anab.* 6.12.2. **καὶ οἱ σὺν Κύρωι ἀναβάντες βάρβαροι:** X. claims that Cyrus was accompanied by 100,000 non-Greeks (1.7.10). After Cyrus' death the Greeks for a time accompanied Ariaeus, but he and the rest of Cyrus' non-Greek force joined Tissaphernes (2.4.9); καί 'even' stresses their disloyalty. Cf. 2.5.39 for the accusation of betrayal and 1.5.16 for a warning by Cyrus of their unreliability. **οὐδὲ ἱππέα οὐδένα σύμμαχον ἔχοντες** 'without even a single horseman to help them'. Cyrus had relied on non-Greek cavalry (1.8.5–6, 9.31); forty Thracian cavalry who were with the Ten Thousand after his death subsequently deserted to the Persians (2.2.7). **ὥστε εὔδηλον . . . οὐδεὶς ἂν λειφθείη** 'so that it was all too clear that, if they won a victory, they would not be able to kill even one man, but if they were beaten, not one of them would be left alive'. The phrasing echoes Clearchus' warning at 2.4.6 (cited Introduction p. 30; cf. *Cyr.* 4.3.5; Plut. *Ant.* 39.7). X. introduces variety in the μέν/δέ clauses: the first participle appears in the nominative while the second agrees with the partitive genitive αὐτῶν, and οὐδ' ἂν ἕνα refers to the enemy, αὐτῶν οὐδείς to the Greeks. **νικῶντες:** νικάω is often used in the present for 'prevail in a battle', and so there is not necessarily a meaningful contrast with the aorist ἡττηθέντων (see 3.2.13n.). **κατακάνοιεν:** Doric κατακαίνω for ἀποκτείνω (Gautier 22–3; add Epicharm. fr. 85 Austin; DK 90 2.13) is confined to X. in classical Attic prose; for the flavour of this and similar Doricisms, see Introduction pp. 30–1.

3.1.3 **ἀθύμως ἔχοντες** = ἄθυμοι ὄντες (*CGCG* 26.11; Smyth 1438). The march back is marked by frequent returns of ἀθυμία (3.3.11, 4.20, 5.3, 4.3.7, 8.21, 6.4.26), which has the same structural role as ἀπορία (2n.). **ὀλίγοι μὲν αὐτῶν . . ., ὀλίγοι δὲ . . ., ἐπὶ δὲ τὰ ὅπλα πολλοὶ οὐκ ἦλθον:** the soldiers' woes are stressed through anaphora; variation in word order and vocabulary (πολλοὶ οὐκ ≈ ὀλίγοι) in the third part gives prominence to ἐπὶ τὰ ὅπλα (= either the whole camp or particular quarters), underlining the breach in security (cf. Aen. Tact. 26.7–10 on the importance of patrols for demoralized armies). The fact that the Greeks' immediate response to news of the arrests had been to run ἐπὶ τὰ ὅπλα (2.5.34) and the more ordered picture of the camp later (32, 40nn.) both suggest that X. has exaggerated the disorder here. **ὅπου ἐτύγχανον** (*sc.* ὄντες) **ἕκαστος** 'where they each happened to be'. For ἕκαστος used in apposition to a plural subject and verb, see Smyth 952; the reading ἐτύγχανεν probably arose by assimilation. **οὐ δυνάμενοι καθεύδειν ὑπὸ λύπης:** for sleeplessness in grief, cf. e.g. Hom. *Il.* 24.4–5. **πόθου πατρίδων, γονέων, γυναικῶν, παίδων:** πόθος is poetic vocabulary; cf. ἐπόθουν εἰς τὴν Ἑλλάδα σώιζεσθαι at 6.4.8, where X. again presents the mercenaries as normal citizens with familial responsibilities rather than as mobile workers who can settle anywhere. The grouping of fatherland with parents, wives and children is common (e.g. Arr. *Anab.* 5.27.6 (with πόθος); Nielsen 2004: 50–1), especially in defensive contexts (e.g. Aen. Tact. *pref.* 2, in a contrast of wars at home and abroad); X. emphasizes the soldiers' belated realization of the riskiness of their aggressive foreign adventure. For the solemn asyndeton, cf. Dem. 14.32 ἑαυτόν, γονέας, τάφους, πατρίδα; Livy 4.28.5 *domos parentes coniuges liberos.* **οὓς,** while agreeing with παίδων, belongs in sense with all four preceding nouns. **οὔποτ' ἐνόμιζον ἔτι ὄψεσθαι:** for the pathos cf. Thuc. 6.30.2 (forebodings felt by family and friends at the departure of a distant expedition). While yearning here leads to despair, Xenophon turns it into a motivation at 3.2.39. **οὕτω μὲν δὴ . . . ἀνεπαύοντο:** μὲν δή (. . . δέ) is a frequent formula of transition (*CGCG* 59.74; *GP* 258); the μέν-clause pithily recapitulates the situation. The imperfect suggests that the theme will be resumed (cf. 11; *CGCG* 33.51).

3.1.4–10 The emotive account of the Greeks' difficulties prepares for the intervention of Xenophon, which is emphasized initially through an analeptic explanation of how he came to serve with Cyrus and then, when the temporal level of 3 is resumed, through a number of marked narrative features (11–14, 15–25nn.). The technique of filling in the background of characters upon their introduction is reminiscent of Homer (cf. *SAGN* II.21), but used more expansively here, though the narration is still compact, with sparse circumstantial detail, predominant use of indirect speech, and perfunctory summaries for two crucial departures (8, 10). The story, which could have been included at any of Xenophon's earlier appearances (Introduction p. 11), is delayed until his decisive intervention.

The presentation of Xenophon is not uniformly positive, in that he ignores a clear warning from Socrates that he may get into trouble with the Athenians for serving with Cyrus (5n.). That warning hints at his future exile, which is later twice overtly mentioned (5.3.7, 7.7.57) – though it is not certain whether this exile was due to his support for Cyrus or his later service with Agesilaus (the authority of Socrates may support the former, but this is not decisive: see Introduction pp. 11–12). Whatever the circumstances of the exile, the negative undertones in Xenophon's presentation here underscore Socrates' piety in recommending that he consult the Delphic oracle; X. thereby defends Socrates from blame for the actions of his associates (as with Critias and Alcibiades at *Mem.* 1.2.12–48). Later in antiquity this scene was cited in praise of the active as opposed to contemplative life (Max. Tyr. 15.9), while Socrates' warnings were turned into a fictional letter (*Ep. Soc.* 5).

3.1.4 **Ἦν δέ τις . . . Ξενοφῶν Ἀθηναῖος:** placement of the verb before the name is normal in 'presentative' sentences (3.3.1n.). The wording (also used at *Hell.* 4.1.29, 5.4.2) evokes a Homeric introductory formula (e.g. *Il.* 5.9 ἦν δέ τις ἐν Τρώεσσι Δάρης; Kahn 1973: 249–50) for minor characters who typically come to a bad end (Tuplin 2003a: 127). The introduction of Themistocles, saviour of the Greeks at Salamis, at Hdt. 7.143.1 (ἦν δὲ τῶν τις Ἀθηναίων ἀνήρ) is a more propitious intertext, though, like Xenophon, Themistocles was later exiled. The inclusion of the ethnic Ἀθηναῖος is in keeping with X.'s practice in introducing characters in *An.*, although patronymics are added for some Athenians (3.3.20n.). Livy's introduction of the Roman saviour Marcius (25.37.2) picks up Xenophon's introduction here (Hornblower *per e-litt.*). **οὔτε στρατηγὸς οὔτε λοχαγὸς οὔτε στρατιώτης ὢν:** triple οὔτε, followed by military ranks of decreasing importance, emphasizes that Xenophon joined the expedition not in a paid military capacity, as readers might expect, but through an aristocratic link of φιλία (Azoulay 2004a; cf. 2.5.14, 22, *Mem.* 1.2.5–8, for the validation of such ties over monetary contracts). It also makes his rapid rise to the post of στρατηγός more impressive. Plutarch (*Mor.* 817e) quotes this sentence to illustrate the point that political ability rather than holding an office is the chief requirement for successful intervention in public affairs. **συνηκολούθει:** cf. Thuc. 6.44.1, also of voluntary accompaniment. **ἀλλὰ Πρόξενος αὐτὸν μετεπέμψατο:** by letter (5). Greek generally avoids the repetition of relative pronouns in successive clauses; these either have no relative pronoun (e.g. 17) or, as here, use a personal pronoun (*CGCG* 50.9; Smyth 2517). The analepsis starts here. **Πρόξενος:** one of the generals arrested by Tissaphernes; a Theban who had been summoned by Cyrus (1.1.11, 2.3), supposedly to fight the Pisidians (9n.); in his obituary (2.6.16–20) X. presents him as ambitious, honest and unable to exercise control. **ξένος** denotes a friend joined by ξενία, 'a bond of trust, imitating kinship and reinforced by rituals, generating affection and obligations between individuals belonging to separate social units' (*OCD*[4] 591). **ἀρχαῖος** implies that the guest-friendship, not Proxenus, is old (cf. *Mem.* 2.8.1 ἀρχαῖον ἑταῖρον); it could have arisen from Proxenus' studies with Gorgias (2.6.16), assuming these were in Athens, or from Xenophon's time as a prisoner at Thebes (Philostr. *VS* 1.12), though this is probably an invention to explain the ξενία; or it could have been inherited. **φίλον αὐτὸν Κύρωι ποιήσειν:** φίλος is regularly used in X. of Persian nobles who receive the king's largesse (Briant 2002, Ch. 8); it is applied rhetorically to all the Greek soldiers at 1.3.19 and 3.2.5(n.). That no mention is made of Cyrus' supposed Pisidian expedition might suggest that Xenophon was not aware of it until he arrived in Sardis, but see 6, 8nn. **ὃν . . . τῆς πατρίδος** 'whom he said he himself regarded as better for himself than his fatherland'. Presumably a quotation from Proxenus' letter (Gera 2013: 87); for the meaning of πατρίς for a Boeotian, see 30n. X.'s other works (esp. *Cyr.*) show the importance he attached to personal leadership and charisma; ironically, attachment to Cyrus leads to Proxenus' death in Mesopotamia and to Xenophon's being stranded there with little prospect of seeing his fatherland again (3, where πατρίδων is emphatically placed first) and ultimately to his being exiled. On Xenophon's motives for leaving Athens see Introduction pp. 10–11.

3.1.5 μέντοι 'however' indicates that Proxenus' invitation is not the whole story of Xenophon's decision to join Cyrus (cf. Slings 1997: 120–1); it is not 'purely temporal' (*GP* 406). **ἀνακοινοῦται:** middle, 'to consider a question together with someone'. Historical presents mark the crucial events of the story: cf. 5 συμβουλεύει, 7 λέγει, 8 καταλαμβάνει. **Σωκράτει τῶι Ἀθηναίωι:** the article marks Socrates out as well known; contrast Ξενοφῶν Ἀθηναῖος at 4. For Xenophon's association with Socrates, see *Mem.* 1.3.8–13, where he is rebuked in a conversation, and Introduction pp. 9–10. It is not known whether Xenophon's father was still alive at this time, i.e. whether Socrates was consulted in preference to him. **ὑποπτεύσας** is here construed like a verb of fearing (μή + optative in historic sequence). X. does not reveal whether this fear was actually expressed by Socrates himself; Cicero (*Div.* 1.54) assumed so, which makes Xenophon's subsequent behaviour seem more rash. **τι πρὸς τῆς πόλεως ὑπαίτιον εἴη** 'it (i.e. Κύρωι φίλον γενέσθαι) might somehow (τι: accusative of respect) be reprehensible in the view of (πρός + genitive) the city'. Socrates' fears hint at Xenophon's eventual exile (4–10n.), but their wording here does not have any implications for the nature of the proceedings against him (probably an impeachment (εἰσαγγελία) for treason brought by a private individual, heard in the assembly in his absence, and leading to exile in lieu of the death penalty (Dreher 2004: 55–60)). **ὅτι ἐδόκει . . . συμπολεμῆσαι:** in 407 BC Cyrus was appointed by his father to a special command in western Asia Minor to support Sparta (*Hell.* 1.4.3, where X. again uses συμπολεμεῖν). προθύμως contrasts Cyrus' wholehearted support for Sparta with the Persians' earlier tactic of playing Sparta and Athens off against each other. **ἐλθόντα** is closely connected in sense to ἀνακοινῶσαι ('go and consult'), and so accusative, the case for subjects of infinitives, rather than dative agreeing with τῶι Ξενοφῶντι (*CGCG* 51.12 n. 1). **ἀνακοινῶσαι:** the active for the consultation of gods, where the communication is more one-sided (cf. 6.1.22, *Hell.* 7.2.20; but note the middle at *Hell.* 7.1.27). As part of his defence of Socrates against the charge of impiety, X. consistently stresses his respect for oracles as sources of practical advice (e.g. over choice of friends, *Mem.* 2.6.8); see Bandini/Dorion 1.50 n. 7. **τῶι θεῶι:** Apollo, as often in Delphic contexts in Thucydides and X. (though note ἡ Πυθία, Herodotus' preferred expression, at *Mem.* 1.3.1). Socrates' further use of ὁ θεός in 7, contrasting with X.'s double use of Ἀπόλλων at 6, none the less suggests that X. is capturing one of Socrates' theological positions, namely his reluctance to name individual gods (cf. *Symp.* 8.9; Pl. *Phlb.* 12c1–3, *Cra.* 400d6–401a5, and the repeated use of ὁ θεός for Apollo in both Pl. *Ap.* and – with one exception – X. *Ap.*); if so, X.'s use of Ἀπόλλων shows that Socrates' theology has not corrupted his associates. **περὶ τῆς πορείας:** the oracle was commonly consulted by individuals seeking advice on journeys (Parker 2004: 147). X. does not report how Socrates framed his advice or what the goal of the πορεία actually was – only that Xenophon was rebuked by Socrates on his return (7n.).

3.1.6 Ἀπόλλω: X. always uses this (old) accusative form, not the generally slightly less common Ἀπόλλωνα. **τίνι ἂν θεῶν θύων . . . ἔλθοι τὴν ὁδόν** 'to which of the gods he should sacrifice . . . to make the journey'. τίνι goes with θύων καὶ εὐχόμενος, ἄν with ἔλθοι and σωθείη. τὴν ὁδόν is internal accusative (*CGCG* 30.12; Smyth 1567) of a noun within the same semantic field as the verb. Xenophon's question presupposes that he should make the journey while acknowledging that it would involve some risk (see 4n. on the question whether Proxenus told him of the supposed expedition against the Pisidians). This form of question was conventional; it does not indicate any lack of piety (Rood 2015a: 150). **ἐπινοεῖ:** the use of the indicative instead of the optative highlights that Xenophon had indeed decided to go and distances X. from his eagerness (*CGCG* 41.13). **σωθείη** 'return safely' (a common meaning of σώιζομαι). **ἀνεῖλεν:** ἀναιρέω is the technical term for oracular responses (probably owing to the practice of divination by lots which were 'taken up' from bowls). **θεοῖς οἷς:** for οἷς θεοῖς 'to which gods' (the entire relative clause is object of ἀνεῖλεν). For the inversion of noun and relative pronoun in such relative clauses, see Probert 2015: 162–7 and cf. already Jebb on Soph. *Trach.* 151–2 (*pace* Diggle 2002, there is no need to change to θεούς). X. reveals only at 6.1.22 that Zeus the King was one of the gods named by the oracle (cf. also 7.6.44).

3.1.7 ὅτι οὐ τοῦτο πρῶτον ἠρώτα . . . ἐπυνθάνετο: τοῦτο points forward and is explained in the πότερον clause, while ὅτι introduces either an indirect statement ('that', with the imperfect indicatives used by Socrates in his direct speech retained: *CGCG* 41.10; Smyth 2623b) or a causal clause which is factually correct (*CGCG* 48.2; Smyth 2241). Either way, the imperfect describes the enquiry from Xenophon's perspective at the time (*CGCG* 33.23, 51), thus highlighting the moment at which he decided to limit the god's possible answers. Though it is often claimed that Xenophon disobeyed Socrates (e.g. Danzig 2007: 32), Socrates' criticism need not imply that he explicitly told Xenophon to ask an either/or question (5n.). X.'s vagueness protects Socrates from the charge of inciting Xenophon and Xenophon from the charge of openly ignoring Socrates' advice (though some criticism of Xenophon's enthusiasm is perhaps implied). **λῷον** 'better' is limited to religious contexts in prose (it is common in oracular inscriptions from Dodona) (Gautier 194–5; Chantraine s.v.). **πορεύεσθαι ἢ μένειν:** Xenophon learns from Socrates' rebuke: he thrice later uses an either/or formulation in consulting the gods (6.1.22, 2.15, 7.6.44), in the last two cases over the question whether to remain with or leave the army (he remained). *Por.* ends with X. advising the Athenians first to make an either/or consultation at Delphi, then to ask to which gods they should sacrifice for success (6.2–3). **ἰτέον εἶναι** 'that he must go' (lit. 'that there must be a going'), impersonal verbal adjective expressing obligation (*CGCG* 37.3; Smyth 2152). **μέντοι** answers the expectation that Socrates will continue to scold Xenophon. For the shift to direct speech, see 3.3.12–19n.

3.1.8 μὲν δὴ . . . οὕτω: transitional summary (3n.). οὕτω (with ἐξέπλει and partly glossed by the intervening phrase) is apologetic. **θυσάμενος:** the middle marks Xenophon as the intended beneficiary of the sacrifice. **οἷς:** i.e. τούτοις τοῖς θεοῖς οἷς; οἷς for οὕς is the result of relative attraction (*CGCG* 50.13; Smyth 2531). **ἐξέπλει:** imperfect for the background action to the key meeting with Cyrus, which is marked by the historical present καταλαμβάνει (commonly used in 'find-passages': Rood 1998a: 114 n. 23). At 6.1.23 X. gives more detail about Xenophon's journey from Ephesus (where he landed) to Sardis; he would have arrived just before the events of 1.2.5. **ἐν Σάρδεσι:** Sardis was where Cyrus gathered his forces (1.2.2–5); formerly capital of Lydia, it was now centre of his special area of command. **μέλλοντας ἤδη ὁρμᾶν τὴν ἄνω ὁδόν** 'already about to set out on the journey upcountry'. μέλλω tends to be used with present rather than future infinitive for agents who are putting a plan into action rather than merely thinking about it (*CGCG* 51.33; Smyth 1959a). ἤδη offers a hint that Xenophon was expecting some sort of expedition upcountry, though not necessarily one against Pisidia (4n.). **συνεστάθη:** aorist passive of συνίστημι 'introduce' (LSJ s.v. IV).

3.1.9 ἐπειδὰν τάχιστα . . . ἀποπέμψει αὐτόν: reports of false statements in indirect speech tend to preserve the mood of the 'original' (the optative would mark the narrator's temporal perspective) (*CGCG* 41.13). Cyrus' promise distances Xenophon from those of his followers who were seeking a position with him in the Persian empire (1.7.7–8). **ἐλέγετο . . . εἰς Πισίδας:** see Introduction p. 3. By whom or exactly when this story was told is here left vague, to spare Cyrus.

3.1.10 μὲν δή: 3n. **οὕτως** (apologetic: 8n.) goes with ἐστρατεύετο. **ἐξαπατηθείς, οὐχ ὑπὸ Προξένου:** the placement of the negative limits its scope to ὑπὸ Προξένου, so as to defend X(enophon)'s friend from the charge of deception and not openly accuse Cyrus. **ᾔδει:** *sc.* Πρόξενος. **πλὴν Κλεάρχου:** Clearchus son of Rhamphias was a prominent Spartan figure in the final part of the Peloponnesian War, as *proxenos* (official representative) and harmost (governor) at Byzantium (*Hell.* 1.1.35, 3.15–18: 411–408 BC). Diodorus (14.12.2–7) claims that he made himself tyrant of Byzantium in 403 BC after killing the magistrates and many wealthy citizens, and then ignored Spartan orders to lay down his power and was defeated by a Spartan force sent out against him. In *An.*, X. reports only that he was in exile when Cyrus invited him to gather troops in the Chersonese (1.1.9), after ignoring a Spartan order not to sail out to fight the Thracians (2.6.2–3). He is presented as emerging as overall leader of the army after Cyrus' death (2.2.5); his obituary (2.6.1–15) casts him as φιλοπόλεμος and as a (sometimes excessively) tough leader (cf. 3.2.30, 31nn.). For his knowledge of Cyrus' plans, see Introduction p. 3. **εἰς Κιλικίαν:** to the east of Pisidia; its capital Tarsus was the site of the mutiny (3.1n.). **σαφὲς πᾶσιν ἤδη . . . ἐπὶ βασιλέα** 'it now (ἤδη) seemed clear to all that the expedition was against the king'. For these suspicions, see 1.3.1, 21, 4.7; Cyrus himself announces at Tarsus that he is marching against an enemy on the Euphrates (1.3.20), and reveals only at the Euphrates that he is marching against the king (1.4.11). **φοβούμενοι . . . καὶ ἄκοντες:** concessive (note the ensuing ὅμως). The earlier narrative has suggested that the soldiers were afraid of the journey *back* without guides and that Cyrus' promises of extra pay were sufficient inducement (1.3.21, 4.13). **δι' αἰσχύνην καὶ ἀλλήλων**

καὶ Κύρου: αἰσχύνη is used 'in a subjective sense, as the . . . mental picture of disgrace' (Cairns 1993: 173 n. 11); the genitives are objective (the soldiers, not Cyrus, feel shame: *CGCG* 30.28). This apologetic claim (cf. Clearchus' defence of the soldiers' loyalty to Cyrus at 2.3.22) points both to group dynamics (the fear of being thought cowardly) and to the willing obedience inspired by Cyrus' virtue (cf. 6.4.8), despite his use of deception. **ὧν** is a connecting relative. The sentence rounds off the sequence that started at 4.

3.1.11–14 The striking new narrative focus on Xenophon continues (cf. Pelling 2013: 57–9). X. reports first a dream that Xenophon had of lightning striking his father's house; then, in indirect discourse, Xenophon's interpretation of his dream; next, in direct discourse, a short internalized self-address. The movement from reflection to action matches 2–3, but unlike the other soldiers Xenophon is stirred to take positive steps to ensure the army's safety (ἀνίσταται at 14, contrasting with ἀνεπαύοντο at the end of 3): he calls together the surviving officers in Proxenus' contingent and delivers the first of three speeches he makes in the course of this night.

Dreams were regularly seen as a means of divine communication (cf. *Eq. mag.* 9.9, *Symp.* 4.33). Though rationalizations were proposed (Hdt. 7.16β.2), Xenophon's reasoning shows one of the mechanisms for sustaining this belief (for another, see *Cyr.* 8.7.21: the soul is most divine during sleep). He suggests that the dream could be either good or bad and that its nature can be deduced from what followed. In other words, whatever happens will support belief in the dream's significance. See further 12, 13nn. The only other dream recorded in *An.* (4.3.8) is likewise dreamt by Xenophon at a time of ἀπορία; it, too, is about confinement.

X.'s inclusion of a dream for a high-status character recalls the techniques of Homer and Herodotus (cf. Harris 2009: 157). Xenophon's dream is symbolic, however, whereas Homeric dreams include figures directly offering (sometimes deceptive) advice or predictions (*Od.* 19.536–53, the only symbolic dream in Homer, includes a figure who explains the meaning). X.'s account specifically interacts with the dream Zeus sends Agamemnon at Hom. *Il.* 2.16–34, rebuking him for sleeping and falsely promising that he will capture Troy, and with its aftermath, where Agamemnon's attempt to test the army's resolve backfires. By contrast, Xenophon's dream from Zeus is ambiguous rather than deceptive and leads to action that boosts rather than undermines his authority (Rinner 1978; 26–32n.).

Whether Xenophon actually had this dream is impossible to say. Its historicity is supported by a modern psychoanalyst (Stein 1984: 553), but X.'s account seems contrived, in that he allows Xenophon both sleeplessness and then sleep (a chance to dream) – a pattern imitated in Greek fiction (Chariton 4.1.1; Heliod. 2.15.2–16.1). A defence of divination attributed to Cicero's brother (Cic. *Div.* 1.25) insists that the dream happened, but does so rather too strongly for comfort ('Shall we say that Xenophon is lying or mad?'). The dream was later cited by Lucian in a defence of his own account of a dream (*Somn.* 17) and turned into an allegory of the immortality of the soul in a poem written by Cardinal Francesco Barberini *c.* 1630 (Rood 2013a).

3.1.11 Ἐπεὶ δὲ ἀπορία ἦν picks up ἐν πολλῆι δὴ ἀπορίαι (2) after the digression. **ἐλυπεῖτο μὲν . . . καθεύδειν:** the presentation of Xenophon as initially unexceptional both lends credibility to his characterization and makes his swift transformation more striking. **ἔδοξεν αὐτῶι:** δοκεῖ μοι/δοκέω are commonly used of dreams. Asyndeton is normal at the beginning of narratives after a preceding signal (here mention of the dream). **σκηπτός,** first attested in Aeschylus and rare in classical Greek prose, is cognate with σκήπτειν 'fall', and used of downward flashes of lightning ([Arist.] *Mund.* 395a14–28 discusses different terms for lightning). **τὴν πατρῴιαν οἰκίαν:** the fact that Xenophon dreams about his father's house picks up the idea of the army's distance from home (4). It has also suggested connections with X.'s exile (see 12n.) or with the ambivalence of the father-complex (Stein 1984; Hughes 1987: 276). **λάμπεσθαι πᾶσα** 'it (*sc.* οἰκία) seemed to shine in its entirety' (πᾶσα in emphatic position; cf. Hdt. 4.79.2). λάμπεσθαι (rare in classical prose) stresses the brightness rather than the destructiveness of the flame, allowing for a positive interpretation of the dream; the verb is common in epic of the gleam of weapons and is used metaphorically in the sense 'shine forth, be famous' (LSJ s.v. 3).

3.1.12 περίφοβος 'very afraid' conveys Xenophon's immediate emotional response to a divine communication, not the feelings induced by his rational interpretation of the dream. **ἀνηγέρθη:** aorist of ἀνεγείρομαι 'wake up'. **τῆι μὲν . . . τῆι δέ** 'in one way . . . in another'. X. describes first Xenophon's positive interpretation, and then, at somewhat greater length, his negative interpretation; the effect is to make Xenophon's subsequent actions more impressive. For similarly ambiguous dreams, cf. Soph. *El.* 644–7; Joseph. *BJ* 6.290–1 (encircling light); Plut. *Pyrrh.* 29.1–3 (thunderbolt), *Mor.* 587a–c (fire blazing from a house where exiles are staying); Artemidorus (2.9) offers a detailed analysis of how, depending on the dreamer's status and situation, lightning can be a source of either distinction or destruction (cf. Hdt. 4.79.1–2 for lightning striking a rich house as a bad portent). The dream's ambiguity might suggest an anticipation of Xenophon's exile (Ma 2004: 336; Parker 2004: 148), but the house is lit up rather than explicitly destroyed by fire. For light in darkness as a mark of salvation, see *Cyr.* 4.2.15 (portent); John 1:5. **ἔκρινεν ἀγαθόν, ὅτι . . . ἰδεῖν ἔδοξε** 'he judged it as auspicious (predicative ἀγαθόν), because . . . he had dreamed he had seen'. ἔκρινεν is aorist rather than imperfect: X. looks back on both the positive interpretation and the dream as complete past events; contrast how the lingering fear caused by the negative interpretation is conveyed by imperfect ἐφοβεῖτο, in keeping with τὸ ὄναρ ἐδόκει, which expresses Xenophon's continuing thoughts about the dream. **ἐν πόνοις ὢν καὶ κινδύνοις:** two nouns (like the cognate verbs) frequently coupled in the same form by X. – a sign of the centrality of active toil to his ethos, here perhaps with a hint of divine recompense. **καὶ ἐφοβεῖτο, ὅτι . . ., μὴ οὐ δύναιτο** 'he was also (adverbial καί in the second clause of a disjunction: *GP* 305) afraid, because . . ., that he could not'. **ἀπὸ Διὸς μὲν βασιλέως** 'from Zeus the King'. Xenophon's reasoning is based on an equation of the Persian king with Zeus, for which cf. Hdt. 7.56.2, 7.220.4; Gorg. DK 82 B5a (Ξέρξης ὁ τῶν Περσῶν Ζεύς); Plut. *Them.* 28.5; Mitchell 2007: 154–5 (iconographic links). Similarly Zeus the King could be thought to support kingship (e.g. Isoc. 3.26; at Dion. Hal. *Ant. Rom.* 2.5.1–2 a prayer to Zeus the King is followed by a lightning portent confirming Romulus as king); the elder Cyrus has close links with him in *Cyr.* (2.4.19, 3.3.21, 7.5.57). X. does not reveal here that 'Zeus the King' was one of the gods to whom Apollo told Xenophon to sacrifice (6n.). **λάμπεσθαι:** now with fire, not the house, as subject.

3.1.13 ὁποῖόν τι μὲν δή ἐστι . . . μετὰ τὸ ὄναρ 'what kind of a thing it is (i.e. what it means) to see such a dream can be judged from what happened after the dream'. τὸ . . . ἰδεῖν (articular infinitive) is subject of ἐστι, and the infinitive σκοπεῖν depends on ἔξεστι. See 11–14n. on X.'s reasoning. **ἐκ τῶν συμβάντων μετὰ τὸ ὄναρ:** Xenophon's immediate response in rousing the army to action and leading it from danger, and the wealth he accrues at the end of *An.*, both support a positive interpretation of the dream. Xenophon does face personal dangers when his leadership comes under attack in the march along the Black Sea coast and in Thrace, but these problems arise after he has escaped from the clutches of the Persian king. If 'the events after the dream' are extended as far as his exile from Athens, then the lightning strike on his father's house may hint at that (but see 12n.). **γίγνεται γὰρ τάδε** 'here is what happened'. The present in this further anticipatory clause refers to the story as present in front of the reader (unlike historical presents, which mark events within the story world); cf. e.g. Hdt. 8.39.2; Joseph. *AJ* 17.284; Longus 3.6.5, 4.27.1. The asyndeton that follows is regular after τάδε. **εὐθὺς ἐπειδὴ ἀνηγέρθη:** at 11 Xenophon 'immediately woke up' and interpreted his dream; now the interpretative process is subsumed in the awakening, since what he does 'immediately on waking up' is address himself. The repetition of εὐθύς adds a sense of urgency. **πρῶτον μέν** is balanced by 15 ἐκ τούτου. **ἔννοια αὐτῶι ἐμπίπτει:** cf. *Cyr.* 1.1.1: ἔννοιά ποθ' ἡμῖν ἐγένετο. The use of direct speech for reporting thoughts (and in particular important decisions) is reminiscent of epic (Hentze 1904) and tragedy (Hutchinson on Aesch. *Sept.* 1034) but unparalleled in extant classical Greek historiography (except possibly at Ctesias F8d.12 Lenfant, an excerpt at two removes from the original); other examples in classical Greek prose are mainly in first-person narrations (Andoc. 1.51; Pl. *Euthphr.* 9c1–8, *Ep.* 7.346e1–7b6 (if authentic)), but see Dem. 19.320 for another third-person example. These passages generally include direct self-questioning, which cannot easily be conveyed in indirect speech (the Demosthenes passage shifts from indirect to direct presentation with πῶς οὖν . . .;). **τί κατάκειμαι** 'Why am I lying down?' (with the implication of idleness). Xenophon's initial rhetorical question is modelled on Homeric deliberative monologues while adapting the second-person language both of military exhortation (Dillery 1995: 73; cf. esp. Callinus fr. 1.1 West: μέχρις τέο κατάκεισθε;) and of dream-figures (Hom. *Il.* 2.23–4 εὕδεις . . . | οὐ χρὴ παννύχιον εὕδειν βουληφόρον ἄνδρα; Pind. *Ol.* 13.67; Plut. *C. Gracch* 1.7 τί δῆτα . . . βραδύνεις; *Luc.* 12.1, *Mor.* 252f). His personal initiative is thereby highlighted. **ἡ δὲ νὺξ προβαίνει:** cf. Hom. *Il.* 10.251–3 for the passing of the night as a reason for alarm in a military crisis. **εἰκός:** *sc.* ἐστι. **εἰ . . . γενησόμεθα** 'if we are going to be'. εἰ with future indicative (rather than ἐάν with subjunctive) is used when fulfilment of the conditional is undesirable, especially in threats and warnings (*CGCG* 49.5; Smyth 2328). **ἐπὶ βασιλεῖ** 'in the power of the king'. **τὶ ἐμποδὼν** (*sc.* ἐστι) **μὴ οὐχὶ . . .** (*sc.* ἡμᾶς) **ἀποθανεῖν:** μὴ οὐ with infinitive (*CGCG* 51.35; Smyth 2742) is standard after a negative verb of hindering ('what prevents?' implies 'nothing prevents'). **οὐχί** for οὐ, with emphatic deictic iota, is a feature of colloquial Attic (Willi 2003a: 244–5) and common in speeches in X. **πάντα μὲν . . . πάντα δέ:** anaphora with μέν/δέ is frequent in X. even when, as here, there is no strong antithesis. **ἐπιδόντας** 'having lived to see', a common nuance of ἐφοράω. **ὑβριζομένους** 'brutally assaulted'. The present participle after two aorists should be taken closely with ἀποθανεῖν, indicating two stages of punishment (first torture, then violent death). ὕβρις and its cognates typically denote violence that undermines the victim's status; the especial disgrace of ὕβρις accompanying death is noted at Aeschin. 2.181. For Persian torture, see Hornblower on Hdt. 5.25.1.

3.1.14 ὅπως δ' ἀμυνούμεθα: the ὅπως-clause with future indicative (regular after verbs of effort or precaution: *CGCG* 44.2; Smyth 2211) is here placed first to mark the logical next step of Xenophon's reasoning.

παρασκευάζεται picks up the focus on preparedness in the account of Cyrus' march, where Cyrus' hopes to catch his brother unprepared (1.1.6, 5.9, cf. 2.3.21) are thwarted (1.2.5, 8.1). **ὥσπερ ἐξόν** 'as if it were possible', accusative absolute (*CGCG* 52.33; Smyth 2076). **ἐγὼ οὖν . . . ταῦτα πράξειν;** 'This being the case, then, what city's general (lit. 'the general coming from what sort of city', with sandwiched interrogative, cf. *Mem.* 2.2.1 τοὺς τί ποιοῦντας) do I expect to do this?' ἐγώ, thrown forward as the new topic, and οὖν mark the transition from Xenophon's diagnosis of the problem to his search for a solution. His reasoning is that he (as an Athenian) should not wait for others (even those from the most powerful city, Sparta) to take the lead. **ποίαν δ' ἡλικίαν . . . ἀναμένω;** 'What sort of age am I waiting for (lit. 'to come to me')?' The use of ποίαν suggests that Xenophon is thinking in terms of age-groups (cf. Lycurg. 1.144 ποία δ' ἡλικία . . .; πότερον ἡ τῶν πρεσβυτέρων;); for his age, see Introduction p. 9. Abstract ἡλικίαν as subject of ἐλθεῖν (here with dative) recalls Homer (cf. e.g. *Od.* 13.59–60 γῆρας | ἔλθηι καὶ θάνατος); the abstract expression underlines Xenophon's impatience at his own passivity (more commonly the person comes εἰς ἡλικίαν). **οὐ γὰρ ἔγωγ' ἔτι πρεσβύτερος ἔσομαι** 'for I will not any longer be an elder'. Xenophon has assumed until now that he will live long enough to join the age-group of πρεσβύτεροι, who might be expected to take responsibility in a crisis. There is an implicit contrast (cf. ἔγωγ') with the actual elders in the army who are not taking appropriate action. **ἐὰν . . . προδῶ ἐμαυτόν:** Xenophon presents inertia in dire circumstances as self-betrayal (cf. Eur. *Andr.* 191; Philostr. *VA* 7.14.11) rather than just surrender (which would be <u>παρα</u>δῶ).

3.1.15–25 Xenophon's speech to the captains of Proxenus' contingent (about twenty men?) is the first of three speeches he makes in the course of this night to successively larger groups: he goes on to address all the surviving generals and captains (35–44) and then the whole army (3.2.8–32). His rhetorical virtuosity in encouraging dejected men (which was regarded by Dio Chrys. 18.15 as a lesson for aspiring statesmen) is shown by the different arguments he uses in the three speeches. The first speech appeals to the captains to set an example individually; the second appeals to an elitist group ethos; the third constructs an image of the whole army as heirs to the values that ensured the Greek victory in the Persian Wars (Rood 2015b). The third speech picks up with more emphasis some of the exhortatory rhetoric found in the first, such as the language of competition (16n.) and appeals to the gods; the gods are mentioned only once in the second speech, but their prominence in the first shows that Xenophon's religious rhetoric is not directed only at the common soldiers. In none of the speeches, however, does Xenophon mention his dream, presumably because a dream alone would not have lent credibility to his call for action (at 4.3.8, by contrast, Xenophon tells Chirisophus of the second dream).

The first speech recapitulates key parts of this scene and of the story so far. Xenophon starts by stressing the bad position in which the Greeks find themselves (15–16 ~ 2–3); he then warns of worse to come if they do nothing (17–18 ~ 13–14). His reflections on the significance of the shift from truce to war (19–22) offer a retrospective interpretation of the negotiations in Book 2. Finally, the speech looks forward to what is to come, underlining the sense of a narrative break at the start of Book 3 (3.1n.). The close contact between the events as presented in X.'s narrative and in Xenophon's speech points to the leadership qualities of Xenophon (cf. Introduction p. 37).

3.1.15 ἀνίσταται: Xenophon's decisive intervention is marked by a historical present; contrast the torpor of the other soldiers (2–3n.). **πρῶτον** goes closely with Προξένου, highlighting Xenophon's limited first step, while anticipating his later speech to all the surviving officers. **ἔλεξεν** 'made an argument, related' occurs in X. about a fifth as often as εἶπεν 'said, uttered', but is preferred in introductions of longer speeches. In classical Attic it is most common in poetry and so may be somewhat elevated (Fournier 1946: 80–91). **οὔτε καθεύδειν δύναμαι** echoes X.'s words at 11. **ὥσπερ οἶμαι οὐδ' ὑμεῖς** 'just as, I suppose, you cannot either', as is confirmed by X. at 3. οἶμαι is parenthetical, as nominative ὑμεῖς (*sc.* δύνασθε) shows. οὐδέ is 'not . . . either' after a preceding negative (*GP* 194). **οὔτε κατακεῖσθαι ἔτι** picks up Xenophon's question τί κατάκειμαι; at 13 (see 17, 25nn. for other echoes of his soliloquy). **ἐν οἵοις ἐσμέν** 'in what sort of a situation we are' (i.e. the situation described by X. at 2).

3.1.16 δῆλον ὅτι 'clearly' (parenthetical: Smyth 2585). **οὐ πρότερον . . . πρίν ἐνόμισαν** 'not until they believed'. For πρίν with indicative after a negative verb, see *CGCG* 47.14; Smyth 2432. πρότερον anticipates πρίν. **τὸν πόλεμον ἐξέφηναν:** the language of open war contrasts with the repeated stress on suspicion and concealment in the account of the negotiations in Book 2 (see 21n.). Contrast Xenophon's rhetoric at 3.2.29(n.). **ἀντεπιμελεῖται:** compound verbs in ἀντι- are common in X., reflecting the importance which he attaches to the principles of rivalry and reciprocity (cf. e.g. *Mem.* 2.6.28 ἀντεπιθυμέομαι, *Hell.* 4.6.3 ἀντεπικουρέω, *Cyr.* 8.3.49 ἀντεπαινέω); many of them were probably coined by X. and are rarely found elsewhere, including ἀντεπιμελ(έ)ομαι (which occurs in some MSS at *Cyr.* 5.1.18 and later only at Lib. *Ep.* 438.5). **ὅπως ὡς κάλλιστα ἀγωνιούμεθα:** for the construction, see 14n. Both the image of warfare as contest and superlatives of καλός are conventional in martial contexts and found in *An.* at other moments of heightened rhetoric (contest: 3.1.21–2, 2.15, 4.44n.,

45n.; cf. 1.7.4, 2.5.10, 5.2.11; κάλλιστ-: 24, 6.3.17; the two motifs together at 4.6.7, 8.9).

3.1.17 καὶ μήν 'and yet'. **εἰ . . . ἐπὶ βασιλεῖ γενησόμεθα** closely echoes Xenophon's soliloquy (13n.). **ὑφησόμεθα:** future middle of ὑφίημι 'yield'. **πείσεσθαι:** future infinitive of πάσχω. **ὅς** 'this is the man who' (connecting relative). **καὶ τοῦ ὁμομητρίου καὶ ὁμοπατρίου** picks up the opening sentence of *An.*, Δαρείου καὶ Παρυσάτιδος γίγνονται παῖδες δύο; the detail makes the king's treatment of Cyrus seem much worse (note the first καί, which is adverbial, 'even'), and so the threat to the Greeks even greater. The terms ὁμομήτριος and ὁμοπάτριος are often combined in contexts that stress close family ties (e.g. Isae. 7.5; Lys. 32.4; Dem. 25.79; Ctesias F15.52 Lenfant (in a Persian context)). **καὶ τεθνηκότος ἤδη** is more pointed if καί is taken as adverbial ('even when he was already dead') rather than as connective ('and already dead'). **ἀποτεμὼν . . . ἀνεσταύρωσεν:** X. had reported that Cyrus had his head and right hand cut off (1.10.1), not that those bodily parts were impaled. Given that the Greeks have been informed only of his death (2.1.3), either Xenophon's statement is filling an earlier narrative ellipse or Xenophon is making these details up. Mutilation and impalement were standard punishments among the Persians and seen as barbaric by Greeks (3.4.5n.), but mutilation of a hand is attested only for Cyrus (see Mari 2014 for the possible symbolism). Plut. *Artax.* 13.2 (probably from Ctesias, cf. F16.64 Lenfant) says that Artaxerxes had Cyrus' head cut off on the battlefield before displaying it himself to his men. **ἡμᾶς** 'as for us' is thrown forward to establish the new topic; though identical with the subject of οἰόμεθα, it can be construed as the subject of παθεῖν (Smyth 1974), but it is more likely that Xenophon changes construction halfway through. **οἷς κηδεμὼν μὲν . . . ἐστρατεύσαμεν δέ:** 'for whom there is no protector, but who marched . . .'; cf. 3.1.4n. κηδεμών is bitterly ironic, since it is often used of those with a duty towards corpses (LSJ s.v. A), especially family members; Xenophon implies that the king will treat the Greeks even worse than he did his brother. **δοῦλον ἀντὶ βασιλέως ποιήσοντες:** ἀντὶ . . . ποιεῖν is used with polar expressions, cf. Hdt. 1.210.2 ἀντὶ μὲν δούλων ἐποίησας ἐλευθέρους. Greek writers commonly conceive of all Persians below the king as slaves, using δοῦλος to cover Persian *bandaka* (Missiou 1993); here Xenophon attributes the same conception to the king himself. X. has nowhere explicitly stated what either Cyrus or the Greeks planned to do to Artaxerxes if captured. For the fear that intended wrongdoing increases punishment in the event of failure, cf. Thuc. 7.64.1. **ἀποκτενοῦντες εἰ δυναίμεθα:** εἰ with oblique optative (for ἐάν with subjunctive) after a purpose construction (ὡς with future participle, a form of indirect thought) in secondary sequence. Xenophon repeats the argument (with the same phrase) at 7.1.28. **ἂν . . . παθεῖν** varies the earlier πείσεσθαι.

3.1.18 οὐκ ἂν ἐπὶ πᾶν ἔλθοι ὡς . . . παράσχοι 'would he not go to any lengths to provide', potential optative followed by purpose clause with another optative (aorist from παρέχω) owing to mood attraction (*CGCG* 40.15; Smyth 2186). **αἰκισάμενος** 'by torturing' ('coincidental' aorist participle: 3.4.42n.) takes a double accusative of person and thing. **πᾶσιν ἀνθρώποις φόβον:** for punishment as a deterrent against foreign aggression, cf. 2.4.3; Hdt. 9.78.2, 116.3. The king's subsequent failure to prevent the Greeks' escape is not to be taken as a sign that *An.* is in fact encouraging an attack on the Persian empire (Introduction p. 21). **τοῦ στρατεῦσαι:** objective genitive (dependent on φόβον) of the articular infinitive. **ἀλλ' ὅπως τοι . . . πάντα ποιητέον** 'No – we must do everything to ensure we do not fall into the power of that man.' See 7n. for the impersonal verbal adjective (here with object πάντα), 14n. for ὅπως with future indicative. Dismissive ἐκείνωι (rather than αὐτῶι) follows from the preceding characterization of the Persian king as dangerous and marks the conclusion to this section of the argument; τοι (originally a second-person pronoun) marks out its special relevance to the addressees (*CGCG* 59.51). Xenophon drums home the point by repetition (cf. 17).

3.1.19 μὲν οὖν, as often, marks a transition (*CGCG* 59.73; *GP* 470–3), here to a new section in which Xenophon outlines why there are grounds for hope. **ἔστε μὲν αἱ σπονδαὶ ἦσαν:** originally Ionic ἔστε was gradually incorporated into Attic; X. uses it synonymously with ἕως (Lillo 2013). The initial negotiations after Cyrus' death focused on whether the Greeks and Persians were in a state of σπονδαί or πόλεμος (2.1.21–3). Clearchus then made σπονδαί at 2.3.10, and again (with an oath) at 2.3.26–8; under their terms the Greeks were not allowed to plunder Persian land as long as the Persians provided a market. **μακαρίζων:** cf. Cyrus' equally astute praise of Greek liberty at 1.7.3 (εὐδαιμονίζω). **διαθεώμενος** suggests thorough and continual inspection; in classical Greek the verb occurs only here and four times in the Platonic corpus. The succeeding subordinate clauses bring out the various sources of Persian strength (quantity and quality of land; supplies; servants; flocks; gold; clothes), all governed by ἔχοιεν (oblique optative in indirect question); variation is achieved by ὡς δὲ ἄφθονα (for ὅσα δέ) and by χρυσὸν δέ, ἐσθῆτα δέ (for ὅσον δὲ χρυσόν, ὅσην δ' ἐσθῆτα). This summary complements earlier descriptions of the Persian empire offered by Cyrus (1.7.6) and by X. (Rood 2010a: 86–7) and matches that offered by Aristagoras at Hdt. 5.49.4–7; while the Greeks have seen only a small part of it, many of its further sources of strength could have been observed in the king's army (and by extrapolation from Cyrus' court).

3.1.20 τὰ . . . τῶν στρατιωτῶν: object of ἐνθυμοίμην (optative in past indefinite clause: *CGCG* 50.21; Smyth 2409), elaborated in the ὅτι-clause ('namely that . . .'). **δ' αὖ** 'on the other hand'. **μετείη** 'there is a share', with partitive genitive οὐδενός (which itself governs partitive ἀγαθῶν). **πριαίμεθα** 'buy', aorist optative from *πρίαμαι. **ὅτου δ' ὠνησόμεθα** 'with which we would buy' (genitive of price: *CGCG* 30.31; Smyth 1372). **ἄλλως δέ πως . . . ἢ ὠνουμένους** 'in any other way . . . than by buying'. **<τοὺς> ὅρκους . . . κατέχοντας** 'I knew that our oaths prevented us from'; supply ᾔδειν from the previous clause. For κατέχω in this sense (LSJ s.v. I.b) with infinitive, cf. Pl. *Phdr.* 254a2 ἑαυτὸν κατέχει μὴ ἐπιπηδᾶν (X. *Mem.* 2.6.11 has ὥστε μή); the 'redundant' negative μή expected with verbs of hindering is here omitted. Bassett 2002: 460 argues that Xenophon ignores Chirisophus' transgression of the oaths (19n.) when he foraged from a village (2.5.37) even though Tissaphernes was providing a market (2.5.30); but the verb used at 2.5.37, ἐπισιτίζεσθαι, need not support this (see 3.4.18n.; Jansen 2014). **ταῦτ' οὖν λογιζόμενος:** οὖν is resumptive, picking up ὁπότε ἐνθυμοίμην. **τὸν πόλεμον:** *sc.* φοβοῦμαι from preceding ἐφοβούμην. Contrast 16, where Xenophon presents the Persians' open declaration of war as a sign that they thought they were well prepared.

3.1.21 ἔλυσαν τὰς σπονδάς: the treaty lasted until the arrest of the generals (2.5.32). Xenophon's suggestion that the Persians' breaking of the treaty means that the Greeks can now exploit Persian goods is rhetorically apt; it need not cast doubt on Clearchus' wisdom in making a truce in the first place. **λελύσθαι μοι . . . ἡ ἡμετέρα ὑποψία** 'I think that their insolence and our suspicion are at an end, too'. The perfect infinitive λελύσθαι indicates that they have been 'ended' (LSJ s.v. II.4) once for all. The repetition of the same word in two different senses or nuances (ἔλυσαν . . . λελύσθαι), which later rhetorical treatises call *paronomasia*, is established rhetorical practice in classical prose (Macleod 1978: 66 n. 8). Here, however, the wordplay arguably results in an obscure expression: ὕβρις and ὑποψία are both presented as aspects of the period of truce but not of war; but Xenophon elsewhere imagines the ὕβρις inflicted on the arrested generals as continuing as he speaks (13, 29nn.). ὕβρις, moreover, has not been used of Persian behaviour in Book 2, while the earlier state of ὑποψία has been presented as mutual (2.4.10, 5.1–2; cf. Clearchus at 2.5.4–5; Wencis 1977: 47). Xenophon, then, is replacing the idea of mutual suspicion with a loaded opposition that casts the Persians' earlier behaviour in a negative light, as the product of a sense of superiority. Now, by contrast, the move into open warfare allows the Greeks to display their prowess. Hude's conjecture ἀπορία for ὑποψία, which is approved by most modern editors, creates a more straightforward expression (cf. Pl. *Prt.* 324e1 λύεται ἡ ἀπορία 'the problem is solved'), but weakens the rhetoric. For the contrast between suspicion and open war, cf. 2.5.1–2; Thuc. 1.146, 5.26.3. **ἐν μέσωι:** contrast the negative use at 2. **ταῦτα τὰ ἀγαθὰ ἆθλα** 'these goods as prizes', with predicative ἆθλα. Both ἀγαθά (2.1.12, *Ages.* 2.8) and ἆθλα (*Hell.* 4.2.5) are stock incentives (*Cyr.* 2.3.2, 7.1.12–13 combine both), with a Panhellenic resonance: cf. Hdt. 5.49.4 (speech of Aristagoras) 'those who live in that continent have more goods (ἀγαθά) than all other peoples put together . . . you could have them all if you set your mind to it'; Gorg. DK 82 A1 'trying to persuade them to make as prizes (ἆθλα) of war not each others' cities but the land of the barbarians'; Arr. *Anab.* 5.26.7 (modelled on X.). See also 16n. on contest imagery. As θεράποντας (19) suggests, the prizes included slaves. **ὁπότεροι . . . ἡμῶν** 'for (*sc.* τούτοις) whichever of the two of us (i.e. Persians or Greeks)'. A prospective relative clause (with ἄν + subjunctive: *CGCG* 40.9). **ἄνδρες ἀμείνονες:** comparative form of ἄνδρες ἀγαθοί, part of the language of 'civic heroism' (Tuplin 2003a: 144), evoking patriotic conflicts such as the Persian Wars (Rood 2004a: 317); in *An.* it is clustered in the speeches in this section (44, 3.2.3, 11, 15, 39), but also applied in the narrative to soldiers killed by the Carduchians (4.1.18, 2.23; cf. 3.5.15n.). **ἀγωνοθέται:** used of the judges at the Olympic Games (Hdt. 6.127.3). **οἱ θεοί:** the prospect of divine support (15–25n.) becomes prominent towards the close of the speech; cf. 23, 24nn. **ὡς τὸ εἰκός:** caution is characteristic of mortal pronouncements about the gods.

3.1.22 οὗτοι: the opponents (3.2.13n.). **ἐπιωρκήκασιν:** perfect indicative of ἐπιορκέω 'swear falsely by'. The basis for the charge of perjury is the killing of the generals: X. has explained that they were killed ὅτι ἐστράτευσαν ἐπὶ βασιλέα ξὺν Κύρωι (2.6.29), thereby offering a rebuttal of sorts to the Persians' claim to have killed Clearchus for breaking the oaths made after Cyrus' death (2.5.38); Clearchus himself had earlier insisted on his own reluctance to engage in τὸν . . . θεῶν πόλεμον (2.5.7). For accusations of perjury against Tissaphernes later in his career, see *Ages.* 1.13, *Hell.* 3.4.11 (again with the argument that the Greeks should be grateful for his oath-breaking). **ὁρῶντες:** concessive. **στερρῶς** 'resolutely'. Attic στερρός and Ionic στερεός occur in tragedy, but are rare in Attic prose (× 5 in X., the Attic form only here). **αὐτῶν:** genitive with ἀπειχόμεθα. **τοὺς τῶν θεῶν ὅρκους:** 3.2.10n. **ἀγῶνα:** continuing the metaphor from 21; cf. 16n. **πολύ:** with μείζονι. **τούτοις:** *sc.* ἐξεῖναι 'than is possible for them'; τούτοις is parallel with the unexpressed subject of ἰέναι (i.e. ἡμῖν).

3.1.23 ἔτι δ' 'moreover'. **τούτων:** genitive of comparison. **καὶ ψύχη . . . φέρειν:** φέρειν depends on ἱκανώτερα (*CGCG* 51.9); ψύχη is plural of ψῦχος 'cold' (contrast ψυχή 'soul'). For endurance of hot and cold as a requirement of the good soldier, cf. e.g. *Hell.* 5.1.15, *Ages.* 5.3, *Cyr.* 8.1.36; for the stereotype that Asiatics lack this quality, see Hippoc. *Aer.* 16, 23. **σὺν τοῖς θεοῖς** links Xenophon's three speeches (42n., 3.2.8, 11, 14). The idiom is particularly common in X. (× 35, mainly in *An.* and *Cyr.*), and otherwise mostly found in serious poetry. **οἱ . . . ἄνδρες** 'the men (we have to face)', i.e. the enemy (Sturz I.239); cf. 3.4.40 for this use of ἄνδρες in blunt military exhortations. **καὶ τρωτοὶ καὶ θνητοί** 'liable to wounding and death'. For the argument from the enemy's vulnerability, cf. Hom. *Il.* 4.510–11 and esp. 21.568–70, where Agenor resolves to face Achilles because he is both τρωτός (a Homeric *hapax*) and θνητός. Xenophon goes one better than Agenor by arguing that the apparently stronger enemy are not stronger at all. Underlying his reasoning is the fact that Persian troops were not as heavily armed as Greek hoplites. **ἤν** = εἰ + ἄν; for the form, see Introduction p. 28. **ὥσπερ τὸ πρόσθεν:** for the claim that the battle of Cunaxa was a victory for the Greeks, cf. 2.1.4, 9; no divine involvement is mentioned in the earlier narrative. In his speech to the whole army Xenophon appeals to this victory more positively, as itself holding the prospect of further success (3.2.14n.). **διδῶσι** 'keep on giving' (present subjunctive).

3.1.24 ἴσως γὰρ . . . ἐνθυμοῦνται is parenthetical (*CGCG* 59.58 on ἀλλὰ . . . γάρ; *GP* 98–9). **πρὸς τῶν θεῶν** 'by the gods', more commonly used at the start of speeches, adds urgency and reinforces the idea of a new beginning (cf. 15–25n. and ἄρξωμεν later in this sentence). **μὴ ἀναμένωμεν:** hortatory subjunctive (*CGCG* 34.6; Smyth 1797), with accusative and infinitive, picking up ἀναμένω (14). In the march upcountry Meno's desire to make the first move was a mark of his ambition (1.4.13–16); here Xenophon has the much more positive idea of inspiring others to excellence. **παρακαλοῦντας:** future participle expressing purpose. **τὰ κάλλιστα ἔργα:** see 16n. for κάλλιστα; equivalent phrases are found in patriotic exhortations (e.g. κάλλιστον ἔργον at 6.3.17; Hdt. 8.75.2; Thuc. 6.33.4) and commemorative epigram (Simon. *FGE* 45 = *Anth. Pal.* 7.296.3–4 οὐδαμά πω κάλλιον . . . | ἔργον). **ἄρξωμεν τοῦ ἐξορμῆσαι** 'let us take the lead in arousing'; articular infinitive in genitive after hortatory subjunctive ἄρξωμεν (in Attic prose the middle is more common in this sense). **φάνητε:** aorist imperative (contrast φανῆτε, aorist subjunctive), with asyndeton and shift from first- to second-person form (because Xenophon is not himself a captain). **ἀξιοστρατηγότεροι** is attested elsewhere only at Arr. *Anab.* 4.11.5 (modelled on this passage) and in Cassius Dio. X. is fond of adjectives in ἀξιο-, often in the comparative or superlative, many of which are first attested in his works and recur later, if at all, only in imperial prose (e.g. ἀξιομακαριστότατον *Ap.* 34; ἀξιοθαυμαστότεροι *Mem.* 1.4.4; ἀξιοτεκμαρτότερον *Mem.* 4.4.10; ἀξιοσπουδαστότεροι *Lac.* 10.3).

3.1.25 ἡγεῖσθαι 'to take the lead' in stirring the army (rather than 'to be leader' in an official sense); cf. 3.2.36n. **οὐδὲν προφασίζομαι τὴν ἡλικίαν** 'I in no way plead my age in excuse'. The focus on Xenophon's youth picks up the end of his soliloquy (14n.). **ἀκμάζειν . . . ἐρύκειν** 'I am at the peak of my power to ward off (final-consecutive infinitive: *CGCG* 51.16)'. ἀκμάζω is generally used of crops etc. rather than of persons, but cf. Alcibiades' first-person use at Thuc. 6.17.1. ἐρύκω is an exclusively Ionic word and frequently used in Homer. Given that X. uses it only here, it may be intended as a further reminiscence of epic diction (23n.). **ἀπ' ἐμαυτοῦ:** the self-centred ending is surprising (Nitsche proposed adding τε καὶ τοῦ στρατοῦ), but it underscores Xenophon's point that the good of the whole will come from tending to the good of the individual (cf. Nicias' view that a good citizen can still be concerned with personal safety (Thuc. 6.9.2); contrast *Cyr.* 8.1.2).

3.1.26–32 Xenophon's speech meets with universal approval with the exception of a single objector, Apollonides (26n.); this reverses the Herodotean pattern of a single wise adviser objecting to a foolish proposal (e.g. Hdt. 7.10). The immediate rejection of Apollonides' suggestion that the Greeks continue dialogue with the Persians resumes the mood of their earlier rejection of the defeatist Phalinus (2.1). Apollonides is next abused as un-Greek because he has pierced ears (31n.), and driven away from the meeting; there is no word of what happened to him subsequently. The passage recalls the Thersites scene at Hom. *Il.* 2.211–77 (cf. Rinner 1978: 146–7): both Apollonides and Thersites are abused for physical features, and both are scapegoats who strengthen the ties among the other soldiers and boost the status of the men who rebuke them, Xenophon and Odysseus.

3.1.26 πλήν 'save that', introducing a new clause, as often with a part of πᾶς preceding (LSJ s.v. B.III). **Ἀπολλωνίδης τις ἦν:** the word order reverses the presentative formula used for Xenophon (4n.). Apollonides is a very common theophoric name. **βοιωτιάζων τῆι φωνῆι** 'who spoke like a Boeotian', presumably in dialect and accent; the phrase is imitated at Arr. *Anab.* 6.13.5, possibly for a deliberate contrast with this scene (Bosworth 1996: 56). The unusual lack of clear ethnic identification in the introduction of a soldier (the only parallels are 5.1.17, 7.14) prepares for the challenge to Apollonides' status when Agasias notes that he has his ears pierced ὥσπερ Λυδόν (31n.). Agasias' comparison does not mean that Apollonides was actually a Lydian, as is often assumed (e.g. *LGPN* s.v.; Hunt 1998: 169, proposing that he had been a slave in Boeotia; Sekunda 2013: 205, suggesting that he put on a Boeotian accent); it is an abusive stereotype, exploiting in a crisis an unusually strong binary understanding of ethnicity (Lee 2007: 72–4; Vlassopoulos 2013: 140–2). If he had anything to do with Lydia, it could be that he was a Boeotian who had served there (Ma 2004: 337) or that he came from a nearby Aeolian area linguistically connected with Boeotia (Lane Fox 2004c: 204). **φλυαροίη ὅστις λέγει:** optative in indirect statement in historic sequence followed by retained indicative in subordinate clause. The indicative distances the reader from empathizing with Apollonides' criticism of the 'nonsense' (9n.). The use of indirect rather than direct discourse may in part be dictated by Apollonides' dialect (Smith 2012: 56); it also prepares for the summary of the later part of his speech, which avoids repetition of the narrative, and ensures that X. does not yield the floor to him. **ἤρχετο λέγειν τὰς ἀπορίας** 'started to list their difficulties'. Apollonides rehearses the grievances given by X. at 2 – indirectly showing how the army might still have been stuck but for Xenophon's intervention, and causing Xenophon to intervene to prevent the return of ἀθυμία. The only other use of the plural of the leitmotif ἀπορία (2n.) in *An.* is at 12; as with other abstract nouns, the plural expresses instances of ἀπορία (Smyth 1000).

3.1.27 ὑπολαβών is regularly used of a speaker who 'takes up' something said by the previous speaker, often in heated conversations. Here (by contrast with 31) Xenophon even interrupts Apollonides, as indicated by μεταξύ and the preceding ἤρχετο λέγειν. **ὧδε:** the adverb of manner draws attention to the tone (here scathing) of a riposte; contrast τάδε at 35(n.). **ὦ θαυμασιώτατε ἄνθρωπε** indicates (feigned?) surprise on Xenophon's part that Apollonides should make these objections, a theme elaborated in the sentence that follows. 'Friendly' addresses of this kind are used by speakers who are dominating a conversation, and the superlative is usually ironic; the addition of ἄνθρωπε is contemptuous when a speaker knows the addressee, as is presumably the case with Xenophon here (given that he is addressing one of Proxenus' λοχαγοί). See Dickey 1996: 117, 141, 152. **οὐδὲ ὁρῶν γιγνώσκεις οὐδὲ ἀκούων μέμνησαι:** proverbial (Fraenkel on Aesch. *Ag.* 1623), though without the verbal repetition found at e.g. Dem. 25.89 τὸ τῆς παροιμίας, ὁρῶντας μὴ ὁρᾶν καὶ ἀκούοντας μὴ ἀκούειν; Matthew 13:13 βλέποντες οὐ βλέπουσιν καὶ ἀκούοντες οὐκ ἀκούουσιν. The first οὐδέ is adverbial, the second connective ('not even . . . nor': *GP* 193). **ἐν ταὐτῶι γε μέντοι ἦσθα τούτοις** 'yet, mind you, you were in the same place as these men'. *GP* 413 comments that γε μέντοι here gives 'a partial ground for the acceptance of a belief', but this misses Xenophon's sarcastic edge. **ὅτε βασιλεύς . . . τὰ ὅπλα:** Xenophon alludes to the Greeks' rejection of Persian demands the day after Cyrus' death (2.1.7–23), rebuking Apollonides for his failure to learn from the arguments used on that occasion. **μέγα φρονήσας:** often of the type of pride that could be thought to attract divine punishment: cf. 6.3.18; Hdt. 7.10ε οὐ γὰρ ἐᾶι φρονέειν μέγα ὁ θεὸς ἄλλον ἢ ἑωυτόν.

See Hau 2012: 593–4 on X.'s use of the phrase. **ἐπὶ τούτωι** refers to Cyrus' death. **πέμπων ἐκέλευε:** as often with verbs of communication, the imperfect directs attention to the addressees' response (here negative, and so the order remains effectively incomplete: *CGCG* 33.51); it does not refer to repeated or continuous demands (X. does report at 2.5.38 a further Persian demand that the Greeks hand over their weapons, but this happens much later). The present participle links the dispatch and the message closely together, cf. 2.3.1 πέμπων τὰ ὅπλα παραδιδόναι ἐκέλευε.

3.1.28 ἐξωπλισμένοι . . . παρεσκηνήσαμεν: Xenophon alludes to an occasion when the Greeks encamped near the king (2.2.15) – but this happened by accident, not on purpose. The perfect ἐξωπλισμένοι 'fully armed' denotes a state of readiness (cf. 2.3.3). The variant ἐξοπλισάμενοι could be supported by 2.1.2 ἔδοξεν οὖν αὐτοῖς . . . ἐξοπλισαμένοις προϊέναι; if so, Xenophon has reversed the chronology, since this arming happens before the arrival of the Persian envoys. **πρέσβεις πέμπων . . . ἔστε σπονδῶν ἔτυχεν:** ἔστε (19n.) with aorist means 'until'. Xenophon distorts events slightly. After the Greeks rejected the Persian demand that they hand over their weapons, the king first requested a treaty (2.3.1); then, agreeing to Clearchus' insistence that the Greeks receive supplies before they accepted a treaty (2.3.5–6), he had them led to villages where they could get supplies (2.3.14). Xenophon wrongly implies here that these supplies were an incentive to make the Greeks agree to a treaty.

3.1.29 ἐπεὶ δ' αὖ οἱ στρατηγοὶ κτλ.: 2.5.32. **ὥσπερ δὴ σὺ κελεύεις:** Xenophon interrupts his narrative with an indignant (note δή and σύ) and elliptical aside; he is perhaps to be imagined gesturing towards Apollonides. **ἄνευ ὅπλων:** this detail (absent from the earlier narrative) underlines their misplaced confidence in the truce; they had in fact been warned not to trust the Persians (2.4.3–4, 5.29). **παιόμενοι, κεντούμενοι, ὑβριζόμενοι:** cf. 13n. for ὕβρις and 3.4.25n. for the asyndeton. Xenophon imagines what is happening to the captured generals at this moment. Ariaeus had claimed that Clearchus was already dead while Meno and Proxenus were held in high honour (2.5.38); that claim is ignored here (cf. 3.1n.). In the mean time, X. has revealed that the other generals had their heads cut off ('the swiftest death') except for Meno, who was tortured for a year (2.6.29). To complicate matters, Ctesias (T7a, F27.69 Lenfant; cf. Plut. *Artax.* 18) suggests that all the generals were sent in chains to Artaxerxes; that Clearchus and the others were kept alive for quite some time; and that they were all then executed except for Meno. Diodorus (14.27.2) seems to follow Ctesias, but adds that Tissaphernes kept Meno 'because he was thought to be ready to betray the Greeks'. **οἱ τλήμονες:** appositional with ἐκεῖνοι. The word belongs to epic and tragedy. **καὶ . . . ἐρῶντες τούτου** 'though very much, I imagine, longing for this (*sc.* τοῦ ἀποθανεῖν)'. The shocking expression of a passion for death (cf. Soph. *Ant.* 220 οὐκ ἔστιν οὕτω μῶρος ὃς θανεῖν ἐρᾶι; Hippoc. *De arte* 7 οὐκ ἀποθανεῖν ἐρῶντες) is softened by parenthetical οἶμαι; the whole clause adds pathos. The same thought in relation to the king's enemies is found at Chariton 6.7.7. **φλυαρεῖν φήις:** cf. 26 φλυαροίη (suggesting that Apollonides had used that same word); the indignant alliteration is kept up with πείθειν and πάλιν. **πείθειν . . . ἰόντας:** ἰόντας agrees with ἡμᾶς, the unexpressed subject of πείθειν, 'try to persuade', which stands first as a bare and dismissive summary of Apollonides' policy, creating an imbalance (τοὺς μὲν ἀμύνεσθαι <u>κελεύοντας</u> ~ πείθειν δὲ . . . <u>κελεύεις</u>, with an incredulous echo of κελεύεις in the previous sentence). πάλιν goes with πείθειν and ἰόντας, not with κελεύεις (*pace* Grote 1903–6: VII.246, who suggests that Apollonides was one of those taking a soft line, ὑπομαλακιζομένους, at 2.1.14).

3.1.30 ἐμοί, ὦ ἄνδρες: the change of addressee is accompanied by asyndeton (δέ would wrongly suggest a connection with σύ in the previous sentence). **μήτε** is co-ordinated with τε ('both . . . not . . . and . . .'). **προσίεσθαι εἰς ταὐτὸν ἡμῖν αὐτοῖς** 'admit into the same service as ourselves', picking up ἐν ταὐτῶι . . . ἦσθα (27). **ἀφελομένους τε τὴν λοχαγίαν:** in the absence of Proxenus, Xenophon assumes that the captains *en masse* have authority to demote Apollonides without consulting the men in his unit. **σκεύη ἀναθέντας ὡς τοιούτωι χρῆσθαι** 'load baggage on him and use him like that (lit. "like such a kind of thing")', i.e. like a pack-animal. Xenophon's justification in the next sentence draws on the common equation of non-Greeks and non-humans; cf. the implication at 5.8.5 that service as a mule-handler is humiliating for a free man. **τὴν πατρίδα** probably refers (despite Agasias' response) to a single city rather than to the Boeotian confederacy (cf. Nielsen 2004). **τὴν Ἑλλάδα** widens the scope, showing the importance for the soldiers of both Greek and local identities (cf. 3.2.7–32n.). **Ἕλλην:** the repetition of Ἑλλ- roots stresses the need for Greeks to live up to what Greece stands for (cf. Gorg. DK 82 B11a.36; Lys. 33.7; Dem. 14.31).

3.1.31 ὑπολαβών: 27n. **Ἀγασίας Στυμφάλιος:** an Arcadian with a snappy style of speech (6.1.30, 6.17–18, 21–4), identified as a friend of Xenophon (6.6.11); for his role in *An.*, see Flower 2012: 92–4. **ἀλλά:** extremely frequent at the start of speeches in X. (*GP* 20), underlining the interactional style of many reported speeches in his works; here it substitutes for Xenophon's assumption that Apollonides is a disgrace to Greece the claim that he has nothing to do with Greece at all (*CGCG* 59.11). **τούτωι γε . . . παντάπασιν** 'this man has nothing to do either with Boeotia or (with any part of) Greece at all'; for the construction with the impersonal verb (genitive of thing and dative of person), see *CGCG* 36.15; Smyth 1467. Given that προσήκω can denote kin relations (3.2.11n.), Agasias may be not simply using a cultural definition of Hellenic identity, but even pretending to disbelieve Apollonides was a Hellene by birth. For the rhetoric (with similar appeal to visual evidence), cf. Ar. fr. 311 K–A οὗτός ἐστ' οὐκ Ἀργόλας. | Μὰ Δί' οὐδέ γ' Ἕλλην, ὅσον ἔμοιγε φαίνεται. **ὥσπερ Λυδόν** 'like a Lydian' does not indicate that Apollonides actually was a Lydian (26n.). Wearing of earrings is associated with women in Greece (Hom. *Od.* 18.297–8; Aen. Tact. 31.7); for men, it is a mark of non-Greek identity (Mayor on Juv. 1.104). Lydians were commonly regarded as effeminate following their conquest by Persia (Hdt. 1.155.4); for their wearing of earrings, see Dio Chrys. 32.3; Barnett 1948, Fig. 20. The abuse of a man wearing earrings at Anac. fr. 388 *PMG* and the presence of earrings in some sixth- and fifth-century vase paintings have been thought to suggest Lydian influence on Greeks in Asia Minor and neighbouring islands, with earrings 'an acceptable part of stylish, if foppish, male dress' (Kurtz and Boardman 1986: 62); but their connotations (oriental, effeminate, or both?) remain controversial. Cf. Arr. *Parth.* fr. 46 Roos, where a Mesopotamian prince with both ears pierced is rebuked by Trajan for avoiding a campaign. **ἀμφότερα τὰ ὦτα τετρυπημένον:** lit. 'pierced with respect to both his ears' (*CGCG* 30.14; Smyth 1601a). ἀμφότερα is presumably for emphasis; there are stories that in the past boys in Greece wore a ring in a single ear (Dio Chrys. 32.3; Isid. *Etym.* 19.31.10).

3.1.32 καὶ εἶχεν οὕτως 'and this was the case' (for ἔχω with adverb, see 3n.). The imperfect brings out that the other Greeks notice Apollonides' pierced ears only after they have been mentioned by Agasias. This suggests that usually he did not wear earrings and/or had his ears hidden behind his hair (cf. Diphilus fr. 67 K–A for hair grown long in order to cover a tattoo). Ps.-Demetrius (*Eloc.* 137) found the brevity (συντομία) of this phrase full of a charm (χάρις) that would have been spoilt by amplification (e.g. if X. had written ἔλεγεν ταῦτα ἀληθῆ, σαφῶς γὰρ ἐτετρύπητο). **παρὰ τὰς τάξεις** presents a more orderly image of the Greek army than X. has suggested earlier (3n.). **τὸν στρατηγόν:** after the arrest of five generals, the only generals left were Chirisophus, Cleanor (47n.) and Sophaenetus (assuming with Roy 1967: 305 that Sosis, who appears only at 1.2.9, is not a general). **ὁπόθεν . . . ὑποστράτηγον:** the ὑποστράτηγος is generally assumed to be a replacement for an absent or dead general. If suffect-officers were in place at this point, it would be another sign that X.'s earlier presentation of the army's disarray is exaggerated. But this is the only appearance of the word in *An.*, and the first in extant Greek (the cognate verb ὑπεστρατήγει is used at 5.6.36 of Neon, whose position is exceptional (Introduction p. 2 n. 4.)). It is possible, then, that an editor, familiar with the Roman use of ὑποστράτηγος as equivalent to *legatus*, inserted this clause through a mistaken inference from 5.6.36; if so, αὖ may have been inserted in **c** to give the three-way opposition greater relief: given that the ὑποστράτηγος clause, if genuine, is parenthetical, δέ is in any case preferable. See further Huitink and Rood 2016: 215–27. **οἴχοιτο** is further ground for suspicion: contrasted with σῶιος εἴη, it should mean 'be dead' (cf. *Cyr.* 5.4.11; Soph. *Aj.* 1128, *Tr.* 83–5), but this usage is rare in prose and odd with ὁπόθεν (which probably means 'from those τάξεις from which'); while οἴχομαι when used as a verb of movement ('be gone') normally has an indication of direction or an accompanying participle.

3.1.33 εἰς τὸ πρόσθεν τῶν ὅπλων: see 3n. on τὰ ὅπλα; cf. the Achaean generals' nocturnal meeting in no-man's-land at Hom. *Il.* 10.194–271. Lee's suggestion (2007: 192) that the generals wanted to be out of earshot of the other troops presupposes that those troops were in their quarters, contrary to the impression given by 3. **σχεδὸν μέσαι ἦσαν νύκτες:** the plural of νύξ is frequently used with reference to part of a night (K–G I.18). The phrase suggests that the night is not quite as far advanced as 13 would lead readers to think. The full meeting of the army occurs at dawn (3.2.1), which (given 12–14 hours of darkness, depending on the chronology (Introduction pp. 41–2)) allows for a surprisingly long time for the intervening scene. Presumably X.'s time signals are schematic, evoking nocturnal discussions among the Achaeans (Hom. *Il.* 2.53–440, 9.13–181) and in the Greek fleet at Salamis (Hdt. 8.57–63), and also the symbolic power of dawn (3.2.1n.).

3.1.34 Ἱερώνυμος Ἠλεῖος is mentioned subsequently when he convenes a meeting (6.4.10), serves as an envoy (7.1.32) and (if it is the same man) is wounded in action (7.4.18). **πρεσβύτατος:** it was a conventional privilege for the oldest to speak first (cf. *Hell.* 4.1.31 ἤρξατο λόγου ὁ Φαρνάβαζος· καὶ γὰρ ἦν πρεσβύτερος, *Mem.* 2.3.15, *Cyr.* 6.1.6, 8.7.10; Pl. *Leg.* 712c8–9), and so perhaps reassuring in a crisis (Dalby 1992: 20); for 'age-based authority' in the army, see Lee 2007: 76–7. **ἤρχετο λέγειν**, rather than signalling a speech that will be interrupted (26n.), here stresses Hieronymus' role as introductory speaker (cf. 7.2.24). **ἡμῖν . . . ἔδοξε:** Hieronymus initially glosses over the fact that it was Xenophon who called them together, though παρακαλέσαι picks up παρακαλοῦντας from Xenophon's speech (24). **ὁρῶσι τὰ παρόντα:** a euphemistic reference to the ἀπορίαι of 2. **βουλευσαίμεθα** is optative in a purpose clause in historic sequence, **δυναίμεθα** in a conditional clause (εἰ = 'in the hope that': *CGCG* 49.25) within the purpose clause (a form of indirect thought). **ἔφη:** 3.3.2n. **ἅπερ καὶ πρὸς ἡμᾶς:** in the event Xenophon introduces significant variations (35–47n.), though it would have been possible for X. to summarize the second speech while indicating additional points (on the model of Thuc. 4.114.3, 120.3).

3.1.35–47 Xenophon's speech (35–44) to all the surviving officers deploys a different style of rhetoric from his first speech. Whereas that speech, addressed to the officers of his own contingent, focused on the desirability and practicality of taking immediate action, and included some direct self-promotion, he assumes a more tentative style in this speech, where he is addressing men who are less well known to him (cf. 45n.). After a brief recapitulation of the seriousness of the army's position, he appeals to the elite status of his listeners, insisting that it is their duty to take action on behalf of the whole army. He does offer guidance as to possible steps to take, but avoids seeming too self-assertive. He thereby succeeds in instructing his audience without arousing enmity: whereas his earlier speech met with disapproval from one outcast, this speech meets with approval from a Spartan general, and he is in due course elected one of the replacement generals.

3.1.35 **τάδε** focuses attention on the content of the following speech, inviting comparison with Xenophon's earlier speech (it carries no connotation of verbatim reporting). **ἀλλὰ . . . μὲν δή** 'well, ...' is a quasi-apologetic concession of the obviousness of Xenophon's first point, preparing for his practical advice (ἡμῖν δέ γε οἶμαι . . .). **πάντες ἐπιστάμεθα:** Xenophon appeals to his audience's assumed knowledge of a continuing Persian plot, even though what follows is based on supposition about Persian plans or, at most, on the Persian embassy to the Greeks at 2.5.35–42 (which had actually accused Clearchus of plotting against Tissaphernes). **βασιλεὺς καὶ Τισσαφέρνης:** the first mention of Tissaphernes since 2.5.40 (contrast the focus on the king alone at 13, 17); he may have been known to some of the officers from his time as satrap of Lydia. **ἡμῖν:** dative of agent (*CGCG* 37.2). **πάντα ποιητέα** echoes 18, but here πάντα is subject rather than object and ποιητέα passive rather than active. **ἐπὶ τοῖς βαρβάροις γενώμεθα:** another echo (with variation) of Xenophon's first speech (17–18 ἐπὶ βασιλεῖ/ἐπ' ἐκείνωι γενησόμεθα). **ἀλλὰ . . . ἐκεῖνοι ἐφ' ἡμῖν** (the same idiom reversed) gives an aggressive turn to Xenophon's earlier rhetoric.

3.1.36 **ἐπίστασθε** is imperative, as εὖ shows (cf. εὖ ἴστε in the next sentence; at 42, by contrast, bare ἐπίστασθε is indicative). Xenophon here shifts from (inclusive) first- to second-person forms, underlining the officers' exclusive responsibility. **τοσοῦτοι . . . συνεληλύθατε** 'in such numbers as are here gathered', i.e. few enough to have the chance to win distinction, but still enough to inspire the troops. **καιρόν** 'opportunity'; the word is used three times in the speech (see 39, 44), signalling the possibility of a turning point in the Greeks' fortunes. **οὗτοι:** the addressee-oriented pronoun (Ruijgh 2006) fits the shift to second-person forms (it is perhaps to be imagined as accompanied by a gesture). **πρὸς ὑμᾶς ἀποβλέπουσι:** Xenophon expresses an ideal of top-down leadership in which vision (cf. ὁρῶσιν, φανεροί) leads to imitation (cf. μιμεῖσθαι); he had not himself waited for another man to take the lead (14). **κἂν μὲν ὑμᾶς ὁρῶσιν . . . φανεροὶ ἦτε:** the officers change from being objects of the soldiers' gaze in the first conditional clause (κἂν μέν . . ., with crasis of καὶ ἐάν) to agents in their own right in the second, where they are subjects of φανεροὶ ἦτε (when we expect a phrase such as ἢν δὲ ὑμᾶς ὁρῶσιν παρασκευαζομένους). The stress on the importance of public display is typical of X.; φανερὸς ἦν is repeatedly used in the defence of Socrates at *Mem.* 1.1–3 and in the obituaries in *An.* (1.9.11, 2.6.19, 23). **παρασκευαζόμενοι:** 14n. **καὶ τοὺς ἄλλους παρακαλῆτε** picks up 24, 34, reflecting the momentum created by Xenophon's intervention.

3.1.37 **ἴσως:** for tact. **τοι:** 18n. **δίκαιόν ἐστιν:** Xenophon retains the impersonal construction (rather than saying δίκαιοί ἐστε) in order to suggest that the principle of reciprocity which operates between leaders and led is based on a general principle of justice and mutual agreement rather than serving the interests of the leaders. The requirement of leaders to excel in return for their privileges recalls Sarpedon's speech at Hom. *Il.* 12.310–28, but Xenophon postpones treating the inevitability of death (which for Sarpedon is an incentive to gain a heroic death in battle) until 43. A supposed imbalance between toils and rewards is later the cause of Arcadian disaffection (6.2.10, cf. 7.6.9). **ὑμᾶς . . . ὑμεῖς . . . ὑμεῖς:** Xenophon underlines by urgent repetition (perhaps accompanied by gestures) that it is the task of the officers to act; his rhetoric is imitated at Arr. *Anab.* 7.9.8. **ταξίαρχοι,** mentioned elsewhere only at 4.1.28, are probably paired with λοχαγοί for rhetorical effect rather than being a distinct rank such as light-armed commanders (Huitink and Rood 2016: 211–15). **ὅτε εἰρήνη ἦν . . . ἐπλεονεκτεῖτε:** yet it was Cyrus' military adventure that itself created the hierarchies (or at least the posts of στρατηγός and λοχαγός, see 36n.) to which Xenophon now appeals, whereas Sarpedon as Lycian king spoke of his reciprocal relations with his subjects (Tuplin 2003a: 127). By using the general term εἰρήνη to refer to any time before the arrest of the generals, Xenophon flatters his audience by extending their sense of entitlement to the time before the expedition (*pace* Lee 2007: 82 n. 13, this sentence does not presuppose the existence of the same λόχοι at that time, though it may suggest that the officers were of higher status (Stronk 27)). In purely financial terms, captains received double and generals four times the pay of ordinary soldiers (to judge from 7.2.36, 3.10, 6.1, 7); what special honours they enjoyed is not specified (contrast mention of double portions for Spartan kings at *Ages.* 5.1, *Lac. Pol.* 15.4). **ἐπεὶ πόλεμός ἐστιν:** ἐπεί is causal ('now that'). See 16n. for X.'s demarcation of war and peace. **ἀξιοῦν δεῖ ὑμᾶς αὐτοὺς . . . εἶναι** 'you must see fit (LSJ s.v. ἀξιόω II.2) yourselves to be'; cf. 5.2.13 οἱ ἀξιοῦντες τούτων (*sc.* τῶν λοχαγῶν) μὴ χείρους εἶναι (which shows the same ethos working bottom up). Many commentators take ὑμᾶς . . . εἶναι as object clause after ἀξιοῦν ('it is proper to expect you to be'; LSJ s.v. ἀξιόω III.2); the oddness of reflexive ὑμᾶς αὐτούς and of an apologetic request in this context tells against this interpretation. **προβουλεύειν τούτων καὶ προπονεῖν:** forethought and toil are two qualities of the ideal Xenophontic leader; their combination is a variant on the common combination of word and deed (45n.). X. is fond of grouping verbs with προ- prefixes (e.g. *Cyr.* 8.1.32, *Hier.* 10.6, 8, *Mem.* 2.10.3); the genitive τούτων depends on this prefix.

3.1.38 ἂν . . . ὠφελῆσαι: for aorist infinitive with ἄν, see 3.2.29n. ὠφελῆσαι is a word often used by X. to emphasize the importance of mutually beneficial relationships between (unequal) partners (e.g. 1.3.4, 5.1.12), and is preferable to the variant ὀνῆσαι (more generally 'do a kindness', e.g. 5.6.20, 6.1.32). **ὅπως . . . ἀντικατασταθῶσιν:** aorist passive of ἀντικαθίστημι; ὅπως with subjunctive (like a purpose clause) after a verb of effort is less common than the future indicative construction (*CGCG* 44.3; Smyth 2214). **ἀντὶ τῶν ἀπολωλότων** 'instead of the ones who are lost'. **ἄνευ γὰρ ἀρχόντων:** at 3.2.29 Xenophon attributes the same thought to the Persians as a motive; see Introduction pp. 21–3 for the importance of leadership in X.'s thought. **ὡς μὲν συνελόντι εἰπεῖν** 'if one may put it briefly', lit. 'for one compressing (LSJ s.v. συναιρέω I.2.b) to say'; limitative ὡς with absolute infinitive (Rijksbaron on Pl. *Ion* 535d6–7) and indefinite use of the dative participle without pronoun (Smyth 1497). The expression (× 8 in X., but in no other extant classical author) qualifies the sweeping tone of οὐδαμοῦ. **οὐδαμοῦ . . . παντάπασιν** 'not . . . anywhere, and definitely not in military affairs'. In his other writings X., like Xenophon here, posits that leadership skills are transferable from one realm to another. **ἡ μὲν γὰρ εὐταξία . . . ἀπολώλεκεν:** the neat antithesis of εὐταξία/ἀταξία is disturbed by imbalance in the verbal parts, perhaps to underline Xenophon's relative inexperience: he knows (from Athens' fate in the Peloponnesian War?) examples of indiscipline, but can only speak of the reputation enjoyed by good discipline. Alternatively δοκεῖ may stress that the thought is commonplace (cf. Soph. *Ant.* 672–6; Antiph. DK 87 B61, with Pendrick). The retreat will serve as a paradigm of good order, but an increasingly imperfect one (cf. Xenophon's warning about indiscipline at 5.8.13–26).

3.1.39 ἤν καὶ . . . ποιῆσαι: Xenophon's style in addressing the officers is tentative (35–47n.): the conditional (with subjunctive protasis: *CGCG* 49.17) leaves it to them to take the initiative, while οἶμαι (repeated from 38) keeps the outcome uncertain.

3.1.40 ἴσως καὶ ὑμεῖς αἰσθάνεσθε ὡς refers back to 3. ἴσως is understated: as X. has described it, the disarray was impossible not to notice. For ὡς, 'how', see 3.2.11n. **ἀθύμως μὲν . . . πρὸς τὰς φυλακάς:** repeating ἀθύμως from 3, but presenting a more ordered picture of the army than earlier (when X. claimed that many did not go to their stations). **οὕτω γ' ἐχόντων:** genitive absolute, probably neuter ('under these circumstances', *sc.* τούτων), as at 3.2.10, rather than masculine (which is still possible despite αὐτοῖς later in the sentence; cf. 1.5.16; Smyth 2073a). **ὅ τι:** accusative of respect with χρήσαιτο. **εἴτε νυκτὸς δέοι τι εἴτε καὶ ἡμέρας:** for the pairing, cf. 6.1.18 χρῆσθαι τῶι στρατεύματι καὶ νυκτὸς καὶ ἡμέρας; here καί before ἡμέρας stresses the greater likelihood of attack by day. Parts of δεῖ occur five times in this speech, underlining Xenophon's appeal to the officers' sense of duty (Barrett on Eur. *Hipp.* 41 notes the increasingly moral colouring of δεῖ in the fourth century).

3.1.41 ἤν δέ τις: 39n. **αὐτῶν:** with τὰς γνώμας. **πείσονται . . . ποιήσουσι:** for πάσχω as functional passive of ποιέω, see also 3.3.13(n.).

3.1.42 ἰσχύς is pleonastic after πλῆθος. Superior barbarian numbers are often presented as less decisive than ἀρετή, both in pre-battle speeches (e.g. Thuc. 4.126.2) and in celebratory narratives, particularly of the Persian Wars (e.g. Thuc. 3.56.5; Andoc. 1.107, with Macdowell; Lys. 2.23; cf. Oakley on Livy 6.13.1); Xenophon, by contrast, stresses morale, as at *Hell.* 7.4.24, partly in keeping with the importance of morale in X.'s leadership theory, partly because his rhetorical aim is to inspire the officers to inspire in turn the common soldiers. **ἥ . . . ποιοῦσα:** agreeing with the second of the preceding nouns, but going in sense with both. **σὺν τοῖς θεοῖς:** cf. 23n.; this is the only mention of gods in the second speech. **ταῖς ψυχαῖς ἐρρωμενέστεροι** 'stouter in their souls', irregular comparative of ἐρρωμένος. **τούτους** picks up ὁπότεροι. **ὡς ἐπὶ τὸ πολύ** 'generally'. **ἀντίοι:** Ionic for Attic ἐναντίος; X. uses both. **δέχονται** 'await the attack of', a common meaning (LSJ s.v. II.2).

3.1.43 ἐντεθύμημαι δ' ἔγωγε: Xenophon's personal contribution, by contrast with the thoughts presumed to be known to all (πάντες ἐπιστάμεθα 35, ἐπίστασθε 42). He offers an optimistic take on the heroic choice: it is precisely the readiness to die nobly in consciousness of the inevitability of death that ensures survival into old age; contrast, e.g., Pind. *Ol.* 1.82–4, where the thought of old age is an incentive to risk death through heroic effort. For weaker versions of Xenophon's reflection, cf. *Cyr.* 3.3.45 μῶρος δὲ καὶ εἴ τις ζῆν βουλόμενος φεύγειν ἐπιχειροίη, εἰδὼς ὅτι οἱ μὲν νικῶντες σῴζονται, οἱ δὲ φεύγοντες ἀποθνήσκουσι (from a speech of the Assyrian king); Sall. *Jug.* 107.1; Hor. *Carm.* 3.2.14, with Nisbet and Rudd; Livy 8.24.4. **ὁπόσῳοι . . . ἐκ παντὸς τρόπου** 'all those who seek to live at all costs' hints at any soldiers who, like Apollonides earlier, are still thinking of negotiation. μα(σ)τεύω is Doric (Gautier 34) and occurs in poetry as well (especially Euripides); it is attested only in X. in classical prose. **οὗτοι μέν:** for μέν following both relative and demonstrative, see *GP* 385. **τούτους ὁρῶ:** variation for the earlier οὗτοι, so as to highlight Xenophon's personal insight.

3.1.44 ἡμᾶς: the variant ὑμᾶς fits the earlier second-person forms (38n.), but the first-person singular observation in 43 leads well into a first-person plural (ἐσμεν) that unites Xenophon and his addressees. **ἄνδρας ἀγαθούς:** 21n. on ἄνδρες ἀμείνονες.

3.1.45 Χειρίσοφος: leader of the official Spartan contingent that arrives by ship at Issus at 1.4.3 and subsequently leader of the vanguard in the retreat. His sudden prominence here is unexpected, as he has been mentioned only three times since his first appearance: he is sent to Ariaeus as envoy at 2.1.5, returns at 2.2.1, and is absent at 2.5.37. He speaks first in the ensuing general assembly (3.2.1n.). After a more elaborate opening sentence, he speaks in short clauses with parataxis (αἱρεῖσθε . . . ἥκετε . . . ἄγετε) and repetition (αἱρεῖσθε, ἑλόμενοι, αἱρεθέντας), in a stereotypically Spartan way (3.2.1n.). **πρόσθεν μέν . . . Ἀθηναῖον εἶναι:** an indirect comment on Xenophon's sudden rise to prominence in the narrative, echoing his postponed introduction (4n.). For knowledge of local identities among the officers, see 31n. **ἐπαινῶ:** X. frequently makes characters use the language of praise (cf. 5.5.8, 6.4, 7.33 *bis*, 6.6.16), thereby aligning *An.* with (and at times distancing it from) works of encomiastic rhetoric such as X.'s own *Ages.* Praise of Xenophon by a Spartan is especially striking given Sparta's enmity with Athens and her military reputation. **λέγεις τε καὶ πράττεις:** for skill in speech and action as attributes of the ideal leader, cf. Hom. *Il.* 9.443 μύθων τε ῥητῆρ' ἔμεναι πρηκτῆρά τε ἔργων; Thuc. 1.139.4. **ὅτι πλείστους εἶναι τοιούτους:** in line with the role of emulation in X.'s ideas about leadership; cf. 3.2.31(n.) μυρίους . . . Κλεάρχους. **κοινὸν . . . τὸ ἀγαθόν:** X. suggests through Chirisophus that, if others emulated Xenophon's self-concern (14, 25nn.), a common good would result.

3.1.46 ἔφη: 3.3.2n. **μὴ μέλλωμεν:** cf. 47. **αἱρεῖσθε:** for the method used, see 47n. Contrast 2.2.5 (οὐχ ἑλόμενοι), where Clearchus is not elected overall leader but chosen because of his leadership skills. **τὸ**

μέσον: the central location of the assembly signals the re-establishment of order after the disarray of 3. **συγκαλοῦμεν:** future. **Τολμίδης ὁ κῆρυξ:** introduced at 2.2.20 as from Elis and κήρυκα ἄριστον τῶν τότε, but subsequently mentioned only at 5.2.18.

3.1.47 ᾑρέθησαν: X. does not reveal how the choice is to be made. Xenophon alludes in a later speech to the soldiers electing leaders (5.7.10, 28), but Chirisophus' instructions ἀπελθόντες . . . αἱρεῖσθε (46) suggest that the replacement generals were chosen separately by the captains of each contingent that needed a general, while not (*pace* Roy 1967: 288) ruling out consultation of the soldiers. **ἄρχοντες:** the vague language stresses the importance of leadership (cf. 38 ἄνευ γὰρ ἀρχόντων κτλ.). The five names that follow are new στρατηγοί, presumably (except for Xenophon) chosen from the existing λοχαγοί. X. gives for each man an ethnic, perhaps in imitation of the formal language of decrees. Despite 38, he does not mention replacement of the λοχαγοί who had been killed or promoted; it may have been decided to reorganize the λόχοι under the remaining λοχαγοί instead. **Κλεάρχου:** 10n. **Τιμασίων Δαρδανεύς:** an exile (5.6.23) from Dardanus in the Troad, across the Hellespont from the area where Clearchus gathered troops (1.1.9). Timasion and Xenophon, as the youngest generals, are chosen as co-leaders of the rear (3.2.37), but Timasion becomes prominent only in the account of the march along the Black Sea coast. **Σωκράτους:** Socrates, an Achaean, receives a brief obituary at 2.6.30. **Ξανθικλῆς Ἀχαιός:** only mentioned twice later (5.8.1, 7.2.1); the name is very rare (attested only once elsewhere in *LGPN*). **Ἀγίου:** either Agias replaced Xenias and/ or Pasion, the two generals who deserted at 1.4.7, or else it may have been Agias rather than Sophaenetus who arrived with a contingent at 1.2.9 (the MSS present Sophaenetus arriving twice). **Κλεάνωρ Ἀρκάς:** from Orchomenus (2.5.37), and πρεσβύτατος (2.1.10, cf. 3.2.37n.) of the ἄρχοντες who deal with the Persian envoys who arrive the day after Cyrus' death, but not one of the original generals. Lendle 94 and Lee 2007: 51 suppose that he was at that meeting as a ὑποστράτηγος (but cf. 32n.), but he is already called a στρατηγός at 2.5.37; it is more likely that he was actually a λοχαγός at 2.5.37 or else that he had already replaced Xenias or Pasion and now took over Agias' troops too (Roy 1967: 289). Ἀρκάς brings out the continuity with Agias; **c**'s reading could be a contamination from 3.2.4. **Μένωνος:** a Thessalian, eponymous character in Plato's *Meno*, and recipient of a very hostile obituary at 2.6.21–9, which portrays him as self-centred, ruthless and corrupt. **Φιλήσιος Ἀχαιός:** mentioned five times subsequently, but not again in Books 3–4; along with Sophaenetus, one of the oldest of the generals (5.3.1). **Προξένου:** see 4n. **Ξενοφῶν Ἀθηναῖος:** held back until last (X. does not mention the replacements in the same order as the obituaries for the dead generals at 2.6). See 4n.

3.2 XENOPHON ADDRESSES THE WHOLE ARMY

At daybreak, as the whole army is assembled, it is addressed by Chirisophus, Cleanor and then Xenophon in directly reported speeches of increasing length and rhetorical bravura (1, 4, 7–32nn.). Xenophon's speech is interrupted by an omen and a vote (9) and followed by two more rounds of votes on practical measures at the instigation of Chirisophus (33) and of Xenophon himself (38).

Triads of speeches are not uncommon in epic and historiography, especially at times of intense crisis (Lang 1984: 22–4), but the present one is unusual, in that the speeches are not oppositional but complementary (*Hell.* 6.3.3–17 is similar but has speeches of even length). They are all designed to jolt the soldiers out of despondency (3.1.2n.). Chirisophus and Cleanor, two of the existing generals (3.1.32n.) and so known to the soldiers, prepare the ground, arguing, like Xenophon at 3.1.15–18, that the Persians cannot be trusted and that the only option left is to fight. Also like Xenophon (3.1.21–2(nn.)), both appeal to the gods and emphasize the terrible fate that will await the men should they fall into the king's hands. Chirisophus' speech is straightforward, while Cleanor drives home the point in strongly moral tones. It is left to Xenophon to explain why the army can look forward to the coming struggle with confidence and to propose practical measures that will ensure success.

The three speeches are alike in appealing to a Panhellenic and hoplite ethos (7–32, 19nn.), even though X.'s mention of the summoning of the whole army presumably includes the peltasts, many of whom were not Greek (see 36n., 4.8.4–7). This restricted focus continues the ethos of Xenophon's earlier speeches (see 3.1.21, 23, 42nn.).

3.2.1 ἥιρηντο: pluperfect, describing the result of the election (3.1.47 aorist ἡιρέθησαν) and functioning as the starting point for a new phase in the narrative; cf. 3.1.2n. **ἡμέρα τε σχεδὸν ὑπέφαινε καὶ ...** 'day had just begun to dawn and . . .' For intransitive ὑποφαίνω, see LSJ s.v. III. Parataxis with τε καί suggests a close connection between two events and is often used with time-markers to emphasize instant action; cf. e.g. 1.8.1; Hdt. 8.56, 83.1. The reference to dawn is symbolic, marking, as often, a new start or a turning point in narrative (Vivante 1979 on Homer; Aesch. *Pers.* 384–7). By placing the reference here rather than at the start of 3.3, the actual beginning of the army's retreat, X. suspensefully situates the lengthy assembly against the expectation that decisive events will soon take place. **εἰς τὸ μέσον:** 3.1.46n. **προφυλακὰς καταστήσαντας:** for the accusative participle, see 3.1.5n. on ἐλθόντα. There is nothing to choose between προφυλακάς (**c**, from προφυλακή 'outpost') and προφύλακας (**f**, from προφύλαξ 'advance guard'); cf. LSJ s.v. προφύλαξ. This precaution (not anticipated in Chirisophus' instructions at 3.1.46) reminds the reader that the Persians are near; cf. the mention of pickets as the first port of call for Persian envoys at 2.3.2, 4.15. **ὁ Λακεδαιμόνιος** underlines the reason for Chirisophus' leadership (37n.) and so for speaking first (even though Cleanor is older) and (together with ὧδε (3.1.27n.)) points to his stereotypically Spartan mode of speaking: as in his previous speech (3.1.45n.), he uses relatively brief, paratactic clauses (for Spartan impatience with long speeches and embellished rhetoric, cf. Hdt. 3.46.2; Thuc. 1.86.1). **ἔλεξεν:** 3.1.15n.

3.2.2 ὦ ἄνδρες στρατιῶται appeals to what the addressees have in common and underlines Chirisophus' call to arms (cf. Dickey 1996: 180; contrast bare ἄνδρες at 4). **χαλεπὰ μὲν τὰ παρόντα:** Chirisophus makes no attempt to assuage the soldiers' fears expressed at 3.1.2. **ὁπότε** 'now that' (causal: LSJ s.v. B). **ἀνδρῶν στρατηγῶν . . . καὶ στρατιωτῶν:** the seemingly otiose ἀνδρῶν emphasizes the generals' valour; contrast Thuc. 4.27.5 εἰ ἄνδρες εἶεν οἱ στρατηγοί. We find the same three ranks at 3.1.2, but in the earlier speeches the common soldiers who died (3.1.2n.) have not been mentioned; Chirisophus reintroduces them with a view to his audience. **πρὸς δ' ἔτι** 'and moreover', with adverbial πρός. **οἱ ἀμφὶ Ἀριαῖον** 'Ariaeus and his men'. **προδεδώκασιν:** the perfect tense emphasizes the irreversible nature of the betrayal (for which see 3.1.2n.) and Ariaeus' responsibility for it (*CGCG* 33.34–5). The betrayal (feared by Clearchus at 2.4.5) is further stressed by Cleanor (5) and then turned into an advantage by Xenophon (17).

3.2.3 ἐκ τῶν παρόντων 'in the present circumstances'. **ἄνδρας ἀγαθούς:** 3.1.21n. **τελέθειν:** for this deliberate Doricism (for γίγνεσθαι), see Introduction p. 30. **ὑφίεσθαι:** 3.1.17n. **πειρᾶσθαι ὅπως . . . σωιζώμεθα:** for the construction, see 3.1.38n. The present subjunctive σωιζώμεθα shows that Chirisophus envisages a long, continuous struggle. **εἰ δὲ μή . . . ἀποθνήισκωμεν** 'if not – at all events let us die nobly'. ἀλλά at the start of a main clause after a negative conditional, often combined with γε in X. and Plato (*GP* 12–13), introduces the only available alternative. **οἶμαι . . . παθεῖν . . . ποιήσειαν:** combining Xenophon's phrase from 3.1.17 with the wish (optative ποιήσειαν, cf. Smyth 1814a for this use in relative clauses) that the Persians may be punished by the gods. For παθεῖν ('be treated') and ποιεῖν ('treat'), cf. 3.3.13n.

3.2.4 Ἐπὶ τούτωι 'on top of that' rather than merely 'after that', suggesting that the next speaker will build on the previous speech. **Κλεάνωρ ὁ Ὀρχομένιος** is earlier called Ἀρκάς (3.1.47n.); the more specific reference here balances Χειρίσοφος ὁ Λακεδαιμόνιος. **ἀλλ':** on ἀλλά at the start of speeches, see 3.1.31n.; here it is assentient, expressing agreement with the previous speaker (*GP* 18). **ὁρᾶτε μέν . . . ὁρᾶτε δέ:** emphatic anaphora, without real antithesis (3.1.13n. on πάντα μὲν . . . πάντα δέ). The separation of the king and Tissaphernes is artificial, as the latter stresses that he acts on behalf of Artaxerxes in his dealings with the Greeks (2.3.17–20); Cleanor singles out Tissaphernes because the soldiers have actually seen him. His forceful style is marked by rhetorical repetitions and fullness of expression: αὐτὸς . . . αὐτὸς . . . αὐτὸς . . .; ἐξαπατήσας . . . ἐξαπατήσας . . . ἐξαπατηθῆναι; καὶ ἐδώκαμεν καὶ ἐλάβομεν; οὔτε . . . οὔτε . . .; his previous speeches (2.1.10–11, 5.39) are similarly forceful. **ἐπιορκίαν καὶ ἀσέβειαν . . . ἀπιστίαν:** strongly moral terms (Hirsch 1985: 31). Perjury (referring to the murder of the generals despite the sworn treaty) is implicitly linked to ἀσέβεια by Xenophon (3.1.22n.) and to ἀπιστία by Clearchus (2.4.7). At *Cyr.* 8.8.3, X. marks the betrayal of the generals as a turning point in Greek perceptions of Persians, claiming that thenceforth Persian ἀπιστία and ἀσέβεια were recognized. **ὅστις** is typifying: 'who is the kind of man who . . .' (Smyth 2496). **λέγων**, a present participle indicating repeated insistence, and the following three aorist participles are concessive. **ὡς** (rather than ὅτι) stresses that the reported speech is insincere (*CGCG* 41.6). **γείτων . . . Ἑλλάδος:** Cleanor reports Tissaphernes' words in front of the generals (2.3.18): γείτων οἰκῶ τῆι Ἑλλάδι (see 3.1.47n. for Cleanor's presence in that scene). **περὶ πλείστου . . . ἡμᾶς** 'he would make it his top priority to save us' (cf. LSJ s.v. περί A.IV). The potential optative echoes Tissaphernes' cautious promise (2.3.18 'I thought it a piece of good fortune if I could somehow persuade the king to allow me to lead you safely back to Greece'), but Cleanor ignores the reason for his caution (his need for the king's consent). **ὀμόσας . . . δεξιὰς δούς:** clasping the right hand (δεξίωσις) was an important way of guaranteeing oaths (Sommerstein and Bayliss 2013: 156–8). Tissaphernes had performed these acts together with the brother of the king's wife (2.3.28), and this had impressed Clearchus as a sign of the king's loyalty (2.4.7, cf. 5.3). **ἐξαπατήσας . . . τοὺς στρατηγούς:** by seizing them in his tent (2.5.32). **καὶ οὐδὲ Δία ξένιον ἠιδέσθη, ἀλλὰ . . .:** a long sentence gets longer still, as Cleanor adds one further and, given οὐδέ 'not even', climactic example of Tissaphernes' ἀπιστία. ξένιος is a common cult-title for Zeus in his capacity as protector of the sanctity of guests (Herman 1987: 125). **<ξένος>:** Castiglioni's addition makes sense of τε and results in a succession of near-synonyms which fits Cleanor's elaborate style. ξένος may have dropped out because of the preceding ξένιον. **ὁμοτράπεζος:** sharing food and libations, as Tissaphernes and Clearchus do (2.5.27), is a powerful symbol of the sacred bond between host and guest. For the sacrilege of breaking such a bond, cf. e.g. Aeschin. 3.224 (using ἀσέβημα); Herman 1987: 67. ὁμοτράπεζος is often used of a 'quasi-official' rank at Persian courts (e.g. 1.8.25; cf. Briant 2002: 308), but is not so here (since Clearchus would have been described as Tissaphernes' ὁμοτράπεζος instead of the other way around). **αὐτοῖς τούτοις ἐξαπατήσας** 'deceiving them through these very means' sums up the various examples of Tissaphernes' treachery. **ἀπολώλεκεν:** 2n. on προδεδώκασιν.

3.2.5 Ἀριαῖος δέ 'as for Ariaeus', a theme-constituent (3.3.16n.) in the nominative, followed by relative clauses, and picked up with καὶ οὗτος 'even that man', the start of the sentence proper (*CGCG* 60.34). **ὃν . . . ἠθέλομεν . . . καθιστάναι, καὶ ἐδώκαμεν καὶ ἐλάβομεν πιστά:** supply μεθ' οὗ with ἐδώκαμεν κτλ. (cf. 3.1.4n.). For the form ἐδώκαμεν (also at *Hell.* 6.3.6) instead of older ἔδομεν (*Cyr.* 6.1.8), see Introduction p. 28. See 2.1.4 for the Greeks' plan to make Ariaeus king after Cyrus' death and 2.2.8 for the exchange of pledges. **μή** is the common negative with infinitives after verbs of swearing (*CGCG* 51.31; Smyth 2725). **αἰδεσθείς:** earlier (2.5.39), addressing Ariaeus directly, Cleanor had made Ariaeus' breaking of his oath to the Greeks the central issue, but here he makes the problematic suggestion that respect for Cyrus is due also after his death (cf. Eur. *Hec.* 311–12): although betraying a tie of friendship was generally viewed as reprehensible, it is precisely because Cyrus died that Ariaeus was forced to look after his own interests. **τιμώμενος μάλιστα ὑπὸ Κύρου ζῶντος:** the present participles refer to continuous actions in the past (contrasting with νῦν). τιμή is a key concept in X.'s view of the mutually beneficial relationship between a leader and his followers, which 'emerges particularly in the bestowal of benefit from the leader to the follower' (Gray 2011: 294); for Cyrus' conception of this, cf. 1.9.28–9. **τοὺς ἐκείνου ἐχθίστους . . . ἡμᾶς τοὺς Κύρου φίλους** polarizes the two camps in terms associated with Cyrus. τοὺς Κύρου φίλους (with Cyrus' name instead of another pronoun and with positive rather than superlative form) has an official, honorific sound; a title used of Cyrus' non-Greek followers by Clearchus (2.2.3) and Cleanor himself (2.5.39, bitterly underlining their betrayal) is now applied to the Greeks.

3.2.6 ἀλλά: a breaking-off formula: 'enough said' (*CGCG* 59.11). **τούτους μὲν . . . · ἡμᾶς δέ:** Cleanor reverses the order of the wish and exhortation found in Chirisophus' speech (3). **ὅ τι ἂν δοκῆι τοῖς θεοῖς πάσχειν:** rather than raising doubts about the Greeks' prospects, Cleanor's surprisingly passive ending gives the gods their due (like the end of Chirisophus' speech; cf. 3.1.21n.) and sets off Xenophon's rousing speech.

3.2.7–32 Xenophon's lengthy speech is carefully constructed. It consists of three parts: (*a*) a brief recapitulation of what the previous speaker has said (8); (*b*) an enumeration of the good prospects (καλαὶ ἐλπίδες) of success (10–26); (*c*) the proposal of practical measures (27–32). Its main purpose is to cajole the soldiers into action and to define a new war aim, σωτηρία 'survival' (8, 15nn.; Dillery 1995: 69–70).

The core of the second part consists of a refutation of the soldiers' fears catalogued at 3.1.2. Xenophon suggests that the perceived problems are in fact advantages. There are particularly close correspondences with 3.1.2 in relation to Ariaeus' betrayal (17), the lack of cavalry (18), guides (20), supplies (21) and uncrossable rivers (22). These correspondences underline Xenophon's capacity to judge his audience.

The refutation is sandwiched between two arguments that respond more loosely to the soldiers' fears: Xenophon first reminds them of the Persian Wars (11–16), and then sketches a picture of the incapacity of the Persian king to control his own subjects, even flaunting (only to reject) the idea that the Greeks might settle in the Persian empire if they so wish (23–6). The section on the Persian Wars emphasizes the soldiers' common identity as Greeks, using verbal repetitions to present them as heirs to the men who saved Greece in the Persian Wars while effectively ignoring the non-Greek peltasts in the army (cf. 3.2n.). It is largely made up of topoi familiar from battle exhortations and Athenian funeral orations (especially Lys. 2.20–47; Pl. *Menex.* 240a–41d), here adapted to remove the exaltation of specifically Athenian glory and so appeal to Xenophon's diverse audience (11, 13nn.). When he turns to deal with the Persian empire, his point is also to reinforce a sense of the army as a coherent Greek community: permanent settlement would primarily be a threat not to the Persians, but to Greek identity. See further 25, 26nn.; Introduction p. 21.

The practical measures which Xenophon proposes in the third part of the speech aim at reinforcing the new command structure (29–32), but first (27–8) he suggests that the army dispose of wagons, tents and other possessions that do not help it to fight effectively or to obtain provisions (the two necessary conditions for achieving σωτηρία: 27n.). This proposal was recalled by Polyaen. *Strat.* 1.49.1; for its psychological effect, cf. Dion. Hal. *Ant. Rom.* 9.31.3 (perhaps inspired by this passage), where a speaker mentions generals who 'by burning their tents and baggage have imposed on their men the necessity of taking whatever they needed from enemy country'.

Xenophon's speech is a virtuoso performance. It contains a high number of syntactic irregularities which mimic extemporaneous speech. It also, however, shows many signs of self-conscious rhetorical sophistication: in true sophistic style Xenophon unashamedly turns the 'weaker case into the stronger' (Arist. *Rhet.* 1402a24), relying on εἰκός-arguments, humour, exaggeration and *reductio ad absurdum.* Other signs of rhetorical sophistication are the repeated use of the abstract concept σωτηρία, which unites the three main parts of the speech (8, 9, 10, 15, 32; cf. Allison 1997: 54–61 on Thucydides' thematic use of this noun), as well as elements associated with Gorgias such as explicit division into parts and the studied use of antithesis and assonance. The rhetorical self-consciousness is most evident in the refutation, which is an excellent example of the 'apagogic' style, according to which each possible source of fear is mentioned in turn and dealt with, only to be dismissed as irrelevant when it is replaced by the next. This is another specifically Gorgianic feature (Spatharas 2001: 405–8; 18, 20nn.); perhaps Xenophon is presented as surpassing Proxenus, a pupil of Gorgias (2.6.16). The apagogic style creates an impression of exhaustivity, which here compensates for Xenophon's unpersuasive treatment of several points. It also allows him to use similar arguments with different emphases: thus he claims first that the soldiers' piety, then that their bravery, will ensure divine support (11n.); he also suggests as grounds for confidence first their Persian Wars inheritance and then their own recent experience of fighting the Persians (16n.). The speech as a whole, then, aims for local effect rather than grand design.

3.2.7 Ἐκ τούτου: both 'after that' and 'on the basis of that (which Chirisophus and Cleanor had said)'. Asyndeton is standard in *An.* when the connection with the previous sentence is established by an anaphoric pronoun (here τούτου); contrast 3.3.6(n.). **Ξενοφῶν ἀνίσταται:** Xenophon's new position as protagonist is shown by the historical present (contrast ἀνέστη at 1, 4); by the omission of an ethnic (ὁ Ἀθηναῖος); and by the lack of any explanation for his role (contrast 3.1.34). **ἐσταλμένος** 'having fitted himself out', perfect middle participle of στέλλω. Although the moment at which Xenophon arms himself is not narrated, the dwelling on his armour (with triple repetition of superlatives of καλός) may recall arming scenes of Homeric heroes before their ἀριστεῖα (Tuplin 2003a: 121). **νομίζων, εἴτε . . . , εἴτε . . .:** as in Xenophon's interpretation of his dream (3.1.12n.), the bad alternative is treated second and at greater length, thereby making Xenophon's subsequent success more striking. The imbalance is reinforced by the pathos of the second clause (see below). There is a further contrast between διδοῖεν οἱ θεοί and impersonal δέοι: the gods are not to be held responsible for failure, only for victory. **κάλλιστον κόσμον:** for a fine appearance as suitable in death, cf. Hdt. 7.209.3; Dion. Hal. *Ant. Rom.* 3.18.2 ὡπλισμένους τε κάλλιστα καὶ τὸν ἄλλον ἔχοντας κόσμον οἷον ἄνθρωποι λαμβάνουσιν ἐπὶ θανάτωι. Xenophon's reasoning fits Chirisophus' rhetoric about the choice of victory or a noble death (3n.). This passage inspired Max. Tyr. 1.10 (on X.'s persuasiveness when equipped θώρακι καὶ ἀσπίδι) and Aelian (*VH* 3.24), though Aelian presents Xenophon's reasoning as a proverbial saying of X.'s and adds that he 'possessed an Argolic shield, an Attic breastplate, a helmet of Boeotian manufacture and a horse from Epidaurus' – a claim that reflects X.'s connoisseurship and Panhellenic connections, but is not tied to this specific occasion. **ὀρθῶς ἔχειν** 'it was right' (ἔχω plus adverb: 3.1.3n.) governs the infinitive τυγχάνειν. **τῶν καλλίστων ἑαυτὸν ἀξιώσαντα** 'having deemed himself worthy of the finest things'. ἀξιώσαντα agrees with the implied subject of τυγχάνειν (i.e. Xenophon). **ἐν τούτοις** picks up τῶν καλλίστων. **τῆς τελευτῆς τυγχάνειν** is a pathetic variation on τελευτᾶν, found in emotionally charged contexts at 2.6.29, *Hell.* 4.4.6. **τοῦ λόγου δὲ ἤρχετο ὧδε:** anticipating the interruption at 9.

3.2.8 τὴν . . . Κλεάνωρ: Xenophon picks up Cleanor's morally charged terms (4n.), but merges the parts played by the king, Tissaphernes and Ariaeus through the generalizing τῶν βαρβάρων, which hints at the stereotype of barbarian faithlessness (cf. Hdt. 8.142.5 βαρβάροισί ἐστι οὔτε πιστὸν οὔτε ἀληθὲς οὐδέν). The first μέν is 'inceptive', as often in the opening of formal speeches (cf. *GP* 383); the second sets up a contrast with ἐπίστασθε δέ. **ἐπίστασθε:** 3.1.35n. **οἶμαι** is parenthetical. **εἰ μὲν οὖν κτλ.:** οὖν is inferential ('so then, if . . .'), μέν looks forward to μέντοι, a more strongly adversative particle than δέ, rejecting rather than balancing the first alternative (cf. *GP* 409). **διὰ φιλίας ἰέναι** 'engage in friendly relations' (LSJ s.v. διά A.IV.b). The replacement of the language of oaths and truces with that of friendship, building on Cleanor's rhetoric (5n.), makes for a *reductio ad absurdum.* **ἀθυμίαν:** 3.1.3n. **τοὺς στρατηγούς . . . οἷα πεπόνθασιν:** the subject of this indirect exclamation (*CGCG* 42.11) is syntactically integrated into the governing clause, as object of ὁρῶντας (prolepsis: *CGCG* 60.37; Smyth 2182). The perfect (a present tense) suggests that the generals are envisaged as still being alive. **δίκην ἐπιθεῖναι**, a forceful variant for δίκην λαβεῖν, presents the Greeks as active agents of just war against the Persians (cf. the same phrase at *Ages.* 2.29); contrast Cleanor's reliance on the gods (6). The phrase is rare outside forensic and intra-state contexts. **σὺν τοῖς θεοῖς:** 3.1.23n. The gods are mentioned first, because their help underpins the other good prospects which Xenophon will list. **πολλαὶ . . . καὶ καλαὶ ἐλπίδες . . . σωτηρίας:** an implicit response to Phalinus' advice at 2.1.19 to resist if there is any hope of getting home safely (τῶν μυρίων ἐλπίδων μία τις . . . σωθῆναι), but to try to save themselves (σώιζεσθαι) any way they can if there is none (μηδεμία σωτηρίας . . . ἐλπίς). Phalinus thought the second alternative applied, but Xenophon now lists many good prospects. The phrases πολλαὶ ἐλπίδες (e.g. Hdt. 3.122.2, 5.30.6, 36.3; Thuc. 8.48.1; Eur. *Med.* 1032–3) and ἐλπὶς/ἐλπίδες σωτηρίας (e.g. *Hell.* 4.8.38; Thuc. 4.96.7,

8.82.1; Eur. *Hel.* 1031; Ar. *Thesm.* 946; [Dem.] 49.46) are often used of deluded or slender hopes; cf. also Nicias at Thuc. 7.77.1: 'we must have hope (ἐλπίδα) – people have in the past been saved (ἐσώθησαν) from more terrible situations' (see 36n. for other links with the closing stages of the Sicilian expedition). The addition of καλαί is therefore not superfluous (cf. e.g. *Eq. mag.* 7.3; Polyb. 2.70.7; Philemon fr. 197 K–A οἱ γὰρ θεὸν σέβοντες ἐλπίδας καλὰς | ἔχουσιν εἰς σωτηρίαν).

3.2.9 Τοῦτο δὲ λέγοντος αὐτοῦ πτάρνυταί τις: sneezing was often regarded as an omen (Lateiner 2005a: 99–100); here it is a good one because it coincides with Xenophon's uttering the word σωτηρίας, as indicated by singular τοῦτο and present λέγοντος. **προσεκύνησαν τὸν θεόν:** Ζεὺς σωτήρ (one of Zeus's Panhellenic cult-titles), as the omen suggests and Xenophon's next remark confirms (and *Anth. Pal.* 11.268.3 suggests that Ζεῦ σῶσον is a standard response to any sneeze). προσκύνησις is a form of worship that involves certain bodily movements of devotion (not just bowing: see Bowie on Hdt. 8.118.4); in Greece it is done for the gods, but the Persians also performed (what Greeks interpreted as) προσκύνησις for their rulers (13n. on οὐδένα . . . προσκυνεῖτε), assisting the Greek belief that all Persians were slaves to the king (3.1.17n.). For an ancient attempt (presumably inspired by this passage) to explain why προσκύνησις is a suitable response to sneezing, see Ath. 2.66c; it is similarly the response to an omen at *Cyr.* 2.4.19 and to a fart at Ar. *Eq.* 638–40. **οἰωνός:** originally 'bird', but in classical times used for all sorts of omens, including chance words (as in the formulaic phrase δέχομαι τὸν οἰωνόν; cf. Lateiner 2005b: 36). **εὔξασθαι . . . τοῖς ἄλλοις θεοῖς θύσειν:** for εὔχομαι 'vow', see LSJ s.v. II. The sacrifice, τῶι Διὶ τῶι σωτῆρι καὶ τῶι Ἡρακλεῖ . . . καὶ τοῖς ἄλλοις δὲ θεοῖς (4.8.25), takes place near Trapezus, the first Greek city the army reaches. **κατὰ δύναμιν:** according to X.'s Socrates (*Mem.* 4.3.16), it is generally accepted practice κατὰ δύναμιν ἱεροῖς θεοὺς ἀρέσκεσθαι. Cf. also *Mem.* 1.3.3; Hes. *Op.* 336; Arist. *Eth. Nic.* 1163b15–18, with Gray 2011: 304–6. **ἔφη:** 3.3.2n. **ἀνατεινάτω τὴν χεῖρα:** the same words (again preceded by ὅτωι δοκεῖ ταῦτα) are used of voting at 33, 38 (cf. ἀράτω τὴν χεῖρα at 5.6.33, 7.3.6), and also (presumably as a Xenophontic mannerism) at Lucian, *Deor. Conc.* 19, *Nav.* 31; *Etym. Magn.* s.v. καταχειροτονία. Besides this political use in the imperative, the phrase was used in religious contexts such as prayers and oaths (e.g. *Cyr.* 6.1.3; Pind. *Ol.* 7.65, *Isthm.* 6.41; Ar. *Av.* 623) – a usage that adds solemnity here. Voting by show of hands was used in the Athenian assembly (Hansen 1991: 147), where it was termed either χειροτονεῖν (not used in *An.*) or ψηφίζεσθαι (used in this sense at 31, 33; originally of voting by casting a pebble); but the procedure does not make the army a *polis* (Introduction pp. 4–6). **ἐκ τούτου:** 7n. **ἐπαιάνισαν:** i.e. made the shout ἰὴ παιών (associated with Apollo and so with healing and protection). This shout was often, as here, used in moments of danger and impending struggle (e.g. *Hell.* 4.7.4; Eur. *IT* 1403–4) or as a refrain after prayers (e.g. Ar. *Pax* 453); occasionally it simply indicated rejoicing (e.g. 6.1.11). **ἤρχετο:** *sc.* τοῦ λόγου (the full expression at 7).

3.2.10 πρῶτον μέν: picked up by ἔπειτα δέ in 11. Throughout, the divisions in Xenophon's speech are clearly signposted, which is characteristic of Gorgias (cf. MacDowell 17–18). The first good prospect is that the gods will probably be on the Greeks' side, a point made earlier by Xenophon (3.1.21) and here prepared by Cleanor (5 οὔτε θεοὺς δείσας). **ἐμπεδοῦμεν . . . ὅρκους** 'we stand true to the oaths sworn to the gods'. ἐμπεδόω is part of the official language used in the context of ratifying oaths (cf. the parodic use at Ar. *Lys.* 211, 233). τῶν θεῶν is objective genitive with ὅρκους (cf. how verbs of swearing can be followed by accusatives of the entity sworn by, e.g. 6.6.17 ὄμνυμι θεοὺς καὶ θεάς). **τὰς σπονδὰς . . . λελύκασιν:** 3.1.21n. **οὕτω δ' ἐχόντων:** 3.1.40n. **εἰκός:** cf. ὡς (τὸ) εἰκός (3.1.21n.), but here the argument from likelihood is logical. On εἰκός-argumentation in early Attic oratory, see Gagarin 1994. **τοὺς μεγάλους . . . βούλωνται:** a common enough sentiment, but with two twists. (*a*) X(enophon), presumably under Socratic influence, regularly associates the alternation between great and small with a lack of piety (6.3.18, *Mem.* 1.4.16, with Ellis 2016); more commonly, it is attributed to divine jealousy of human arrogance, prosperity or happiness (e.g. Soph. *Aj.* 131–3; Hdt. 1.32.1, 3.40.2–3, 7.10ε; Thuc. 7.77.3) or else to less transparent divine laws (e.g. *Hell.* 6.4.23, a speech of Jason of Pherae: ὁ θεὸς . . . πολλάκις χαίρει τοὺς μὲν μικροὺς μεγάλους ποιῶν, τοὺς δὲ μεγάλους μικρούς; Soph. *El.* 916–17; Dion. Hal. *Ant. Rom.* 7.3.4; and, without involvement of the gods, Hdt. 1.5.4). (*b*) Here the use of σώιζειν rather than μεγάλους ποιεῖν avoids the idea of circularity found in many formulations of this sentiment, assimilating it to the rhetoric of salvation in this speech. **κἄν:** 3.1.36n. **εὐπετῶς** 'easily' – a characteristic of divine action (cf. e.g. Hom. *Il.* 22.18–19: τοὺς δὲ σάωσας | ῥηϊδίως).

3.2.11 ἔπειτα δέ, ἀναμνήσω γάρ . . . ἵνα εἰδῆτε: ἔπειτα δέ does not syntactically qualify a clause: Xenophon inserts a parenthetical, anticipatory γάρ-clause (3.1.24n.), but proceeds to treat it as the leading clause, making ἵνα εἰδῆτε depend on it (instead of saying εὖ ἴστε). ἀναμνήσω, followed by a double accusative, is future indicative rather than aorist subjunctive, the former being common when speakers announce a transition to a new topic (cf. 14 ἐρῶ; Pelliccia 1995: 325–7). **τοὺς τῶν προγόνων τῶν ἡμετέρων κινδύνους:** the Persian invasions of 490 and 480–479 BC. Greek does not usually employ possessive pronouns when ownership is clear, but explicit references to 'our ancestors' may be formulaic in Athenian funeral orations (cf. Lys. 2.6 τῶν ἡμετέρων προγόνων, with Todd), and here take on Panhellenic significance: Xenophon's audience consists of Greeks from many different cities and in fact includes men whose ancestors fought on the side of the Persians (cf. Flower 2012: 180). **ὡς ἀγαθοῖς τε . . . σῴζονταί τε . . . οἱ ἀγαθοί** 'how brave . . . and that . . . the brave are saved'. ὡς followed by an adjective that denotes a measurable quality often introduces an indirect exclamation rather than an indirect statement (*CGCG* 42.11). Xenophon provides in advance the conclusion his audience should draw from the ensuing story; προσήκει, a word with kinship connotations (cf. οἱ προσήκοντες 'family relations'), suggests that the Greeks' bravery derives from their ancestors. Whereas Xenophon's previous point was that the gods deliver the pious (10n.), he now suggests that they favour the brave. **ἐλθόντων . . . στόλωι:** Darius sent an expedition to Greece in 490 BC in revenge for Athenian involvement in the Ionian revolt, in particular the burning of Sardis (Hdt. 5.97–105). Emphasis on the size of the invading army (here stressed through a παν- compound; cf. 3.3.13n.) is commonplace (e.g. Lys. 2.20; Pl. *Menex.* 240a; Isoc. 4.71). The Persian army was traditionally multi-ethnic, but the explicit reference to the Persian allies here is pertinent, because it both taps into Xenophon's audience's recent experiences at Cunaxa (1.8.9) and foreshadows the fact that they will have to pass through the territory of many different peoples. **αὐτοὶ Ἀθηναῖοι τολμήσαντες ἐνίκησαν:** at Marathon. The Athenians' 'daring' lay in their willingness to fight αὐτοί 'by themselves', i.e. before help from allies arrived (though they did in fact receive help from Plataea). Both daring (e.g. Lys. 2.22) and fighting alone (e.g. Pl. *Menex.* 240c; [Dem.] 60.10; Walters 1981) were patriotic topoi of Athenian funeral orations that provided X(enophon) with suitable analogies for the present situation (cf. 3.1.16n.); significantly, he does not add the standard rider in fourth-century rhetoric on Marathon (for which see Marincola 2007: 115), namely that the Athenians secured the 'salvation of all Greeks'. Xenophon's rhetoric need not, then, be explained by Athenocentrism (Loraux 2006: 191) or seen as apologetic, the exiled X. showing the Athenians that he exalted Athenian glory (Luccioni 1947: 34 n. 28); cf. Flower 2012: 181.

3.2.12 εὐξάμενοι . . . ἔδοξεν αὐτοῖς: nominative participle, as if 'they decided' follows, but Xenophon shifts to the impersonal expression. The vow mirrors the vow just made to Zeus Soter and other gods (9); it is otherwise mentioned (with variations) only by Plut. *Mor.* 862b–c; Ael. *VH* 2.25; and Σ Ar. *Eq.* 660a. **ὁπόσους κατακάνοιεν:** indirect speech for ὁπόσους ἂν κατακάνωμεν. For κατακαίνω, see 3.1.2n. Herodotus (6.117.1) puts the number of Persian casualties at 6,400. **καταθύσειν:** the compound verb, often used of sacrificing animals, creates a (Gorgianic) jingle with κατακάνοιεν (the simple verb is used later in the sentence). **ἔτι καὶ νῦν ἀποθύουσιν:** the prefix ἀπο- signals the repayment of a debt. The sacrifice was held on the sixth day of the Athenian month Boedromion (i.e. late summer). Mention of it here reinforces the rhetoric about a small army being victorious over a much larger one (45,000 goats should have been sacrificed by now); suggests continuity between the past and the present (cf. Due 1989: 31–8 on ἔτι καὶ νῦν in *Cyr.*); and foreshadows the festival for Artemis that Xenophon himself set up during his exile at Scillus (5.3.9–13).

3.2.13 ἔπειτα: the asyndeton connects the two expeditions more closely (contrast 11). **Ξέρξης . . . Ἑλλάδα:** in 480 BC. τήν shows that Xenophon refers to a generally known fact. For the uncountability of Xerxes' army, cf. Lys. 2.27; Herodotus (7.60.1) gives a global figure of 1,700,000 for his ground forces, but claims to be unable to give a precise breakdown. **ἐνίκων** 'were victorious'; for imperfects that denote a state rather than incomplete action, see *CGCG* 33.18; Smyth 1887. The imperfect is typically used in listing victories; the aorist ἐνίκησαν (11) is used in a context in which there is some stress on the battle itself (specified by ὑποστῆναι . . . τολμήσαντες) (cf. Rood 1998a: 242–3). **τούτων:** the demonstrative pronoun οὗτος is the standard way of referring to one's opponent in Attic courts, and is repeatedly used of the Persians in this speech (14, 17, 21, 23). **καὶ κατὰ γῆν καὶ κατὰ θάλατταν:** this formulaic phrase (× 15 in X.) groups together the victories at Plataea on land in 479 BC and at Salamis by sea in 480 BC (obscuring the fact that Xerxes himself returned to Asia before Plataea). Xenophon departs from their chronological order so as to highlight the victory on land (the salient point in the present circumstances). Grouping the battles also appeals to his Panhellenic audience (note the shift from 'the Athenians' to οἱ ἡμέτεροι πρόγονοι): though neither battle was fought by a single city (cf. *Hell.* 6.5.34), Salamis came to be seen as an Athenian victory, Plataea as a Spartan one (in Athenian funeral orations, Plataea is given relatively short shrift and presented as having come about through Athenian persuasion (Lys. 2.44–7) or Athenian and Spartan cooperation (Pl. *Menex.* 241c)). **ὧν . . . τὰ τρόπαια** 'as tokens (predicative τεκμήρια) of these things (ὧν = connecting relative) it is possible (ἔστι: 39n.) to see the trophies'. References to trophies are another stock element of funeral orations (e.g. Gorg. DK 82 B5b, 6; Lys. 2.20, 25; Pl. *Menex.* 240d). In due course, the Ten Thousand will erect trophies over the Persians (4.6.27, 6.5.32). **ἡ ἐλευθερία τῶν πόλεων:** the Persian Wars are traditionally represented as a fight for freedom over slavery (e.g. Thuc. 2.36.1; Lys. 2.26, 44, 47; Pl. *Menex.* 240e; cf. 3.1.17n.). **ἐγένεσθε καὶ ἐτράφητε** suggests both that the soldiers are the natural heirs to the generation that fought the Persian Wars and that they have an obligation to preserve the values their ancestors taught them; the idea that citizens should repay the cost of their upbringing to the *polis* through military service was commonplace (e.g. Lys. 2.70; Isoc. 6.108; Lycurg. 1.53; cf. Liddel 2007: 140–1). **οὐδένα . . . προσκυνεῖτε:** 9n. Hdt. 7.136.1 is the classic expression of this cliché. δεσπότην (predicative: 'as master') is used to describe a relation of ownership, especially of slaves (e.g. *Oec.* 12.18), and so contrasts with ἐλευθερία.

3.2.14 τοιούτων μέν ἐστε προγόνων 'such are the ancestors from whom you are sprung'. προγόνων is predicative (note the lack of article). **οὐ μὲν δή** (*GP* 393) often corrects an assumption (here spelt out in the ὡς-clause, which is anticipated by τοῦτό γε). **ἀλλ'** 'on the contrary' introduces a more relevant point. Athenian funeral orations similarly shift from the Persian Wars to the current generation (Lys. 2.67–8; Pl. *Menex.* 246a), but without pre-emptive moves against any possible misunderstanding of the rhetoric; Xenophon adapts this rhetoric for his downcast Panhellenic audience. The rhetorical move he rejects was familiar from Homer (e.g. *Il.* 4.370–400: Agamemnon disparages Diomedes by praising his father Tydeus). **οὔπω πολλαὶ ἡμέραι ἀφ' οὗ** 'it is only a few days since' (in fact about forty-five): supply εἰσι with πολλαὶ ἡμέραι; ἀφ' οὗ is formulaic for 'since', so agreement between οὗ and ἡμέραι is not required. **τούτοις τοῖς ἐκείνων ἐκγόνοις:** the remote demonstrative pronoun ἐκεῖνος for the Persians of the past, οὗτος for the current opponents. **πολλαπλασίους ὑμῶν αὐτῶν . . . σὺν τοῖς θεοῖς:** rather than being an adjective with ἐκγόνοις in the dative, πολλαπλασίους is used substantivally ('many more men') and functions as object of ἐνικᾶτε. The word implies comparison, and so a genitive follows. Each word drives home the analogy with the Persian Wars (πολλαπλασίους ~ παμπληθεῖ (11), ἀναρίθμητον (13); ἐνικᾶτε ~ ἐνίκησαν (11), ἐνίκων (13); σὺν τοῖς θεοῖς ~ εὐξάμενοι τῆι Ἀρτέμιδι (12)). The battle of Cunaxa is presented as a resounding victory, with due rhetorical exaggeration; see 3.1.23n.

3.2.15: for Xenophon's style here, see Introduction pp. 35–6. **δή** indicates that Xenophon regards the point as obvious (3.1.2n.). **περὶ τῆς Κύρου βασιλείας:** Xenophon does away with Cleanor's point that the situation can still be understood in terms of Cyrus' cause (5n.), preparing for his depiction of the current phase of the struggle as defensive. His picture of selfless Greeks obscures the fact that they were mercenaries for whom material gain and other rewards were at stake. **ὁπότε:** 2n. **περὶ . . . σωτηρίας** is formulaic in the context of battles (Thuc. 6.69.3, 7.61.1, 70.7, in relation to the Athenian force in Sicily) and deliberations (Thuc. 5.87, 88; Ar. *Eccl.* 396–7; [Arist.] *Ath. Pol.* 29.2, 4, with Rhodes 1972: 231–5); the underlying idea that wars on foreign soil are really defensive and so should inspire greater bravery in the troops is a recurring theme in battle exhortations (e.g. Thuc. 4.95.2, 7.64, with Luschnat 1942: 55; Leimbach 1985: 74; see 3.4.46n.). **ἀγών:** for the contest imagery, see 3.1.16n. **δήπου** 'surely'. **προσήκει:** 11n. **προθυμοτέρους:** another topos of battle exhortations (e.g. Thuc. 6.68.4, 7.66.1), picking up the τόλμα-rhetoric at 11.

3.2.16 ἀλλὰ μήν 'moreover'. **σὺν τῶι πατρίωι φρονήματι:** the point is driven home by τὸ πλῆθος ἄμετρον and ἐτολμήσατε, which echo the earlier presentation of the Persian Wars (11n.). **πεῖραν ἤδη ἔχετε:** for rhetorical appeals to the advantage of experience of the same enemy, see Hdt. 9.46.2 (Athenian experience of the Persians); Kraus on Livy 6.7.4. **οὐ θέλουσι . . . δέχεσθαι:** for the form θέλουσι, see 3.5.8n. Ascribing a lack of fighting spirit to the enemy is standard rhetoric in battle exhortations (e.g. Thuc. 5.9.6). At Cunaxa, the Persian contingent opposite the Greeks was soon in full flight, according to X.'s presentation of events (1.8.21, 10.4). **καὶ . . . ὄντες** 'even though they are' (concessive); πολλαπλάσιοι echoes πολλαπλασίους (14). **προσήκει** through its kinship connotations (11n.) picks up the earlier linking of the audience's recent success in fighting the Persians and their ancestors' achievements in the Persian Wars; the emphasis has now shifted from the Greeks' debt to their inheritance (σὺν τῶι πατρίωι φρονήματι) to the confidence produced by experience.

3.2.17 μηδὲ μέντοι . . . εἰ 'again, do not think you are worse off (ἔχω plus adverb: 3.1.3n.) in this respect, if . . .'. μηδέ adds a fresh point, μέντοι gives force to the addition; the combination is rare (*GP* 410, with 413–14 on positive καὶ . . . μέντοι). τοῦτο points forward to εἰ, which is occasionally used instead of ὅτι to present a (distasteful) fact as a supposition (Wakker 1994: 291–2). For μεῖον, see 3.4.34n. **οἱ Κύρειοι** 'those (*sc.* enemies, from 16 τοὺς πολεμίους) connected with Cyrus'. This reference to the troops under Ariaeus is a suitable starting point for Xenophon's *refutatio* (7–32n.) as it picks up the two previous speeches (2, 5nn.). For the adjectival form, cf. 1.10.1 τὸ Κύρειον στρατόπεδον; Thuc. 5.67.1 οἱ Βρασίδειοι, with *CT*. The phrase has been rejected by modern editors (see the apparatus) because the first hand of **C** had a different (now illegible) reading and because X. elsewhere (× 4 in *Hell.* and *Ages.*) and Isocrates (4.144) apply Κύρειος/Κύρειοι to the remnants of the Ten Thousand in Spartan service (later in antiquity it became a way of referring to the Ten Thousand as a whole (Polyaen. *Strat.* 7.16.1; Lib. *Or.* 18.79)). But the phrase need not have had a specific connotation either when X. wrote *An.* or during the expedition itself; the reference to non-Greek troops is clear from the context; and Κύρειοι (suggesting their special status as troops selected by Cyrus himself) makes for a good rhetorical climax after the dismissal of the king's army, increasing the indignation at their betrayal. **ἀφεστήκασιν**: Xenophon prepares for his next argument by speaking of desertion rather than betrayal, as before. **κακίονες:** Xenophon adds a tactical argument to Cleanor's moral one (5n.), namely that defectors are cowards and so better in the enemy's ranks than the Greeks'. The casuistical flavour is characteristic of sophistic argumentation. **ἔφυγον γοῦν:** γοῦν 'at any rate' offers (minimal) evidence for the preceding statement (*CGCG* 59.54; *GP* 451). Xenophon conflates their flight in the battle of Cunaxa (1.9.31–10.1) with their later decision to go over to the king. **τοὺς δ' ἐθέλοντας φυγῆς ἄρχειν** 'men who are willing to take the lead in flight', thereby perverting their proper duty of leading the charge; the implication is that they may flee again, and that the other divisions of the enemy army will then follow. ἐθέλοντας ironically plays on the positive connotations of volunteering (for which see 3.3.18n.). **πολὺ κρεῖττον:** *sc.* ἐστί. For the argument that deserters are better in enemy ranks, cf. Dio Cass. 41.35.2 τίς δ' οὐκ ἂν εὔξαιτο τοιούτους ἐκείνωι στρατιώτας ὑπάρξαι; Xenophon formulates this argument as a general statement, making its validity seem absolute and, perhaps, addressing anyone in his audience who may be contemplating defection. **ἐν τῆι ἡμετέραι τάξει:** not just variation for σὺν ἡμῖν (ταττομένοις): Xenophon implies that cowardly barbarians destroy the archetypal Greek τάξις (cf. 1.2.18, 5.4.20, 8.13). Cf. the abuse of barbarian disorder in speeches at Thuc. 4.126.5 οὔτε γὰρ τάξιν ἔχοντες αἰσχυνθεῖεν ἂν λιπεῖν τινὰ χώραν; Dio Cass. 38.45.4.

3.2.18 εἰ δέ τις ὑμῶν ἀθυμεῖ introduces the next source of fear that Xenophon will dispel, in accordance with the apagogic style (7–32n.). **οἱ μύριοι ἱππεῖς:** the article is dismissive, referring to 'the' 10,000 enemy horsemen the soldiers have, according to Xenophon, conjured up in their imagination. Earlier X. mentions reports of 6,000 horsemen in the king's army (1.7.11). **ὑπὸ μὲν γὰρ ἵππου . . . ἀπέθανεν:** the point is unpersuasive: soon the lack of cavalry will cause major problems (3.3.8, 9nn.; also e.g. 5.6.8, 6.5.29, 7.6.29), which Xenophon tries to overcome by establishing a makeshift cavalry contingent (3.3.19, 20nn.). The argument is presented in hyperbolic terms and with 'a welcome sense of humour' (Usher 1969: 78), which indicates that Xenophon is just doing his best to assuage the soldiers' fears (Rood 2004a: 314); cf. Crassus at Dio Cass. 38.45.5, telling his soldiers not to fear barbarian shouting: φωνή τε γὰρ οὐδένα πώποτε ἀνθρώπων ἀπέκτεινε. **οἱ δὲ ἄνδρες . . . γίγνηται** 'but the men are the ones who do whatever happens in battles'. The articles are generic (*CGCG* 28.6; Smyth 1122–3). Xenophon prudently does not spell out what actually happens in battles.

3.2.19 οὐκοῦν very occasionally introduces a new step in an argument (*Mem.* 3.8.9, with *GP* 435), here that horses are not just useless but actually detrimental. Given that MSS constantly confuse οὐκοῦν and οὔκουν, it is possible to read a rhetorical question: οὔκουν . . . ; 'isn't it so that . . .?' **πολύ,** repeated twice in anaphora, is hyperbolic. **ὀχήματος** 'foundation': six times in X., but otherwise attested in Attic only in tragedy, lyric parts of comedy and Plato, mostly in the late dialogues. It may be a pompous poeticism, covering over the weakness of the argument, but its use in X. and Plato may also indicate that, like other originally Ionic neuters in -μα, the word had become part of 'Great Attic' (see Introduction pp. 27–8). **κρέμανται** 'hang on', a graphic exaggeration, though Persian and Greek horsemen sat on cloths or rode bareback and had no stirrups, and so were easily unseated if their horses suddenly reared (cf. *Eq.* 7.5–7; Evans 1986–7: 100). **τὸ καταπεσεῖν:** articular infinitive, functioning as the object of φοβούμενοι (*CGCG* 51.39; Smyth 2034a). **ἐπὶ γῆς βεβηκότες:** the lack of an article lends the phrase a solemnity (contrast *Cyr.* 5.2.15 ἐπὶ γῆς 'on earth' with *Cyr.* 4.5.54 ἐπὶ τῆς γῆς 'on the ground') that contrasts with the frivolous κρέμανται. As often, the perfect of βαίνω means 'stand firm' (LSJ s.v. A.2; cf. the etymologically related βέβαιος). The alleged advantage of hoplites over cavalry may owe something to rhetorical contrasts (e.g. Thuc. 4.10.4) between land-battles, which are determined by courage, and sea-battles, which are unpredictable (the association of horses or chariots with ships was a literary and artistic commonplace; see Kowalzig 2013: 46 n. 27 for references). **προσίῃι** 'attacks' (LSJ s.v. πρόσειμι (εἶμι) 2). **ὅτου:** for τούτου ὅ (relative attraction: 3.1.8n.). **ἑνὶ μόνωι:** the asyndeton is apt: Xenophon suddenly thinks of another point, and adds it as an afterthought (a gesture may be envisaged). **φεύγειν:** for asyndeton following the explicit announcement of a point, see 3.1.11n. The climactic word, intended to raise a laugh, occupies the first position in the clause. But there is irony here, as it is precisely the impossibility of pursuing the enemy which makes the lack of cavalry so problematic: see 3.3.15, and compare the soldiers' fears at 3.1.2(n.).

3.2.20 εἰ δὲ δή ('but suppose that actually', cf. e.g. Thuc. 3.40.4, 6.37.1) **. . . θαρρεῖτε . . . ὅτι δὲ . . . τοῦτο ἄχθεσθε, σκέψασθε:** εἰ governs θαρρεῖτε (here plus accusative, 'are confident about') and ἄχθεσθε, the ὅτι-clause depends on τοῦτο ἄχθεσθε, and the main clause starts at σκέψασθε. Xenophon's loose way of connecting arguments is characteristic of the apagogic style (7–32n.): he first concedes that the previous argument is invalid or irrelevant, then introduces the next source of fear which he will dismiss. **κρεῖττον** again signals Xenophon's attempt to turn a definite disadvantage into a positive asset (cf. 17, 21). **φανερός:** 3.1.36n. The implication here is that Tissaphernes' subsequent betrayal shows that his earlier offer to guide the Greeks was deceptive. **οὓς ἂν ἡμεῖς ἄνδρας λαβόντες . . . κελεύωμεν** 'men whom we capture and order'. ἄνδρας, the antecedent of οὕς, is incorporated into the relative clause (*CGCG* 50.15; Smyth

2536). **τι περὶ ἡμᾶς ἁμαρτάνωσι** 'make a mistake in anything that concerns us'; τι underlines the complete powerlessness of the guides as envisaged by Xenophon. **περὶ τὰς ἑαυτῶν ψυχὰς καὶ σώματα ἁμαρτάνουσι:** περὶ τοῦ σώματος/τῆς ψυχῆς (κινδυνεύω) is a common phrase in oratory to refer to the risk of capital punishment (e.g. Antiph. 2.1.4, 2.4.5, 6.1), but this amplified form, with both terms for 'life', appears to be unique (for the pathos, cf. Dio Cass. 40.64.3). For the use of a single article with two nouns that form a close unity, see Smyth 1143. Xenophon's theory is put into practice at 4.1.23–5.

3.2.21 τὰ δὲ ἐπιτήδεια is thrown forward as the new topic (cf. 3.1.14(n.) ἐγὼ οὖν). **πότερον** still depends on σκέψασθε (20). **ὠνεῖσθαι κρεῖττον:** contrast κρεῖττον Τισσαφέρνη: the occurrence of κρεῖττον is now predictable and so appears after the focus of the sentence, ὠνεῖσθαι (*CGCG* 60.23). **ἧς:** relative attraction (3.1.8n.). **μικρὰ μέτρα πολλοῦ ἀργυρίου:** a succinct and euphonic antithesis. μικρὰ μέτρα is in apposition to τὰ ἐπιτήδεια (see Smyth 981 on 'partitive apposition'). Even under Cyrus, the Greeks had trouble buying sufficient food at the market attached to the army because of the high prices (1.5.6); see further 3.1.2n. The issue of provisions is raised again by Xenophon at 34(n.). **μηδὲ τοῦτο ἔτι ἔχοντας:** with ἔχοντας supply ἡμᾶς (subject accusative with ὠνεῖσθαι). τοῦτο refers back to ἀργυρίου. μηδέ is used under the influence of ὠνεῖσθαι, which, if negated, would take μή, not οὐ (Smyth 2737). **αὐτούς** 'ourselves'. **ἥνπερ κρατῶμεν:** the full thought at 39. **ὁπόσωι** 'as large as'; supply χρῆσθαι from the main clause. Clearchus, by contrast, mentioned a potential lack of provisions as a reason to stick with Tissaphernes (2.5.9), and the Greeks will in fact occasionally experience dangerous shortages (4.1.9, 7.3).

3.2.22 εἰ δὲ ταῦτα μὲν . . . κρείττονα (*sc.* ἐστι)**:** the same rhetorical move as at 20(n.), but with a different formulation. ταῦτα (proleptic: 8n.) prepares for the contrast with τοὺς δὲ ποταμούς. **ἄπορον** 'a difficulty' (cf. LSJ s.v. ἄπορος II for τὸ ἄπορον). But Xenophon also hints at the adjective's regular meaning 'impassable' (e.g. ἄποροι in the following sentence). **μεγάλως:** with ἐξαπατηθῆναι. **διαβάντες:** see 2.4.13–24, where the Greeks suspected that the Persians tried to coax them into crossing the Tigris. **εἰ ἄρα:** ἄρα in conditionals indicates surprise (Wakker 1994: 346), here that felt by the soldiers when they discover that what seemed a problem is in fact a sign of stupidity on the part of the enemy. **μωρότατον** 'as a very foolish thing' (predicative); the superlative only here in X. **πεποιήκασιν:** the perfect of an act that cannot be undone (*CGCG* 33.34). **προσιοῦσι** 'for people who go . . .' A regular generic use of the dative participle in geographical descriptions (Smyth

1497). The implication is that the Greeks will be compelled to march to the sources of a river and so live off the land of the Persians longer. In the event, they march beyond the sources of the Tigris (4.4.3), though they no longer follow the river after 3.5 (where a plan to cross it is dismissed); but in the mean time they have to cross the Zapatas (3.3.6) and, with considerable difficulty, the Centrites (4.3.3–34). Rivers remain a problem later in the march, too (5.6.9–10). Cf. the river image at *Hell.* 4.2.12.

3.2.23 εἰ δὲ . . . φανεῖται: on the function of εἰ δέ, see 18n. Here the suggestion is that even with two points conceded, all is not lost. For εἰ with future indicative (διήσουσιν from διίημι 'let through' (LSJ s.v. 2)), see 3.1.13n. **οὐδ' ὣς ἡμῖν γε ἀθυμητέον** 'not even so do *we* need to despair'. For the impersonal construction, see 3.1.7, 35nn. ὥς is demonstrative (= οὕτως: LSJ s.v. ὡς A.a.2–3), γε limitative (*CGCG* 59.53; *GP* 140), suggesting that others might despair in such a situation. **Μυσούς** stands in prolepsis (8n.). The Mysians were a people of Hellespontine Phrygia, most of whom, according to *Hell. Oxy.* 24.1, were 'autonomous and not subject to the king'. **οὓς . . . εἶναι:** Xenophon's boast has an epic ring to it (e.g. Hom. *Il.* 2.248–9 οὐ γὰρ ἐγὼ σέο φημὶ χερειότερον βροτὸν ἄλλον | ἔμμεναι), and supports his argument that if the king would like to be rid of the Mysians, he would *a fortiori* want to be rid of the Greeks; cf. *Hell.* 4.8.5 for a similar argument involving free cities in Persia. **βασιλέως ἄκοντος:** this phrase (3.3.4n.) makes for the type of rhetorical jingle of which Xenophon is fond in this speech. **πολλάς τε . . . πόλεις:** the archaeological evidence suggests that this is a rhetorical overstatement (Tuplin 2004a: 179). The pairing of εὐδαίμων and μέγας is formulaic in descriptions of cities (× 11 in *An.*; cf. 3.4.7n.); found already in Herodotus (5.31.3 (of an island), 8.111.2) and Aristophanes (*Av.* 37), it recurs in later historiography, and its stylistic effect is discussed at Ps.-Aristid. *Rh.* 2.69 Patillon. **Πισίδας:** see Introduction p. 3. X. often links them with the Mysians as the prime examples of peoples within the Persian empire who kept their independence and were enough of a nuisance to require occasional military intervention (1.9.14, *Hell.* 3.1.13, *Mem.* 3.5.26); Clearchus had suggested to Tissaphernes that the Greek mercenaries could help him against both (2.5.13). **Λυκάονας δὲ καὶ αὐτοὶ εἴδομεν** 'as for the Lycaonians, we have even seen for ourselves'. X. reported that Cyrus allowed the Greeks to plunder Lycaonia as they marched through it (1.2.19), but not the observation Xenophon makes here about the Lycaonians' use of mountain strongholds. Xenophon is thus shown to have a superior ability to draw lessons from the army's experiences (cf. Rood 2014: 78). Much less is known about the Lycaonians from Greek sources than about the Mysians and Pisidians (Tuplin 2004a: 179–81): hence Xenophon appeals to autopsy for the former and to general knowledge for the latter (cf.

repeated ἐπιστάμεθα). **τὴν τούτων χώραν καρποῦνται:** τούτων refers to the Persians. The picture Xenophon sketches here is almost one of 'internal colonization', with the Lycaonians taking over the exploitation of Persian soil (Tuplin 2004a: 179). A fictitious story about the Chaldaeans ravaging Armenian territory from their mountain strongholds at *Cyr.* 3.2 is perhaps inspired by his experience with the Lycaonians.

3.2.24 καὶ ἡμᾶς δ' ἂν ἔφην ἔγωγε: for καὶ . . . δέ, see 3.3.2n. The use of the counterfactual construction ('I would (almost) say') is explained by ἀλλὰ . . . δέδοικα (25). γε qualifies the entire phrase rather than ἐγώ alone (*GP* 122); the pronoun, used in a late position in the clause, need not be emphatic (Dik 2003). **μήπω φανεροὺς εἶναι . . . ὡς αὐτοῦ που οἰκήσοντας:** ὡς with future participle here indicates pretence rather than purpose (*CGCG* 52.39): countering the soldiers' earlier fear that the king might try to keep them within his empire (2.4.4), Xenophon argues that they should give the king the impression (cf. φανερούς; also εἰ ἑώρα at the end of this section) that they may settle in the Persian empire, and so coax him into helping them leave. Xenophon does not regard permanent settlement as a genuine alternative to returning to Greece. Cf. 2.4.22 for Persian fears that the Greeks may permanently settle in their lands, and Hdt. 2.103.2 for an example of part of an invading army settling abroad. **οἶδα:** boldly presented as a certainty, the following claim does not convey what Xenophon thinks may actually happen, but encouragingly suggests that the soldiers' distress at being in Persia is matched by the king's distress at having them there. **πολλοὺς μὲν . . . ἐκπέμψειν:** for the repetition of ἄν without a verb, see Smyth 1766; for the genitive of the articular infinitive with purpose value, see *CGCG* 51.46; Smyth 2032e. Xenophon imagines a scenario in which the king allows the Mysians safe passage out of his realm and offers them hostages as a security against deception (a common practice: Amit 1970: 133–4). The emphatic anaphora of πολλούς underlines the king's putative desperation, but is somewhat empty, as the quantity of guides and hostages matters less than their quality (cf. 7.4.24 for a bad sort of hostage). **ἀδόλως** is a common word in treaties and oaths of peace (e.g. 2.2.8, 3.26, *Hell.* 3.4.6; cf. Thuc. 5.18.9, 23.2, 47.8, all citations of actual treaties). **ὁδοποιήσειέ γ':** the most far-reaching and costly measure the king would take – road-building – is stressed by γε. The formulation may suggest knowledge of royal roads (Tuplin 2004a: 173 n. 62). Xenophon later envisages the Greek cities on the coast of the Black Sea repairing or building roads for the Ten Thousand to be rid of them (5.1.13–14). **καὶ εἰ** 'even if' stresses the king's eagerness: four-horse chariots would require wide roads of high quality. But while such chariots were used in Assyrian and Persian armies (cf. 1.8.10 for scythed chariots at Cunaxa), the idea of Mysians possessing them is fanciful. The Greeks associated four-horse chariots above all with the heroic past (hence τέθριππος is frequent in tragedy (e.g. Eur. *Hipp.* 1212)) and with the Panhellenic games (e.g. Hdt. 6.103.2). **οἶδ' ὅτι** is parenthetical (cf. 3.1.16n.). **τρισάσμενος** 'thrice-pleased' does not recur until late antiquity, but the formation is of a familiar type; cf. e.g. τρίσμακαρ/τρισμακάριος, τρισόλβιος, found in epic and drama.

3.2.25 ἀλλὰ γάρ: with ἀλλά Xenophon breaks off the current topic (6n.), with γάρ he explains why (*CGCG* 59.57). His fear does not concern what will happen if they actually settle (never a serious proposal), but what will happen if they linger long enough to give the king the impression that they will. **ἄν** = ἐάν. **ζῆν . . . βιοτεύειν:** the use of near-synonymous verbs is a Gorgianic touch (e.g. DK 82 B11.7 ἀνόμως ἐβιάσθη καὶ ἀδίκως ὑβρίσθη). βιοτεύω is common in X., but otherwise rare in classical prose. The dangers of Persian luxury are a familiar theme in fourth-century texts, e.g. *Cyr.* (Gera 1993: 59–60, 76–7); for the specific connection between luxury and idleness, cf. Isoc. 4.132 (on Greek subjects of Persia in Asia Minor). **καὶ Μήδων . . . καὶ Περσῶν:** the combination of names is unusual in Greek and found in military contexts (Simon. *FGE* 11, 13 West; Thuc. 1.104.2; Tuplin 2003b: 352). The Persians took over power from the Medes (3.4.8n.), but Medes continued to form part of the ruling elite (Briant 2002: 24–7); in *Cyr.* Median ornamentation corrupts Persian simplicity. Any of these associations (military victory, elite status, fine living) may explain their pairing here; the amplification continues in the two paired expressions that follow, each with an increasing number of syllables. **καλαῖς καὶ μεγάλαις:** this frequently combined pair of adjectives is applied to women in Homer (× 3 in the *Odyssey*) and later authors (e.g. [Arist.] *Ath. Pol.* 14.4; Heliod. 7.2.1); it associates female beauty with height (Tuplin 2004a: 156; *pace* Llewellyn-Jones 2010, μεγάλαις cannot mean 'fat'). Given that female beauty was seen by the Greeks as a hallmark of the Persian court (Briant 2015: 326–30), the phrase offers another fanciful suggestion of the ready availability of elite women. **γυναιξὶ καὶ παρθένοις:** except in medical writings, a rare expression; here it is a vaunt of sexual potency. Marriage and sexual violence were part of the imagery, and doubtless the reality, of Greek colonization (Dougherty 1993: 61–80). **ὁμιλεῖν**, used of a variety of social relations, here has sexual overtones (cf. e.g. *Mem.* 2.1.24 παιδικοῖς ὁμιλῶν). **μὴ ὥσπερ οἱ λωτοφάγοι:** μή is repeated after the long intervening conditional clause. The Lotus Eaters were encountered by Odysseus during his return to Ithaca; those of his companions who ate from the lotus plant forgot about their journey home and had to be forced on board ship by Odysseus (Hom. *Od.* 9.83–104). They were placed by geographers on the north coast of Africa (Hdt. 4.177). Xenophon is either using λωτοφάγοι of Odysseus' companions, casting himself as Odysseus, or suggesting that the tribe was composed of (descendants of?) travellers who forgot to return home. Dwelling among the Lotus Eaters was used as an image for yielding to pleasure (e.g. Pl. *Rep.* 560c5; Heraclit. *All.* 70.3). Here too the allusion's connotations are negative: by settling in the Persian empire the Greeks will forget their true identity (Dillery 1995: 62). For another explicit Odyssean allusion, see 5.1.2; cf. Lossau 1990; Gray 2011: 143–4.

3.2.26 εἰκὸς καὶ δίκαιον: the terms do not carry their full semantic force; the phrase is a solemn way of saying 'expedient' (cf. Thuc. 5.90; Pl. *Crat.* 438e6). **ἀφικνεῖσθαι καὶ ἐπιδεῖξαι:** the present infinitive of an enterprise which may not be completed, the aorist of what they can certainly do if they arrive back home. **ἑκόντες πένονται** 'they are poor on purpose'. Demaratus in Herodotus (7.102.1) tells Xerxes that 'poverty has always been endemic to Greece' – but he then insists that Greeks keep it at bay through their ἀρετή. Poverty could also be viewed positively, as a source of hardiness (e.g. Ar. *Plut.* 558–61; Pl. *Rep.* 556c8–e1). But while Xenophon is in one way appealing to that ideal, his rhetoric is not serious, as is shown by his concluding appeal to greed (39n.), which matches the behaviour throughout the expedition of the Greek soldiers (who are motivated by greed) and of Xenophon himself (who desires wealth in order to be able to help others). It also runs counter to proposals to alleviate poverty, whether by economic reforms (*Por.*) or by migration to the western parts of the Persian empire (Isoc. 4.131–3, 5.120–3). **ἐξὸν . . . ὁρᾶν:** ἐξόν (concessive accusative absolute participle) is commonly used of feasible but rejected opportunities (cf. 2.5.22, 6.6, 5.6.3); for accusative κομισαμένους after αὐτοῖς, see 3.1.5n. on ἐλθόντα; πλουσίους goes with τοὺς πολιτεύοντας and is predicative ('to see them being prosperous'). Xenophon continues with the idea of settling in the Persian empire, but again at the level of fantasy. He is not substituting a non-serious plan for immediate settlement with a serious long-term plan, along the lines proposed by Isocrates, to solve the problem of poverty (which, unlike in the previous clause, is here conceived as restricted to particular groups within Greece). **ἀλλὰ γάρ:** 25n. **τἀγαθά:** 3.1.21n. **δῆλον ὅτι:** parenthetical. **τῶν κρατούντων ἐστί:** the generalization (while keeping open the possibility of a future attack on Persia) concludes the second section of the speech by repeating its main theme, the need to fight and win now.

3.2.27 τοῦτο δὲ δεῖ λέγειν explicitly sets up the final section, where Xenophon considers how the army can ensure success. **ὡς ἀσφαλέστατα** underlines Xenophon's leadership credentials (cf. its repeated use by Clearchus in the mutiny scene (1.3.11)); when he consulted the oracle (3.1.6), by contrast, his (aristocratic and individual) ambitions were to make the journey κάλλιστα καὶ ἄριστα. **εἰ . . . δέοι:** the potential conditional prudently presents this as a remote possibility (*CGCG* 49.8). **πρῶτον μέν:** 10n. It is picked up by ἔπειτα and then by ἔτι δέ (28). **ἔφη:** 3.3.2n. **κατακαῦσαι . . . συμφέρηι:** the way in which the baggage wagons and animals 'act as general' (see 2.2.13 for another striking metaphorical use of στρατηγεῖν) is explained in the following ἀλλά-clause. The animals still determine the march formation (36n.) and, even after a cull (4.1.12–14), the route (4.1.24, 2.10, 6.17); they also remain vulnerable to attack (4.2.13, 5.12) and weather conditions (4.5.4). The wagons will have carried most of the items which Xenophon will nominate for destruction and perhaps other spare gear and provisions (cf. 1.7.20, 10.18); cf. 3.4.32n. for difficulties caused by the loss of the wagons. **τὰς σκηνὰς συγκατακαῦσαι**: the infinitive still depends on δοκεῖ μοι. The troops started the expedition with tents because they thought they were marching on Pisidia (3.1.4n.), where spring was rainy and cool; from now on, they sleep under the open sky except when they are able to quarter in villages (e.g. 4.5.25) (Lee 2007: 122). **αὖ** 'in their turn'. **ὄχλον . . . ἄγειν** 'a trouble . . . to bring along' (presumably on pack animals after the destruction of the wagons). The tents may have consisted of leather panels (cf. 1.5.10), but other details are uncertain (e.g. how many men they housed); within a mercenary army differences might be expected. Cf. van Wees 2004: 107; Lee 2007: 122–3. **συνωφελοῦσι . . . ἔχειν:** Xenophon suggests that only two aims matter in the current situation; in line with his remarks on the Greeks' physical endurance at 3.1.23, he does not mention the protection tents might have provided against extreme weather conditions. For the general's duty to secure access to provisions, see 1.3.11, *Mem.* 3.2.1.

3.2.28 ἔτι δέ 'and moreover'. **τῶν ἄλλων . . . ἀπαλλάξωμεν:** hortatory aorist subjunctive (3.1.24n.). Superfluous items may have included extra sets of clothing and certain tools (cf. Lee 2007: 123) as well as goods plundered along the way (1.2.19, 2.4.27). **πλὴν ὅσα** 'except for everything which' (= πλὴν τοσούτων ὅσα). Some sort of common store of booty must still have been kept (3.3.18n.). **πολέμου . . . ἔχομεν:** the same two aims as 27(n.). **ἵν' . . . σκευοφορῶσι:** Xenophon adds a consideration about maximizing the size of the fighting force to his earlier considerations about manoeuvrability and speed. The implication is that there were not many non-combatant baggage-handlers. **κρατουμένων** 'of those who are conquered' is best taken as a possessive genitive with πάντα, thrown forward to balance ἢν δὲ κρατῶμεν. ἀλλότρια is predicative. **γάρ** belongs to the whole sentence: keeping their possessions is pointless whether they lose or win; cf. Livy 9.23.13, where a general in similar straits orders the burning of a camp while promising that the losses 'will be made up for by spoils'. **ἐπίστασθε** is indicative (cf. 3.1.36n.). The thought is indeed a cliché: Aristotle (*Pol.* 1255a7) presents it as a generally agreed practice that the spoils of war belong to the victors; cf. 5.6.13, 32, *Cyr.* 5.2.23; Pl. *Leg.* 626b3–4 for similar formulations. **ἢν δὲ κρατῶμεν:** after formulating the negative outcome as a general statement in the μέν-clause, Xenophon applies the positive outcome only to the current situation. **καὶ τοὺς πολεμίους . . . νομίζειν** 'we must regard even the enemy as our pack-bearers (predicative σκευοφόρους)', *sc.* because they would have too many possessions to carry by themselves. The image is humiliating for the enemy (cf. 3.1.30n.).

3.2.29 λοιπόν: another explicit division marker (10n. on πρῶτον μέν; cf. Gorg. DK 82 B11a.19 τὸ δὲ λοιπόν ἐστιν), here reinforced by καὶ μέγιστον and so climactic. **ὁρᾶτε γὰρ κτλ:** Xenophon explains (γάρ) why the point is important before stating the point itself (30 δεῖ οὖν). The importance of the point is established by the claim that the Persians seized the generals so that the Greek army would destroy itself through ἀταξία; this inferred motivation is in line with Xenophon's own reasoning at 3.1.38(n.) and more plausible to his audience because the Persians' alleged hope almost came true (3.1.3n.). The point itself is that the generals must be vigilant and the whole army disciplined. **καὶ τοὺς πολεμίους:** prolepsis (8n.). καί is here climactic (*GP* 316–17), emphasizing the surprising shift to the enemy's considerations. **οὐ πρόσθεν . . . ἐτόλμησαν** implies both that the Persians previously lacked daring (cf. 11, 16(nn.)) and that their current daring in 'bringing on the war' (the elaborate expression (LSJ s.v. ἐκφέρω II.7) is mocking) is based solely on the expectation that the leaderless Greeks will disintegrate. **ὄντων μὲν τῶν ἀρχόντων** 'as long as we had our commanders'. *Sc.* possessive ἡμῖν; understanding ὄντων as 'were alive' is less likely (cf. Kahn 1973: 243 n. 19). **καὶ ἡμῶν πειθομένων** anticipates the argument that discipline depends on a collaborative effort of commanders and common soldiers. The inclusive first-person plural subtly suggests that Xenophon knows how to follow as well as how to lead. **λαβόντες δὲ . . . ἐνόμιζον:** rather than keeping the μέν- and δέ-clauses both dependent on νομίζοντες, Xenophon starts a new main clause; ἐνόμιζον throws the Persians' false expectations into greater relief. **ἀναρχίαι . . . ἀπολέσθαι:** ἄν goes with the infinitive, representing a potential construction (ἀπόλοιντο ἄν) in indirect discourse (*CGCG* 51.27; Smyth 1848). The basic sense of ἀναρχία is 'lack of a leader' (LSJ s.v. I; cf. Demades fr. 15 de Falco = Plut. *Mor.* 181f, comparing Alexander's army after his death to the blinded Cyclops).

3.2.30 δεῖ: 3.1.40n. **πολὺ . . . ἢ πρόσθεν:** the anaphora of πολύ (to be connected with ἐπιμελεστέρους and εὐτακτοτέρους, respectively) and the repetition of νῦν and πρόσθεν at the end of each clause (cf. the repetition of ἢ τότε at 5.8.19) drive home the need for change. ἐπιμέλεια ('attentiveness') is a key term in X.'s theory of good leadership (Sandridge 2012: 51–7): it includes paying attention to one's own safety (cf. *Cyr.* 1.6.5), and so here may hint that the former generals were careless; it also means being attentive to subordinates (cf. *Cyr.* 2.1.11, *Eq. mag.* 6.3, *Mem.* 3.9.10–11), which creates obedience and loyalty (because the soldiers know that their leader wishes the best for them and that they are being watched); cf. 3.1.37n. Of the former generals, Clearchus relied only on coercion (2.6.8–12), Proxenus was too soft (2.6.19), and Meno won obedience by complicity in the soldiers' wrongdoings instead of by making them better (2.6.27) (cf. Gray 2011: 38–9).

3.2.31 ψηφίσασθαι depends on δεῖ. For the verb, see 9n. on ἀνατεινάτω τὴν χεῖρα. **τὸν ἀεὶ ὑμῶν ἐντυγχάνοντα** 'whoever of you happens to be there on each given occasion'; for the generic use of the articulate participle, see *CGCG* 52.48; Smyth 2052. **σὺν . . . κολάζειν:** Xenophon stresses the collaborative nature of the relationship between leaders and followers, but acknowledges that some form of coercion may be necessary. This realistic touch is characteristic of X. (cf. *Mem.* 3.5.5–6, *Hier.* 10.1–3, *Eq. mag.* 7.10). ἀταξία was considered a grave punishable offence in Sparta (*Hell.* 3.1.9) and elsewhere (*GSW* II.238–43). **ἐψευσμένοι ἔσονται:** for the (regular) periphrastic construction of the future perfect middle-passive, see *CGCG* 20.7. **τῆιδε . . . τῆι ἡμέραι:** the idea of a single decisive day is a rhetorical commonplace, found e.g. in pre-battle speeches (*Cyr.* 3.3.37; Thuc. 5.9.9); here it marks a new start in a long campaign. **μυρίους . . . Κλεάρχους:** despite the implied criticism of Clearchus (30n.), his stern discipline is here held up as a positive example. For the rhetorical use of names in the plural, cf. e.g. Hdt. 4.143.2 Μεγαβάζους . . . τοσούτους; Lib. *Decl.* 10.1.37 πολλοὺς ἔδει Θεμιστοκλέας εἶναι τῆι πόλει.

3.2.32 ἀλλὰ γάρ: 25n. **καί** signals impatience (cf. *GP* 316) and so conveys the impression that Xenophon suddenly wakes up to the urgency of the situation. **περαίνειν** probably means 'bring (the speech) to a conclusion' rather than 'put words into action'; for the rare absolute use, cf. *Hell.* 6.2.30. **ὥρα:** *sc.* ἐστί. **ἴσως . . . παρέσονται:** the first time in the assembly that the proximity of the enemy is openly acknowledged. **ἐπικυρωσάτω:** the word (only here in X.) is associated with the Athenian assembly (Thuc. 3.71.1, 5.45.4; cf. Eur. *Or.* 862). **ἔργωι περαίνηται** 'it may be accomplished in action', a different sense of περαίνω from its previous occurrence (*paronomasia*: cf. 3.1.21n.). **εἰ . . . διδάσκειν:** for ταύτηι 'this way', cf. LSJ s.v. οὗτος C.8.4.c. Used absolutely, διδάσκειν means 'explain, show by argument' (LSJ s.v. II).

For openness to better suggestions, cf. *Mem.* 4.8.11; Hom. *Il.* 14.107–8; Ap. Rhod. 1.665–6. X. makes such openness a conspicuous characteristic of the elder Cyrus (*Cyr.* 4.4.8, 6.2.24, 39, 4.19, 8.3.2). **τολμάτω**, together with adverbial καί, acknowledges that some soldiers may be reluctant. **ὁ ἰδιώτης:** ὁ is generic. ἰδιώτης, generally used of anyone not occupying an office or taking an active part in affairs, here excludes the elected commanders of the army (cf. 1.3.11 οὔτε στρατηγοῦ οὔτε ἰδιώτου). The term was used in Athens for citizens who occasionally spoke on their own initiative in the assembly (Rubinstein 1998: 141–3). Neither here nor at 37–8 do any of the private soldiers step forward. **κοινῆς σωτηρίας:** the pithy phrase summarizes the key theme of the speech. The emphasis on the importance of the collective contrasts with the end of Xenophon's first speech (3.1.25n.); there he was addressing captains, here the whole army.

3.2.33 Μετὰ ταῦτα: for the asyndeton, see 7n. **εἶπεν:** 3.1.15n. on ἔλεξεν. **ἀλλ':** 4n. Here it is adversative, rejecting Xenophon's proposal to open the floor. **τινος ἄλλου δεῖ** 'anything else is needed' (lit. 'there is a lack of something else' (LSJ s.v. δέω B.1)). **καὶ αὐτίκα** 'in a moment, too'. After Xenophon's mention of the enemy (32n.), a sense of urgency pervades these last exchanges. **ποιεῖν:** i.e. make further suggestions (as Xenophon had proposed). **καὶ ὅτωι . . . ἅπαντες:** the same sequence at 9(n.), but here with asyndeton before ἀνέτειναν, which reflects the speed with which the proposal is ratified (rather than 'a certain naive awkwardness' (*GP* xlv)).

3.2.34 πάλιν εἶπε Ξενοφῶν: after πάλιν, Xenophon is the expected subject and stands after the verb in an unmarked position. Contrast Χειρίσοφος εἶπεν (33): after Xenophon's invitation to speak, it is expected that someone will, and so the salient information, Χειρίσοφος, comes before the verb (*CGCG* 60.23). **προσδεῖν:** the fact that Xenophon takes up Chirisophus' invitation to say what else is needed 'in addition to what Xenophon had said' marks out his distinctive insight. He may have deliberately omitted the points he is about to make in the hope that someone with more experience would take up the baton (he becomes notably more cautious in what follows). **τὰ ἐπιτήδεια:** taking care of provisions comes first, as one of a general's most important duties (27n.). Earlier (21), Xenophon had argued that it was better to take provisions from the enemy rather than to buy them; now he thinks of a concrete opportunity to do so. **ἀκούω** 'I have heard/been told' (*CGCG* 51.19). As elsewhere (3.3.16n.), the introduction of information in a speech by Xenophon rather than in the earlier narrative highlights his strategic grasp; how he obtained the information is left unclear. **οὐ πλέον . . . ἀπεχούσας:** the negative formulation ('no more than') implies that the villages can easily be reached; contrast the use of the same phrase at 3.3.11 (n.) when the army actually reaches the villages (after journeying 25 stades).

3.2.35 οὐκ ἂν οὖν θαυμάζοιμι: with οὖν, Xenophon draws the inference that, since it is clear (cf. δῆλον ὅτι at 34, i.e. to everyone, also the enemy) that they must move, the enemy has probably settled on a strategy of pursuit. The potential optative conveys a cautious suggestion (*CGCG* 34.13; Smyth 1826). Throughout this part of the speech, Xenophon is careful to stress the uncertain outcome of his proposals. **εἰ . . . ὥσπερ οἱ δειλοὶ κύνες . . . εἰ καὶ αὐτοί:** the article is standard with generalizing plurals (*CGCG* 28.6; Smyth 1123). After the sonically expressive simile (note the frequency of δ- and κ-sounds), εἰ is repeated for clarity; the connection between the *comparatum* and *comparandum* is established by adverbial καί ('they themselves, too', with αὐτοί picking up οἱ πολέμιοι) rather than οὕτως. The qualification of the dogs as δειλοί continues the rhetoric of 16; but the Persians fall short of the dogs (ἐπακολουθοῖεν suggests greater hesitation than διώκουσι) while the Greeks are braver than the 'passers-by' (they 'march away' (ἀπιοῦσιν) rather than flee (φεύγουσιν)). The simile (which is imitated by Dio Chrys. 8.17) resembles the dog simile at Hom. *Il.* 17.725–9, but X., the author of a treatise on hunting with hounds (*Cyn.*), is in any case fond of dog similes (and Socrates often draws analogies between man and dog; e.g. *Mem.* 2.7.13–4, 4.1.3), often specifying the character of the dog involved (cf. e.g. *Hell.* 2.4.41, *Cyr.* 1.4.15, 21, with *SAGN* IV.475).

3.2.36 ἴσως continues the tentative tone. **ἀσφαλέστερον:** 27n. on ὡς ἀσφαλέστατα. **πλαίσιον:** a πλαίσιον was originally a rectangular frame used in construction (Dover on Ar. *Ran.* 800); for metaphors as indicative of a military linguistic register, see Introduction p. 32. Here it is a rectangular formation with hoplites on all sides protecting the baggage carts and camp-followers in the middle. It was not a new formation for armies on the march: X. notes that ethnic contingents in the Persian army employed it, though without non-combatants in the centre (1.8.9), while Thucydides mentions its use by Brasidas when he extricated a Spartan army from mountainous Lyncestis (4.125.2–3) and by the Athenians in their unsuccessful withdrawal from Syracuse (7.78.2) – both significant intertexts for *An.* (see 3.3.12–18, 4.3, 38–43nn. for the former, 3.1.2, 2.8, 15, 4.20, 5.16nn. and Ehrhardt 1994 for the latter). While earlier the army marched in a long line whose width could be varied to impress the enemy (2.4.26), the new formation provided a clear structure for the retreating army, with defence for the non-combatants and reassurance for the soldiers that their supplies and any remaining loot were well protected (cf. 7.8.16). Xenophon does not specify the position of the light-armed troops, although in the retreat they will play a vital role in co-ordination with the hoplites (3.3.7, 8, 4.3, 15, 28, 38nn.; Best 1969: 56–78). **ἡμῖν:** for the accusative participle after the dative, see 3.1.5n. **τῶν ὅπλων:** for ὅπλα = ὁπλῖται (a common usage), see LSJ s.v. ὅπλον III.4. **ἵνα . . . εἴη:** a purpose clause with an oblique optative in primary sequence is occasionally found in tentative proposals; cf. 2.4.4 (as here, with a subjunctive in some MSS) and *Cyr.* 3.1.11 (K–G II.383). **ὄχλος** is a general term for the non-combatants in the army in X. (attendants, slaves, captives, male and female companions; cf. Lee 2007: 259–73). **ἐν ἀσφαλεστέρωι:** the repetition (cf. ἀσφαλέστερον) underscores the interdependence of the army's components. **νῦν ἀποδειχθείη:** aorist passive of ἀποδείκνυμι 'settle'; the following indirect questions are subject. Xenophon stresses the need to make a decision about the leadership structure now, since the situation is critical. **τίνας χρὴ . . . κοσμεῖν** 'who should lead the square and organize the front'. Not a tautology: the commander(s) of the vanguard (the most prestigious position) will also steer the whole formation in the right direction. Plural τίνας for the front (as well as for the back and sides) seems to require a minimum of eight commanders in total, while only seven have been elected. Since the first printed edition, τίνα has often been printed, by error or conjecture, but it imposes a false precision: Xenophon keeps all options open before nominating Chirisophus for the front position. Diodorus' claim (14.27.1) that Chirisophus was sole leader is due to misinterpretation of ἡγεῖσθαι here or at 37 (cf. 3.1.25n.) and perhaps recollection of 6.1.32, where he *is* elected leader; for Chirisophus' position, cf. further 3.3.3, 4.38nn.; Stylianou 2004: 72. **ἐπὶ τῶν πλευρῶν ἑκατέρων** 'on each of the two flanks'. πλευρά, originally a 'rib' or 'flank' of a body (and applied to a ship's frame at Thgn. 513), is found in a military sense first in X. (× 4, all in *An.* 3, where formations are a particular concern); cf. synonymous πλευρόν, used twice in *Cyr.* (and earlier at Soph. *Aj.* 874 of one side of a naval encampment). The rare adjectival plural ἑκατέρων (again at 37) stresses that the flanks are separate units. **ὀπισθοφυλακεῖν** 'command the rear' (LSJ s.v. II); cf. 3.3.7n. on ὀπισθοφύλακες. **τοῖς τεταγμένοις** refers to the troops rather than the generals.

3.2.37 εἰ μὲν οὖν . . . ἐχέτω: for μὲν οὖν, see 3.1.19n. Xenophon makes the same request as at 32(n.). **εἰ δὲ μή:** Xenophon is to be imagined as briefly pausing before this sentence; compare 38, where the narrative explicitly reports a pause. **ἡγοῖτο:** cautiously expressed as a wish rather than an order; some MSS make Xenophon sound more imposing, reading imperative ἡγείσθω here and/or hortatory subjunctive ὀπισθοφυλακῶμεν later on. **καὶ Λακεδαιμόνιος:** adverbial καί presumably implies 'in addition to all his other qualifications' (left unspecified) (cf. *GP* 296–7). Being Spartan is a qualification because, since the battle of Plataea (13n.),

Spartans had a reputation for being the best at hoplite warfare (Cartledge 1977: 11), and because Sparta was the supreme power in Greece at this time. **τῶν δὲ πλευρῶν . . . ἐπιμελοίσθην** 'may two of the oldest generals have command over each of the flanks', i.e. two pairs of two: ἑκατέρων should have a distributive meaning with numerals (cf. e.g. *Cyr.* 8.3.9, where εἰς τετρακισχιλίους is divided into δισχίλιοι . . . ἑκατέρωθεν). This interpretation has the advantage of giving all seven generals a role. Cobet's emended text, δύο τὼ πρεσβυτάτω στρατηγώ, is accepted by many editors and taken to mean 'may the two oldest generals have command over the two flanks' (i.e. one general on each flank); but τὼ δύο would be expected for 'the two', and the definite description 'the two oldest generals' does not fit the distributive meaning of ἑκατέρων. That Xenophon describes four in a group of seven generals as 'the oldest' (also at 3.3.11(n.)) can be explained by the importance of age-based status in Greece (cf. 3.1.14n.); later X. calls Sophaenetus and Philesius τοὺς πρεσβυτάτους τῶν στρατηγῶν (5.3.1), and Sophaenetus alone πρεσβύτατος . . . τῶν στρατηγῶν (6.5.13) (cf. also 3.1.47n. on Cleanor). It is also an astute rhetorical move, flattering those left on the flanks. **οἱ νεώτατοι:** the rear was less prestigious, but in a retreat it was the area of greatest danger and so offered an opportunity to win distinction. In the following narrative X. will focus above all on Chirisophus as leader of the vanguard and on Xenophon in the rear. **τὸ νῦν εἶναι** 'for the time being'. εἶναι is absolute infinitive, with limitative value (*CGCG* 51.49; Smyth 2012c); τό qualifies νῦν, turning the punctual adverb into an expression for a period of time (cf. Rijksbaron 2006a).

3.2.38 πειρώμενοι: Xenophon presents the first formation emphatically as a trial, proposing revisions on 'each given occasion' (ἀεί, as at 31); the present participle indicates a prolonged process of trial and error. For revisions of the formation, see 3.3.12–19, 4.19–23nn. **εἰ . . . λεξάτω:** for the rhetorical move, see 32n. on εἰ . . . διδάσκειν. **ὅτωι . . . χεῖρα:** the same formulaic phrase at 9(n.). **ἔδοξε ταῦτα:** the formula (for the asyndeton, cf. 33n. on καὶ ὅτωι . . . ἅπαντες), used five times in *An.*, sometimes of decisions by the generals alone, recalls that used to introduce Athenian decrees on inscriptions: ἔδοξεν (τῆι βουλῆι καὶ) τῶι δήμωι (e.g. ML 25, 52). But here it is a formula of 'participatory', not necessarily ideologically democratic, approval (Hornblower 2004a: 244).

3.2.39 νῦν τοίνυν emphatically marks the transition from argumentation to the final appeal, in which Xenophon underlines the need to put theory into practice immediately; this closural use (found also at 3.1.37) is frequent in Lysias (e.g. 18.23, 27.16, 30.30) and Demosthenes (e.g. 19.311, 24.209). **ὅστις τε . . . ὅστις τε . . . καὶ εἴ τις δέ:** triple anaphora with a slight variation in the last member to bring out the tentativeness of the last suggestion; not everyone would be willing to acknowledge a financial motivation. The repetition of πειράσθω acknowledges the effort required. **τοὺς οἰκείους ἐπιθυμεῖ ἰδεῖν** looks back to 3.1.3. **ἀνὴρ ἀγαθός:** 3.1.21n. **οὐ γάρ ἔστιν . . . τυχεῖν:** ἔστιν = ἔξεστιν, as the accent shows. The negative formulation emphasizes that the soldiers must now dispel any other thought. Unlike Xenophon's practical proposals, the need for bravery is non-negotiable. **ζῆν ἐπιθυμεῖ . . . ἐστί:** it is not enough merely to try to be brave, the army must also try to win. The rhetoric echoes Chirisophus' speech (3n.). **χρημάτων ἐπιθυμεῖ:** this consideration has not been mentioned before and clashes with the idea that the only aim now is a safe return and in particular with Xenophon's proposal to burn all superfluous possessions (including, no doubt, booty (28n.)). But the point is a natural one in the case of mercenaries and also a topos of battle exhortations (cf. *Cyr.* 3.3.45); here it leads to a closing recapitulation of the argument made at 28. **τῶν μὲν γὰρ νικώντων** (*sc.* ἐστί) **τὸ κατακαίνειν** 'for it is for the victors to do the slaying'; for the possessive genitive with εἰμί, see Smyth 1304.

3.3 THE RETREAT BEGINS

The Greek army sets off on its retreat with a new leadership and a new strategy in place following the meetings of the officers and of the whole army described in 3.1–2. Since the death of Cyrus (1.8.27), it has advanced about 250 miles north, gradually moving up out of the Mesopotamian plain, while all the time maintaining contact with the Persian army under Tissaphernes. The remainder of Book 3 describes a march up the Tigris valley of about a hundred miles into still higher and narrower land. The army's dealings with the Persians now move from the atmosphere of tension and suspicion that pervades Book 2 to open warfare.

The army's first goal is some villages Xenophon mentioned as lying 20 stades away (3.2.34); Xenophon's warning (3.2.35) that the Persians may continue to press them in their retreat raises the expectation that the army may encounter further difficulties. The army's performance under its new leadership is measured against Book 2 through repeated echoes of the earlier narrative – in particular, echoes of the aftermath of the seizure of the generals (2.5), which is the previous day in historical terms, but separated in narrative terms by the obituaries (2.6) and by the long night scene (3.1–2). Xenophon emerges as an innovative and successful leader, but he is not perfect: like Thucydides' Demosthenes and Gylippus (*CT* II.188, III.550), he makes mistakes but learns from them (Nussbaum 1967: 44; Flower 2012: 131).

X.'s focus throughout is on the Greeks rather than the Persians. It is clear that the Persians could have attempted to prevent the Greeks crossing the Zapatas (a wide river, cf. 6n.). As it is, they seem to have been content to let them get as far away as possible from the centre of Persian power, while continuing to harass them. They then increase their pressure on the Greeks when it becomes clear that the army has not disintegrated following the arrest of the generals. Finally, when this proves ineffective, they leave them to the warlike Carduchians to deal with. The brief parallel narrative of Diodorus does focus more on Tissaphernes' reasoning at this point: 'Tissaphernes, following with his army, clung to the Greeks, but he did not dare to meet them in battle face to face, fearing as he did the courage and recklessness of desperate men; and although he harassed them in places well suited for that purpose, he was unable to do them any great harm, but he followed them, causing slight difficulties, as far as the country of the people known as the Carduchians' (14.27.3). This account of Tissaphernes' reasoning is probably inferred from X.'s narrative and designed to show up the Greeks' courage.

3.3.1 Τούτων λεχθέντων: long speeches and debates are commonly rounded off by a capping formula (a verb of speaking in the aorist participle) marking progression to a new scene; contrast present ἀριστοποιουμένων later on. For the asyndeton, see 3.2.7n. **κατέκαιον . . . σκηνάς:** as Xenophon had proposed, in the same order (3.2.27). Contrast their state of despondency the previous evening, when few soldiers lit fires (3.1.3). κατέκαιον and the following imperfects denote durative and repetitive actions: X. describes a large number of activities in broad strokes, the perfunctory narrative mirroring the soldiers' haste. In contrast to the similar scene at 4.1.14, no disobedience is recorded here. **τῶν δὲ περιττῶν . . . ἀλλήλοις** 'they shared with one another whatever anyone needed of the excess baggage'. τῶν περιττῶν is a partitive genitive (*CGCG* 30.29; Smyth 1306), δέοιτο is optative in a past indefinite construction (3.1.20n.). While the burning of unnecessary items (mentioned in the following clause) is in line with Xenophon's recommendations (3.2.28n.), the communal spirit shown here goes beyond them. This spirit reappears in the exchange of wood and food in the winter march through Armenia (4.5.6 μετεδίδοσαν ἀλλήλοις ὧν εἶχον ἕκαστοι); towards the end of *An.*, by contrast, the officers are reluctant to share loot (7.8.11 ἵνα μὴ μεταδοῖεν τὸ μέρος). **ἠριστοποιοῦντο:** the army had two main meals, ἄριστον ('breakfast') and δεῖπνον ('dinner'). Often the army would march before eating (Lee 2007: 209), but here it eats first. Like the fires, the meal marks a return to normality after the army's disturbed state the previous evening (3.1.3). **ἀριστοποιουμένων δὲ αὐτῶν** restates (in a genitive absolute) ἠριστοποιοῦντο. Rather than being an example of 'naïve repetition' (Russell 1991: 289), the participle provides a frame of reference for the upcoming discourse (cf. Denniston 1952: 95–6 for parallels in Herodotus and Plato). The phrase μετὰ δὲ ταῦτα ἀριστήσαντες (6) then marks temporal progression and opens a new scene. **ἔρχεται . . . λέγει:** the word order is that of 'presentative sentences', which introduce a new participant to the scene (*CGCG* 60.30). X. often uses the historical present in *An.* to segment his narrative, marking the most important stages of the march and highlighting the crucial events in the main storyline (*CGCG* 33.55; Sicking and Stork 1997: 147–56). Hence the frequent appearance in the historical present of verbs of movement and speaking. **Μιθραδάτης** was introduced as a loyal companion of Cyrus in X.'s account of the immediate aftermath of the arrest of the generals the previous day, when he comes with Ariaeus and Artaozus to the Greek camp (2.5.35); in the interpolated list of rulers at 7.8.25 he is described as the ruler of Lycaonia and Cappadocia, but the reliability of that list is suspect. Keeping his focus on the Greeks, X. mentions him as he arrives at the Greek army (for the technique, cf. 2.1.7 with historical present ἔρχονται, 3.17, 4.8; Introduction p. 38). He does not explain (and may not have known) why Mithradates joined Ariaeus and Artaozus, who had sent a message together at 2.4.15, or what happened to either of his companions from the previous day. The name Mithradates is itself derived from the god Mithras and is common in Greek accounts, e.g. as the foster-father of the elder (Hdt. 1.110.1, where the form is Mitra-) or slayer of the younger Cyrus (Plut. *Artax.* 11.5). MSS often vary between the forms 'Mithradates' and 'Mithridates'; for the likely Old Persian stem, see Schmitt 2002: 63–4. **σὺν ἱππεῦσιν ὡς τριάκοντα:** the number enhances the verisimilitude of the narrative, while the approximation increases the eyewitness effect. Mithradates makes two further appearances, with progressively larger forces (3.3.6, 4.2); the sequence culminates in the appearance of Tissaphernes with a still larger army (3.4.13). **τοὺς στρατηγούς**, if taken as representing Mithradates' actual words, shows that he assumes the Greeks have a regular board of generals (even though he could not have learnt of the replacements, except perhaps through a spy); on his earlier approach to the army, by contrast, he had asked to meet εἴ τις εἴη τῶν Ἑλλήνων στρατηγὸς ἢ λοχαγός (2.5.36). **εἰς ἐπήκοον** 'within hearing distance', with καλεσάμενος. The detail implies an atmosphere of suspicion, cf. 2.5.36–8, 4.4.5, 7.6.9. **λέγει:** no interpreter is mentioned, probably because X. is selective (contrast 2.5.35) rather than Mithradates bilingual. **ὧδε** hints at the discrepancy between Mithradates' conciliatory tone and his intentions (cf. 3.1.27n.).

3.3.2 ὦ ἄνδρες Ἕλληνες: this address (3.5.5n.) when used by Persian speakers could either be flattering, singling out the Greeks' special valour (cf. 1.7.3), or menacing, emphasizing their isolation in a hostile land (cf. 2.3.18, 5.38). **Κύρωι πιστὸς ἦν . . . καὶ νῦν ὑμῖν εὔνους** (*sc.* εἰμί): cf.

2.4.16, where a messenger announces he has been sent by Ariaeus and Artaozus, πιστοὶ ὄντες Κύρωι καὶ ὑμῖν εὖνοι; but here Mithradates overtly equates *past* faithfulness to Cyrus with *present* loyalty to the Greeks, perhaps because his need to establish his loyalty is stronger following the arrest of the generals; cf. Cleanor's warnings to the Greeks not to let themselves be deceived again (3.2.6) in view of Tissaphernes' lack of faith (3.2.4 ἀπιστίαν). For Greek perceptions of the Persian ideology of faithfulness, see Briant 2002: 324–5; Petit 2004: 183–7. **ὡς ὑμεῖς ἐπίστασθε:** cf. 2.5.35, where Ariaeus, Artaozus and Mithradates are introduced as men who were Κύρωι πιστότατοι; the knowledge of Mithradates' addressees coincides with readers' knowledge. At the same time, the appeal to the past leaves open Mithradates' loyalty in the present, especially after Xenophon's appeal to audience knowledge of barbarian ἀπιστία at 3.2.8 (ἐπίστασθε δὲ καὶ ὑμεῖς). **καὶ ἐνθάδε δ' εἰμί** 'and besides, I am actually here': in the particle combination καὶ . . . δέ, a favourite of X.'s (*c.* × 265), καί serves as the connective, while δέ is adverbial, emphasizing the word in front of it and presenting it as distinct from the preceding items in the list (Rijksbaron 1997). Mithradates thus adds another weighty reason why the Greeks should trust him, namely his very presence. **σὺν πολλῶι φόβωι διάγων:** σύν is used extensively by X., esp. in *An.* and *Cyr.*, though in Attic it had largely been replaced by μετά by *c.* 400 BC (Mommsen 1895: 365; Gautier 49); σύν remained the usual preposition in the *koine.* For the intransitive use of διάγω in the sense 'pass time (continuously)', see LSJ s.v. II.2. Mithradates' (pretended) fear is that the Persian king and Tissaphernes may accuse him of disloyalty for having dealings with the Greeks. **εἰ οὖν ὁρώιην . . . ἔλθοιμι ἄν:** Mithradates can see that the Greeks are planning something, but is uncertain what (cf. τί ἐν νῶι ἔχετε). Through his vague talk of a rescue plan (σωτήριόν τι, resonating with the salvation language from the preceding assembly scene: 3.2.7–32n.), he tries to extract information from the Greeks while remaining noncommittal about his own plans (note the potential optative). **καί** is adverbial ('also'). **". . . λέξατε οὖν" ἔφη**: X. often inserts a 'superfluous' ἔφη in directly reported speeches, at strong breaks or changes of direction, as here (cf. 3.1.34, 46 *bis*, 2.9, 27, 3.13, 5.6). **ὡς φίλον τε καὶ εὔνουν** (*sc.* ὄντα) 'considering that I am friendly and loyal' (for subjective ὡς + participle, see *CGCG* 52.39; Smyth 2086). **κοινῆι:** the alleged desire to accompany the Greeks on their return recalls earlier discussions with Ariaeus (2.2.10–11) as well as Tissaphernes' offer to escort them (2.3.29). There Tissaphernes had the excuse that he was himself returning to his own satrapy; Mithradates' only justification is his protestation of loyalty.

3.3.3 καὶ ἔλεγε Χειρίσοφος: one general is spokesman for all, as at 2.5.39, 5.4.4. For Chirisophus' style of speaking, see 3.1.45, 2.1nn. **εἰ μέν τις**

ἐᾶι . . . ἢν δέ τις κτλ.: there is a strong balance between the two clauses (διαπορεύεσθαι ~ διαπολεμεῖν, with the δια-prefix expressing determination to continue to the end; ὡς ἂν δυνώμεθα ἀσινέστατα ~ ὡς ἂν δυνώμεθα κράτιστα), but also a progression: Chirisophus first addresses what the Persians may do now (εἰ + present indicative), then issues a threat about the Greeks' response if at any one point (ἤν + subjunctive) they are hindered. **ἀσινέστατα:** in keeping with the Greeks' earlier oath to march without harming the land (ἀσινῶς) so long as the Persians provided a market (2.3.27). For Ionic/Attic ἀσινής, see Introduction p. 28. **ἀποκωλύηι:** exact parallels for ἀποκωλύω τινά τινος do not seem to exist, but for the genitive of separation with this verb, see e.g. *Hier.* 8.1 τὸ ἄρχειν οὐδὲν ἀποκωλύει τοῦ φιλεῖσθαι. With the variant reading ἐπι- (which would nicely suggest hostility), the genitive should be one of 'space within which' ('on our route'), but this use of the genitive is mostly poetic and only occurs once in *An.* (1.3.1 ἰέναι τοῦ πρόσω; cf. Joost 1892: 130). For X.'s use of the prefix ἀπο-, see Balode 2011: 24–9, 157–8.

3.3.4 ἄπορον picks up the key ἀπορία-motif (3.1.2n.). **βασιλέως ἄκοντος:** so too an anonymous speaker had claimed during the mutiny at Tarsus that the Greeks could not leave unnoticed ἄκοντος . . . Κύρου (1.3.17) and Phalinus had suggested that they had no hope of safety ἄκοντος βασιλέως (2.1.19). Xenophon, by contrast, had pointed to the example of the Mysians who lived prosperously within the king's lands βασιλέως ἄκοντος (3.2.23), thereby fortifying the Greeks against this sort of rhetoric. **ἔνθα δὴ ἐγιγνώσκετο . . . ὑπόπεμπτος εἴη** closely mirrors an earlier scene where the Greeks come to recognize that a Persian envoy is giving disingenuous advice (2.4.22 τότε δὴ καὶ ἐγνώσθη ὅτι οἱ βάρβαροι τὸν ἄνθρωπον ὑποπέμψειαν). The parallel supports the reading ὑπόπεμπτος 'sent on a secret mission' (attested elsewhere only at Σ Thuc. 4.46.5) over the less precise ὕποπτος. In both passages the passive of γιγνώσκω unobtrusively suggests the whole army's realization while the imperfect signals that that realization was gradual and δή that it follows naturally from what preceded (3.3.11n. on ἔνθα δὴ πάλιν ἀθυμία ἦν). **καὶ γάρ** introduces, after Mithradates' insincere speech, a second reason (the presence of one of Tissaphernes' kinsmen) for the Greeks' suspicions (γάρ is connective, and καί 'also' is adverbial: *GP* 108). Imperfect παρηκολούθει 'was accompanying him' suggests that the Greeks only now become aware of the significance of the kinsman's presence. **τῶν Τισσαφέρνους τις οἰκείων** 'one of Tissaphernes' relatives'. The position of τις gives emphasis to Tissaphernes' name. The omission of the relative's name (cf. 3.4.13n. on ὁ βασιλέως ἀδελφός) may suggest that the Greeks did not know it, but X. does not explain how they recognized the man in the first place (he is presumably not the brother mentioned at 2.5.35). **πίστεως ἕνεκα:**

Tissaphernes' desire to keep a check on Mithradates ironically exposes his lack of faith towards the Greeks.

3.3.5 δόγμα ποιήσασθαι: a formal term for a resolution by an official political body (e.g. *Hell.* 6.5.2; Diod. Sic. 11.76.5, 18.56.7; Dion. Hal. *Ant. Rom.* 8.87.3), used of the army as a whole at 6.4.11. **πόλεμον ἀκήρυκτον:** of a particularly hostile state of war where there is no communication even by heralds (cf. e.g. *Hell.* 6.4.21; Hdt. 5.81.2, with Hornblower). While the two sides earlier communicated by heralds (2.1.7, 3.1), now the generals have seen through Mithradates and want no dealings with Persians whatsoever. **ἔστ'** = ἕως (3.1.19n.), here with oblique optative in indirect discourse. **διέφθειρον . . . διέφθειραν** 'tried to corrupt . . . corrupted'. An 'aside' (still representing the generals' thoughts, as γάρ indicates; cf. 3.4.42, 5.12(nn.)) detailing earlier unsuccessful attempts ('conative' imperfect: *CGCG* 33.25; Smyth 1895) at persuading the soldiers to desert and the actual desertion of a captain. Alternatively the imperfect could be habitual, indicating an opposition between seduction of the masses and the more serious corruption of an officer (Nussbaum 1967: 34). The lack of a subject with διέφθειρον makes for a harsh transition, but effectively conveys the generals' perspective ('they' can only be 'the enemy'). διαφθείρω has connotations of the destruction of will power and moral fibre, and often means 'bribe'; this sense is more common in oratory than in historical writing (Harvey 1985: 86–7). **Νίκαρχον Ἀρκάδα:** at 2.5.33 an Arcadian named Nicarchus, 'holding his entrails in his hands', brought back news of the arrest of the generals and the attack on the men who had accompanied them to Tissaphernes' tent. Despite the apparent gravity of that wound, this Nicarchus (here specified as a captain) is probably the same man: the initial account of the wound may have been exaggerated (Masqueray) or his men may have carried him (Hyland 2010: 250, with useful data on abdominal wounds). **ᾤχετο . . . ὡς εἴκοσι:** cf. 2.2.7 for an earlier case of desertion. Lee 2007: 190 n. 92 suggests that the men were able to slip away because they were on guard duty. Hyland 2010: 250–1 argues that they were aiming to escape rather than desert, but there is no reason to reject X.'s version of events.

3.3.6 Μετὰ δὲ ταῦτα indicates a greater textual boundary than μετὰ ταῦτα (contrast 3.2.7n. on ἐκ τούτου; see in general Buijs 2005: 138–48); here it marks the return to the main storyline after the aside at 5 (cf. 1.2.27, 2.4.23, 6.4.12). **ἀριστήσαντες:** for the aorist, see 1n. on τούτων λεχθέντων. **διαβάντες τὸν Ζαπάταν ποταμόν:** despite the earlier stress on the problem of crossing rivers (3.1.2, 2.22), X. does not explain how this river *c.* 400 feet (120 m) wide (2.5.1) was crossed; like some rivers omitted altogether (the Lesser Zab (T1) 50 miles south of this point, the Khosr (3.4.7–12n.), the Khabur (T7)), it may have been either forded or bridged (see T1). **ἐπορεύοντο:** the imperfect is suitable for marches that are seen as preparing for the main action rather than as important events in themselves; it is rarer in *An.* than the aorist (used at e.g. 3.4.10, 13). See Rood 2010b: 58; also Buijs 2007 on *Hell.* and *Ages.* **τεταγμένοι:** overcoming the danger of ἀταξία (3.1.29, 2.29). **τὰ ὑποζύγια . . . ἔχοντες:** i.e. in the πλαίσιον formation proposed by Xenophon at 3.2.36(n.). **ἐπιφαίνεται πάλιν ὁ Μιθραδάτης:** for the historical present and the word order, see 1n. on ἔρχεται . . . λέγει. The close parallels with 1 underline the frustrating feeling that the previous rebuff of Mithradates has not been enough. **ὡς διακοσίους . . . εἰς τετρακοσίους:** ὡς means 'around', while εἰς signifies an upper limit ('as many as') and so is suitable with unexpectedly large numbers (LSJ s.v. εἰς III); here it conveys a sense of climax. **καὶ τοξότας καὶ σφενδονήτας:** the Persian cavalry are now accompanied by archers and slingers, both of whom are effective from a distance. The ideological opposition between the Persian use of the bow and the Greek use of the spear was important for Greeks (Hall 1989: 85–6); in practice both sides made some use of both. Slingers could be seen as servile (the elder Cyrus at *Cyr.* 7.4.15) since they supported other troops rather than acting independently. But they were able to release missiles at high speed (see 16(n.)) and were particularly effective in difficult terrain (*GSW* v.56–61). **μάλα ἐλαφροὺς καὶ εὐζώνους** 'very nimble and flexible'. The specification prepares, after the reference to the slow-moving pack-animals and camp-followers, for the effectiveness of these Persian troops. ἐλαφρός is used in X. of other non-Greek troops at 4.2.27, and elsewhere in contexts of dancing, hunting and youth; in epic it is an epithet of limbs and animals. εὔζωνος, lit. 'well-girdled', is used in epic always of women and in Herodotus and Thucydides only in measuring distances covered by a fast traveller. X. uses it six times in *An.*, initially of light-armed non-Greek troops but later also of hoplites operating without their shields; it becomes the standard word for light-armed troops in Polybius (× 73).

3.3.7 ὡς φίλος ὤν 'as if he were a friend'. **ἐπεὶ δ' ἐγγὺς ἐγένοντο:** plural, as Mithradates and his men are now together treated as the subject; cf. the similar shift to the plural at 4.5.33. **ἐξαπίνης:** X. uses both this form and ἐξαίφνης (Introduction p. 29). **καὶ ἱππεῖς καὶ πεζοί:** apposition, 'both . . . and . . .'. **ὀπισθοφύλακες** 'rearguard', i.e. the rear division (not a separate unit guarding the rear), here including the archers and javelin-throwers mentioned in the following γάρ-clause. This and cognate forms (cf. 3.2.36 ὀπισθοφυλακεῖν) are first attested in (and rare outside) X. **ἀντεποίουν . . . οὐδέν** 'they could do nothing in return'. **οἵ τε γὰρ Κρῆτες . . . ἐτόξευον:** the Cretans must be the 200 archers who came with Clearchus (1.2.9); cf. further 3.4.16–17, 4.2.28. Cretans were renowned for archery (cf. Pl. *Leg.* 625d6–7; Diod. Sic. 5.74.5); they are attested in the armies of Athens (Thuc. 6.25.2, 43; cf. Ar. *Ran.* 1356), Sparta (*Hell.* 4.2.16) and Alexander (Arr. *Anab.* 2.9.3); cf. Launey 1987: 280. While most Greeks used bows made from a single piece of wood, with a range of *c.* 200 yards (180 m), the Cretans probably used composite bows made of wood and horn laminated together, which achieved greater torsion and had a range of *c.* 250 yards (230 m). Given that the Persians used composite bows too, the explanation for the Cretans' shorter range may lie in the fact that their arrows were heavier (Snodgrass 1964: 144–5; see further 3.4.17n.). **καὶ ἅμα** 'and besides' (see Rusten on Thuc. 2.42.1), with κατεκέκλειντο. **ψιλοὶ ὄντες** 'because they were unprotected'. ψιλοί, lit. 'bare', like γυμνῆτες (3.4.26), can be used, as here, of troops not protected by shields, in contrast to peltasts, though both terms can also include peltasts in contrast to hoplites (Best 1969: 44–6). **εἴσω τῶν ὅπλων:** i.e. within the hollow of the πλαίσιον. For the meaning of τὰ ὅπλα, see 3.2.36n. **κατεκέκλειντο** 'were shut in'. The pluperfect refers to a continuous past state; it leaves it unclear whether that state resulted from an initial strategic decision or whether the archers had first tried (as at 3.4.26) to increase their range by operating outside the πλαίσιον (their preferred location, as the verb implies). That formation now serves to protect them and not only (as Xenophon foresaw at 3.2.36) the non-combatants. **οἱ δὲ ἀκοντισταί:** it is not unusual for δέ to be coordinated with τε after a considerable gap (*GP* 513); there is no need for **f**'s τε. The term 'javelin-throwers' appears three times in *An.*, apparently referring to the same soldiers as are elsewhere called 'peltasts' (cf. 4.3.27, 5.2.12). **βραχύτερα . . . ἢ ὡς ἐξικνεῖσθαι** 'too short to reach' (lit. 'shorter than so as to reach'); result clauses introduced by ἢ ὥσ(τε) invariably take an infinitive (*CGCG* 46.8; Smyth 2007). **τῶν σφενδονητῶν** is genitive with ἐξικνεῖσθαι by analogy with verbs of 'touching' and 'hitting' such as ἅπτομαι (*CGCG* 30.21; Smyth 1345).

3.3.8 Ξενοφῶντι ἐδόκει: X. does not mention any consultation with Timasion, the other leader of the rearguard (3.1.47n.); in the sequel (3.3.11), the generals find fault with Xenophon only. **διωκτέον εἶναι:** for the impersonal verbal adjective, see 3.1.7n. **καὶ ἐδίωκον:** imperfect for an action that immediately follows upon the previous one (*CGCG* 33.52). **διώκοντες** restates ἐδίωκον so as to emphasize the failure of the pursuit.

3.3.9 οὔτε γὰρ ἱππεῖς ἦσαν τοῖς Ἕλλησιν justifies the Greeks' fear of their own lack of cavalry (3.1.2); cf. the lesson Xenophon draws at 15, and contrast his rhetorical attempt to dismiss that fear at 3.2.18(n.). **ἐκ πολλοῦ** 'at a great distance'. **οἷόν τε ἦν** 'it was possible' (impersonal use, as at 15).

3.3.10 καὶ φεύγοντες . . . εἰς τοὔπισθεν τοξεύοντες 'even in flight . . . shooting behind them'. This is the only literary reference to Persian use of these steppe nomad tactics, later associated with Parthians (e.g. Verg. *G.* 3.31 *fidentemque fuga Parthum uersisque sagittis*; Hor. *Carm.* 1.19.11–12 *versis animosum equis Parthum*); cf. Tuplin 2010: 158–65. For iconographic evidence, in Greece and elsewhere, see Rostovtzeff 1943. Despite his interest in horsemanship, X. does not stress the skill involved in the manoeuvre. **προδιώξειαν** 'moved forward in pursuit' (optative of repeated action: *CGCG* 50.21; Smyth 2568). The verb means 'pursue in advance (of others)' on its only other occurrence in pre-Byzantine Greek (Thuc. 6.70.3), but its sense here is easy (cf. e.g. προβαίνειν 'move forward') and (as opposed to **c**'s διώξειαν) offers a fitting contrast with ἐπαναχωρεῖν.

3.3.11 οὐ . . . σταδίων: X. uses stades to measure journeys shorter than a parasang (Rood 2010b: 54). The negative formulation 'no more than' brings out the disappointingly short distance (*c.* 3 miles) covered in an entire day (ὅλης); at 3.2.34(n.), by contrast, Xenophon had encouraged the troops by placing these villages at οὐ πλέον εἴκοσι σταδίων. Xenophon had also enticingly called the villages 'fine', while here X. offers no comment. **Ἔνθα δὴ πάλιν ἀθυμία ἦν:** a return to the mood of 3.1.3; that this response is unsurprising is suggested by 'evidential' δή (*CGCG* 59.44; van Ophuijsen 1993: 140–6). **Χειρίσοφος καὶ οἱ πρεσβύτατοι:** i.e. all the generals except for Timasion, Xenophon's colleague at the rear (see 3.2.37n. on τῶν δὲ πλευρῶν . . . ἐπιμελοίσθην). X. stresses by contrast Xenophon's youth, playing on a conventional association of youth with rashness (Dover 1974: 102–5) that his subsequent leadership will undermine. **ἐδίωκεν:** the underlying direct speech had ἐδίωκες: as usual, the imperfect is not replaced by a present oblique optative (διώκοι), because this could easily lead to confusion (*CGCG* 41.10; Smyth 2623b). **τῆς φάλαγγος:** Homer uses φάλαγξ (almost always in the plural) of a line of troops. The use of the singular referring to a whole hoplite formation is first attested in X. and may reflect the increasing technicality of military terminology. The basic meaning of the word may have been 'log' (as at Hdt. 3.97.3); for similar military metaphors relating to building materials (πλαίσιον, πλίνθιον), see 3.2.36, 4.19nn.

3.3.12–19 A long speech by Xenophon which shifts from indirect to direct speech after one sentence. X. makes liberal use of this technique, with or without ἔφη, and even occasionally switches to direct speech mid-sentence (there are at least thirty other examples in *An.*: cf. e.g., with increasing boldness, 2.1.9, 5.5.24, 1.3.16), but the technique is attested from Homer onwards and is quite frequent in the later orators (cf. Combellack 1939; Bers 1997: 179–87). Sudden shifts into direct speech are a common phenomenon of spoken language, but not necessarily 'naïve' (West 1990: 8) or simply a 'reflex that can occur without artistic calculation' (Bers 1997: 6 n. 11): the clustering of the device in *An.* suggests that it is especially used in dramatic sections of the narrative. Here, the direct speech starts at the point at which Xenophon takes the initiative, defending himself against the accusation, whose 'rightness' is acknowledged less prominently in indirect speech.

Xenophon's presentation of events contains extensive verbal repetition of the earlier narrative. There are parallels for this technique in Thucydides (Luschnat 1942; Hunter 1973), but it is more striking here, where the commander is himself the author. There are some slight but significant adjustments. (*a*) The Greeks were not able to harm the enemy: Xenophon *sees* at 12 exactly what X. has narrated at 7. (*b*) Their failure is due to the greater range of the enemy missiles: Greek inferiority in the narrative (7 βραχύτερα) is recast in Xenophon's speech as enemy superiority (15). (*c*) The Greeks try to pursue the Persians, but are not able to go far from their own army (15 ~ 8–9). In the speech the strategic point is reformulated as a general statement (15 οὐχ οἷόν τε (*sc.* ἐστί) ~ 9 οὐχ οἷόν τε ἦν), preparing for the proposals Xenophon makes to overcome the problem. (*d*) Hence the Greeks are unable to catch the enemy (15 ~ 9). Xenophon's speech again turns the specifics of the narrative into a general strategic point (οὐδ' εἰ ταχὺς εἴη πεζὸς πεζὸν ἂν διώκων καταλαμβάνοι ~ οὔτε οἱ πεζοὶ τοὺς πεζοὺς . . . ἐδύναντο καταλαμβάνειν). It presents the Greeks' inability to pursue first, in the μέν-clause, not second, in a γάρ-clause, as in the narrative; this chiastic arrangement obscures any personal responsibility Xenophon may have had for the initial strategic failure.

Xenophon's specific suggestions that the army institute units of slingers and cavalry (16n.) highlight the fact that the πλαίσιον-formation has still left the rear exposed. By contrast, when Brasidas used this formation in a retreat (3.2.36n.), he added a detached rear unit – but he did not have mounted archers to face. The experiences of the Ten Thousand here may in turn have helped Agesilaus on his return from Asia Minor in 394 BC with a larger cavalry force (and with X. in attendance) to develop a more effective solution to the problem of pressure on the πλαίσιον, namely cavalry units at both front and rear that could offer rapid support to whichever part came under attack (*Hell.* 4.3.4; Spence 1993: 141–51). Xenophon's advice was recalled by Polyaen. *Strat.* 1.49.2.

3.3.12 ὀρθῶς αἰτιῷντο: an unusual instance of a general accepting responsibility for a mistake before remedying it; cf. Thuc. 7.5.3. **ἔφη:** the insertion of a verb of speaking delays the following reported words, so that ἠναγκάσθην comes as an emphatic climax. **ἠναγκάσθην:** necessity is a standard defence; cf. e.g. 5.5.16–17; Gorg. DK 82 B11.7; Antiph. 5.79.

3.3.13 κακῶς . . . ποιεῖν picks up κακῶς . . . πάσχοντας (πάσχω often functions as the passive of ποιέω). **παγχαλέπως:** the παν- compound rather than the variant with πάνυ (cf. 5.2.20, 7.5.16 for similar wavering in the MSS) is appropriate here because it has a higher (perhaps archaizing or poetic) register than πάνυ, a later, typically Attic, word (Thesleff 1954: 57). In prose, παγχάλεπος occurs in Antiphon (2.2.3), whose language is often rather contrived, and in Plato's late, more solemn, style (× 11); X. himself uses various other παν- compounds (esp. πάμπολυς and πάγκαλος) in his historical writings while excluding them almost entirely from his conversational works; see Introduction p. 29.

3.3.14 τοῖς οὖν θεοῖς χάρις: the omission of ἔστω is standard with this phrase (cf. *Oec.* 8.16, *Cyr.* 7.5.72, 8.7.3), though it is much rarer than English 'Thank God that . . .'. χάρις is a key term in the principle of reciprocity underlying the Greeks' relations with the gods. For Xenophon's rhetorical appeals to the gods, see 3.1.15–25n. **οὐ σὺν πολλῆι ῥώμηι ἀλλὰ σὺν ὀλίγοις:** the preceding narrative specified *c.* 200 cavalry and *c.* 400 light-armed troops. For the rhetorical opposition between small and large Persian forces, see e.g. 2.2.12, 4.3; here it foreshadows the increase of Persian troops at 3.4.2, raising the question of what would have happened if that larger force had appeared before Xenophon's reforms. Cf. the counter-factual at 4.1.11 ('if more (*sc.* Carduchians) had gathered at that time, much of the army would have been in danger of destruction'), with Grethlein 2012: 31.

3.3.15 οἱ μὲν πολέμιοι suggests that ἡμεῖς δέ will follow, but instead the Greeks' disadvantage is presented less bluntly. **ὅσον** 'over such a distance as', with implied antecedent τοσοῦτον; it is best interpreted as an accusative of 'extent' or 'space traversed' (*CGCG* 30.16; Smyth 1581). **ἀντιτοξεύειν** is used at 5.2.32, but otherwise not in classical prose; it may have been coined by X. (cf. 3.1.16n. on ἀντεπιμελεῖται). **οἱ ἐκ χειρὸς βάλλοντες:** the ἀκοντισταί of 7. **ἐν ὀλίγωι δέ:** *sc.* χωρίωι (cf. 9). **ἐκ τόξου ῥύματος:** lit. 'a bow's drawing away', i.e. as far as an arrow can fly. Probably taken from Aeschylus' metonymy τόξου ῥῦμα (*Pers.* 147), the phrase occurs only here and was noted by Pollux (*Onom.* 1.164); cf. the imitation ἐς τόξου ῥῦμα (Arr. *Parth.* fr. 58 Roos; Eunapius fr. 93 *FHG*).

3.3.16 ἡμεῖς . . . δεῖ 'as for us, we need . . .' After speaking about the enemy, Xenophon moves to a discussion of what the Greeks should do about them. The nominative should be construed as a 'theme-constituent', which announces the entity about which the following predication is made, and which is itself outside the structure of the sentence. This is a common feature of spoken language (*CGCG* 60.34; Slings 1997: 196). **σφενδονητῶν . . . δεῖ:** not anticipated by Xenophon in his speech to the army. **τὴν ταχίστην:** lit. 'by the quickest route' (as at 1.2.20), here 'as quickly as possible'. Greek uses many elliptical phrases with feminine adjectives as adverbial expressions of space and time (e.g. τῆι ὑστεραίαι 20); such expressions often require feminine nouns like ὁδός and ἡμέρα to be supplied (Smyth 1027b), but they can be free-standing, especially when without the article (e.g. 3.4.17 μακράν). **ἱππέων:** cf. 3.1.2, 3.9. **ἀκούω . . . Ῥοδίους:** the first mention of Rhodians in the army, and so a sign of Xenophon's grasp of the army's resources. The creation of a unit of slingers has been taken to show the versatility of Greek hoplites (Rawlings 2000: 240), but Rhodians were particularly renowned as slingers, cf. Thuc. 6.43; Launey 1987: 246. In any case these Rhodians may have been camp-followers, which would explain why X. offers a special inducement (Whitby 2004: 217–18). X.'s formation of this Rhodian unit was recalled in a speech attributed to Alexander at Arr. *Anab.* 2.7.8. **φασιν** 'they say', a generalizing third person, typical of the ethnographic mode, but here artfully presented by X. in a speech by Xenophon rather than in the narrative. Xenophon is not relying on any specific information about this group of Rhodians, but on general knowledge about Rhodians. **καὶ διπλάσιον φέρεσθαι τῶν Περσικῶν σφενδονῶν:** owing to the different sort of missile used, as X. explains at 17. καί is adverbial.

3.3.17 χειροπληθέσι: lit. 'hand-filling', i.e. as large as can be held in the hand; this is the earliest extant use of the word. Diod. Sic. 19.109.2 mentions slingers using stones weighing 1 mina (*c.* 1 lb), which would be the size of a tennis ball, according to *GSW* v.2 n. 4; larger sling-stones are depicted on Persian seals and reliefs (Root 2007: 203–7). Xenophon displays detailed knowledge about sling bullets and their range, thus further establishing his authority as a competent military leader. **σφενδονᾶν:** the Persians are understood as subject from ἐκεῖναι, which refers to τῶν Περσικῶν σφενδονῶν. **οἱ δέ γε Ῥόδιοι:** δέ γε is a favourite particle combination of X.'s; here, it is strongly adversative (*GP* 155). **καὶ ταῖς μολυβδίσιν** 'lead bullets too' (i.e. in addition to other sorts of projectile). This is the first literary reference to the use of lead bullets; they were moulded into acorn shapes and often bore an inscription. It is estimated that they had a range of more than 400 yards (365 m); if so, X.'s claim that they carried twice as far as stones is plausible (Vegetius 2.23 mentions targets for slung stones being set at 200 yards (180 m)). Foss 1975 published a lead bullet inscribed with the name Tissaphernes (see Weiss and Draskowski 2010: 125–6 for a second example), and argued that Tissaphernes learnt the technique from his contact with the Ten Thousand; Briant 2002: 1037–8 is sceptical.

3.3.18 ἦν οὖν αὐτῶν κτλ.: following his observation that Rhodians are good slingers, X. proposes finding out how many of the Rhodians (αὐτῶν, partitive genitive with τίνες) have slings. He then suggests that, once this figure is known, they secure a supply of slings, both (καὶ τούτοις μὲν . . .) by buying them (through a sort of compulsory purchase order) and (τῶι δὲ . . . ἐθέλοντι) by getting volunteers to make others; he also (καὶ τῶι . . . ἐθέλοντι) suggests that they secure a supply of people to use the slings by asking for volunteers. The whole passage must be referring to Rhodians, i.e. τῶι . . . ἐθέλοντι is in both cases any Rhodian (at 3.4.15 it is presupposed that slingers are Rhodians). Presumably the reason why X. proposes that the army buy the slings (rather than give money to the owners if they serve as slingers) is that no soldiers at this stage are being paid a daily wage; the proposal presupposes the existence of a common store of booty (attested later at e.g. 4.7.27, 5.1.12) that could be exchanged for cash. The Rhodians get money for their slings (αὐτῶν ἀργύριον: for the genitive of object bought, cf. *Mem.* 1.6.11) and for making them (<u>ἄλλο</u> ἀργύριον), and those who serve get relief from various duties (<u>ἄλλην</u> τινὰ ἀτέλειαν). Cobet's conjecture τούτοις (referring back to τίνες, cf. e.g. *Cyr.* 8.1.3 διὰ <u>τί</u> . . .; διὰ <u>τοῦτο</u> . . .) best makes sense of the passage. The fatal objection to the readings τούτωι and τούτων τῶι is that neither τούτωι nor τῶι (without a generalizing participle; cf. τῶι ἐθέλοντι with the note below) can refer to a *group* of people. **πέπανται:** X. occasionally (× 6) uses perfect πέπαμαι (from *πάομαι) instead of κέκτημαι; see Introduction p. 28. It was deemed noteworthy by Byzantine scholars (cf. *Etym. Magn.* s.v. πολυπάμμων: καὶ πασάμενος πολλάκις Ξενοφῶν λέγει ἀντὶ τοῦ κτησάμενος). **τῶι δὲ . . . ἐθέλοντι . . . τῶι . . . ἐθέλοντι:** for the repetition with generic participle (*CGCG* 28.25; Smyth 2052), cf. 5.6.20. The verb is commonly used for volunteering for a military enterprise (cf. Rutherford 1881: 57 on the cognate noun ἐθελοντής), cf. perhaps the inscription ΕΘΕΛΟΝΤΟΣ, 'of one who is willing', on a lead bullet published by Weiss and Draskowski 2010: 127 (who take it as genitive of a personal name). **ἐν τῶι τεταγμένωι** 'in the position assigned to them' (the same expression occurs at *Cyr.* 6.2.37). **ἀτέλειαν:** perhaps freedom from keeping watch or other military duties such as gathering supplies. The proposal was probably made not so much because slinging was hazardous (Lee 2007: 55 n. 72) or low-status (Hunt 1998: 187 n. 5), but simply as an incentive (cf. e.g. *Ages.* 1.24 for the effective use of incentives as a sign of good leadership). **ἱκανοί** here denotes quality, not quantity. Its use with verbs of helping and harming is distinctive of X. (× 11 with ὠφελέω and εὖ/κακῶς ποιέω) and a sign of the practical orientation of his ethical vocabulary.

3.3.19 ὁρῶ, like ἀκούω (16), underlines Xenophon's ability both to obtain and to use information (cf. 3.4.41n. on ὑπὲρ αὐτοῦ τοῦ ἑαυτῶν στρατεύματος) – two attributes of the good general. **τοὺς μέν τινας παρ' ἐμοί:** τινας is in apposition. Xenophon seems to have a small personal supply of horses. It is not clear if he travelled with them from the outset. **τοὺς δὲ τῶν Κλεάρχου καταλελειμμένους** 'others, those left behind from the horses belonging to Clearchus'. Perhaps they were left by the forty horsemen who deserted to the Persians by night at 2.2.7. **αἰχμαλώτους σκευοφοροῦντας . . . σκευοφόρα:** X. has not previously mentioned the capture of enemy horses (for a later instance, see 3.4.5n.). The soldiers who had captured the horses are made to accept in return σκευοφόρα, which are proper pack-animals (especially donkeys and mules), with flatter backs than horses and therefore better for carrying gear (Griffith 2006: 203), but less prestigious.

3.3.20 ἔδοξε ταῦτα: 3.2.38n. **ἐδοκιμάσθησαν** 'were passed as fit to serve' (LSJ s.v. II.2.b). Though the verb and cognate noun are used of the scrutiny of sacrificial animals (Hdt. 2.38.1) and cavalry (*Hell.* 6.4.31) outside Athens, X.'s language may reflect institutional procedure at Athens (Rhodes on [Arist.] *Ath. Pol.* 45.3), where the council had responsibility for the scrutiny of some military classes, including horses and cavalry (49.1–2) and πρόδρομοι and ἅμιπποι (49.1), as well as of newly enrolled citizens (42.2) and office holders (45.3). The δοκιμασία for horses and cavalrymen is not explicitly attested for Athens before the fourth century, but its earlier existence can perhaps be inferred from fifth-century vase paintings (Feyel 2009: 53–73). **τῆι ὑστεραίαι:** the scrutiny must have involved manoeuvres for which daylight was necessary. **σπολάδες καὶ θώρακες αὐτοῖς ἐπορίσθησαν** 'jerkins and breastplates were provided for them'. The σπολάς was a sleeveless leather or cloth jacket hung from the shoulders (Poll. *Onom.* 7.70), probably here an undergarment (Aldrete *et al.* 2013: 60); the θώραξ was a breastplate made from bronze or from laminated cloth to which bronze plates could be fixed; see *Eq.* 12.1–7 for X.'s prescriptions of defensive armour for cavalrymen. Another view is that the σπολάς is an alternative outer-garment to the θώραξ (as perhaps at 4.1.18; for καί as 'or', see *GP* 292); if so, θώρακες could be a gloss on σπολάδες (cf. Poll. *Onom.* 7.70 'Xenophon used σπολάς instead of θώραξ'). But as cavalrymen did not carry shields, a σπολάς alone would have provided poor protection (see further 3.4.48n. on θώρακα . . . τὸν ἱππικόν). X. does not explain where the equipment came from (despite reporting the destruction of surplus gear at 1). **ἵππαρχος ἐπεστάθη** 'was appointed as cavalry commander'. The only use of this term in *An.*; it was used at Athens ([Arist.] *Ath. Pol.* 61.4, with Rhodes), and X. wrote a separate treatise, *Hipparchicus* (*De equitum magistro*), on the training of cavalry commanders.

He does not explain how Lycius was chosen (at 3.4.21 the same verb is used in the active with the generals as subject). **Λύκιος . . . Ἀθηναῖος** appears first here; subsequently he leads a charge (4.3.22–5) and is with Xenophon on Mt Theches (4.7.24). The inclusion of both patronymic and ethnic is unusual: patronymics are included elsewhere in *An.* for two Athenian captains who appear once (4.2.13), but not for other participants in the expedition, including Xenophon (3.1.4n.) and four other Athenians. Possible explanations for the patronymic here are the identity of the father Polystratus, probably the defendant of [Lys.] 20 (Davies 1971: 468), a participant in the oligarchic coup at Athens in 411 BC, and the similar social background of X. and Lycius (Tsagalis 2009: 471–3).

3.4 THE ARMY CARRIES ON UP THE TIGRIS

The army continues its journey following the institution, at Xenophon's suggestion, of new units of cavalry and slingers. In this section it returns to the Tigris, following a route up river past some striking ruins (7–12n. (*c*)) and some well-stocked villages, through terrain that gradually becomes hillier; all the time it is followed by a Persian presence that becomes more and more imposing.

X.'s narrative continues to provide a commentary on the Greeks' strategic strengths and weaknesses, and on the advice offered by Xenophon in his speech to the whole army. The narrative brings out the advantages of cavalry and slingers (4, 16–18), but also shows that the army makes further adaptations in response to repeated Persian pressure: a significant change is made to the marching formation when the Greeks have to deal with narrowing terrain (19–23); further modifications are made when they enter hilly country with the Persians still in pursuit (28), and when the Persians send a detachment ahead and occupy a hill below which the road runs (38–43). Doctors are appointed (30), and there is mention of the Cretan archers practising an apparently new mode of shooting (17).

Whereas earlier changes were explicitly attributed to Xenophon, there is at first no mention by name either of Xenophon or of any other general, and little focus on the generals as a group (cf. also 32n. on ἐδίδαξεν . . . ἡ ἀνάγκη). Xenophon is, however, implicitly to the fore, in that it is his strategy that is being put to the test, and the action described takes place primarily in the rear, the area most heavily under pressure from the Persians – and the section where Xenophon himself is placed. A shift occurs when the Persians block the Greeks' path from the front. In response, there is first a consultation between Chirisophus and Xenophon, in which the latter proposes yet another tactical innovation (38–43n.), and then an ascent of a ridge in which Xenophon's personal leadership is foregrounded by contrast with a named subordinate (47–9) – two episodes that foreshadow the narrative texture of Book 4, where the interaction of Chirisophus and Xenophon will again be prominent as the army faces dangers in mountainous terrain both ahead and in the rear.

The first part of this chapter (1–37) stands out because of the relative overtness of the narratorial voice. During the uneasy peace described in Book 2 and the first part of the retreat (3.3n.) X. tells the story mostly from the Greeks' perspective and restricts the information he offers to what was known to the Greeks at the time; this mode of telling the story is resumed in the final section of this book and in the account of the army's encounters with unfamiliar tribes in Book 4. Here, by contrast, X. inserts narratorial comments (as marked by the use of the present tense) on the qualities of Persian weapons and the disadvantages of the formation the army uses, which the Ten Thousand or their generals then discover for themselves (17n. on μεγάλα . . . τόξα . . . ἐστιν, 19n. on ἀνάγκη γάρ ἐστιν, 20n.). He also uses the present tense to explain why the Persians retreat every night (34–6n.). A narratorial analepsis (2n. on τοσούτους γὰρ ἤιτησε Τισσαφέρνην) explains why Mithradates' troops increase in number and partly analeptic and partly proleptic statements are inserted which describe what happened generally during this part of the retreat or contain information which the Ten Thousand themselves did not know (17, 34–6n.). He also reveals a Persian manoeuvre before the Ten Thousand find out (37; contrast 3.5.1–2). This sort of unrestricted narratorial knowledge was common in ancient historians; its adoption at this point perhaps reflects the fact that open warfare against the Persians was a familiar historiographical topic.

3.4.1 τῆι ἄλληι 'on the next day'. **πρωϊαίτερον** 'earlier' (*sc.* than usual). **χαράδραν:** placed first as the new topic. See T2. **ἔδει:** αὐτούς (i.e. the Greeks) is better omitted because they are the default subject of ἔδει διαβῆναι. **ἐφ' ἧι** 'with a view to which', with ἐφοβοῦντο. The overt expression of their fears raises the question why the Persians did not try to prevent the crossing (cf. 3.3n.); possible reasons for their failure are their confidence in victory on the plain (2) and the problem of using cavalry in the ravine (cf. 5).

3.4.2 διαβεβηκόσι 'once they were across' (contrast preceding aorist διαβῆναι for the crossing itself; see *CGCG* 33.7). **πάλιν ἐπιφαίνεται ὁ Μιθραδάτης** echoes 3.3.6 ἐπιφαίνεται πάλιν ὁ Μιθραδάτης; see 3.3.1n. on ἔρχεται . . . λέγει for the word order and on σὺν ἱππεῦσιν ὡς τριάκοντα for the pattern of Persian appearances with larger forces. **ἔχων . . . εἰς τετρακισχιλίους:** since 3.3.6 the number of cavalry has increased fivefold and that of archers and slingers tenfold. For the qualification εἰς, emphasizing the larger number (cf. ensuing τοσούτους), see 3.3.6n. **τοσούτους γὰρ ἤιτησε Τισσαφέρνην:** a narratorial analepsis (cf. 3.4n.), offering information that could have been learnt from the high-status captives taken at 5 or else inferred subsequently by X. on the basis of his knowledge of the relative status of the two men. **ὑποσχόμενος . . . καταφρονήσας:** there is again no need to assume Persian informants for either Mithradates' promise or his feeling of contempt. The full report here builds on the increasingly negative portrayal of Mithradates, encouraging still more scepticism about his earlier protestations of friendship to the Greeks (cf. 3.3.2n.). His promise to 'hand over' the Greeks implies a belief that they will surrender rather than fight to the death. His overconfidence prepares for his subsequent failure (cf. Lys. 2.27 Ξέρξης . . . καταφρονήσας . . . τῆς Ἑλλάδος) while pointing to the difference that Xenophon's plans make: Mithradates wrongly assumes that he alone will have learnt from the earlier battle. For the negative connotations of καταφρονέω (used only here in *An.*) in X., see Hau 2012. **ἄν** = ἐάν. **ἐν τῆι πρόσθεν προσβολῆι:** as described at 3.3.7–11. **ὀλίγους ἔχων:** cf. 3.3.14(n.) σὺν ὀλίγοις. **ἔπαθε . . . ποιῆσαι** picks up 3.3.7, 12. The chiastic μέν/δέ clauses produce a juxtaposition of antithetical οὐδέν and πολλά (Smyth 2915a). Each clause offers a reason for Mithradates' contempt; ἐνόμιζε in the second clause hints that he had not in fact harmed the Greeks as much as he supposed (not least because the harm he had done had inspired Xenophon's tactical innovations).

3.4.3 ἐπεὶ δὲ . . . διαβεβηκότες resumes the narrative level of διαβεβηκόσι (2). In action–reaction pairs articulated with ἐπεί, the subject of the main clause (here Mithradates) is implied to have noticed the action in the ἐπεί-clause (Rijksbaron 1976: 160); this fits οἱ Ἕλληνες, reflecting Mithradates' external perspective. **ὅσον ὀκτὼ σταδίους:** the relatively long distance (about a mile) which Mithradates allows the Greeks to advance (underlined by ὅσον 'as much as': LSJ s.v. IV.1) before crossing himself reflects his concern that they might launch a counter-attack. **παρήγγελτο . . . τῶν ὁπλιτῶν:** the focus switches to the Greeks. τούτοις is to be understood as antecedent to οὕς; πελταστῶν and ὁπλιτῶν, partitive genitives, depend on it. The pluperfects παρήγγελτο and εἴρητο ('the instructions were') could cover orders given either before or while Mithradates crossed (unlike the English pluperfect, the Greek pluperfect does not imply a past-in-the-past: *CGCG* 33.40 n. 1); placement of the information here highlights how the Greeks frustrate Mithradates' expectations. **ὡς ἐφεψομένης ἱκανῆς δυνάμεως** gives the grounds why, in the opinion of those giving the orders (for subjective ὡς with participle, see *CGCG* 52.39; Smyth 2086), the cavalry should feel confidence (θαρροῦσι); X. stresses the co-operation of the different branches of the army (a key element in its successful retreat) and the development in the Greeks' 'running out' tactics since 3.3.8–10 (cf. Lee 2007: 74 n. 199). *Hell.* 3.4.23 (= *Ages.* 1.31) presents Agesilaus using the same tactics against Tissaphernes at Pactolus during his Asiatic campaign (3.3.12–19n.): the youngest hoplites and peltasts are ordered to run and the cavalry to charge 'on the assumption that (ὡς) he himself and the whole army would follow (ἑπομένου)' (cf. Anderson 1970: 117–18; also Brasidas' tactics at Thuc. 4.125.3).

3.4.4 ὁ Μιθραδάτης: this turns out to be his final mention in *An.*; cf. 3.5.1n. **κατειλήφει:** pluperfect of καταλαμβάνω 'catch up'; the ellipse of Mithradates' crossing (left suspended at 3 διέβαινε) and the omission here of the object αὐτούς both reflect the Greeks' perspective (cf. 3n. on ἐπεί). **ἤδη** 'now' is another sign of the Greeks' perspective, stressing the moment at which they need to act on their orders; cf. 34. **ἐσήμηνε** 'the signal was given', with subject (i.e. ὁ σαλπιγκτής, cf. 4.3.29, 32) understood (LSJ s.v. σημαίνω A.II.2); cf. 36 ἐκήρυξε. Of the Greek historians X. is most attentive to the use of signals in warfare (on which see Krentz 1991, esp. 115–16). **ἔθεον ὁμόσε οἷς εἴρητο** 'those who had been instructed ran to attack'. The implied antecedent of οἷς εἴρητο (the select light and heavy infantry, picking up 3) supplies the subject for ἔθεον (immediative imperfect: 3.3.8n. on καὶ ἐδίωκον). θέω ὁμόσε is found elsewhere only in X.'s accounts of the Pactolus battle (3n.) and twice in Dionysius of Halicarnassus. **καὶ οἱ ἱππεῖς ἤλαυνον:** successive clauses linked by καί form an unobtrusive chiasmus, highlighting the distinctive contribution of the new cavalry unit. **οὐκ ἐδέξαντο, ἀλλ' ἔφευγον:** a common negative–positive mode of expression; cf. 4.2.7, *Hell.* 4.3.17, 6.5.31, 7.5.12; here it brings out the blow to Persian expectations.

3.4.5 ἐν ταύτηι τῆι διώξει: the shift to abstraction (cf. 16 ἀκροβολίσει) after the run of short clauses allows for overt analysis of the advantages gained by Xenophon's tactical reforms. **τοῖς βαρβάροις:** dative of disadvantage. **πολλοὶ . . . εἰς ὀκτωκαίδεκα:** the greater precision about the number of cavalrymen captured underlines their greater importance (cf. Thuc. 3.87.3; Isoc. 8.118). X. does not mention what happens to the horses of these cavalrymen; presumably they were incorporated in the new cavalry unit (cf. 3.3.19). **ἐν τῆι χαράδραι:** owing to the difficulties faced by horses in uneven terrain (1n.). **ζωοὶ ἐλήφθησαν:** the verb ζωγρεῖν is more commonly used for 'take alive' (cf. 4.7.22), but the fuller expression is paralleled at *Hell.* 1.2.5 ζωὸν ἔλαβεν, where the relative numbers of captives and fatalities are again stressed. ζωός is an Ionicism and Doricism (Gautier 55); Attic prefers ζῶν. **αὐτοκέλευστοι . . . ᾐκίσαντο** 'unprompted, the Greeks disfigured'. In battles between Greeks, corpses were normally returned under treaty, while mutilation was seen as barbaric (cf. 5.4.17, scalping by the 'barbaric' (5.4.34) Mossynoecians;

Hdt. 9.79.1 τὰ πρέπει μᾶλλον βαρβάροισι ποιέειν ἤ περ Ἕλλησι, with Flower/Marincola); οἱ Ἕλληνες signposts the departure from ordinary Greek values, while αὐτοκέλευστοι exculpates their leaders (the word is found only here in classical Greek, but is common later). **ὡς . . . ὁρᾶν** 'so that it might be as frightening as possible for the enemy to see'. The Greeks may also have been motivated by a desire to avenge Mithradates' betrayal (Tuplin 2004c: 27 n. 10; cf. 3.3.2–3 and the motive attributed to him in this chapter at 2).

3.4.6 οὕτω πράξαντες 'after faring thus' could be taken as euphemistic (eliding the Greeks' cruelty) or as sarcastic (pointing up the contrast with the Persians' expectations). **τὸ λοιπὸν τῆς ἡμέρας:** this phrase is used (as at 16 and 30) when the army has overcome a difficulty earlier in the day's march; in these sections X. gives no indication of the distance the army covered (contrast the regular stages–parasangs formula: 10n.). **ἐπὶ τὸν Τίγρητα ποταμόν:** the Tigris was familiar to the Greeks from earlier stages of their retreat (2.4.13–28). X. mentions the army's arrival at the river before mentioning the city situated on it (7). He uses the same technique throughout the march between the Euphrates and Trapezus on the Black Sea coast (1.5.4, 2.4.13, 25; cf. cities 'across' rivers at 1.5.10, 2.4.28). Before the crossing of the Euphrates, by contrast, X. mentions the city before the river (1.2.7–8, 13, 23). The shift in technique suggests that rivers now provide a more familiar landmark than cities and also pose the greater strategic challenge.

3.4.7–12 X.'s account of the army's stops at Larisa and Mespila, two cities once held by Medes but subsequently captured by the Persians, raises a number of problems best considered together. For a detailed treatment of the whole section, see Tuplin 2003b: 371–89.

(*a*) *The Assyrian background.* 'Larisa' is the Assyrian city Kalhu, the Calah of Genesis 10:11–12, best known as Nimrud, the capital built by Ashurnasirpal II in the first half of the ninth century BC, and 'Mespila' is Nineveh, the palace built by Sennacherib towards the start of the seventh century BC (see T3–4). Both cities had been conquered and partly destroyed by the Medes and Babylonians in 614–612. X.'s account shows no knowledge of this Assyrian background, even though Herodotus alludes to Nineveh's capture by the Median king Cyaxares (1.106.2), Ctesias offers a narrative of its fall (F1b Lenfant = Diod. Sic. 2.24–7), and X. includes Assyrians in *Cyr.* His failure to include this background in *An.* may owe something to the nature of his information – probably not a written source (*pace* Cawkwell 2004: 52–3) but local inhabitants or captives who obscured (perhaps through ignorance) the Assyrian past. Two indications of the difficulty X. faced in integrating this information with the literary tradition on Assyria are Herodotus' sketchy Assyrian coverage and Ctesias' location of Nineveh on the Euphrates rather than the Tigris (F1b = Diod. Sic. 2.1–28, with Lenfant 235 n. 107).

(*b*) *Medes and Persians.* While the circumstances and aftermath of the fall of the Assyrian empire are obscure, there is archaeological evidence for continued settlement at both Nimrud and Nineveh, and so the possibility of a capture by a Persian king cannot be excluded (Briant 2002: 23 prefers to think of Persians contributing to the Medo-Babylonian attack). The only other evidence for a Persian attack on Nineveh comes in the *Stathmi* of Amyntas, a surveyor in Alexander's army (*FGrH* 122 F 2 = Ath. 12.529e–30a): 'in Nineveh there was a high mound, which Cyrus pulled down during his siege while raising a mound against the city'; this evidence seems independent of X. (*pace* Briant 2002: 879), and so perhaps offers slight support for the historicity of the capture. The circumstances of the two cities' capture (which Grote 1903–6: VII.257 n. 1 found 'of a truly Oriental character', cf. 8, 12nn.) may be of thematic importance. Higgins 1977: 95 suggests that their conquest 'only owing to chance acts of nature' testifies to Persian weakness (cf. Tuplin's suggestion (1991: 51) of a 'mildly anti-Persian source'). But the acts of nature are attributed to divine support – support which, according to Xenophon's earlier rhetoric (3.1.15–25, 2.10nn.), the Persians have now forfeited (Tuplin 2003b: 383).

(*c*) *The descriptions of the sites.* For both Larisa and Mespila X. offers a selective account of the imposing city walls and other notable constructions. He does not mention other features that could have been visible from outside (the gates or the moat and the River Khosr at Nineveh) or features within the cities (the palaces with their decorative panels and bull-colossi, the hanging gardens of Nineveh); indeed, there is no sign that the army entered either city. No fully inhabited city in Mesopotamia receives any such description in *An.* (Tuplin 2003b: 385); the nearest equivalent is the description of the Median Wall (2.4.12). These descriptions do, however, have precedents in Herodotus' accounts of the walls of Babylon and Ecbatana and of the pyramids of Egypt, though X. does not press this intertextual link through Herodotean concepts such as θαῦμα, ἔργα or the transience of greatness (any stress on which is weakened by the exclusion of the Assyrian past).

3.4.7 πόλις ἦν ἐρήμη μεγάλη: both Larisa at 7 and 9 and Mespila at 10–11 are described with imperfects and some pluperfects, showing that X. is reporting the perspective of the participants in the march rather than the state of the city at the time of narration (Rijksbaron 2012: 353–61 gives further examples of this use of the imperfect). ἐρήμη μεγάλη marks a contrast with the common description of cities as μεγάλη καὶ εὐδαίμων and/or οἰκουμένη (3.2.23n.); cf. the polarized classification of Greek rhetorical precepts on topographical descriptions (e.g. Theon *Prog.* 79.9 τόπος . . . ἔρημος ἢ οἰκούμενος). It need not denote absolute desertion: X.'s account of the capture of the city does not imply destruction; during the march upcountry the army came on a πόλις ἐρήμη μεγάλη called Corsote (1.5.4) but was still able to gain ample provisions there (see further 9n. on ἐπὶ ταύτης . . . ἀποπεφευγότες); and ἔρημος is often used in the sense 'unguarded' (*HCT* III.439). **ὄνομα:** the regional shift in X.'s technique for arrivals at cities and rivers (6n.) is accompanied by a change in the way he glosses names: up to the Euphrates, he twice glosses river names explicitly with ὄνομα (1.2.23, 4.4) and twice explains them implicitly through aetiologies (1.2.8, 13), while between the Euphrates and the Black Sea he glosses the names of cities either as here with ὄνομα (cf. 1.5.4, 10, 2.4.13, 25, 28, 3.4.10) or with ἐκαλεῖτο (4.7.19). This shift confirms that rivers are presented as the more familiar landmark in this section of the march. **Λάρισα:** Larisa was a common Greek toponym (πολλαὶ . . . αἱ Λάρισαι Strabo 13.3.2, cf. 9.5.19; Paus. 2.24.1) to which X. probably assimilated a local name or phrase: possible candidates are Akkadian *al šarruti* 'capital city' (Barnett 1963: 25, but see Dalley 1993: 144) and the biblical toponym Resen. **ᾤκουν . . . Μῆδοι:** 7–12n. τὸ παλαιόν and similar phrases (cf. ποτε in 10) typically conjure up a vague idea of pastness in contexts where chronological precision is not important; here τὸ παλαιόν shows that (unlike the other imperfects) ᾤκουν does not describe conditions at the time the army passed the cities. **τοῦ δὲ τείχους κτλ.:** the physical description matched the site reasonably well prior to its destruction in 2015 (for a survey of archaeological evidence, see Postgate and Reade 1976–80). For the wall, the height of 100 feet is accurate if the measurement is taken from the level of the plain; the thickness (25 feet) fits some sections but is too small for others; while the perimeter length of two parasangs (*c.* 6 miles: 10n.) slightly exceeds modern estimates of 4.5–5 miles. The use of parasangs suggests that X. is either reproducing local sources (cf. 2.4.12 on the Median Wall: μῆκος δ' ἐλέγετο εἶναι εἴκοσι παρασάγγαι) or self-consciously orientalizing. **κρηπὶς δ' ὑπῆν λιθίνη:** strong stone foundations in major Asiatic and Egyptian monuments are noted at Hdt. 1.93.2, 2.170.2; cf. the metaphorical use by Darius at Aesch. *Pers.* 814–15 κακῶν | κρηπὶς ὕπεστιν. **τὸ ὕψος εἴκοσι ποδῶν** 'of 20 feet in height' (accusative of respect modifying descriptive genitive, as in 9); X. varies the construction after the nominatives τὸ εὖρος and ὕψος with predicate πόδες.

3.4.8 ταύτην: asyndeton with anaphoric pronoun (3.2.7n. on ἐκ τούτου) is particularly common after the presentative formula πόλις ἦν. **βασιλεὺς**

ὁ Περσῶν: readers would presumably think of the elder Cyrus, who conquered the Median empire in 550 BC (and who is named in Amyntas' account, cited above). **τὴν ἀρχὴν ἐλάμβανον:** the imperfect casts the downfall of the empire as a gradual process which included the capture of Larisa as one of its stages. X. focuses on Persian acquisition of an empire, not on freedom (contrast Hdt. 1.127.1). **Ἥλιος δὲ . . . οἱ ἄνθρωποι** 'Helios, putting a cloud in front (of the city), made it invisible until the inhabitants left it.' Helios was an all-seeing sun-god invoked in oaths (Hom. *Il.* 3.277); his worship was associated with non-Greeks (Ar. *Pax* 406–8) and later assimilated with that of Persian Mithra (Briant 2002: 250–2). ἀφανίζειν πόλιν, usually 'destroy a city' (as at 3.2.11), here refers to an unusual meteorological event (like the thunder at Mespila at 12), i.e. a prolonged mist; Tacitus (*Ann.* 13.41.3) similarly describes how a city in Armenia suddenly covered by a dark cloud (*atra nube coopertum*) was believed to be delivered up to destruction by the gods. Helios' hostile use of clouds may derive from Assyrian omens (clouds portend a city's destruction at *Shumma Alu* 2 33 Freedman; cf. *Enuma Anu Enlil* 24 III.65 van Soldt 'If the Sun weeps . . . (and when) you observe the sky there is darkness . . . one king will defeat another') or from conflation of solar and storm deities (cf. Assyrian sun-god Šamaš shown with rain-clouds in British Museum tile 115076; Psalms 104:2–3; Polyaen. *Strat.* 7.2; Philo *FGrH* 790 F 2 (10.7); the cult of Zeus Helios). While in Greek accounts cloud-gathering was mainly the province of Zeus (hence Schenkl's emendation), the Sun could produce clouds by evaporation (Xenophan. DK 21 A46; Hippoc. *Aer.* 8; cf. Eustathius II.86, III.341 Van der Valk) or to avoid seeing pollution (Ps.-Callisth. 1.41 (battle of Issus) αὐτὸς ὁ ἥλιος . . . συννεφὴς ἐγένετο; Lucan 7.5–6). Modern editions print the sixteenth-century emendation ἥλιον δὲ νεφέλη προκαλύψασα ἠφάνισε ('a cloud, covering the sun, made it (i.e. the sun) invisible'), but (*a*) as object, ἥλιον (δέ) provides a weak antithesis to βασιλεὺς ὁ Περσῶν; (*b*) the focus on the city, the implicit object of ἐξέλιπον, is diluted if ἥλιον is object in the preceding clause; (*c*) the cloud performs two similar actions; (*d*) the cloud's agency is surprising (despite Homeric metaphors of enveloping clouds of grief or death (*Il.* 17.591, 20.417–18)); (*e*) elsewhere in classical Greek (Eur. *IT* 312; Aen. Tact. 32.9) the active of προκαλύπτω means 'put over as a cover' (the sense 'cover' occurs later in antiquity). **ἑάλω:** aorist of ἁλίσκομαι 'be taken'.

3.4.9 παρὰ ταύτην τὴν πόλιν . . . δύο πλέθρων: the πυραμὶς λιθίνη is a ziggurat, which would be easily assimilated to the pyramid, a more familiar monument (Reade 2002: 167 probably unnecessarily infers from πυραμίς that the ziggurat had already eroded considerably when Xenophon saw it). παρά 'alongside' is accurate if the πόλις is taken as the citadel, discounting the perimeter walls, on the inner side of which the ziggurat itself lay. The width X. gives may be correct for the lowest section that could be seen above the walls (allowing 100 feet (30 m) for a πλέθρον); his figure for the height is also reasonable if it applies to the height as seen by the army from the west as it passed between the Tigris and the city (Reade 2002: 167). **ἐπὶ ταύτης . . . ἀποπεφευγότες** 'on this were many of the barbarians, who had taken refuge from nearby villages'. ἀποπεφευγότες is a participle, not a periphrastic pluperfect with ἦσαν, which would have required ἐπί with accusative (Aerts 1965: 47). The Greeks could not have known about the origins of all the peoples on the ziggurat (e.g. if some had come from the city – a possibility not strictly ruled out by X.'s phrasing), though they could have drawn conclusions from the state of the nearby villages.

3.4.10 ἐντεῦθεν δ' ἐπορεύθησαν σταθμὸν ἕνα παρασάγγας ἕξ: a σταθμός is a 'stage', a day's march; a παρασάγγης (in origin perhaps the distance travelled in one hour) is a Persian measure of distance, rated between 21 and 60 (or even more) stades; the ratio 30 stades to the parasang is found in Herodotus (2.6.3, 5.53) and in interpolated summaries at *An.* 2.2.6, 5.5.4, 7.8.26. If X. had a fixed measure in mind, *c.* 3 miles is a reasonable estimate (Nimrud is *c.* 20 miles from Nineveh). The combination of stages and parasangs is used twenty-four times in Book 1 with Cyrus as subject of the verb ἐξελαύνει; subsequently it is used less regularly and with the Greeks as subject of the verb, usually for periods of uninterrupted and completed marching; its use here (the first since 2.4.28) indicates a brief return to the standard style of march. See Rood 2010b. **τεῖχος ἔρημον μέγα πρὸς [τῆι] πόλει κείμενον:** for ἔρημον, see 3.4.7n. on πόλις ἦν ἐρήμη μεγάλη. The city walls of Nineveh enclose two high mounds, Kouyunjik and Nebi Yunus; there was a further section of external defences. It is unclear (cf. Tuplin 2003b: 387–9) which part of the site X. refers to as the τεῖχος (probably here 'fort' rather than 'wall') and which as the πόλις. The placement of Mespila across the Tigris on the site of Mosul (Rawlinson 1850: 419 n. 1; *Barr.* 89 F4) can, however, be excluded (see 6n. on ἐπὶ τὸν Τίγρητα ποταμόν for cities explicitly 'across', πέραν, rivers). There also seems to be textual corruption; the simplest solution, followed here, is deletion of τῆι before πόλει, on the grounds that the city has not yet been mentioned. **Μέσπιλα:** the origins of this name for Nineveh are obscure. It has been connected with Mosul (the city across the river from Nineveh, see the previous note) and with Akkadian *mušpalum* ('low ground', perhaps via Aramaic *mšpyl'*), which is found in an inscription relating to Nineveh (Reade 1998–2001: 428), though nowhere used as a toponym (Dalley 2013: 241 n. 63). Tuplin 2003b: 372 speculates that X. assimilated the name to Μέσπιλα on the basis of the presence of medlar trees (μέσπιλα are 'medlars', cf. μεσπίλη 'medlar tree'). The toponym (spelt Μίσπιλα) is used elsewhere only by two grammarians, both citing X. **Μῆδοι . . . ὤικουν** contrasts with the order in 7 (ὤικουν . . . Μῆδοι); the Medes are here placed first as they are now the expected answer to the question about the city's former inhabitants (cf. 3.2.34n.). X need not be implying that it was now totally deserted. **κρηπίς:** here not a foundation but an outer stone wall with a higher mud-brick wall immediately behind it (Tuplin 2003b: 377). In an inscription on a clay prism Sennacherib prided himself on the structure of this 'great wall – the one called "wall whose radiance casts down the enemy"': 'I made a foundation upon limestone and made it 40 bricks thick. I raised its height to 180 courses of brickwork' (translation from Dalley 2013: 213). **λίθου ξεστοῦ κογχυλιάτου:** X.'s description matches Sennacherib's palace inscriptions, which mention 'fossiliferous limestone, whose structure is as finely granulated as cucumber seeds' (translation from Russell 1997: 300), as well as Layard's discoveries at the site (Layard 1853: 446). It suggests close observation (although there was a moat between the walls and the river); for scientific interest in fossils in the fifth century BC, see Xenophanes DK 21 A33.5; Hdt. 2.12.1. Pausanias (1.44.6) claims that this type of stone is found within Greece only in Megara. X.'s adjective reappears only in Philostr. *VA* 2.20 (a description of a palace in India, evidently modelled on X.); a scholion on 3.4.10 offers the gloss κογχυλίας λίθος.

3.4.11 ἑκατόν is accurate if the 50 feet of the κρηπίς are included in the height. **ἓξ παρασάγγαι:** a considerable exaggeration; modern estimates for the perimeter are 7–7.5 (rather than *c.* 18) miles. **λέγεται:** the attribution of the story to people outside the story-world of *An.* (shown by the present tense) suggests that it is familiar and endowed with some prestige; there is no suggestion of unreliability. λέγεται is used elsewhere in *An.* for 'mythical' events located in Greek spheres of influence (1.2.8, 13, 6.2.1, 2); for an ethnographic comment on the inhabitants of a land bordering Greek territory (6.4.2); and for recent and contemporary events in Persian settings – a usage confined to Books 1–2 (1.2.9, 14, 8.24, 28, 2.6.29). In Books 3–4, by contrast, where the Greeks move through unknown landscapes, X. does not otherwise attribute information to people outside the story-world (except possibly at 3.5.15(n.) ἔνθα θερίζειν [καὶ ἐαρίζειν] λέγεται). The variant ἐλέγετο would point to guides or other locals as sources, but this word is used in *An.* only of events or geographical features in the immediate story-world (with the exception of 7.2.22, where the story is of pressing significance for the Greeks). **Μήδεια:** the name (meaning 'Median woman') is shared with the (mythical) Medea, often seen as eponym of the Medes, who fled to Media from Athens (e.g. Hdt. 7.62.1). **βασιλέως:** the last Median king was Astyages. **ἀπώλλυσαν:** for the imperfect, see 8n. on τὴν ἀρχὴν ἐλάμβανον.

3.4.12 οὔτε χρόνωι . . . οὔτε βίαι: i.e. neither by prolonged siege nor by direct assault, elaborating on οὐδενὶ τρόπωι (8) in the Larisa story. **ἐμβροντήτους ποιεῖ** 'made thunderstruck' (with an implication of mental disturbance). The present tense is used in quick summaries of events that are off the main storyline (cf. Rijksbaron 1991: 1–2). For the impact of lightning, cf. *Hell.* 4.7.7 'a thunderbolt fell on the camp, and some men died after being hit (πληγέντες), others from the shock (ἐμβροντηθέντες)'; *GSW* III.119–22. In classical Greek ἐμβρόντητος is mostly used metaphorically with the sense 'silly', 'senseless' ([Pl.] *Alc.* 2.140c8 ἠλιθίους τε καὶ ἐμβροντήτους), often abusively in comedy (cf. Wankel on Dem. 18.243). The reading βροντῆι κατέπληξε is probably a gloss on the more unusual expression, which is imitated at Dio Chrys. 27.2. **καὶ οὕτως ἑάλω:** the use of the same phrase as at 8 points to the parallel fates of the two cities.

3.4.13 ἐπορεύθησαν σταθμὸν ἕνα: the stage–parasang framework resumes (1on.), but here, unusually, with a single stage and no indication of arrival at a destination (as at 1.2.6, 4.1, 4, 6, the only other single stages). X. thereby prepares for the sudden disruption to the framework (εἰς τοῦτον δὲ τὸν σταθμόν) caused by the appearance of Tissaphernes and a brief military action; the day's march is resumed at 16. **Τισσαφέρνης ἐπεφάνη** contrasts in both tense and order with ἐπιφαίνεται ὁ Μιθραδάτης (2), underlining that Tissaphernes is the expected culmination of the escalating Persian opposition. **οὕς τε αὐτὸς ἱππέας ἦλθεν ἔχων:** the roughly 500 cavalrymen with whom Tissaphernes came to inform on Cyrus (1.2.4). ἔχων governs οὕς as well as its implied antecedent and each limb of the paratactic structure τε . . . καὶ . . . καὶ . . . καὶ πρὸς τούτοις; the convoluted structure brings out the size of Tissaphernes' force. **τὴν Ὀρόντα δύναμιν:** see 2.4.8. Orontas was a member of a family dynasty that held the satrapy of Armenia (3.5.17n.) and a major figure in the western part of the Persian empire in the fourth century: in the 380s BC he served as commander of the Persian army in Cyprus, and in the late 360s (perhaps around or soon after X. composed *An.*) he was involved (perhaps while he was holding a senior position in Mysia) in a revolt against the king (see Osborne 1973; Stylianou on Diod. 15.90.3). **τοῦ τὴν βασιλέως θυγατέρα ἔχοντος:** the marriage (which had been imminent at 2.4.8) reflects a common Persian method of strengthening bonds between the royal family and the nobility (Brosius 1996: 70–82). The daughter's name was Rhodogyne (Plut. *Artax.* 27.7; *OGIS* 391–2). Greek authors regularly avoided naming respectable Greek women, but X. refers by name to high-status foreign women in *An.* (the king's mother Parysatis and the Cilician queen Epyaxa) and *Cyr.* (Mandane, Panthea) and also to high-status Greek women within the Persian empire (Hellas in *An.*, Mania in

Hell.). So the non-naming of Rhodogyne can be attributed either to her lack of importance for the plot or to X.'s lack of knowledge. **οὓς Κῦρος ἔχων ἀνέβη βαρβάρους:** 3.1.2n. on καὶ οἱ σὺν Κύρωι ἀναβάντες βάρβαροι. **ὁ βασιλέως ἀδελφός:** see 2.4.25, where X. specifies that he is a νόθος 'bastard' and that he had brought troops from Susa and Ecbatana. For another Persian elite male introduced not by name but by connection to the king, see 2.3.17, 28 ὁ τῆς βασιλέως γυναικὸς ἀδελφός; cf. the unnamed brothers of Ariaeus and Tissaphernes at 2.4.1, 5.35; also 3.3.4(n.) τῶν Τισσαφέρνους τις οἰκείων. **πάμπολυ ἐφάνη** brings out the visual impact of the army; see 3.3.13n. for the παν- compound and Clarke 2006 for the use of φαίνομαι without participle or infinitive in the sense 'be clearly', i.e. as if with participle. Cf. Clearchus' use of a ruse ὥστε τὸ στράτευμα . . . δόξαι πάμπολυ εἶναι (2.4.26).

3.4.14 ἐπεὶ δ' ἐγγὺς ἐγένετο: as at 3.3.9 (ἐπεὶ δ' ἐγγὺς ἐγένοντο . . .), but here with Tissaphernes as subject, preparing for the account of his tactics. **ὄπισθεν:** i.e. in the Greeks' rear (which is where the Persians in pursuit would have been anyway), contrasting with the new flanking move (εἰς τὰ πλάγια παραγαγών). Tissaphernes was relying on the Persians' superior numbers but not exploiting them in hand-to-hand combat. **ἐμβαλεῖν . . . διακινδυνεύειν:** both negative clauses mark out Tissaphernes as cowardly (cf. 3.2.16(n.) οὐ θέλουσι . . . δέχεσθαι; contrast the Greeks' τόλμα at 3.2.11, 16(nn.)); the first refers to his refusal to launch a direct assault (LSJ s.v. ἐμβάλλω II) now, the second gives the long-term thinking underlying his refusal. Mithradates is not slighted when he adopts a similar strategy at 3.3.7.

3.4.15 διαταχθέντες: the δια- prefix implies distribution at intervals to increase the spread of missiles (by contrast with the enforced shooting from within the square at 3.3.7). **οἱ Ῥόδιοι:** 3.3.16n. While the account of Persian strategy is focused on Tissaphernes, the Greek light-armed troops act without the need for precise orders. **οἱ [Σκύθαι] τοξόται:** given that Scythians are mentioned nowhere else in *An.*, Σκύθαι should be deleted as an intrusive gloss, probably deriving from the familiar use of Scythian archers as a police force at Athens or from the generic use of Σκύθαι in the sense ἱπποτοξόται attested at Ael. *Tact.* 2.13. **οὐδεὶς ἡμάρτανεν ἀνδρός:** the lack of article here suggests that each hit 'a man' almost at random (for the 'unmissability' topos, cf. Dion. Hal. *Ant. Rom.* 5.24.3, 8.86.8; Plut. *Crass.* 24.4 'the compactness and denseness of the Romans did not allow even anyone who wished to miss a man (οὐδὲ τῶι βουλομένωι διαμαρτάνειν ἀνδρός)'; Dexippus *FGrH* 100 F 25.5). After two verbs in the aorist describing the beginning of the fight, the imperfect tense marks what happened in its progress. **οὐδὲ γὰρ . . . ῥάιδιον ἦν:** owing to the size of the Persian army.

The tone of the aside is sardonic. **καὶ ὁ Τισσαφέρνης . . . ἀπεχώρει:** καί is the first word of the main clause; it is co-ordinated with the following καί, not with the two preceding uses of καί in the ἐπεί-clause. X. again makes Tissaphernes seem cowardly by attaching the detail μάλα ταχέως ἔξω βελῶν (for omission of article with prepositional phrases, see Smyth 1128) to him rather than his army and by using the immediative imperfect ἀπεχώρει.

3.4.16–18 καὶ τὸ λοιπὸν τῆς ἡμέρας . . . τῆι ἀκροβολίσει: this is a difficult passage, probably in large part owing to textual problems. X. first implies a contrast between the current and the earlier exchange of missiles and then picks up earlier passages discussing the relative distances covered by Greek and Persian bows (3.3.7, 16, 17(nn.)) in order to show that the difference was caused by two new factors, one prepared by the earlier narrative (the Rhodian slingers), one not previously announced (the Cretans' use of Persian arrows); in so doing he moves from the specific narrative context to a more general register, but both the temporal structure and the logic of the passage are hard to grasp. The running translation with glosses supplied below divides this section into five parts: (*a*) argues that words are missing in 16; (*b*)–(*c*) suggest that this gap should contain an explanation that the Cretans were now able to shoot further because they began using Persian arrows, which were of a similar size to but lighter than their own; (*d*) highlights an awkwardness that may point to further textual problems.

(*a*) story-now (16): 'The rest of the day the one side (οἱ μέν = the Greeks) made their way while the other side (οἱ δ' = the Persians) followed. And the barbarians no longer (οὐκέτι, i.e. by contrast with the earlier engagements) harmed them in the long-range fighting at that time; for the Rhodians slung further than the Persians and <. . .> (most of) the archers.' The text of the last sentence in the MSS will not do (whether or not one reads πλείστων before τοξοτῶν): οἵ τε Ῥόδιοι needs a second clause with a new subject (emending τε to γε to remove this need replaces one problem with another); and while some editors, taking καί as adverbial, translate the second half of the sentence 'slung further than the Persians, even than (most of) the archers' (i.e. further than the Persian archers shot their arrows), this seems impossibly compressed. Some mention of the Cretan archers (preparing for 17) is also expected: hence Madvig's addition of <οἱ Κρῆτες ἐτόξευον>. But given that the Cretans were (probably owing to their heavier arrows) previously shooting less far than the Persians (3.3.7(n.)), it is hard to understand why they should now be shooting *further* than the Persians just because they were (as, in the MSS, emerges later in the passage) using their arrows.

(*b*) general (17): 'Persian bows are also (καί) big (i.e. like the Cretans')'. A very abrupt comment, and both the emphatic position of μεγάλα and the presence of καί are hard to explain without prior mention of the size of the Cretans' bows and arrows.

(*c*) story-general (17): '. . . so that whichever arrows were captured were useful for the Cretans, and they continued using the enemy's arrows, and they would practise shooting far by discharging upwards'. διετέλουν χρώμενοι requires a stronger statement that the Cretans started using the Persian arrows than the preceding χρήσιμα ἦν (i.e. something like ἐχρῶντο δὲ αὐτοῖς οἱ Ἕλληνες at 4.2.28; cf. Polyb. 18.28.9; Plut. *Thes.* 8.1). It could mean 'used continuously', but some indication of the time frame would be expected (as at *Hell.* 7.3.2–3).

(*d*) story-general (17): 'And many sinews as well as lead were found (ηὑρίσκετο) in the villages for use for the slings.' The connection of thought is that slingers as well as archers had supplies. But which villages? The imperfect demands a wider reference than just the villages (3.3.11) where the unit of slingers was instituted. Since then, X. has mentioned villages only at 9, but he did not specify that the army passed through them. ἐν ταῖς κώμαις here also reads awkwardly before the clear sequence κώμαις ἐπιτυχόντες . . . ἐν ταῖς κώμαις in 18 (where the article in the second phrase refers back to the first); it may none the less be a general reference to villages, with the definite article presupposing knowledge of their importance in the Persian empire. Another possibility is to move this sentence to after ἦν γὰρ πολὺς σῖτος ἐν ταῖς κώμαις in 18 (for the ensuing repetition cf. ἐν (. . .) τῶι πεδίωι at 3.5.1–2); this change would make good sense of the general ὥστε χρῆσθαι in 18 and align the imperfect ηὑρίσκετο with its use elsewhere in *An.* for the immediate story-now (4.4.13, 5.4.28, 29, 7.5.14).

(*e*) story-now (18): 'And that day, when the Greeks were making camp after coming across villages, the barbarians went away, having the worse of it (μεῖον ἔχοντες) in the long-range fighting (τῆι ἀκροβολίσει, picking up τῆι τότε ἀκροβολίσει in 16, where the statement of Persian inferiority is not as strong).'

The probability that these difficulties are due to textual corruption is strengthened by comparison with sections where general and specific material is more tightly integrated (34–6(n.), 4.2.28). Confusion in the MSS may have been caused by the repetition of key words and phrases (τῆι ἀκροβολίσει, τοξ- roots, ὥστε, χρῆσθαι, ἐν ταῖς κώμαις); ὁπόσα δ' in some MSS at 17 may point to scribal hesitation about the correct division of clauses.

3.4.16 ἐσίνοντο: for Ionic/Attic σίνομαι, see Introduction p. 28; the variant ἐπέκειντο (a more common word in Attic prose) must have arisen from a gloss. **τῆι τότε ἀκροβολίσει:** τότε reinforces the contrast with earlier engagements while also preparing for the damage the Persians are able to inflict when the Greeks' march is disrupted (19–23n.). The rare abstract noun ἀκροβόλισις is found three times in X. (18 below and *Cyr.* 6.2.15), then not until his imitator Arrian; ἀκροβολισμός (twice each in *Hell.* and Thucydides) became the standard form.

3.4.17 μεγάλα... τόξα... ἐστιν: present tense, indicating an ethnographic statement; for stress on the size of Persian (composite) bows (3.3.7n.), cf. Hdt. 7.61.1 'the Persians had short spears, long bows (τόξα . . . μεγάλα), and arrows made from reeds'. **ὥστε χρήσιμα . . . τοξεύμασι:** for reuse of enemy missiles, cf. the use of the even larger Carduchian arrows as javelins (4.2.28); Kelly 2012: 275 lists further examples. X.'s insistence on the point (with χρήσιμα picked up by χρώμενοι and χρῆσθαι) matches his concern in the Socratic works with making good use of material goods (Pomeroy on *Oec.* 1.8). **ὁπόσα ἁλίσκοιτο:** optative in past indefinite construction (3.1.20n.); ὁπόσα is followed by partitive τῶν τοξευμάτων. The odd application of ἁλίσκομαι 'capture' to missiles that the Persians deliberately discharged against the enemy with no intention of regaining them increases the sense of Greek cunning; earlier in the march they had used enemy arrows for firewood (2.1.6). **τοῖς Κρησί:** dative with χρήσιμα, but juxtaposed with τῶν τοξευμάτων owing to the Cretans' renown as archers (3.3.7n.). **ἐμελέτων . . . μακράν:** ἱέντες (used absolutely: LSJ s.v. ἵημι I.3.b) emphasizes the mode of shooting, τοξεύειν the overall action. μακράν 'far' (for the form, see 3.3.16n. on τὴν ταχίστην; LSJ s.v.) goes with τοξεύειν. Upward shots were a Persian technique (Hdt. 7.226) adopted not for easy recovery of the arrows but for an optimum combination of distance and momentum as they fell. **νεῦρα . . . καὶ μόλυβδος:** νεῦρα are not bowstrings (νευραί in classical prose) but sinews for use as sling-cords (so the ὥστε-clause goes with both νεῦρα and μόλυβδος). These supplies are probably linked with local agriculture, with the lead being taken from tools (Ma 2010: 428), rather than military stockpiles (Briant 2002: 1038). **ἐν ταῖς κώμαις:** 16–18n. (*d*). **ὥστε χρῆσθαι:** the infinitive suggests the use of the produce over a period of time; contrast ὥστε χρήσιμα ἦν, which refers to the immediate use of specific Persian arrows (*CGCG* 46.4, 7). **εἰς τὰς σφενδόνας** 'for the slings' (εἰς with accusative expressing goal: Smyth 1686.1d).

3.4.18 καὶ ταύτηι μὲν τῆι ἡμέραι: a stronger expression (e.g. resumptive μὲν οὖν, or δ' αὖ as at 4.3.1) might be expected for the return to the main narrative level, but cf. 4.1.11, 14, 2.7 for καὶ . . . μέν with temporal phrases rounding off an episode after background material. **κατεστρατοπεδεύοντο:** the villages (T5) were probably collections of huts without defences, but they may have been situated in good defensive positions (cf. 33). **τῆι ἀκροβολίσει:** τότε probably entered the MSS from 16: it would point to a contrast with subsequent fighting, but the exchanges at 25–6 seem too far off. **ἔμειναν . . . καὶ ἐπεσιτίσαντο:** cf. similar delays for provisioning at 1.4.9, 5.4 in the march up and 4.7.18 in the retreat. ἐπισιτίζομαι is a general military term for provisioning on campaign, whether the food is provided by allies, bought from a market or looted from stores; here the last option is most likely. **πολὺς σῖτος:** similarly well-stocked villages are found further up the Tigris (31, 5.1). X. confirms Xenophon's observations on the advantages for the Greeks in being able to exploit any land they should control (3.2.21); he shows no concern for how the villagers survived the destruction of their food reserves. **ἐπορεύοντο . . . καὶ Τισσαφέρνης εἵπετο:** varying οἱ μὲν ἐπορεύοντο, οἱ δ' εἵποντο (16); the focus on Tissaphernes also contrasts with ἀπῆλθον οἱ βάρβαροι earlier in 18.

3.4.19–23 As with the introduction of slingers and a cavalry corps to make the rear less exposed to attack (3.3.12–19n.), the Greeks make further modifications to the πλαίσιον-formation in the light of experience, here attributed to the generals rather than to Xenophon specifically (21). The problem that now emerges is that the formation was too broad and inflexible to cope with occasional narrowing of the road owing to terrain; this problem would become acute when, as here, there was pressure from the enemy behind. The generals seek to overcome it by introducing flexible λόχοι along the flanks which would hold back whenever the line of march became too narrow, and then, as the line expanded, fill any gap that emerged, dividing if necessary into smaller units so as to fill the required width (21, 22). It later becomes clear that the extra protection on the flanks is not enough: further adaptations are required when the Persians attack from above (28) or block the path in front (38–43).

In keeping with the perhaps artificial exactness of much military writing, X. offers a precise technical description that draws on the language used in materialistic explanations of natural phenomena (19(n.) ἀνάγκη, ἐκθλίβεσθαι, 20(n.) διάσχηι . . . διασπᾶσθαι, κενόν) and is marked by verbal repetition. He formulates the problem in universalizing terms (marked by the use of the present tense), stressing that the Greeks are responding to both physical and logical necessity (four ἀνάγκη-words in 19–20), which threatens a return to their earlier disarray (19 ἀτάκτους, 20 ἀθυμεῖν), but is overcome by cool strategic reasoning. In formulating the solution, by contrast, he focuses on the specific measures adopted at the time while using the same order of exposition as in his account of the problem: (*a*) drawing together of the wings: ἢν συγκύπτηι τὰ κέρατα τοῦ πλαισίου (19) ~ ὁπότε μὲν συγκύπτοι τὰ κέρατα (21); (*b*) narrowing of the front at crossing-points: γεφύρας (19), ὁπότε δέοι γέφυραν διαβαίνειν ἢ ἄλλην τινὰ διάβασιν (20) ~ εἰ δὲ καὶ διαβαίνειν τινὰ δέοι διάβασιν ἢ γέφυραν (23); (*c*) confusion/no confusion: ταραττομένους (19) ~ οὐκ ἐταράττοντο (23); (*d*) drawing apart of the wings/flanks: ὅταν δ' αὖ διάσχηι τὰ κέρατα (20) ~ ὁπότε δὲ διάσχοιεν αἱ πλευραὶ τοῦ πλαισίου (22); (*e*) middle empty/full: κενὸν γίγνεσθαι τὸ μέσον τῶν κεράτων (20) ~ τὸ μέσον ἀνεξεπίμπλασαν . . . ὥστε ἀεὶ ἔκπλεων εἶναι τὸ μέσον (22). X.'s efforts to provide a neatly symmetrical account lead, however, to a formulation of the role of the new units that is compressed and has been variously interpreted.

A similar theoretical concern with marching structures is shown in *Cyr.*: see esp. 1.6.43, 2.4.2–4, 6.3.3–4 for adjustment to narrow terrain; also 4.5.37, 5.3.37, 4.45–6, and cf. *Eq. mag.* 2.9, 7.11.

3.4.19 οἱ Ἕλληνες ἔγνωσαν: contrast 21, where X. gives the generals credit for the solution. **πλαίσιον ἰσόπλευρον** is object of ἔγνωσαν and subject of the ὅτι-clause (cf. 3.2.8n), while **πονηρὰ τάξις** is predicate. ἰσόπλευρον = 'with equal flanks', i.e. equal in length or depth; the closest parallels to X.'s usage are late (glosses on νηὸς ἐΐσης/νῆας ἐΐσας at Σ Hom. *Od.* 3.431; Ps.-Zonar. ε 629.6 Tittmann). The adjective has always been taken in the sense 'equal-sided' (common from Plato's *Timaeus* onwards), implying that the πλαίσιον proposed by Xenophon at 3.2.36(n.) was a square (a formation that later technical writers and lexicographers, citing this passage, call a πλινθίον (Arr. *Tact.* 29.7–8; *Suda* π 1778 Adler; cf. Ael. *Tact.* 37.8–9)); but (*a*) a square formation makes no sense for an army on the march (as opposed to a static army under cavalry attack) and runs counter to other indications in the narrative (e.g. the metaphor 'tail' (38(n.); *HCT* IV.343)); (*b*) the problem the Greeks identify would occur with *any* inflexible πλαίσιον, and the solution X. describes is not a change from square to oblong πλαίσιον at pinch points; (*c*) elsewhere in *An.* πλευρά is specifically 'flank'. Arrian (who imitated X.'s phrase at *Anab.* 4.5.6) was evidently misled by the mathematical sense of ἰσόπλευρος. **πολεμίων ἑπομένων:** the same phrase at 20. The repetition underlines the fact that it is the Persians' continued pressure that has caused the problem Xenophon had not foreseen. Genitives absolute are occasionally postponed when, rather than offering background information, they make explicit the conditions under which the preceding observation holds true; this type of postponement is particularly common in *An.* in claims about the position or status of the enemy (cf. 24 τῶν πολεμίων ὄντων ἱππέων; 36 ἀκουόντων τῶν πολεμίων; 40 πολεμίων ἐπιφαινομένων; also 2.4.6, 4.6.12, 5.6.9, 6.3.12). **ἀνάγκη γάρ ἐστιν:** the present tense brings out that the problem observed is universal; this perspective is maintained in the conditional ἢν μὲν συγκύπτηι and in the corresponding ὅταν δ' αὖ διάσχηι in 20. The use of ἀνάγκη for the process of drawing apart compressed bodies of troops matches its use in fifth-century scientific writing of 'a chain of cause and effect implicit in the material world', e.g. in the creation of thunder and lightning (Dover on Ar. *Nub.* 376–8, with references). **συγκύπτηι** 'bend towards one another' (a body metaphor), only here and at 21 in X. **κέρατα:** the wings of the front and rear lines (by contrast with πλευραί, used of the flanks of the whole formation). Wings rather than flanks are specified here because the trouble starts as the front wings converge. **ὀρέων ἀναγκαζόντων ἢ γεφύρας:** the terrain starts to become slightly narrower further south (3.3n.), but this is the first time X. reports mountains impinging on the march (T6). Bridges play some role in the narrative before the army crosses to the left bank of the Tigris (2.3.10, 4.13, 17–24) but are mentioned in Book 3 only here and at 3.5.8–12, when a proposal to bridge the Tigris is rejected. Here X. is probably alluding to fixed bridges over ditches, streams and stretches of marshland. For river crossings, see further 3.2.22, 3.6nn. **ἐκθλίβεσθαι** 'be squeezed out of position' (rather than 'be cramped, crowded' (LSJ s.v. ἐκθλίβω)), a graphic expression derived from medical and scientific descriptions of compressed elements (e.g. Hippoc. *Flat.* 10; Arist. *Gen. an.* 783a16). **πιεζομένους** refers to physical pressure, while **ταραττομένους** includes mental disturbance. **δυσχρήστους** picks up from 17(n.) the stress on utility (marked by cognate χρήσιμα and χρῆσθαι). For X.'s fondness for δυσ- compounds, see 3.5.16n. **ἀτάκτους ὄντας** 'since they are disordered' (causal).

3.4.20 δ' αὖ 'in turn', i.e. once they were through the narrow space (emphasizing how the divergence is a logical consequence). **διάσχηι . . . διασπᾶσθαι** 'draw apart . . . disperse'; the δια- prefix implies separation. The register of διασπάω is both military (e.g. Thuc. 5.70 ἵνα . . . μὴ διασπασθείη . . . ἡ τάξις) and scientific (e.g. Emp. DK 31 B63 διέσπασται μελέων φύσις). X. suggests that it is impossible for troops in such straits to restore their previous positions by themselves. **κενόν** is also used of 'void' by the atomists (e.g. Democr. DK 68 B125). **ὁπότε δέοι . . . ἔσπευδεν:** X. shifts from the universal present tenses to an iterative imperfect (with optative in the sub-clause) for details specific to this expedition; cf. 1.5.2–3, with *CGCG* 61.4–6. **γέφυραν . . . ἢ ἄλλην τινὰ διάβασιν:** the phrasing implies that a γέφυρα is the most desirable form of διάβασις (cf. 2.6.6 εἰς παιδικὰ ἢ εἰς ἄλλην τινὰ ἡδονήν). διάβασις is used in X. of a place (4.3.17) or means (2.3.10 – not 'bridge', *pace* LSJ) of river-crossing, and also for crossing of difficult terrain (*Cyn.* 10.19 τὰς διαβάσεις τῶν ναπῶν). See further 23n. **βουλόμενος . . . πρῶτος:** an understandable but self-defeating instinct for self-preservation, cf. Thuc. 7.84.3 πᾶς . . . διαβῆναι αὐτὸς πρῶτος βουλόμενος, of the Athenians' disastrous attempt to cross the River Assinarus in their retreat from Syracuse; contrast the beneficial desire to be 'first' at 4.3.29, 7.11–12, and the open cynicism of Meno in crossing the Euphrates first at 1.4.14–16. **εὐεπίθετον ἦν ἐνταῦθα τοῖς πολεμίοις** 'under such circumstances it was easy for the enemy to attack', i.e. by rapid cavalry attacks on unsettled parts of the army; the confusion would also make protection against missiles harder.

3.4.21 οἱ στρατηγοί: 19n. on οἱ Ἕλληνες ἔγνωσαν. **ἓξ λόχους ἀνὰ ἑκατὸν ἄνδρας:** ἀνά is distributive ('100 men each': Smyth 1682.2c). For one hundred as the size of a λόχος, cf. 4.8.15 (with the qualification σχεδόν); at one point in the march up, by contrast, two λόχοι amount (if the text is sound) to a hundred men (1.2.25). Numbers across companies must in practice have varied unless the army was reorganized when new marching arrangements were introduced by the new board of generals. **πεντηκοντῆρας . . . ἐνωμοτάρχους:** the nouns (both of which are used as predicates after ἄλλους: 'others as . . .') signify officers in charge of units, the πεντηκοστύς (the name of which suggests a group of fifty) and the ἐνωμοτία ('sworn group'), probably twenty-five men (X. does not clarify its size, as Arr. *Tact.* 6.3 notes). The only other mention in *An.* of ἐνωμόταρχοι/ἐνωμοτίαι is 4.3.26; πεντηκοντῆρες do not reappear. The mention of these sub-officers here is due to the role their units play in 22; there is no reason to suppose that other λόχοι did not have them. The titles are found elsewhere only in Spartan armies (*Lac.* 11.4, with Lipka; Thuc. 5.66.3, 68.3, with *HCT*; Lazenby 2012: 6–13), and so are perhaps the result of Chirisophus' input (Anderson 1970: 234). But the match with the Spartan model is loose: the larger Spartan unit μόρα is not mentioned here, and if not the ratio, then at least the size of the units is almost certainly different. **οὗτοι** (the six special λόχοι) **δὲ πορευόμενοι** is a theme-constituent (3.3.16n. on ἡμεῖς . . . δεῖ); the entire iterative description (until 23 οὗτοι) of the units' movements at moments of contraction (ὁπότε μέν . . .) and divergence (ὁπότε δέ . . .) comes under its scope, but the following main clauses have οἱ λοχαγοί as their subject. **ὑπέμενον ὕστεροι οἱ λοχαγοί** 'the captains would wait behind' (with predicative ὕστεροι), i.e. together with their λόχοι, thus providing space and cover for the wings to draw together in an orderly way. λοχαγοί are specified because they are the orchestrators of the manoeuvre. **ὥστε μὴ ἐνοχλεῖν τοῖς κέρασι** confirms that the initial problem (compression at the wings) was solved; the implication is that the special units were normally placed close to the wings. **τοτὲ δὲ . . . τῶν κεράτων** 'but sometimes they would be leading them (i.e. the companies, supplied as object from the theme-constituent) along outside the wings'. For παρα- denoting movement 'along', see Balode 2011: 101–6 (LSJ s.v. παράγω I.2 is misleading). τοτὲ δέ without preceding τοτὲ μέν (conventionally so accented: see Fraenkel on Aesch. *Ag.* 100), like ὁ δέ without preceding ὁ μέν, introduces an explanatory aside: cf. *GP* 166; *Hell.* 1.2.14 οἱ αἰχμάλωτοι Συρακόσιοι . . . νυκτὸς ᾤχοντο εἰς Δεκέλειαν, οἱ δ' εἰς Μέγαρα; Pl. *Phlb.* 35e 3–4 εἴ τις . . . ἀλγεῖ, τοτὲ δὲ χαίρει (after preceding ὑπέμενον, τότε 'at that time' lacks a clear temporal reference; it is not used in the sense 'next'). Here the aside indicates that at times (but exceptionally) the special units did not need to hold back to avoid congestion, because they were already outside the wings when the contraction happened (23 suggests that they would be reacting to problems elsewhere); they would evidently have to stop when they reached the bottleneck. The flexibility of the special units may explain why X. does not expressly indicate their normal position: his main concern (picking up 19–20) is their innovative response at those moments when the army's cohesion was most threatened. The best reconstruction is that the special units were positioned on the outer flanks of the πλαίσιον (so that it was no longer ἰσόπλευρον), where they could support the whole formation, react quickly to narrowing terrain, and fall back without causing problems inside the oblong. At 43, '300 of the select troops', i.e. three of the λόχοι, are presented as a unit regularly under Chirisophus' control near the front of the πλαίσιον (where the compression would begin), and this may imply that the other three were a unit too (see 43n. for 300-strong units). This reconstruction (Grote 1903–6: VII.257; Pelling *per e-litt.*) rejects the common view that the new units had a fixed position *within* the main formation. Some scholars (e.g. Lendle; Lee 2007: 88) place them all in the rear (dismissing the implication of 43), others three rear centre and three front centre, suggesting that the latter would move either (Mather/Hewitt) back inside the πλαίσιον (but this makes no military sense anyway) or (Masqueray, reading τοὺς δέ (*sc.* λόχους)) to the sides (but this further requires insertion of οἱ μέν, 'some' (of the λόχοι), with ὑπέμενον and deletion of οἱ λοχαγοί, which must none the less be supplied as subject of παρῆγον, and presupposes a clear division that X. has not mentioned).

3.4.22 πλευραί: X. specifies the flanks (rather than the wings, as at 20) because he is describing how the special units, now placed ὕστεροι (21), respond to the flanks' divergence. **τὸ μέσον:** the space between the wings, presumably in the rear, where the formation was most exposed to enemy attack. **ἀνεξεπίμπλασαν** 'would fill up again', a *hapax*. ἀνεκ- compounds are very rare (ἐξανα- being the preferred order), but here the ἀνα- prefix ('re-') is placed first because ἐκπίμπλημι 'fill up' is a standard and therefore indivisible term. Krüger's ἂν ἐξεπίμπλασαν, with iterative ἄν, destroys the balance with the other straight imperfects. **εἰ μὲν στενότερον . . . κατ' ἐνωμοτίας:** the smaller units cover a wider front because of the way they are deployed: see Figures 1–3. How they returned to the flanks once the disturbance was over is not explained.

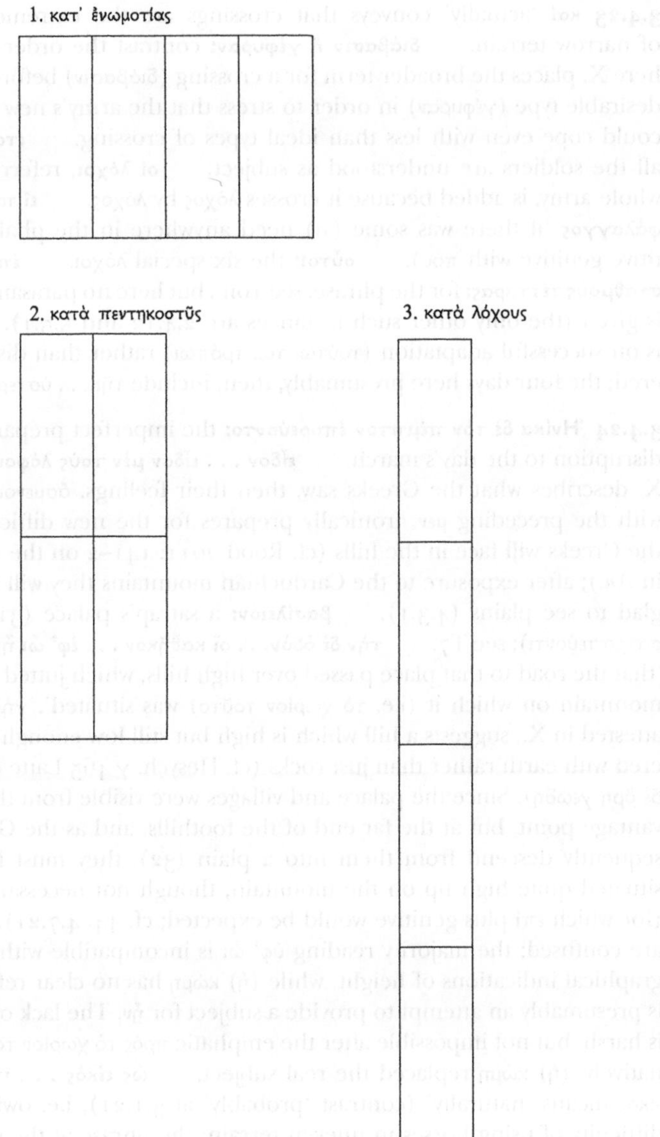

Figures 1–3 The formations described at 3.4.22. Each rectangle represents a unit of twenty-five men (three wide, eight deep, plus one leader).

3.4.23 **καί** 'actually' conveys that crossings are the extreme example of narrow terrain. **διάβασιν ἢ γέφυραν:** contrast the order at 20(n.); here X. places the broader term for a crossing (διάβασιν) before the most desirable type (γέφυραν) in order to stress that the army's new formation could cope even with less than ideal types of crossing. **ἐταράττοντο:** all the soldiers are understood as subject. **οἱ λόχοι**, referring to the whole army, is added because it crosses λόχος by λόχος. **εἴ που . . . τῆς φάλαγγος** 'if there was some (τι) need anywhere in the phalanx' (partitive genitive with που). **οὗτοι:** the six special λόχοι. **ἐπορεύθησαν σταθμοὺς τέτταρας:** for the phrase, see 10n., but here no parasang distance is given (the only other such instances are 2.4.12 and 5.5.1). X.'s stress is on successful adaptation (τούτωι τῶι τρόπωι) rather than distance covered; the four days here presumably, then, include τῆι . . . ὑστεραίαι at 18.

3.4.24 **Ἡνίκα δὲ τὸν πέμπτον ἐπορεύοντο:** the imperfect prepares for the disruption to the day's march. **εἶδον . . . εἶδον μὲν τοὺς λόφους ἄσμενοι:** X. describes what the Greeks saw, then their feelings. ἄσμενοι, together with the preceding μέν, ironically prepares for the new difficulties that the Greeks will face in the hills (cf. Rood 2011: 141–2 on the word's use in *An.*); after exposure to the Carduchian mountains they will be equally glad to see plains (4.3.1). **βασίλειον:** a satrap's palace (31n. on τῶι σατραπεύοντι); see T7. **τὴν δὲ ὁδὸν. . . οἳ καθῆκον . . . ἐφ' ὧι ἦν [ἡ κώμη]** 'that the road to that place passed over high hills, which jutted out of the mountain on which it (i.e. τὸ χωρίον τοῦτο) was situated'. γήλοφος, first attested in X., suggests a hill which is high but still low enough to be covered with earth rather than just rocks (cf. Hesych. γ 465 Latte ὄχθαι, τινὲς δὲ ὄρη γεώδη). Since the palace and villages were visible from the Greeks' vantage point, but at the far end of the foothills, and as the Greeks subsequently descend from them into a plain (32), they must have been situated quite high up on the mountain, though not necessarily on top (for which ἐπί plus genitive would be expected; cf. 44, 4.7.21). The MSS are confused: the majority reading ὑφ' ὧι is incompatible with the topographical indications of height, while (ἡ) κώμη has no clear referent and is presumably an attempt to provide a subject for ἦν. The lack of a subject is harsh, but not impossible after the emphatic πρὸς τὸ χωρίον τοῦτο; alternatively, (ἡ) κώμη replaced the real subject. **ὡς εἰκὸς . . . ἱππέων:** ὡς εἰκός means 'naturally' (contrast 'probably' at 3.1.21), i.e. owing to the difficulty of using horses in uneven terrain; the phrase at the same time suggests that the Greeks are ignoring the danger posed by the Persian light-armed troops. For the position and function of the genitive absolute, see 19n.

3.4.25 **ὡς ἐπὶ τὸν ἕτερον ἀναβαίνειν** 'so as to go up to the next one'. For ὥσ(τε) with infinitive implying intended result, i.e. with the idea of purpose (*CGCG* 46.9; Smyth 2267), cf. 1.8.10, 4.3.29. **ἐπιγίγνονται οἱ βάρβαροι:** presentative order with historical present (as at 2(n.)), underlining the suddenness of the Persians' reappearance. οἱ βάρβαροι prepares for the use of the whip (see below). **εἰς τὸ πρανές** 'downhill'. **ἔβαλλον, ἐσφενδόνων, ἐτόξευον:** asyndeton with verbs in the imperfect appears in vivid battle-narratives at *Cyr.* 7.1.38, *Hell.* 2.4.33 ἠκόντιζον, ἔβαλλον, ἐτόξευον, ἐσφενδόνων, 4.3.19 (= *Ages.* 2.12) ἐωθοῦντο, ἐμάχοντο, ἀπέκτεινον, ἀπέθνῃσκον – a passage praised by Ps.-Longinus (*Subl.* 19.1): 'the words come out without connections and as it were pour forth, almost outstripping the speaker himself'. The effect here is to convey the sense of a sudden barrage of stones, sling-bullets and arrows. **ὑπὸ μαστίγων:** ὑπό with genitive expressing accompanying circumstance (*CGCG* 31.8; Smyth 1698.1b). For the use of whips by Persians (generally against people of low status), see Hdt. 7.22.1, 223.3, with Xerxes' words at 103.4. Whipping was seen as tyrannical (cf. [Arist.] *Ath. Pol.* 35.1) and suitable only for slaves (cf. Hdt. 4.3.4). It is surprising to find it mentioned in *An.* only in a scene where the Persians have the advantage of higher ground (Tuplin 2004a: 174): X. may be suggesting that the Persian army has been scared by the Greeks' unexpected versatility or (better) highlighting the urgent effort of the Persian light-armed troops at this moment (in keeping with the pattern of increasing Persian military effort in the course of the book) and so the particular suffering of the Greeks. Whatever the explanation, there is an implied contrast with the Greeks' willing acceptance of military authority.

3.4.26 κατετίτρωσκον καὶ ἐκράτησαν . . . καὶ κατέκλεισαν: fast-paced paratactic clauses with repetition of κ- and τ-sounds (hence the compound κατετίτρωσκον 'wound heavily'; cf. καταθύσειν at 3.2.12(n.)) convey how, despite the newly instituted tactics, the Greeks' earlier disadvantages (cf. εἴσω τῶν ὅπλων κατεκέκλειντο 3.3.7(n.)) return now that the Persians are occupying higher ground. **γυμνήτων:** 3.3.7n. on ψιλοὶ ὄντες. **ἄχρηστοι:** cf. 17(n.) for the stress on utility and 17n. on ὥστε χρῆσθαι for the indicative with ὥστε. **καὶ . . . καί**, together with the delayed subject, underlines the impotence even of the new slingers.

3.4.27 σχολῇ μὲν . . . ταχὺ ἀπεπήδων: ὁπλῖται ὄντες is causal. X. emphasizes the hoplites' struggle uphill by a historical present; a contrast with the enemy's easy flight is suggested by variation in clause length and word order and by the expressive ἀπεπήδων 'kept leaping back' (the verb is rare in military narratives).

3.4.28 τὸ ἄλλο στράτευμα 'the rest of the army'. **ταὐτὰ ἔπασχον:** i.e. the same as during the initial downhill march at 25–6. **ἔδοξεν αὐτοῖς:** the following τοὺς στρατιώτας may suggest that X. meant αὐτοῖς to refer to the generals. **πρὶν . . . ἀνήγαγον:** a πρίν-clause recording a future strategic decision would normally have an optative (or subjunctive with ἄν), but X. presents it as a fact (using the aorist indicative), treating the division's move as the next step in the story. **ἀπὸ τῆς δεξιᾶς πλευρᾶς:** the side nearer to the mountain. **πελταστάς:** after the institution of mobile hoplite λόχοι (19–23), the new modification involves the even more mobile light-armed troops.

3.4.29 οὗτοι: the Greek peltasts. **οὐκέτι ἐπετίθεντο:** contrasting with 26, 28. **δεδοικότες μὴ . . . οἱ πολέμιοι:** the Persians are subject of ἀποτμηθείησαν, while οἱ πολέμιοι (now referring to the Greeks: see 34n.) are subject of γένοιντο.

3.4.30 οὕτω τὸ λοιπὸν τῆς ἡμέρας πορευόμενοι: the phrase underlines the Greeks' successful adoption of a new tactic (cf. 6n. on τὸ λοιπὸν τῆς ἡμέρας). **οἱ μὲν . . . οἱ δέ:** hoplites and peltasts. **ἐπιπαριόντες** 'marching alongside (παρα-) on higher ground (ἐπι-)'. **ἰατροὺς κατέστησαν ὀκτώ:** X. does not specify who made this decision; whether this was a new or supplementary medical unit (the stress suggests the former); or whether the doctors were soldiers, slaves or local captives. The evidence for doctors serving with Greek armies is slender (Salazar 2000: 68–74), but in line with his practical concern for troops' well-being X. pays more attention to medical treatment of wounds than either Herodotus (7.181.2 is exceptional) or Thucydides; cf. *Lac.* 13.7 for doctors in the Spartan army; *Cyr.* 1.6.15, 3.2.12, 5.4.17–18, 6.2.32, 8.2.24–5. **πολλοὶ . . . οἱ τετρωμένοι** picks up 26 πολλοὺς κατετίτρωσκον.

3.4.31 ἄλευρα, οἶνον, κριθάς: asyndeton is often used in lists of types of produce (cf. 4.4.9, 5.3.9, 6.6.1; Ar. *Thesm.* 420 ἄλφιτον, ἔλαιον, οἶνον; also inscribed inventories such as ML 76). See Denniston 1952: 100. **ἵπποις συμβεβλημένας** 'collected for the horses'; perfect participle of συμβάλλω (LSJ s.v. A.I.2). **συνενηνεγμένα ἦν:** pluperfect passive of συμφέρω (similar in sense to συμβάλλω). **τῶι σατραπεύοντι:** dative of either agency ('by') – a usage found above all with a perfect or pluperfect passive, as here (*CGCG* 30.50) – or advantage ('for': *CGCG* 30.49). The produce had been collected either as a supply depot (Briant 2002: 372) or as tribute payment (Tuplin 1987b: 141–2); cf. the presence of wine and barley in Persian depots in Bactria (Naveh and Shaked 2012: C3:40, C4:22–3, 40). The Persian empire was divided by Darius into about twenty administrative units known as satrapies (cf. Hdt. 3.89.1, though there were changes of detail over time). X. gives no details, but at this point the army was probably in the satrapy of Media (which according to the interpolated list at 7.8.25 had Arbacas, perhaps to be identified with the Arbaces of 1.7.12, as its satrap). The verb σατραπεύω (which appears first in X.) is used at *Hell.* 3.1.10 loosely of a governor subordinate to an actual satrap; the use here need not, then, signify accurate knowledge of local Persian administration. **τὸ πεδίον:** T8.

3.4.32 ἐδίδαξεν . . . ἡ ἀνάγκη: the principle seen at 19–23 is here expressed more abstractly, continuing the focus on trial-and-error. The motif of ἀνάγκη as a teacher aligns X.'s account with Greek narratives of technological and cultural advance (Rood 2015b: 109, with references). While the generals are not here given credit for the solution, X.'s language also excuses their failure to anticipate the problems. **πολλοὶ . . . οἱ ἀπόμαχοι** caps 30 πολλοὶ γὰρ ἦσαν οἱ τετρωμένοι, showing the knock-on effect of the presence of the wounded when the army was actually on the march. ἀπόμαχος 'out of action' is attested first here (cf. also 4.1.13), then not until Arrian. **οἱ ἐκείνους φέροντες:** the wounded would earlier have travelled in wagons (like Ariaeus at 2.2.14). X. mentions later that troops were carried back to camp after an engagement (4.5.22, 5.2.32) and that the sick were put on board a ship when the army reached the Black Sea (5.3.1). Apart from that, he offers hints that, when the pace of the march increased, wounded men were left behind (4.5.11) unless Xenophon himself intervened (5.8.6–11). See Sternberg 2006: 130–43; Lee 2007: 245–7; and cf. Thuc. 7.75.3–4. **οἱ τῶν φερόντων τὰ ὅπλα δεξάμενοι:** the Greeks held on to equipment tenaciously owing to their lack of sufficient replacements (Lee 2007: 130; cf. 5.8.7). X. does not, however, mention here what happened to the weapons of the wounded: Hunt 1998: 167 suggests that the men may have been carried on their shields wearing their armour.

3.4.33 πολὺ γὰρ διέφερεν . . . ἤ 'it was far different . . . from' (see LSJ s.v. διαφέρω III.4 for this impersonal use with accusative and infinitive), here with the implication 'better . . . than'. Defending from a set position contrasts with the earlier fighting; it need not imply that the village itself had any defences of its own. **ἀλέξασθαι** 'defend themselves'. ἀλέξω (× 9 in X.) is largely Ionic and Doric (Gautier 53); in Attic it is found twice in tragedy.

3.4.34–6, like 16–18 and 19–23(nn.), moves between the specific narrative context, more general observations about what happened during this part of the retreat, and narratorial explanation in the present tense. Here the transitions between the temporal layers are made clear through a tight use of ring-composition: (*a*) story-now: when it was now (34 ἤδη) getting late, it was time for the enemy to withdraw; (*b*) story-general: for (γάρ) they never camped nearby; (*c*) general: for (γάρ) a Persian army is (ἐστί, indicating a narratorial comment) at a disadvantage at night; (*b'*) story-general: therefore (τούτου ἕνεκα) they used to camp far away from the Greeks; (*d'*) story-now: when the Greeks discovered (ἐπεὶ δὲ ἐγίγνωσκον 36) that they were about to withdraw, the order to pack up was given. The events of the story-now are focalized through the Greeks, implicitly in 34 and explicitly in 36, but in the general sections an external perspective is adopted.

3.4.34 **Ἡνίκα . . . δείλη:** ἡνίκα-clauses at the start of a sentence (also used at 24, 3.5.2, 4.1.5) set the scene with an imperfect marking simultaneity with the main clause, and usually contain an explicit time-marker (here δείλη) (cf. Buijs 2005: 93–4). ἤδη 'now' marks the Greeks' perspective (cf. 4n.). **ὥρα ἦν:** according to Greek expectations, based on prior experience, suggesting that Persian tactics are becoming familiar. **τοῖς πολεμίοις:** the designation πολέμιοι frequently occurs in contexts in which the narrative is focalized through the Greeks (occasionally the Persians; cf. 29), either explicitly (e.g. in fearing clauses (1), purpose clauses (5) or indirect perception (19, 41)) or, as here, more implicitly (especially with phrases that imply a point of view centred on the spatial location of the Greeks; e.g. 29 ἐγένοντο ὑπὲρ τῶν ἑπομένων πολεμίων; ἐπετίθεντο οἱ πολέμιοι; 3.5.2 οἱ πολέμιοι ἐπιφαίνονται; cf. also 6, 24, 27). **οὔποτε:** that is, at no point during the retreat so far. **μεῖον:** μείων is a Doric comparative (for Attic ἐλάττων, ἥττων: Gautier 32–3), which X. uses often, especially in *An.* and *Cyr.* (for the linguistic similarities of these works, see Introduction pp. 15, 30). **οἱ βάρβαροι τοῦ Ἑλληνικοῦ:** with the latter, a genitive of separation with ἀπεστρατοπεδεύοντο, supply στρατοπέδου (as often). The external perspective prepares for X.'s observation on a problem that affects non-Greeks in particular. **ἑξήκοντα σταδίων:** genitive of comparison with μεῖον. During their last unchecked march (10) the Greeks covered six parasangs, or *c.* 180 stades. X. normally uses stades rather than parasangs to measure the distance between the Greek and Persian armies.

3.4.35 **πονηρὸν . . . ἐστι:** cf. 19 πονηρὰ τάξις. The verbal repetition may be pointed, in that Persians, unlike the Greeks, do not take measures to remedy the situation. The explanation is given as a general statement, and so there is a shift from the imperfect to the present, and from specific τῆς νυκτός and οἱ βάρβαροι to general νυκτός and στράτευμα Περσικόν. Cf. Plut. *Ant.* 44.1 (with Pelling) and Dio Cass. 40.24.2 on similar problems in Parthian armies. **οἵ τε γὰρ ἵπποι κτλ.:** this passage recurs, with verbal and structural modifications, at *Cyr.* 3.3.26–7, there explaining why non-Greek armies usually dig trenches around their camps (here the Persians may not have time to dig trenches, preferring instead to locate their camp farther away). X.'s concern with cavalry encampment is apparent at 7.2.21 (the Thracian ruler Seuthes keeps his horses bridled at night to enable a quick get-away), *Cyr.* 8.5.8–9 (the elder Cyrus always kept the cavalry near the centre of the camp to have more time to prepare in emergencies; cf. Tuplin 2010: 177). **αὐτοῖς δέδενται:** dative of agent or advantage. This and the following perfect describe the horses' state of rest during the night. **πεποδισμένοι εἰσί** 'are hobbled'. The same practice is attributed by Tacitus (*Ann.* 4.25.2) to the Numidians in North Africa and noted (with allusions to X.) in nineteenth-century descriptions of the Ottoman empire (Introduction p. 13). Among Greeks, it is seldom mentioned and only outside the context of war; cf. Hom. *Il.* 13.36–8 and perhaps [Theoc.] *Id.* 25.103–4. **εἰ λυθείησαν:** the apodosis is to be supplied from τοῦ μὴ φεύγειν ἕνεκα. X. means that a horse may accidentally 'be freed' from its tether, in which case the precaution of tying its feet together prevents it from straying. **ἐάν τέ τις θόρυβος γίγνηται:** τε corresponds to οἵ τε γὰρ ἵπποι earlier: after describing a general problem, X. adds further problems which arise in case of an attack (cf. the parallel passage at *Cyr.* 3.3.27 καὶ εἴ τις ἐπ' αὐτοὺς ἴοι). **δεῖ . . . χαλινῶσαι:** Πέρσηι ἀνδρί is dative of advantage (*CGCG* 30.49; LSJ s.v. δεῖ I.c needlessly assume that δεῖ in X. is sometimes construed with a dative instead of an accusative); the saddling (cf. 3.2.19n.) and bridling are carried out by an attendant (left unexpressed). **δεῖ . . . ἀναβῆναι:** riders should be able to mount quickly, ideally without making the horse crouch first (*Eq.* 6.16–7.4), but this is hard for Persian cavalrymen armed with scale cuirasses and bronze thigh-pieces and helmets (1.8.6, *Cyr.* 7.1.2; Hdt. 9.22.2), though managed by Cyrus (1.8.3); cf. *Eq. mag.* 1.6, *Eq.* 7.12 for groom-assisted mounting 'in the Persian manner'. The shift of subject to the 'Persian man' is made easier by the fact that ἀναβῆναι depends on a different δεῖ from both previous infinitives. The MSS readings are unsatisfactory: δή puts undue emphasis on χαλινῶσαι, δέ awkwardly groups χαλινῶσαι and ἀναβῆναι together, while δεῖ without δέ would easily be taken with χαλινῶσαι as well. For the anaphora δεῖ . . . δεῖ δέ . . . (without preceding μέν), cf. e.g. Andoc. 1.18; Denniston 1952: 86. **θωρακισθέντα:** presumably direct-reflexive ('having harnessed himself') rather than passive ('having been harnessed', i.e. by an attendant); *Cyr.* 3.3.27 has middle θωρακίσασθαι, but the morphological variation is paralleled by e.g. αὐλίζομαι, ηὐλισάμην/ηὐλίσθην ('prepare oneself for the night'). **ἀπεσκήνουν** 'used to camp apart' (habitual imperfect) picks up ἀπεστρατοπεδεύοντο (34) and effects the transition from the universal statement back to the story-world (34–6n.).

3.4.36 ἐπεὶ δὲ ἐγίγνωσκον: a resumptive summary, signalled, as often, by ἐπεί (Buijs 2005: 162), which then forms the springboard for the next phase of the action. **διαγγελλομένους** 'passing the word of command from man to man' (LSJ s.v.). X.'s usual words for this are παρεγγυάω (e.g. 4.1.17, 7.24) and παραγγέλλω (e.g. 1.8.22); middle διαγγέλλομαι is not attested elsewhere (the passage is cited in *Suda* δ 517 Adler), but it belongs to a common type of reciprocal middle: cf. e.g. διακελεύομαι 'exhort one another', διαλέγομαι 'converse' (Allan 2003: 86 n. 138); see Introduction pp. 31–2 on its likely provenance and effect here. The Persians may have wanted to conceal their plans from the Greeks: cf. *Eq. mag.* 4.9 'departures . . . are less likely to be noticed by the enemy if the orders are given by passing them along (ἀπὸ παραγγέλσεως) rather than through a herald (ὑπὸ κήρυκος) or in writing beforehand'. **ἐκήρυξε:** *sc.* ὁ κῆρυξ (4n. on ἐσήμηνε). The Greeks use a herald because they want the Persians to hear: their purpose is to see if the Persians will indeed retreat once they start moving. **ἐπέσχον** 'refrained from' (LSJ s.v. ἐπέχω IV.2.b, with genitive). **ἀπῇσαν:** the imperfect keeps the action in suspense, waiting to be confirmed in the following sentence (ἀπιόντας ἤδη). **οὐδὲ γὰρ . . . πορεύεσθαι** 'for, in fact, they did not usually think (ἐδόκει, *sc.* αὐτοῖς) that it was profitable for them to march during the night'. This sentence moves on the same general plane as ἀπεστρατοπεδεύοντο (34) and ἀπεσκήνουν (35), summarizing the situation that has obtained until now and will continue for two more nights. οὐδὲ γάρ brings out that it both serves as an explanation for why the Persians retreat now and is an additional comment on their habit (also noted by Curt. Ruf. 3.3.8) of not marching by night (see *CGCG* 59.66 on the positive equivalent καὶ γάρ, and cf. οὐδὲ γάρ at 15, *Hell.* 4.8.22, 5.1.13, *Symp.* 4.32). The reading λυσιτελεῖν αὐτοῖς is probably a gloss on λύειν αὐτούς, a poetic phrase of the same meaning. Impersonal λύει 'it is profitable' is also construed with the accusative (instead of the expected dative) at Soph. *El.* 1005 and Eur. fr. 661.28–9 *TrGF*, but the phrasing is so rare that a deeper corruption may be suspected. **κατάγεσθαι** 'return to camp', a sense attested at *Hell.* 4.5.18, *Symp.* 8.39, *Cyr.* 8.5.17; the verb's reqular classical usage is 'put in to shore' (e.g. 5.1.11).

3.4.37 σαφῶς 'clearly', with ἑώρων, which marks the transition back to the Greeks' perspective. **ἀπιόντας ἤδη** 'finally departing' (the particle signals that this was later than the Greeks expected). **ἐπορεύοντο:** unlike the Persians (36n.), the Greeks march into the night (cf. 7.3.37 for the Greek practice of putting slow troops in front during night marches to minimize the chance of the army separating). **ἀναζεύξαντες:** ἀναζεύγνυμι, lit. 're-yoke', used absolutely = 'break camp' (cf. 4.6.1) – an action normally taken for granted, but here mentioned in order to stress Greek speed by contrast with the Persians' cumbersome camping arrangements. **ὅσον:** 3n. **γίγνεται:** the historical present of verbs with non-human agents is rare, but in this case human agency is implied; cf. Thuc. 3.74.1 μάχη αὖθις γίγνεται, with Rijksbaron 2011: 7. It highlights the new and unexpected situation. **οὐκ ἐφάνησαν οἱ πολέμιοι:** Greek perspective (cf. 34n. on τοῖς πολεμίοις). **τῆι δὲ τετάρτηι:** turning points in the narrative are also marked by X. as occurring 'on the fourth day' at *Hell.* 3.4.21 (= *Ages.* 1.29), 4.5.3, 6.5.20, and see 31 in this chapter; the pattern may owe something to the 'three times X, but the fourth time Y'-motif found in Homer (e.g. *Il.* 16.784–6). **νυκτὸς προελθόντες:** the Persians' night march comes as a surprise after 35. As the sequel shows, the body of the Persian army closes in on the Greeks from behind, while they send a division around the Greek army to occupy mountainous terrain in front of it. **καταλαμβάνουσι . . . οἱ βάρβαροι:** T9. The brief clause, with the verb (a historical present: 3.1.8n. on ἐξέπλει) in front, mirrors the speed of the Persian manoeuvre; a relative clause then elaborates the specifics. **ὑπερδέξιον:** a standardized military term for 'higher ground' (first in X. and Aeneas Tacticus, common in Hellenistic historiography); originally it must have meant 'higher ground on the right', the side poorly protected by shields carried in the left hand (*GSW* IV.76–8; Whitehead on Aen. Tact. 1.2). **ἧι** 'the route whereby'. **ἔμελλον . . . παριέναι** expresses the intentions of the Greeks, as perceived by the Persians. **ἀκρωνυχίαν:** in apposition to χωρίον ὑπερδέξιον. ἀκρωνυχία, a technical term for 'spur' (of a mountain), literally means 'tip of the toe(-nail)' (cf. expressions for 'on tiptoe' at e.g. Eur. *El.* 840 ὄνυχας ἔπ' ἄκρους στάς, *Cycl.* 159; for the ἀκρο- compound, cf. e.g. Aen. Tact. 15.6 ἀκρολοφία 'mountain ridge'). It is found again at 38 and *Hell.* 4.6.7, and occasionally in later authors (e.g. Philostr. *Her.* 33.41) in imitation of X., but with the weakened meaning 'mountain-top' (cf. *Suda* α 1027 Adler, where 38 is cited). The metaphor is based on basic physical resemblance (cf. the common use of πούς for the 'foot' of a mountain): the spur is like the tip of a toe (or distal phalanx bone), which juts out from the inset of the foot (the mountain: κορυφή/ἄκρον at 41, 44, 49) via a ridge (the middle and proximal phalanx bone: the 'way of approach', ἔφοδος (41)). The technical term (replaced by λόφος at 39, 41, 44) clarifies the tactical problem to be resolved in the ensuing scene. **ὑφ' ἥν** 'along the base of which' continues the Persian perspective, figuring the κατάβασις as stretching out below the Persians' vantage point.

3.4.38–43 The looming danger is first noticed by Chirisophus, the commander of the front. In response, he is presented as calling on Xenophon almost as a matter of course, bypassing the generals on the flanks and ignoring Timasion, the other general in the rear. The ensuing conversation foregrounds Xenophon's awareness of the tactical possibilities offered by the terrain (41n. on ὑπὲρ αὐτοῦ τοῦ ἑαυτῶν στρατεύματος): building on the earlier flanking move by peltasts in response to pressure exerted by the Persians from a hill to the rear (26, 28), he proposes to use three of the mobile hoplite λόχοι instituted at 21 as a detachment to seize higher ground ahead; Brasidas had used his separate hoplite unit (3.3.12–19n.) in a similar way to clear a blocked pass (Thuc. 4.128.1; cf. Whitby 2004: 233). Chirisophus – a less flexible Spartan than Brasidas – lacks such awareness and yields to Xenophon's authority. Xenophon is marked out in this way as the best possible leader for the next phase of the journey, which continues across mountainous terrain, where a similar flexibility and readiness to split the army will be required.

The episode is retold by Polyaenus (*Strat.* 1.49.3) and appears to have impressed Roman historians: Cato (*FRHist* fr. 76 = Gell. 3.7) describes a military tribune in the First Punic War seeing, then volunteering to seize, a hill so as to clear the road ahead, and Livy (7.34.3–8) describes a similar incident during the First Samnite War, with further echoes of this episode (Rood 2018).

From here until the end of the chapter the narrative moves at breakneck speed: the thematic focus on the need for speedy action is stylistically enacted by predominantly paratactic connections with δέ, καί and ἐνταῦθα (contrast the earlier careful segmentation of the narrative by means of ἡνίκα/ἐπει(δή)-clauses) and a relatively high frequency of historical presents. The use of direct speech and the description of the Greeks and Persians witnessing the race to the summit (45n.) further heighten the dramatic intensity.

3.4.38 οὐρᾶς: lit. an animal's 'tail', here the rear of a marching army (cf. Max. Tyr. 6.3, with reference to X.). The metaphor is frequent in X. (see e.g. 6.5.5, *Hell.* 6.5.18, *Cyr.* 2.3.21, 4.3, *Lac.* 11.9; cf. 42n. on τοῦ στόματος), but not otherwise found until Polybius; it may belong to a technical military register. **κελεύει** 'requested'. The verb need not imply that Xenophon is Chirisophus' subordinate (*pace* Cawkwell 2004: 63; see 3.2.36n. on τίνας χρὴ . . . κοσμεῖν). **τοὺς πελταστάς:** Chirisophus' plan is to try to dislodge the Persians using the peltasts' greater mobility uphill.

3.4.39 μέν looks forward to αὐτὸς δέ. **οὐκ ἦγεν:** negated imperfects often express refusal (Smyth 1896). **προσελάσας** implies that Xenophon is on horseback, and so prepares for 46–9. **ὁ δὲ λέγει αὐτῶι:** as often, changes of speaker are signalled clearly at the start of a conversation, and then less obtrusively by ἔφη (40, 42), except for decisive turns (41 καὶ λέγει). **ἔξεστιν ὁρᾶν:** a lesson not lost on Xenophon, who in fact will see more than Chirisophus (41n.). For Chirisophus' style of speaking in brief, mostly paratactic clauses, see 3.2.1n. on ὁ Λακεδαιμόνιος. **προκατείληπται . . . παρελθεῖν:** ἡμῖν is dative of disadvantage (*CGCG* 30.49). Chirisophus merely repeats what he has seen (38): he diagnoses the problem, but does not come up with a plan of action. **εἰ μὴ . . . ἀποκόψομεν:** for the future indicative, see 3.1.13n. on εἰ . . . γενησόμεθα. ἀποκόπτω (lit.

'hew off') is used elsewhere in similar contexts (4.2.10, 17); see also 3.5.2n. on κατέκοψαν.

3.4.40 ἀλλά: Chirisophus changes the topic; see 3.2.6n. **τί οὐκ ἦγες:** the imperfect implies 'when you had the chance' (the aorist is normal with τί οὐ: *CGCG* 38.33). **λέγει ὅτι:** the information is reported in indirect speech because it is already familiar to readers from 39. **"ἀλλὰ μὴν . . ." ἔφη:** interactional ἀλλὰ μήν ('don't worry', correcting the implications of an earlier utterance before moving on to a more relevant point: *CGCG* 59.60) in combination with ἔφη is enough to mark the change of speaker from Xenophon to Chirisophus (cf. *Mem.* 3.10.14, 4.2.36, *Oec.* 15.10; contrast 42 ἀλλὰ . . . ἔφη ὁ Χειρίσοφος). **βουλεύεσθαι** raises the expectation of a protracted conversation, but in fact Chirisophus immediately accepts Xenophon's first suggestion. **πῶς τις . . . ἀπελᾶι:** the formulation holds the middle ground between the confident πῶς ἡμεῖς ἀπελῶμεν ('how are we going to?') and the tentative πῶς τις ἂν ἀπελαύνοι ('how might anyone?'); τις leaves open the possibility that either Xenophon or Chirisophus will execute the plan. For ἄνδρας, see 3.1.23n.

3.4.41 ὁρᾶι: the crucial observation is given in the historical present and in a main clause (contrast 38 ἐπειδὴ . . . ἑώρα). **ὑπὲρ αὐτοῦ τοῦ ἑαυτῶν στρατεύματος** 'precisely above their own army'; for this nuance of predicative αὐτός, see *CGCG* 29.12. The narrator did not report that the spur of the mountain was further along the road than the main summit, thus underlining Xenophon's distinctive tactical insight; cf. 3.2.23n. on Λυκάονας δὲ καὶ αὐτοὶ εἴδομεν, 3.16n. on ἀκούω . . . Ῥοδίους; Rood 2014: 80–1. **ἵεσθαι . . . ἐπί** expresses rapid movement (cf. Arist. *Hist. an.* 629b24, of a lion). **ἀλλά:** 3.2.6n. Xenophon rushes on to discuss the practical implementation of the plan. **ἐθέλω** 'I volunteer' (for this sense, cf. 3.3.18(n.) τῶι . . . ἐθέλοντι); contrast εἰ βούλει 'if you prefer' earlier on.

3.4.42 ἀλλά: 3.1.31n.; here it is corrective: not Chirisophus but Xenophon is to make the decision. **δίδωμί σοι . . . ἑλέσθαι** 'I leave it up to you to choose' (cf. LSJ s.v. δίδωμι I.4). **εἰπὼν . . . ὅτι νεώτερός ἐστιν** 'with the remark that he was younger', a modal aorist participle for an action that coincides with the main verb (*CGCG* 52.5, 42). The final speech turn is perfunctorily rendered in indirect speech, as the narrative presses on. For age as an argument, see 3.2.37n. on τῶν δὲ πλευρῶν . . . ἐπιμελοίσθην. **αἱρεῖται** and the following historical present κελεύει set the decisive action in motion. **οἱ:** dative of the indirect-reflexive pronoun, referring to the subject of κελεύει (*CGCG* 29.18). **τοῦ στόματος:** the use of στόμα 'mouth' of a military 'front' is first attested in X. (cf. 5.2.26, 4.22, *Hell.* 3.1.23, 4.3.4); relevant antecedents may be the use of στόμα to denote the point of a weapon (e.g. Hom. *Il.* 15.389; Eur. *Supp.* 1206) and the military use of κατὰ στόμα 'face to face' (Hdt. 8.11.1; Eur. *Heracl.* 801). Eustathius (I.743.7–10, IV.335.8–10 Van der Valk) cited X.'s usage as parallel to Homeric πολέμου/πτολέμοιο στόμα (*Il.* 10.8, 19.313), connecting it to his use of οὐρά for the 'rear' (38n.), but the Homeric expression more plausibly refers to war's deadly jaws (Hainsworth on *Il.* 10.8). **μακρὸν γὰρ ἦν** 'for it was too far': for μακρόν with the implication 'too', see *Ages.* 7.1. The remark can be understood as still belonging to Xenophon's speech, with ἦν representing ἐστί ('free' indirect discourse); by anchoring the tense to his own temporal perspective the narrator presents Xenophon's opinion as a fact (see 3.1.2(n.) ἐννοούμενοι ὅτι . . . ἦσαν).

3.4.43 ἔλαβε: to replace the peltasts he sent with Xenophon. **αὐτῶι:** i.e. Xenophon, with συνέπεσθαι (contrast οἱ at 42). The following καί is adverbial. **τοὺς τριακοσίους . . . τῶν ἐπιλέκτων** refers to three of the six λόχοι, consisting of a hundred men each, formed earlier (21n.). The soldiers of those λόχοι are here together called the ἐπίλεκτοι, a word first attested in fourth-century literature and inscriptions (Tritle 1989), sometimes with the sense 'elite corps'; it reflects the growing specialization of Greek warfare. 300 is a common number for select military units, especially in Sparta (e.g. *Lac.* 4.3; Hdt. 7.205.2; Thuc. 4.125.3). **ἐπὶ τῶι στόματι** 'near the front' (LSJ s.v. ἐπί B.I.1.a).

3.4.44 ὥρμησαν ἁμιλλᾶσθαι: for ὁρμάω with infinitive, see LSJ s.v. II.1. For ἁμιλλάομαι expressing energetic movement in the face of obstacles, cf. Eur. *Or.* 456; Plut. *Arat.* 22.1, *Luc.* 28.3 (perhaps drawing on this passage); the verb also resonates with the language of athletic contests (cf. *Eq.* 8.6, *Cyr.* 1.4.15 and, in a military context, *Hell.* 7.2.14). For the depiction of war as a contest, see 3.1.16n., and the next note.

3.4.45 πολλὴ μὲν κραυγὴ . . . τοῖς ἑαυτῶν διακελευομένων: the first διακελευομένων belongs with τοῦ Ἑλληνικοῦ στρατεύματος, an *ad sensum* construction (cf. *Hell.* 3.3.4 ἡ πόλις . . . εἵλοντο; *CGCG* 27.6). The sentence continues the presentation of the race to the summit as a sporting event; compare the cheering audience at athletic games at 4.8.28 ἔνθα πολλὴ κραυγὴ καὶ γέλως καὶ παρακέλευσις ἐγίγνετο. While drawn from real-life experience of the psychological impetus provided by spectators (cf. 4.7.11, 8.27), the positing of an internal audience is also a tried method in ancient historiography for making battle scenes visually and emotionally compelling (the rhetorical term is *enargeia*; cf. e.g. Thuc. 7.71, with Plut. *Mor.* 347a–c and Hornblower 2004b: 344–6; also Walker 1993; Introduction p. 38). The anaphora and verbal repetition (with a chiastic ordering of the final participial phrases) suggest that the race to the top hangs in the balance until the end.

3.4.46 παρεκελεύετο 'kept encouraging them' (iterative imperfect) suggests that the following directly reported speech represents a number of different exhortations. The urgency of the situation is reflected by the abruptness with which it is introduced: in classical Greek direct speech after παρακελεύομαι or verbs with a similar meaning normally requires an additional verb of speaking (e.g. Thuc. 4.94.2 παρεκελεύετό τε καὶ ἔλεγε τοιάδε) or at least an introductory pronoun (e.g. *Cyr.* 3.3.43 τοιάδε παρεκελεύετο). **νῦν . . . νῦν . . . νῦν . . .**: the anaphora and asyndeton produce a forceful staccato effect (cf. Soph. *OT* 596–7, *El.* 1368–9); the shift of construction in the final limb makes for an impressive climax. **ἐπὶ τὴν Ἑλλάδα . . . ἁμιλλᾶσθαι** echoes the narrative's ἁμιλλᾶσθαι ἐπὶ τὸ ἄκρον (44): Xenophon adapts the common trope that wars abroad are fought in defence of the homeland (3.2.15n. on περὶ . . . σωτηρίας) to fit the *nostos* theme. **πρὸς παῖδας καὶ γυναῖκας:** *sc.* νομίζετε ἁμιλλᾶσθαι. The lack of the article is standard in formulaic phrases, especially when they involve kinship terms (cf. e.g. 1.4.8, 3.1.3, 4.1.8, 5.3.1). The order 'children and wives' is the normal one and may reflect Greek priorities (*CT* on Thuc. 4.123.4); X. reverses it when talking about barbarians (Rehdantz on 7.8.9). The same sequence of motifs is found at Aesch. *Pers.* 403–4 (an exhortation before the battle of Salamis): ἐλευθεροῦτε πατρίδ', ἐλευθεροῦτε δὲ | παῖδας γυναῖκας; for appeals to families, see also 3.1.3n. **ὀλίγον πονήσαντες . . . τὴν λοιπὴν** (*sc.* ὁδόν: 3.3.16n. on τὴν ταχίστην) **πορευσόμεθα:** Xenophon justifies his claim that this battle will ensure the Greeks' return home. The shift to first-person plural forms emphasises the army's shared toils, but lays Xenophon open to the charge that those toils are not in fact shared (47n. on ἐξ ἴσου). For the decisive battle as a trope of military exhortations, see Albertus 1908: 67–8. The Greeks will indeed soon be rid of Tissaphernes – but he will be replaced by other enemies in Book 4.

3.4.47–9 After Xenophon has proved himself a more insightful tactician than Chirisophus, there follows a vignette which casts him as an effective leader of the rank and file. See 5.8.1–12 for another instance of the soldiers rebuking one of their own after Xenophon has shown the way, and 7.3.45 for Xenophon's remark (after dismounting) that his troops will run faster and with greater enthusiasm if he, too, marches on foot; noble Persians, by contrast, consider it shameful to be seen going on foot (*Cyr.* 4.3.23). Frontinus (*Str.* 4.6.2) offers a colourful retelling of the vignette, under the heading of the commander's *affectus et moderatio,* in which the (unnamed) grumbler (*obmurmurantem*) is actually put on the horse and Xenophon is reluctant to remount. For a similar incident involving a Spartan mercenary commander in the First Punic War, see Diod. Sic. 23.14.2.

3.4.47 Σωτηρίδας . . . ὁ Σικυώνιος appears only here in *An.*; he must have belonged to one of the three λόχοι under Chirisophus' command. Like him, he is from the Peloponnese, where Soteridas was a common name (*LGPN* III.A lists thirty-two individuals, though none from Sicyon itself, but only one non-Doric Σωτηρίδης, the less plausible reading of **c**). His introduction as '*the* Sicyonian' perhaps hints that he was a notorious figure (articles are normally used only if a person has been mentioned before or is generally well known (3.1.5n. on Σωκράτει τῶι Ἀθηναίωι)). **ἐξ ἴσου** 'on an equal footing'. Soteridas' objection smacks of ἀταξία (3.2.31n. on σὺν . . . κολάζειν); X(enophon)'s own idea is that worthy leaders are right to enjoy greater benefits; cf. 3.1.37n. on ὅτε εἰρήνη ἦν . . . ἐπλεονεκτεῖτε, and *Ap.* 21 for the claim that people who excel are not thought to deserve an equal share (ἰσομοιρία), but more; see Danzig 2012: 516–17 on X.'s views of 'proportional justice'. **ἐφ' ἵππου** 'on horseback': contrast ἐπὶ τοῦ ἵππου 'on his horse' (46). **ὀχῆι:** the verb, also used of people riding in carriages, suggests a lack of effort. **κάμνω τὴν ἀσπίδα φέρων:** the hoplite shield was shallow and saucer-shaped, about a yard (90 cm) in diameter and 15 lb (6.8 kg) in weight (Lee 2007: 111). Its unwieldiness was notorious; see 5.8.23 for another soldier's complaint about having to carry a shield (διεμάχετο ὡς κάμνων ἀσπίδα μὴ φέρειν).

3.4.48 καὶ ὃς . . . ὠθεῖται: καί, rather than δέ, and the historical present underline the decisive rapidity of Xenophon's response. In the fixed phrase καὶ ὅς, ὅς is a form of the article (*CGCG* 28.29). **ἀφελόμενος:** middle, as Xenophon takes the shield for himself. A struggle was probably involved, as the shield would have been either carried on the left arm (with the arm through a double grip) or slung on the shoulder (Lee 2007: 111). **ἔχων**, omitted by **f**, is needed to emphasize that Xenophon held on to the shield the entire time. **θώρακα . . . τὸν ἱππικόν:** the implication that cavalrymen had heavier body armour than hoplites (found also at Plut. *Phil.* 6.8) is plausible: cavalrymen (who did not carry shields) could wear bronze cuirasses for protection without loss of mobility, while hoplites tended to wear lighter fabric or leather cuirasses (Spence 1993: 60–5; Lee 2007: 112 offers estimates of their weights). For cavalry armour, see also 3.3.20n. **ὑπάγειν**, dependent on παρεκελεύετο, represents imperative ὑπάγετε, a colloquial Attic expression for '(get a) move on' (again at 4.2.16 ἐκέλευσεν ὑπάγειν; cf. Ar. *Nub.* 1298 ὕπαγε, τί μέλλεις, *Ran.* 174; Eur. *Cycl.* 52), later adopted in the *koine* (e.g. Matthew 4:10 ὕπαγε Σατανᾶ); the usual military meaning is 'withdraw slowly' (e.g. Hdt. 4.120.2, 4; Thuc. 4.126.6).

3.4.49 παίουσι . . . λοιδοροῦσι: the historical presents and the polysyndeton underline the violence of the soldiers' response, which is to be taken as a sign of loyalty to Xenophon. Hitting and stoning are likewise manifestations of the soldiers' anger at 5.7.21 ("παῖε παῖε, βάλλε βάλλε"). Unlike Apollonides (3.1.30), Soteridas is allowed back into the fold. **βάσιμα ἦν** 'it was passable', i.e. for horses; the use of neuter plural adjectives where a singular is expected, as at e.g. Hdt. 3.109.1 οὐκ ἂν ἦν βιώσιμα ('it would not be liveable'), is rare in Attic prose outside Thucydides (K–G 1.67). The variant βατά (used at 4.6.17) could equally be correct (both words are rare, ἱππάσιμος being the more common term). **καταλιπὼν τὸν ἵππον:** presumably with a slave in attendance (he is back on horseback at 3.5.4); for the suppression of such attendants in Greek historians, see Hunt 1998.

3.5 THE ARMY AT THE CROSSROADS

After the scene in which Greeks race Persians to the top of the mountain is concluded, the army reaches a fertile plain along the Tigris (T10), but finds the route blocked by mountains; the Persians unexpectedly return, kill some Greeks (the first fatalities mentioned since the beginning of the retreat) and start to burn villages in the plain. These new pressures lead to a return of the mood of ἀθυμία and ἀπορία (3, 7) and ultimately to the generals' decision to strike north through the mountains for Armenia. Following this move, the narrative will take on a different texture as the focus shifts from the tense relations of Greeks and Persians to the army's desperate fight for survival against the tribes of the Carduchian and Armenian highlands. In keeping with his narrative focus on the Greeks, X. does not here mention any further movements on Tissaphernes' part, though at the end of *An.* the remnants of the Ten Thousand join the Spartans to fight him over the Greek cities in Asia Minor (7.8.24, cf. 6.1). Knowledge of this war (rather than a separate source) lies behind the specification in Diodorus' account of the retreat that Tissaphernes at this point departed with his army for Ionia (14.27.4).

X. carefully prepares for this decisive shift in the narrative by showing how the sort of energetic response with which the Greek leadership dealt with earlier setbacks is no longer effective. While the soldiers' earlier despondency was dispelled by the rousing rhetoric of Chirisophus, Cleanor and Xenophon (3.2), an attempt now by Chirisophus and Xenophon to lift their morale is inconclusive (5–6); some of the advice Xenophon had offered in his speech to the entire army also starts to seem less persuasive (7n. on ὡς μηδὲ . . . τοῦ βάθους). And while earlier impasses were overcome by introducing tactical innovations proposed by Xenophon (3.2.7–32, 3.12–19, 4.38–43) or the generals (3.4.19–23, 28), there now follows a meeting of all the officers (the first one since

3.1, and the first one that involves the new leadership), in which it is not Xenophon or the other generals but a nameless Rhodian who comes up with a plan – only for it to be dismissed by the Greek leadership (8–12). The Greeks' plight is further underlined by their subsequent decision to retrace their steps, the only time during their retreat to the sea that they are said to do so; X. marks the moment by offering a rare glimpse of the way in which the Persians perceive the Greeks (13n. on ὅμοιοι ἦσαν θαυμάζουσι).

The generals then learn from some captives about their position in relation to some of the major east–west and north–south routes through the Persian empire (15). This account, rendered in indirect speech, rounds off the first part of the retreat, retrospectively shedding some light on the route that the Greeks have been following.

3.5.1 ἔνθα δή introduces the predictable result of the Greek victory in the race to the top (see 3.3.11n., and 4.1.8 for a similar sequence), which consists in two simultaneous actions by the two groups involved in the race, articulated in a μέν/δέ sequence. **οἱ μὲν βάρβαροι**, like οἱ δὲ Ἕλληνες, repeats the designation used at 3.4.37 (ring-composition), though here referring only to two small contingents. **ἔφευγον:** immediative imperfect (3.3.8n. on καὶ ἐδίωκον). **εἶχον**, a durative imperfect, emphasizes that the contingent led by Xenophon continues to occupy the summit; a lacuna obscures the moment when they come down into the plain (3–4n.), but at 4 Xenophon has descended from the mountain, presumably together with the troops stationed there. **οἱ δὲ ἀμφὶ Τισσαφέρνην καὶ Ἀριαῖον . . . ᾤχοντο:** the imperfect leaves open the Persians' destination and possible return. Ariaeus, who here makes his final appearance in *An.*, has not been seen since 2.5.35–42, but his troops are implicitly included in Tissaphernes' forces (3.4.13(n.) οὓς Κῦρος ἔχων). X.'s formulation suggests that he holds a position of command next to Tissaphernes, perhaps promoted at the expense of Mithradates; his rehabilitation is confirmed by his later career (*Hell.* 4.1.27; *Hell. Oxy.* 16, 22.3). **οἱ δὲ ἀμφὶ Χειρίσοφον . . . ἐστρατοπεδεύσαντο:** the body of the Greek army continues on the main road past the mountain and descends into the plain beyond it, where it takes up quarters in one of the villages; aorist ἐστρατοπεδεύσαντο rounds off the sequence; a new scene starts with ἡνίκα δ' at 2 (see 3.4.34n.). **ἦσαν δὲ . . . παρὰ τὸν Τίγρητα ποταμόν:** for the imperfect, see 3.4.7n. on πόλις ἦν ἐρήμη μεγάλη. The repetition, with variation, of μεστῆι/πλήρεις πολλῶν ἀγαθῶν emphasizes the prosperity of this plain, which is located at a major crossroads in the Persian empire (see 3.4.16–18n.(*d*) for other well-stocked villages in this region). It helps explain the Greeks' desire for plundering (2) and, together with the repetition of εἰς τὸ πεδίον/ἐν τούτωι τῶι πεδίωι and the naming of the Tigris, evokes the relatively favourable conditions here (by contrast with the mountains to come).

3.5.2 Ἡνίκα δ' ἦν δείλη: given past Persian performance (3.4.34n.), the Greeks probably did not expect them to reappear for the rest of the day. **κατέκοψαν** 'cut to pieces'. The graphic verb throws into relief the Greeks' first reported losses since the retreat began. See 3.4.39n. for another κόπτω-verb outside the context of regular warfare. **ἐν τῶι πεδίωι:** the third occurrence of ἐν (τούτωι) τῶι πεδίωι brings out the fact that they are stuck in the plain and so especially vulnerable to cavalry attacks. **καθ' ἁρπαγήν:** scattering is a common and dangerous consequence of plundering; cf. *Hell.* 3.4.22 (= *Ages.* 1.30); Thuc. 6.52.2; Aen. Tact. 16.7. Since neither Xenophon nor Chirisophus takes part (3–4), it is likely that various groups of soldiers acted on their own initiative; compare 5.4.16 for another irresponsible raiding party, which X. explicitly says was 'not ordered by the generals'. **καὶ γάρ** 'in fact' introduces subsidiary information that explains what happened during the raids before the Persians appeared (cf. 3.4.36n. on οὐδὲ γὰρ . . . πορεύεσθαι); the fact that significant quantities of livestock were captured becomes relevant at 9. **νομαὶ . . . βοσκημάτων:** νομή, lit. 'land allotted for pasture', is here used of the herds which graze the land. In Attic, βόσκημα is at first virtually confined to tragedy, but it enters prose in the first half of the fourth century and remains part of the *koine*; X. uses it regularly (× 20) (cf. Introduction pp. 28–9). **διαβιβαζόμεναι** 'as they were being taken across', i.e. by the local inhabitants on rafts or boats (see 7 for the depth of the river), presumably for protection from the Greeks.

3.5.3–4 This is a difficult passage, probably owing to textual problems: (*a*) οἱ μὲν ἀμφὶ Χειρίσοφον ἀπῆισαν ἐκ τῆς βοηθείας (4) comes out of the blue: no mention has been made of troops under the command of Chirisophus having *left* the camp *to go* to the rescue; (*b*) the exact troop movements in the sequence καὶ οἱ μὲν ἀμφὶ Χειρίσοφον . . . ἔλεγεν are unclear. For *(b)*, see 4n. *(a)* is best solved by positing a lacuna. The missing section would have told how Chirisophus came to the rescue from the village (1), and may have given details about Xenophon's descent from the mountain, which is otherwise reported very briefly (4 ἐπεὶ κατέβη; ἐπεί usually signals information which has already been mentioned or anticipated (3.4.36n.)). The best place for the lacuna is at the start of 3, because ἐνταῦθα usually introduces a reaction to unexpected circumstances (e.g. 3.4.25, 41, 5.13), here Tissaphernes' change of tactics in response to Chirisophus' rescue mission. Less satisfactory proposals are to read instead of βοηθείας (× 2) either βαθείας (*sc.* γῆς), understood as 'plain', an unparalleled meaning which (in contradiction to 7) takes the Greeks back to the hills, or βοηλασίας 'cattle-lifting', a Homeric *hapax* (*Il.* 11.672) which implausibly makes οἱ ἀμφὶ Χειρίσοφον (used at 1 of the whole army except Xenophon's contingent) correspond with τῶν Ἑλλήνων . . . τῶν ἐσκεδασμένων ἐν τῶι πεδίωι (2).

3.5.3 **καίειν ἐπεχείρησαν:** in order to stop Greek access to the supplies stored in the villages (cf. Tissaphernes' threat at 2.5.19). ἐπεχείρησαν implies that they did not succeed in burning all the villages (cf. 13 τὰς ἀκαύστους κώμας). **καί** 'and so' (*CGCG* 59.20). **ἠθύμησαν:** an ingressive aorist (*CGCG* 33.29). **τινες** presumably refers to the troops encamped in the village, who see smoke from the fires. As at 3.1.3, the troops' despair is a foil to the more energetic response of Xenophon. **ἐννοούμενοι** is construed like a verb of 'fearing' (μή). Contrast the much longer catalogue of woes introduced by ἐννοούμενοι at 3.1.2(n.). **τὰ ἐπιτήδεια** placed in front of εἰ (prolepsis: 3.2.8n. on τοὺς στρατηγούς . . . οἷα πεπόνθασιν) emphasizes the Greeks' concern about provisions. **καύσοιεν**, a future optative, represents καύσουσι in direct thought; for the tense, see 3.1.13n. on εἰ . . . γενησόμεθα. **λαμβάνοιεν** represents a deliberative subjunctive (πόθεν λαμβάνωμεν; 'from where are we to take?').

3.5.4 **καί** introduces two further (and, given the imperfects ἀπῆισαν and ἔλεγεν, simultaneous) Greek responses in different parts of the plain (the point of the μέν/δέ contrast): Chirisophus and his men withdraw, while Xenophon, after his descent from the mountain, addresses his own men. **οἱ μὲν ἀμφὶ Χειρίσοφον ἀπῆισαν:** the unstated reason for Chirisophus' departure may be that he could not stop Tissaphernes from burning the villages; in addition, the lacuna may have reported that the scattered soldiers who survived the Persian attack had regrouped under his command. **παρελαύνων τὰς τάξεις . . . ἔλεγεν:** Xenophon has retrieved his horse from its attendant (3.4.49n.) and, as at 3.4.46, speaks while riding down the lines (τάξεις, referring to the peltasts and 300 hoplites under his command (3.4.43)). **ἡνίκα <τοῖς> ἀπὸ τῆς βοηθείας ἀπήντησαν [οἱ Ἕλληνες]** 'exactly when they (i.e. Xenophon and his τάξεις) fell in with those returning from the rescue mission'. For the rare use of ἡνίκα with an aorist, cf. *Cyr.* 7.1.25. The text printed here is tentative, but the main MS text, which should mean 'exactly when the Greeks (i.e. Chirisophus and his men) on their way from the rescue mission fell in (with Xenophon)', is unlikely to be right: *(a)* ἀπαντᾶν is almost always used with either a dative object or an indication of destination; a bare adverbial phrase designating the source is unparalleled; *(b)* οἱ Ἕλληνες is an unparalleled designation for part of the Greek army in a context where it meets another part; it may have been added, under the influence of the following vocative, to provide a subject.

3.5.5 **ὦ ἄνδρες Ἕλληνες:** this rare form of address is used mostly by non-Greek speakers (3.3.2n.), but occasionally by Greeks addressing multi-ethnic Greek audiences, especially when they appeal to common Greek values and oppose them to non-Greek ones; cf. Hdt. 7.158.1, 9.82.3; Gorg. DK 82 B7; Alcid. *Od.* 1; Aeschin. 3.117. All these speakers position themselves as authoritative outside observers; Xenophon too begins by addressing his audience with 'you' (ὑμετέραν), before switching to inclusive 'we' (ἡμᾶς). **ὑφιέντας τὴν χώραν ἤδη ὑμετέραν εἶναι** 'that they are now actually giving up the country to be yours'. ὑφιέντας (itself dependent on ὁρᾶτε, and with its subject left unexpressed, perhaps as a sign of Xenophon's urgency) is construed with an infinitive denoting purpose or result on the analogy of δίδωμι (*CGCG* 51.16; cf. e.g. 3.4.42). **ἃ γὰρ . . . ὡς ἀλλοτρίαν** 'for what they were trying to achieve at the time when they were making the truce, namely that we were not to burn the king's territory – now they are burning it themselves, as if it belonged to someone else'. An anacoluthon which reflects Xenophon's spirited style: ἃ . . . διεπράττοντο is set up as if something like 'they do not abide by it themselves' will follow, but instead Xenophon starts again at νῦν and makes χώραν from the previous clause the object of καίουσιν. **ὅτε ἐσπένδοντο:** the Greeks had sworn an oath not to harm Persian land in any way if the Persians provided a market (see 3.1.19n. on ἔστε μὲν αἱ σπονδαὶ ἦσαν). **διεπράττοντο:** the verb is commonly used in the aorist or perfect to describe what one 'secures' in the context of negotiations (cf. e.g. 2.3.20, 25, 29, 5.30); the conative imperfect (*CGCG* 33.25; Smyth 1895) here prepares for the stress on their failure. **μὴ καίειν:** the infinitive, though influenced by διεπράττοντο (cf. 2.6.28 στρατηγεῖν διεπράξατο), is in apposition to ἅ, specifying the stipulation that is meant; supply ὑμᾶς (or ἡμᾶς) as subject (cf. 4.2.19). **ὡς ἀλλοτρίαν:** continuing his earlier statements that victors gain the possessions of the vanquished (3.1.21, 2.28, 39(nn.)), Xenophon now claims that Tissaphernes' treatment of the land constitutes an admission of Persian inferiority – but the point is an uneasy one, because the indication that the land is now 'Greek' is that it is being destroyed by the Persians. Cf. Plut. *Demetr.* 7.4, *Flam.* 5.3 for the idea that ravaging a territory is an acknowledgement that the land no longer belongs to the ravager. **ἀλλ' ἐάν που . . . πορευομένους:** using the break-off ἀλλά (3.2.6n.) and reverting to a conventional interpretation of the 'winner-takes-all' motif, Xenophon suggests that Tissaphernes' action will be pointless because the Persians *will* need to store (καταλείπωσι; also in this sense at 5.3.6) their provisions (ἐάν is understated), and the Greeks will come and get them wherever they are. Xenophon makes the Greeks seem more menacing by describing their approach from the Persians' point of view (ὄψονται; cf. 3.2.24 εἰ ἑώρα).

3.5.6 "ἀλλ' ὦ Χειρίσοφε" ἔφη: the vocative (as well as the resumed *inquit* formula (3.3.2n. on ". . . λέξατε οὖν" ἔφη)) indicates that Xenophon, as he rides along the (now converged) lines, has reached Chirisophus. **δοκεῖ μοι . . . ὑπὲρ τῆς ἡμετέρας:** if Xenophon's proposal is sincere, he is assuming that Chirisophus will take seriously the claim that the land now effectively belongs to the Greeks. It is more likely that he knowingly makes an unrealistic proposal so as to engage Chirisophus in a game of verbal jousting, thereby showing to the soldiers that even during this crisis their commanders can afford to be light-hearted. **οὔκουν ἔμοιγε δοκεῖ** 'well, that is not quite *my* view': οὔκουν introduces an emphatic negation (*CGCG* 59.33). Chirisophus echoes Xenophon's words δοκεῖ μοι only to give his own spin to them. Such repetitions with a twist are typical of 'capping games' in which two speakers vie to go one better than each other; this playful and improvised performance technique is widely reflected in tragic and comic stichomythia, Platonic dialogue and sympotic poetry (Collins 2004). For the playful relationship between Xenophon and Chirisophus, cf. their joshing at 4.6.7–19; X. describes an argument at 4.6.3 as their μόνον διάφορον. **ἀλλὰ καὶ ἡμεῖς . . . καίωμεν:** this laconic put-down is intended to outdo Xenophon with the wildly unrealistic suggestion that they should actually burn the land themselves (thereby underlining the fact that the Persians are now burning their own land). The abrupt end to the dialogue suggests that Chirisophus wins the 'capping game', but the omission of any report of the soldiers' response leaves open the question whether it has the desired effect on morale. **θᾶττον** 'soon enough', i.e. sooner than one would expect.

3.5.7 **σκηνάς** 'quarters', i.e. houses in the villages which they occupied – a common military usage (cf. the use of σκην- verbs for 'quartering' in a village/city at 3.4.32; Aen. Tact. 22.3). **περὶ . . . ἦσαν** 'were busy about', a common idiom (LSJ s.v. περί C.3). **στρατηγοὶ . . . καὶ λοχαγοί:** for the lack of the article in standard pairings such as these, see 3.4.46n. πρὸς παῖδας καὶ γυναῖκας. **ἐνταῦθα** 'there', i.e. at the meeting. **πολλὴ ἀπορία** echoes 3.1.2 ἐν πολλῆι δὴ ἀπορίαι. **ἔνθεν μὲν . . . ἔνθεν δὲ . . .** 'on one side . . . on the other' (LSJ s.v. ἔνθεν I.1). The sentence is focalized through the attendees of the meeting (as signalled by the imperfect, as at 1(n.)). **ὑπερύψηλα:** this compound adjective occurs first here and then not until X.'s imitator Arrian. X. coined several such adjectives, including ὑπέρδασυς, ὑπέραισχρος (both at *Cyr.* 2.2.28), ὑπερίσχυρος (*Cyr.* 5.2.2), ὑπέρφοβος (*Eq.* 3.9); a possible model may have been ὑπέρπολυς (first at Aesch. *Pers.* 794, then twice at *Hell.* 3.2.26). The 'super high' mountains include the Carduchian mountains to the north through which the Greeks will eventually have to pass (15n.). **ὡς μηδὲ . . . τοῦ βάθους:** ὡς = ὥστε, μηδέ is adverbial ('not even'). With ὑπερέχειν supply τοῦ ὕδατος (cf. the full expression at *Cyr.* 7.5.8). **πειρωμένοις:** for the dative participle (of persons judging or observing), see Smyth 1487. The hoplite spears here referred to were perhaps as long as 8.2 feet (2.5 metres) (Lee 2007: 115). Xenophon's promise that the Tigris could, if necessary, be crossed at its source (3.2.22) is wearing a bit thin; the Greeks will have assumed that they were still a long way from there. For the implications of the water levels of the Tigris for the chronology, see Introduction p. 41.

3.5.8–12 The impasse is broken by the arrival of an anonymous Rhodian (8n.) with a plan to build a floating bridge of inflated skins. The plan, which is outlined in detail in direct speech (8–11), must have been inspired by the rafts made from inflated skins (*keleks*) used on Mesopotamian water channels since at least the period of the Assyrian empire (when they appear on reliefs) and presumably seen by the Greeks earlier in the retreat (cf. σχεδίαις διφθερίναις at 2.4.28, though these may be leather-covered round boats known as *quffas* (cf. Hdt. 1.194.2) rather than *keleks* (Mark 2005: 72)). Similar rafts are attested elsewhere (e.g. in Roman Gaul (Rougé 1959)), but not in classical Greece (see Hornell 1946: 20–34; Casson 1971: 3–5). The idea of joining such rafts together to form a bridge may have stemmed from memory of the pontoon bridges built over the Hellespont by Xerxes (cf. 10n.). Such bridges are next attested in the fourth century AD, when Ammianus Marcellinus (24.3.11, 25.6.15) reports that they were used by the Roman emperor Julian to cross canals in Mesopotamia, but that a proposal to bridge the Tigris in this way was thwarted by the strength of the current; an *ascogefyrus* 'skin-bridge' is described at Anon. *De rebus bellicis* 16.

For all the detail offered by the Rhodian, his proposal was 'wisely rejected', as Edward Gibbon noted (1994: I.949 n. 107), given the presence of enemy cavalrymen on the opposite bank (12): when the Greeks later cross a fordable river against similar opposition, they rely on an element of surprise (4.3.16–23), while Alexander crossed the River Jaxartes on rafts only with the help of catapult protection (Curt. Ruf. 7.9.2–10).

The inclusion of a speech outlining a bold proposal that is ignored (cf. Thuc. 3.30) allows for further commentary on the Greeks' ability to adapt to local circumstances, even as the generals' objections show that resourcefulness is no longer enough. The slowing down of the narrative and the delaying of the key information (the Persian cavalry) that shows that the proposal is futile also creates suspense: the possibility of a direct route home is raised only to be dismissed. And the very futility of this proposal may excuse Xenophon for having no better solution to the army's ἀπορία.

3.5.8 ἀπορουμένοις δ' αὐτοῖς: the participle picks up ἀπορία (7); for this use, see 3.3.1n. on ἀριστοποιουμένων δὲ αὐτῶν. The phrasing ironically sets up the expectation that a genuine solution is now to follow: cf. Hdt. 1.75.4 (a river crossing), 4.179.2 οἱ (i.e. Ἰήσονι) ἀπορέοντι . . . φανῆναι

Τρίτωνα, 7.213.1; Pl. *Prt.* 321c3. **προσελθών** makes clear that the speaker is a common soldier who joins the meeting at his own initiative; contrast the use of ἀνίσταμαι for the introduction of speakers already present (e.g. 3.2.1, 4, 7). **τις ἀνὴρ Ῥόδιος:** one of seven unnamed characters in *An.* who are given direct speech (Tuplin 2014: 88); some of these are common soldiers who express the *vox communis* (1.3.16–19, 6.4.18; cf. *Cyr.* 4.1.11 and de Jong 1987 on Homeric τις-speeches), but others, like the Rhodian here, make strikingly individual contributions (cf. the Macronian peltast at 4.8.4). As Tuplin notes, their anonymity creates an air of authenticity, suggesting that X(enophon) forgot their names. But non-naming may also reflect low status: Rhodians are elsewhere in *An.* mentioned only as slingers (3.3.16n.). If it is to be inferred that the speaker here is a slinger, this may suggest that he is exceeding his area of expertise. His ethnicity may also highlight his acquisitiveness: Hellenistic historians (Polyb. 31.31.1–3; Diod. Sic. 31.36) comment on the Rhodians' eager receipt of largesse, and ps.-Aristotle (*Oec.* 1348a35–1353a4) includes four Rhodians in a catalogue of statesmen who devised clever financial scams. Rhodes was also renowned for technical innovations from Hellenistic times (Mygind 1999). **ἐγὼ θέλω:** X. sometimes uses θέλω (the standard form in the *koine*) instead of ἐθέλω after vowels to avoid hiatus (cf. 3.2.16). Despite the positive connotations of 'volunteering' (for a similar use of the verb, see 3.4.41n.), the fact that the speech opens with an emphatic reference to the speaker himself, without his identity being known (at least to the narratee), does not inspire confidence in his authority. **κατὰ τετρακισχιλίους ὁπλίτας** '4,000 hoplites at a time'. The reason for this number becomes clear later (11n.). The Rhodian makes no mention of the other members of the army who need to be put across. **ἐμοὶ . . . ὑπηρετήσητε** 'minister to my needs'. The Rhodian casts the generals as subordinate (ὑπηρετέω originally = 'serve as a rower'). The emphatic form ἐμοί (rather than μοι) underlines the *quid pro quo* nature of his proposal. **τάλαντον μισθόν:** μισθόν is predicative. When the army still received wages, they at first earned 1 daric per month, later 1.5 darics (1.3.21). If 1 talent equals 300 darics (as suggested at 1.7.18), the Rhodian is asking for the exorbitant sum of 300 months' pay at the standard rate or 200 at the increased rate. For the presence of money in the army, see 3.3.18n. on ἦν οὖν αὐτῶν κτλ.

3.5.9 **ἐρωτώμενος . . . δέοιτο:** the generals pointedly do not mention the money. **"ἀσκῶν" ἔφη:** the surprising answer is emphasized by postpositive ἔφη (*CGCG* 60.5). **πολλὰ δ' ὁρῶ ταῦτα πρόβατα καί . . .** 'many are the sheep and . . . that I see here', with predicative πολλά, and ταῦτα used in a local sense (in which case the article is often lacking: LSJ s.v. οὗτος B.I.3, C.I.5). The various kinds of livestock listed are, at least in part, the βοσκήματα from 2. ὁρῶ ironically evokes Xenophon's status as privileged viewer (cf. his use of ὁρῶ for his sight of unexploited resources at 3.3.19(n.), 5.1.11, 6.31; also 3.4.41(n.)); it emerges that the Rhodian has either not seen the Persians across the river or not realized their significance. **ἀποδαρέντα καὶ φυσηθέντα** 'skinned and inflated'. φυσηθέντα is loosely added, as if the antecedent were 'skins' rather than 'animals'. Earlier the Greek soldiers had improvised rafts by stuffing their tent covers with straw (1.5.10; cf. Arr. *Anab.* 3.29.4; Curt. Ruf. 7.9.4); the use of fresh inflated skins allowed for greater buoyancy and reduced the chance of splitting. **ῥαιδίως:** the breathless series of participles which follows at 10 is suggestive of the supposed ease of the project which the Rhodian here advertises. But 'ease' is often deceptive (Rood 1998a: 34), and the plan in fact requires considerable skill: Ammianus Marcellinus (25.6.15) mentions *architecti*, while in February 1733 a 'European engineer' constructed a large float buoyed by inflated skins, which allowed 15,000 Persian troops to cross the Tigris in a morning, but which broke up soon afterwards (Jones 1773: 48).

3.5.10: ζεύξας τοὺς ἀσκοὺς . . ., ὁρμίσας ἕκαστον ἀσκὸν . . ., διαγαγὼν καὶ ἀμφοτέρωθεν δήσας: participial phrases expressing successive actions (see Denniston 1952: 104 for enumerations in which only the last item is preceded by καί), with the object changing from 'the skins', to 'each skin', and then (implicitly) to the whole line of skins with the final two participles. διαγαγὼν implies that the Rhodian will put the line of skins into the water, and will then 'bring across' one end of it, for instance by tying it to a boat; once that is done, the ends are fastened to poles or the like on both banks of the river (ἀμφοτέρωθεν). **λίθους ἀρτήσας καὶ ἀφεὶς** 'by fastening stones to them and dropping them': two modal aorist participles (cf. 3.4.42n. on εἰπών) co-ordinated by καί, modifying ὁρμίσας. Fastening more than one stone to each skin would help to trap the air. **ἐπιβαλῶ ὕλην καὶ γῆν ἐπιφορήσω:** the long sentence is rounded off by two chiastically ordered main clauses. Herodotus (7.36.5) describes in similar language the addition of brushwood and compacted earth during the construction of Xerxes' pontoon bridges over the Hellespont: ὕλην ἐπεφόρησαν . . . καὶ . . . γῆν ἐπεφόρησαν (cf. Hammond and Roseman 1996: 93–4, 100). Though the use of brushwood to provide a platform for buoyed rafts is attested, the intertextual reference to Herodotus, if intended, perhaps brings out the grandiosity of the Rhodian's presentation of his proposal.

3.5.11 μὲν οὖν: οὖν introduces the two-part conclusion, balanced by μέν/δέ. The Rhodian attempts to take away the objections which he thinks the generals may have. **αὐτίκα μάλα εἴσεσθε:** verification will be instantaneous, because the strength of the bridge does not depend on that of the structure as a whole, but on that of each skin: if the first men to step on the bridge do not sink, the generals will 'know' that it is sound. The Rhodian optimistically supposes that it can be ensured that the skins will remain airtight; that they will all bear the same load even though they will be from animals of varying size; and that the whole structure will withstand repeated use as well as the strong currents of the Tigris (cf. Whitby 2004: 235). **πᾶς γὰρ . . . σχήσει:** an elegant chiasmus, with variation of aspect in the two futures of ἔχω (George 2016) and of construction with the 'preventing' verbs (for which cf. *CGCG* 51.36). Imperfective ἕξει emphasizes that at any one time each skin (distributive πᾶς) will be keeping two men from sinking (differently George 2016: 623–4); it is followed by an articular aorist infinitive in the genitive, modified, as usual with 'preventing' verbs, by μή. Perfective σχήσει suggests that providing a surface for the bridge will once for all prevent slipping; it is followed by a result clause with present infinitive, implying that non-slipperiness will be a general feature of the bridge. δύο ἄνδρας justifies the promise (8) to take across 4,000 men at a time.

3.5.12 τοῖς στρατηγοῖς: despite the presence of the λοχαγοί (7), only the generals decide. **τὸ μὲν ἐνθύμημα . . . ἀδύνατον:** the clever plan is contrasted with its unpracticability (a variation on the common λόγος/ἔργον contrast). χαρίεις is used of anything that evokes a response of gladness or gratitude (cf. e.g. the colloquial reply χάριέν γε at Ar. *Eccl.* 680), but may carry a hint of irony or condescension (cf. e.g. *Cyr.* 1.4.13; Pl. *Grg.* 484c6). **γάρ** suggests that the sentence still represents the considerations of the generals (for a similar perspectival usage of γάρ, see 3.3.5, 4.42(nn.)). **οἱ κωλύσοντες:** articulate future participles denote persons likely and able to do something (Smyth 2044); **πολλοὶ ἱππεῖς** is in apposition. The presence of cavalrymen across the river may indicate that the Persians planned to drive the Greeks into the Carduchian mountains (contrast the unhindered crossing of the Zapatas at 3.3.6(n.)); assuming the cavalrymen were visible, the Rhodian's oversight is considerable. **οἳ . . . ποιεῖν:** the generals' perspective is further reflected in the emphatic placement and exaggeration of εὐθὺς τοῖς πρώτοις 'the very first' and οὐδέν (the Greeks could have made the preparations required for the bridge, though Persian archers and cavalry could have made its construction difficult and landings impossible (8–12n.)). **ἂν ἐπέτρεπον** 'would allow' is a present counterfactual (as suggested by the imperfect rather than the aorist: *CGCG* 34.16 n. 3; Smyth 1788), marking the generals' perception at the time that the plan to cross the river was not feasible. The effect is ironical: the Rhodian could have dispensed with his long technical exposition.

3.5.13 Ἐνταῦθα 'in these circumstances'. **μέν** similarly sets up contrasts which do not materialize at e.g. 4.5.9, 8.10. **ἐπανεχώρουν εἰς τοὔμπαλιν:** the Greeks turn back the way they came, i.e. towards the south; this is the only recorded time when they retrace their steps during the retreat to the sea. **[ἢ πρὸς Βαβυλῶνα]:** assuming ἤ means 'or', these words must be a clarifying gloss based on the geographical information given below (15); they seem out of place because τοὔμπαλιν ἤ more naturally means 'in the opposite direction from', which makes no geographical sense. The **b** reading ὡς πρὸς Βαβυλῶνα 'as if (they were going) to Babylon' indicates an elaborate but implausible attempt by the Greeks to deceive the Persians; it is probably an emendation to justify the mention of Babylon. **εἰς τὰς ἀκαύστους κώμας**, in apposition to εἰς τοὔμπαλιν, suggests that Tissaphernes burnt the villages only in the northern part of the plain. **κατακαύσαντες ἔνθεν ἐξῇσαν:** κατα- is intensifying ('to the ground'); supply τὴν κώμην as the antecedent of ἔνθεν (a petrified expression for 'from where'). **ὥστε** configures the Persians' response as a consequence of the Greeks' actions, not as their intended goal – which may well have been precisely to confound the Persians (burning the village in which they camped is not an implementation of Chirisophus' earlier proposal (6), which, even if serious, concerned other villages). By refraining from mentioning the Greeks' purpose, X. prepares for the discourse of 'wonder' in the next sentence. **προσήλαυνον** suggests that the Persians were on horseback. **ὅμοιοι ἦσαν θαυμάζουσι:** lit. 'they were like people who were wondering', i.e. 'they seemed to be wondering'. The sentence conveys the Greek interpretation of the striking sight of stationary Persian cavalrymen gazing at them. X. regularly uses the discourse of 'wonder' (θαῦμα) with a view to activating readers' reflection (Baragwanath 2012: 632); here they are invited to share the Persians' bewilderment (and so are distanced from the Greek army). θαυμάζουσι, a correction in one MS (probably by conjecture), yields an idiom used in the context of inferences drawn from outward behaviour (e.g. Pl. *Men.* 80d3 ὅμοιος εἶ οὐκ εἰδότι 'you seem not to know'; Plut. *Artax.* 8.4); with the readings θαυμάζειν and θαυμάζοντες, ὅμοιός εἰμι takes the constructions of verbs of 'believing' or 'knowing', but this is unparalleled. But the corruption could lie elsewhere (see the apparatus). **ὅποι ποτὲ τρέψονται . . . ἐν νῷ ἔχοιεν:** the more pressing concern (note ποτε 'where on earth . . .') retains the indicative of the corresponding direct speech; the more general concern takes the optative (*CGCG* 41.13). For Persian uncertainty about the Greeks' plans, cf. Mithradates' question, asked when communications were still open, τί ἐν νῷ ἔχετε; (3.3.2).

3.5.14 ἀμφὶ τὰ ἐπιτήδεια: ἀμφί was displaced by περί in fourth-century Attic prose (see 7 περὶ τὰ ἐπιτήδεια), but X. uses it often (especially in *An.*

and *Cyr.*), presumably under the influence of Ionic and Doric (Mommsen 1895: 366; Gautier 49–50; cf. Photius *Lex.* α 1377). **οἱ δὲ στρατηγοὶ πάλιν συνῆλθον:** the addition καὶ οἱ λοχαγοί bolsters the parallel with 7 (the reference of πάλιν), but X. never uses two articles in the phrase (οἱ) στρατηγοὶ καὶ λοχαγοί in *An.* (× 7; cf. 7n.). **τοὺς αἰχμαλώτους:** it is presented as a matter of course that the Greeks took some local inhabitants captive; this is the first recorded time that they make use of them as guides, as Xenophon had proposed (3.2.20). To refer to prisoners of war, X. uses either αἰχμάλωτοι or the present participle (οἱ) ἁλισκόμενοι (though in *An.* only in the spurious summary 4.1.3). The perfect participle ἑαλωκότας, transmitted in some MSS, is used in classical times almost exclusively to refer to people 'convicted' of crimes (e.g. Isae. 5.13; Dem. 23.28, 35), and is not used with any frequency for prisoners of war until Greek historians of the Roman era. **ἤλεγχον τὴν κύκλωι πᾶσαν χώραν τίς ἑκάστη εἴη** 'questioned them as to the whole territory (accusative of respect: *CGCG* 30.14; Smyth 1601a) around them, what each region was'. τὴν . . . χώραν is used proleptically (3.2.8n. on τοὺς στρατηγούς . . . οἷα πεπόνθασιν); with ἑκάστη, *sc.* χώρα, assuming a slight shift in meaning. ἐλέγχω suggests a question-and-answer mode of interrogation.

3.5.15 This elaborate indirect speech, which summarizes the answers that the various prisoners gave, offers a rare broader vision of the position of the Ten Thousand within the Persian empire at a key point in the narrative (the next clear geographical pointer, this time in the form of a narratorial comment, comes at 4.3.1). The irregular south–east–west–north direction of the description leaves the Carduchians to the last, preparing for the addition of some rather discouraging ethnographic details (a positive reason for heading north is only revealed at 17 below) (cf. *SAGN* III 175–6). **ὅτι τὰ μὲν . . . ἥκοιεν** 'that the areas to the south lay on the route that led to Babylon and to Media, through which they had come'. Broader τὰ μέν, by contrast with ἡ δέ for the other three routes, is used for the areas the army has crossed because it has not been following a single direct route. With τῆς (possessive genitive) *sc.* ὁδοῦ; for the perfective use of present ἥκω, cf. *CGCG* 33.18. The presentation departs from the linear order (one would pass through Media before reaching Babylon), because, as often, the longer constituent (Μηδίαν, δι' ἧσπερ . . .) is put at the end. **πρὸς ἕω:** for the variant ἠῶ, see Introduction p. 24. **ἐπὶ Σοῦσά τε καὶ Ἐκβάτανα:** presumably the eastern part of Herodotus' 'Royal Road' (5.52–3) from Sardis to Susa is meant, though X. does not overtly show any consciousness of Herodotus' description (Tuplin 2004d: 356). Near Arbela, not far to the south-east from the Greeks' present location, the road split into two, one going east through the mountains to Ecbatana, the other south-east towards Susa (Graf 1994: 179); it is not clear if X.

compressed the prisoners' account or was unaware of how far Susa lay to the south of Ecbatana: the coupling of the two sites again at 2.4.25 may suggest the latter (cf. Tuplin 2003b: 358 n. 15). **ἔνθα θερίζειν [καὶ ἐαρίζειν] λέγεται** offers the sort of apparently incidental information that is sometimes attached to toponyms in historical and geographical texts, especially when they deal with unfamiliar settings (*SAGN* II.140–1, 158–9); given that the information is irrelevant (see Introduction pp. 41–2 for the chronology), it should be taken as a narratorial comment rather than as part of the prisoners' reported speech (with present λέγεται retained from the corresponding direct speech). The antecedent of ἔνθα may be either Σοῦσά τε καὶ Ἐκβάτανα or Ἐκβάτανα alone. The close τε καί connection suggests the former, but this requires an awkward chiasmus (taking ἐαρίζειν with Σοῦσα and θερίζειν with Ἐκβάτανα) to fit other Greek accounts of the king's seasonal migrations (on which see Tuplin 1998; Llewellyn-Jones 2013: 74–95), which present him spending the summer in (mountainous) Media or specifically its capital Ecbatana, the spring (if specified, as at *Cyr.* 8.6.22; Plut. *Mor.* 78d, 604c) in Susa, and the winter in Babylon or Susa. It is better, then, to take the clause with Ἐκβάτανα alone, omitting (with several MSS) καὶ ἐαρίζειν. But the whole clause may be an interpolation: it is rare for such information to interrupt a speech; descriptions of the king's migrations elsewhere include winter; and other sources which mention only Susa and Ecbatana (Ael. *NA* 10.6; Ath. 12.513f; Σ Ar. *Equ.* 1089b; cf. Dio Chrys. 6.1) treat Susa as the winter residence. Interpolation could have been inspired by Greek interest in the king's migrations, and perhaps even by *Cyr.* 8.6.22, which was picked up in the Byzantine era by Zonaras, *Epitome* 3.26. **διαβάντι:** the use of the standard geographical formula for travellers (3.2.22n.) is ironical in this context. **ἐπὶ Λυδίαν καὶ Ἰωνίαν φέροι:** the order of the description matches the route, as Lydia lies immediately to the east of Ionia. Since this is the only route said directly to lead to an area of Greek settlement, the army's inability to cross the river is further emphasized. **Καρδούχους:** first mentioned here, and often thought to be related to the Kurds, who now inhabit the same mountains (though also a wider area). They appear otherwise only in later accounts of the Ten Thousand (Diod. Sic. 14.27.3–4; *FGrH* 109 F 1) and in a few geographical writers or grammarians who are similarly dependent on X. The journey through their land (4.1–2) is remembered by the soldiers as the most difficult section of the march (4.3.2). Definition of routes in terms of inhabitants rather than toponyms ('Carduchia') was commonly used for regions without strong political centres (*SAGN* III.176); here the character of the inhabitants gives the technique added point.

3.5.16 τούτους δὲ ἔφασαν οἰκεῖν: infinitives with φημί are a standard way of continuing indirect speech after ὅτι-clauses (*CGCG* 41.16); here there is also a shift in the quality of the information: infinitives are often used for hearsay reports (*CGCG* 51.19 n. 1) and are common in ethnographic statements (cf. 15 θερίζειν λέγεται). **ἀνὰ τὰ ὄρη** 'all over the mountains' (with distributive ἀνά: *CGCG* 31.8) raises the expectation of continuous guerilla warfare. **πολεμικούς:** the appellation 'warlike' (more commonly in other authors μάχιμος) is frequently applied to peoples who do not live in organized *poleis*, and especially to mountain-dwellers, as associations between tough terrain and a tough way of life were commonly made (cf. the superlatives at 5.2.2, 7.2.22, *Cyr.* 3.2.7; Livy 9.13.7, with Oakley). The prisoners carefully build up the Carduchians as the least attractive option; this creates suspense while being psychologically realistic (they probably do not wish to be taken there themselves). **βασιλέως οὐκ ἀκούειν:** compare the Pisidians and Mysians (3.2.23n.). **καὶ ἐμβαλεῖν:** this and the following two infinitives still depend on ἔφασαν. **δώδεκα μυριάδας:** in apposition to στρατιάν. 120,000 is a frequent numeral in Near Eastern and Egyptian contexts (see Tuplin 1997: 154 n. 88 for examples from X. and the Bible; also Hdt. 2.158.5; Plin. *HN* 36.66); the intended size of the king's force at Cunaxa had been 1,200,000 (1.7.12). **οὐδένα ἀπονοστῆσαι:** for the proverbial pattern of a large expedition with no survivors to describe unmitigated military disaster, cf. Exodus 14:28; Hdt. 3.26.2; Diod. Sic. 11.23.2, 22.9.3; Joseph. *AJ* 2.344; Paus. 10.23.13. ἀπονοστῆσαι, the only νόστος-word in *An.*, recalls epic (e.g. Hom. *Od.* 13.6 of Odysseus' return; see 3.2.25n. on μὴ ὥσπερ οἱ λωτοφάγοι for other Odyssean themes in *An.*) and the end of the Sicilian expedition in Thucydides (7.87.6 ὀλίγοι ἀπὸ πολλῶν ἐπ' οἴκου ἀπενόστησαν, the only use of the verb in that author; cf. Rood 1998b: 242–6). The implicit parallel with the Ten Thousand is ominous. **διὰ τὴν δυσχωρίαν:** δυσχωρία is rare in fourth-century authors, but common in X. (× 12) and Hellenistic historiography. X. frequently uses δυσ- compounds to convey a sense of hostile landscapes (cf. δυσπορία 4.3.7, δύσβατος 5.2.2); for the uncanny effect here, see Purves 2010: 83. **ὁπότε μέντοι . . . σπείσαιντο:** optative in a temporal clause in indirect speech, representing ὁπόταν σπείσωνται (*CGCG* 41.20). σπένδομαι is construed with πρός instead of the more regular dative only here in X.; cf. e.g. Thuc. 5.17.2. The information given by the prisoners raises the possibility that a truce with the Carduchians is possible, an option which will be further explored by the Greeks at 4.1.8. The satrap of the plain in which the Greeks currently find themselves is probably (but not necessarily: Tuplin 2003b: 360) the same as the satrap mentioned at 3.4.31. **καὶ ἐπιμειγνύναι . . . ἑαυτούς:** καί is adverbial: the intermittent truces 'even' lead to further dealings between the people of the plain and the Carduchians. σφῶν and ἐκείνων are independent partitive genitives ('some of . . .') and function as subjects of ἐπιμειγνύναι (Smyth 1318); reflexive σφῶν and ἑαυτούς (representing ἡμῶν and ἡμᾶς) refer to the subject of the main clause (ἔφασαν), i.e. the inhabitants of the plain (*CGCG* 29.18), while ἐκείνους and ἐκείνων refer to the Carduchians (cf. *CGCG* 29.33; Smyth 1261). Intransitive ἐπιμείγνυμι is often used to refer to commercial and cultural exchanges between ethnically different peoples (cf. *Cyr.* 7.4.5; Hdt. 1.185.7, 2.104.4; Thuc. 1.2.2, 146, 2.1); it usually occurs in the middle voice, but (as at Thuc. 1.2.2) the active is used here because the reciprocity is expressed lexically by pronouns.

3.5.17 τοὺς ἑκασταχόσε φάσκοντας εἰδέναι 'those who claimed to know the country in each direction'. ἑκασταχόσε is distributive: one man knows one way, another another. The generals keep all the knowledgeable prisoners apart so that they can have the right guides on hand, but still leave unclear the direction of travel they have decided. **ἀναγκαῖον εἶναι:** as before, the Greeks respond to necessity (3.4.19–23, 32nn.), but the tone here is defeatist and apologetic: the Greeks will pass through the lands of people who have never done them harm (compare Xenophon's defence at 5.5.16 of their having taken provisions 'out of necessity' (ἀνάγκηι)). **ἐμβάλλειν** ominously echoes ἐμβαλεῖν (16); the conative present is used because the success of the undertaking is not guaranteed. **γὰρ . . . ἔφασαν:** X. only now reveals the information acquired during the interrogation which tips the balance in favour of going north. **εἰς Ἀρμενίαν . . . πολλῆς καὶ εὐδαίμονος:** the large (πολλῆς) satrapy of Armenia comprised most of what is today eastern Turkey, Armenia and Georgia (a subdivision 'western Armenia' is mentioned at 4.4.4); for its ruler, Orontas, see 3.4.13n. For the adjective εὐδαίμων (often, as here, combined with an adjective denoting greatness), see 3.2.23n. on πολλάς τε . . . πόλεις. Strabo (11.14.4) describes Armenia as a collection of mountains, plateaux and plains, some of which are 'very fertile' (σφόδρα εὐδαίμονες), and X. frequently comments on the ease with which the Greeks manage to secure provisions (e.g. 4.4.2, 7) – though heavy snowfall and confrontations with the local inhabitants make passing through Armenia still very challenging. **εὔπορον** 'easy to pass through', but also suggestive of εὐπορία, an antonym of the Greeks' present state of ἀπορία.

3.5.18 ὁπηνίκα καὶ δοκοίη τῆς ὥρας 'at a point in time which actually seemed good'. τῆς ὥρας is partitive genitive dependent on ὁπηνίκα ('when'). Normally, sacrifices are made immediately before a departure to verify whether it has the approval of the gods, but here the generals are keen to avoid delay in case the sacrifices are not at once favourable. **τὴν . . . ὑπερβολὴν τῶν ὀρέων:** X. is the first known author to use the noun ὑπερβολή for 'crossing' a mountain (1.2.25, 4.6.5; cf. the verb ὑπερβάλλω) and, as here, for a 'mountain pass' (also at 4.1.21, 4.18, 6.6, 24). The noun is used in both senses in Hellenistic historians (e.g. Polyb.

3.34.6, 39.10). **ἐπειδὴ δειπνήσειαν:** as at 3.1.3, 4.6.22, 6.3.21, 4.10, 26, a late dinner is the mark of a long and arduous day.

* * *

> It was here that we were to bid a final farewell to the Greeks who had accompanied us from the outset of the journey. . . . They turned north . . . and fought their way through the land of the Carduchi, which are the Kurds, until they reached the sea, while we, having a ferry-boat at our disposal and a smaller force to handle, passed over the Tigris into the Tûr 'Abdîn. So at length we parted, and Cheirisophus in advance with the light-armed troops scaled the hills of Finik and led slowly forward, leaving Xenophon to bring up the rear with the heavy-armed men. Their shields and corselets glittered upon the steep, they climbed, and reached the summit of the ridge and disappeared . . .
>
> 'Effendim!' Fattûh broke into my meditations. 'Effendim, the boat is ready.'
>
> 'Oh Fattûh,' said I, 'the Greeks are gone.'
>
> Gertrude Bell, *Amurath to Amurath* (1911: 300)

BIBLIOGRAPHY

Works cited by author's name without date will be found in the Abbreviations list on pp. xi–xiii. Journal abbreviations follow those in *OCD* or *L'Année philologique.*

Adams, R. 1972. *Watership Down*, London

Adrados, F. R. 2005. *A history of the Greek language from its origins to the present*, Leiden

Aerts, W. J. 1965. *Periphrastica: an investigation into the use of εἶναι and ἔχειν as auxiliaries or pseudo-auxiliaries in Greek from Homer up to the present day*, Amsterdam

Ainsworth, W. F. 1844. *Travels in the track of the Ten Thousand Greeks: being a geographical and descriptive account of the expedition of Cyrus and of the retreat of the Ten Thousand Greeks, as related by Xenophon*, London

Albertus, J. 1908. *Die παρακλητικοί in der griechischen und römischen Literatur*, Strassburg

Aldrete, G. S., S. Bartell, and A. Aldrete. 2013. *Reconstructing ancient linen body armor: unraveling the linothorax mystery*, Baltimore

Allan, R. J. 2003. *The middle voice in ancient Greek: a study in polysemy*, Amsterdam

Allison, J. W. 1997. *Word and concept in Thucydides*, Atlanta

Almagor, E. 2012. 'Ctesias and the importance of his writings revisited', *Electrum* 19: 9–40

Amit, M. 1970. 'Hostages in ancient Greece', *RFIC* 98: 129–47

Anderson, J. K. 1970. *Military theory and practice in the age of Xenophon*, Berkeley

1974. *Xenophon*, London

1986. 'Xenophon at Corinth', in M. del Chiaro, ed. *Corinthiaca: studies in honor of D. A. Amyx* (Columbia, MO) 36–9

Avery, H. C. 1973. 'Themes in Thucydides' account of the Sicilian expedition', *Hermes* 101: 1–13

Azoulay, V. 2004a. 'Exchange as entrapment: mercenary Xenophon?', in Lane Fox 2004a: 289–304

2004b. *Xénophon et les grâces du pouvoir: de la charis au charisme*, Paris

Badian, E. 2004. 'Xenophon the Athenian', in Tuplin 2004b: 33–53

Bakker, E. J. (ed.) 1997. *Grammar as interpretation: Greek literature in its linguistic contexts*, Leiden

Balode, S. 2011. *Verbs of motion with directional prepositions and prefixes in Xenophon's* Anabasis, Lund

Baragwanath, E. 2012. 'The wonder of freedom: Xenophon on slavery', in Hobden and Tuplin 2012: 631–63

2016.'Knowing future time in Xenophon's *Anabasis*', in A. Lianeri, ed. *Knowing future time in and through Greek historiography* (Berlin and Boston) 119–39

Barnett, R. D. 1948. 'Early Greek and oriental ivories', *JHS* 68: 1–25

1963. 'Xenophon and the Wall of Media', *JHS* 83: 1–26

Bassett, S. R. 2001. 'The enigma of Clearchus the Spartan', *AHB* 15: 1–13

2002. 'Innocent victims or perjurers betrayed? The arrest of the generals in Xenophon's *Anabasis*', *CQ* 52: 447–61

Bell, G. 1911. *Amurath to Amurath*, London

Bers, V. 1984. *Greek poetic syntax in the classical age*, New Haven

1997. *Speech in speech: studies in incorporated* oratio recta *in Attic drama and oratory*, Lanham, MD

Best, J. G. P. 1969. *Thracian peltasts and their influence on Greek warfare*, Groningen

Blass, F. W. 1892. *Die attische Beredsamkeit, Abt.* II: *Isokrates und Isaios*, 2nd edn, Leipzig

Bonner, R. J. 1910. 'The name "Ten Thousand"', *CPhil* 5: 97–9

Bosworth, A. B. 1996. *Alexander and the East: the tragedy of triumph*, Oxford

Boucher, A. 1913. *L'Anabase de Xénophon (Retraite des dix mille)*, Paris and Nancy

Bradley, P. J. 2010. 'Irony and the narrator in Xenophon's *Anabasis*', in Gray 2010a: 520–2

Breitenbach, H. R. 1967. 'Xenophon von Athen', in *RE* IX.A.2: 1567–2052

Brennan, S. G. 2005. *In the tracks of the Ten Thousand: a journey on foot through Turkey, Syria and Iraq*, London

2008. 'Chronological pointers in Xenophon's *Anabasis*', *BICS* 51: 51–61

2011. 'Apologia in Xenophon's *Anabasis*', PhD thesis, Exeter

2012. 'Mind the gap: a snow lacuna in Xenophon's *Anabasis*?', in Hobden and Tuplin 2012: 307–39

Briant, P. 2002. *From Cyrus to Alexander: a history of the Persian empire*, trans. P. Daniels, Winona Lake, IN

2015. *Darius in the shadow of Alexander*, trans. J. M. Todd, Cambridge, MA

Brosius, M. 1996. *Women in ancient Persia, 559–331* BC, Oxford.

Buijs, M. 2005. *Clause combining in ancient Greek narrative discourse: the distribution of subclauses and participial clauses in Xenophon's* Hellenica *and* Anabasis, Leiden

2007. 'Aspectual differences and narrative technique: Xenophon's *Hellenica* and *Agesilaus*', in R. J. Allan and M. Buijs, eds. *The language of literature: linguistic approaches to classical texts* (Leiden and Boston) 122–53

Buxton, R. F. (ed.) 2016. *Aspects of leadership in Xenophon* (Newcastle upon Tyne: *Histos* Supplement 5), https://research.ncl.ac.uk/histos/documents/SV5.html

Cairns, D. L. 1993. *Aidōs: the psychology and ethics of honour and shame in ancient Greek literature*, Oxford

Caragounis, C. C. (ed.) 2010. *Greek: a language in evolution. Essays in honour of Antonios N. Janaris*, Hildesheim

Cartledge, P. A. 1977. 'Hoplites and heroes: Sparta's contribution to the technique of ancient warfare', *JHS* 97: 11–27

Casson, L. 1971. *Ships and seamanship in the ancient world*, Princeton

Castiglioni, L. 1932. *Studi intorno alla storia del testo dell'*Anabasi *di Senofonte*, Milan

Cawkwell, G. L. 2004. 'When, how and why did Xenophon write the *Anabasis*?', in Lane Fox 2004a: 47–67

Chiron, P. 2014. 'L'abeille attique', in Pontier 2014: 295–318

Clarke, P. 2006. 'Appearance and belief in *Theaetetus* 151d–187a', in F.-G. Herrmann, ed. *New essays on Plato: language and thought in fourth-century Greek philosophy* (Swansea) 125–48

Collins, D. 2004. *Master of the game: competition and performance in Greek poetry*, Washington, DC

Colvin, S. 1999. *Dialect in Aristophanes and the politics of language in ancient Greek literature*, Oxford

2014. *A brief history of ancient Greek*, Oxford

Combellack, F. M. 1939. 'Omitted speech formulas in Homer', *University of California Publications in Classical Philology* 12: 43–56

Cousin, G. 1905. *Kyros le jeune en Asie Mineure (Printemps 408–Juillet 401 avant Jésus-Christ)*, Paris and Nancy

Crespo, E. 2010. 'The significance of Attic for the continued evolution of Greek', in Caragounis 2010: 119–36

Dalby, A. 1992. 'Greeks abroad: social organisation and food among the Ten Thousand', *JHS* 112: 16–30

Dalley, S. 1993. 'Nineveh after 612 BC', *Altorientalische Forschungen* 20: 134–47

2013. *The mystery of the Hanging Garden of Babylon: an elusive world wonder traced*, Oxford

Dandamaev, M. A., and V. G. Lukonin. 1989. *The culture and social institutions of ancient Iran*, trans. P. L. Kohl, Cambridge

Danzig, G. 2007. 'Xenophon's wicked Persian, or What's wrong with Tissaphernes? Xenophon's views on lying and breaking oaths', in Tuplin 2007: 27–50

2012. 'The best of the Achaemenids: benevolence, self-interest and the "ironic" reading of the *Cyropaedia*', in Hobden and Tuplin 2012: 499–539

Davies, J. K. 1971. *Athenian propertied families, 600–300 BC*, Oxford

Davies, M. 2013. 'The hero at the crossroads: Prodicus and the Choice of Heracles', *Prometheus* 39: 3–17

De Meo, D. 1986. *Lingue tecniche del Latino*, 2nd edn, Bologna

Delebecque, E. 1946–7. 'Xénophon, Athènes et Lacédémones: notes sur la composition de l'Anabase', *REG* 59–60: 71–138

1957. *Essai sur la vie de Xénophon*, Paris

Denniston, J. D. 1952. *Greek prose style*, Oxford

Dickey, E. 1996. *Greek forms of address: from Herodotus to Lucian*, Oxford

Diggle, J. 2002. 'Xenophon, *Anabasis* 3.1.6–8 and the limits of "inverse attraction"', *SIFC* 20: 83–6

Dik, H. 2003. 'On unemphatic "emphatic" pronouns in Greek: nominative pronouns in Plato and Sophocles', *Mnemosyne* 56: 535–50

Dillery, J. 1995. *Xenophon and the history of his times*, London

2016. 'Response and further thoughts', in Buxton 2016: 243–77

Dorion, L.-A. 2013. *L'Autre Socrate. Études sur les écrits socratiques de Xénophon*, Paris

Dougherty, C. 1993. *The poetics of colonization: from city to text in archaic Greece*, New York and Oxford

Dover, K. J. 1974. *Greek popular morality in the time of Plato and Aristotle*, Oxford

1997. *The evolution of Greek prose style*, Oxford

Dreher, M. 2004. 'Der Prozess gegen Xenophon', in Tuplin 2004b: 55–69

Due, B. 1989. *The* Cyropaedia: *Xenophon's aims and methods*, Aarhus

Dürrbach, F. 1893. 'L'Apologie de Xénophon dans l'"Anabase"', *REG* 6: 343–86

Ehrhardt, C. T. H. R. 1994. 'Retreat in Xenophon and Thucydides', *AHB* 8: 1–4

Ellis, A. 2016. 'A Socratic history: theology in Xenophon's rewriting of Herodotus' Croesus *logos*', *JHS* 136: 73–91

Erbse, H. 2010. 'Xenophon's *Anabasis*', in Gray 2010a: 476–501 (Germ. orig. 1966)

Evans, J. A. S. 1986–7. 'Cavalry about the time of the Persian Wars: a speculative essay', *CJ* 82: 97–106

Falappone, M. 1979. 'Note di biografia senofontea', *QS* 5: 283–91

Farrell, C. A. 2012. 'Laconism and democracy: re-reading the *Lakedaimoniōn Politeia* and re-thinking Xenophon', in J. Paul, ed. *Governing diversities: democracy, diversity and human nature* (Newcastle upon Tyne) 10–35

Ferrario, S. B. 2012. 'Historical agency and self-awareness in Xenophon's *Hellenica* and *Anabasis*', in Hobden and Tuplin 2012: 341–76

2014. *Historical agency and the 'great man' in classical Greece*, Cambridge

Feyel, C. 2009. *Dokimasia. La place et le rôle de l'examen préliminaire dans les institutions des cités grecques*, Nancy

Flower, M. A. 2012. *Xenophon's* Anabasis, *or* The expedition of Cyrus, Oxford

Foss, C. 1975. 'A bullet of Tissaphernes', *JHS* 95: 25–30

Fournier, H. 1946. *Les verbes 'dire' en grec ancien*, Paris

Gagarin, M. 1994. 'Probability and persuasion: Plato and early Greek rhetoric', in I. Worthington, ed. *Persuasion: Greek rhetoric in action* (London) 46–68

George, C. 2016. 'Verbal aspect and the Greek future: ἕξω and σχήσω', *Mnemosyne* 69: 597–627

Gera, D. L. 1993. *Xenophon's* Cyropaedia*: style, genre, and literary technique*, Oxford

2013. 'Letters in Xenophon', in P. Rosenmeyer, O. Hodkinson, and E. Bracke, eds. *Epistolary narratives in ancient Greek literature* (Leiden) 85–103

Gibbon, E. 1994 [1776–88]. *The history of the decline and fall of the Roman empire*, 3 vols., London

Gillies, J. 1790 [1786]. *The history of ancient Greece: its colonies and conquests, from the earliest accounts till the division of the Macedonian empire in the East*, 5 vols., Basel

Glombiowski, K. 1994. 'The campaign of Cyrus the Younger and the retreat of the Ten Thousand: chronology', *Pomoerium* 1: 37–44

Graf, D. F. 1994. 'The Persian Royal Road system', in H. Sancisi-Weerdenburg *et al.*, eds. *Achaemenid history* VIII: *Continuity and change* (Leiden) 167–89

Gray, V. 1989. *The character of Xenophon's* Hellenica, London

(ed.) 2010a. *Oxford readings in classical studies: Xenophon*, Oxford

2010b. 'Introduction', in Gray 2010a: 1–28

2010c. 'Interventions and citations in Xenophon's *Hellenica* and *Anabasis*', in Gray 2010a: 553–72

2011. *Xenophon's mirror of princes*, Oxford

2014. 'Le style simple de Xénophon', in Pontier 2014: 319–37

Green, P. 1994. 'Text and context in the matter of Xenophon's exile', in I. Worthington, ed. *Ventures into Greek history* (Oxford) 215–27

Grethlein, J. 2012. 'Xenophon's *Anabasis* from character to narrator', *JHS* 32: 1–18

2013. *Experience and teleology in ancient historiography*, Cambridge

Griffith, M. 2006. 'Horsepower and donkeywork: equids in the ancient Greek imagination. Part one', *CPhil* 101: 185–246

Grote, G. 1903–6 [1846–56]. *A history of Greece*, 10 vols., London

Gwynn, A. 1929. 'Xenophon and Sophaenetus', *CQ* 23: 39–40

Hall, E. 1989. *Inventing the barbarian: Greek self-definition through tragedy*, Oxford

Hammond, N. G. L., and L. J. Roseman. 1996. 'The construction of Xerxes' bridge over the Hellespont', *JHS* 116: 88–107

Hansen, M. H. 1991. *The Athenian democracy in the age of Demosthenes: structure, principles and ideology*, Oxford

Harris, W. V. 2009. *Dreams and experience in classical antiquity*, Cambridge, MA

Harvey, F. D. 1985. '*Dona ferentes*: some aspects of bribery in Greek politics', in P. A. Cartledge and F. D. Harvey, eds. *Crux: essays in Greek history presented to G. E. M. de Ste Croix on his 75th birthday* (London) 76–117

Hau, L. I. 2012. 'Does pride go before a fall? Xenophon on arrogant pride', in Hobden and Tuplin 2012: 591–610.

Hentze, C. 1904. 'Die Monologe in den homerischen Epen', *Philologus* 63: 12–30

Herman, G. 1987. *Ritualised friendship and the Greek city*, Cambridge

Hiersche, R. 1970. *Grundzüge der griechischen Sprachgeschichte*, Wiesbaden

Higgins, W. E. 1977. *Xenophon the Athenian: the problem of the individual and the society of the polis*, Albany, NY

Hirsch, S. W. 1985. *The friendship of the barbarians*, Hanover and London

Hobden, F., and C. J. Tuplin (eds.) 2012. *Xenophon: ethical principles and historical enquiry*, Leiden

Høeg, C. 1950. 'Ξενοφῶντος Κύρου Ἀνάβασις: œuvre anonyme ou pseudonyme ou orthonyme?', *C&M* 11: 151–79

Hoffmann, O., and A. Debrunner. 1969. *Geschichte der griechischen Sprache* I: *Bis zum Ausgang der klassischen Zeit*, 4th edn, revised by A. Scherer, Berlin

Hornblower, S. 2004a. '"This was decided" (*edoxe tauta*): the army as *polis* in Xenophon's *Anabasis* – and elsewhere', in Lane Fox 2004a: 243–63

2004b. *Pindar and Thucydides: historical narrative and the world of epinikian poetry*, Oxford

Hornell, J. 1946. *Water transport: origins and early evolution*, Cambridge

Horrocks, G. 2010. *Greek: a history of the language and its speakers*, 2nd edn, Oxford

Hughes, J. D. 1987. 'The dreams of Xenophon the Athenian', *Journal of Psychohistory* 14: 271–82

Huitink, L. 2019. '*Enargeia*, enactivism and the ancient readerly imagination', in M. Anderson, D. Cairns and M. Sprevak, eds. *Distributed cognition in antiquity* (*The Edinburgh history of distributed cognition* 1) (Edinburgh) 169–89

Huitink, L., and T. C. B. Rood. 2016. 'Subordinate commanders in Xenophon's *Anabasis*', in Buxton 2016: 199–242

Humble, N. 2011. 'Xenophon's *Anabasis*: self and other in fourth-century Greece', in P. Crowley, N. Humble and S. Ross, eds. *Mediterranean travels: writing self and other from the ancient world to contemporary society* (Oxford) 14–31

Hunt, P. 1998, *Slaves, warfare and ideology in the Greek historians*, Cambridge

Hunter, V. J. 1973. *Thucydides the artful reporter*, Toronto

Huss, B. 1999. *Xenophons* Symposion: *ein Kommentar*, Stuttgart

Hyland, J. 2010. 'The desertion of Nicarchus the Arcadian in Xenophon's *Anabasis*', *Phoenix* 64: 238–53

Jansen, J. N. 2014. 'Greek oath breakers? The arrest of the generals in Xenophon's *Anabasis* reexamined', *Mnemosyne* 67: 122–30

Jones, W. 1773. *The history of the life of Nader Shah, extracted from an eastern manuscript*, London

Jong, I. J. F de. 1987. 'The voice of anonymity: *tis*-speeches in the *Iliad*', *Eranos* 85: 69–84

Joost, A. 1892. *Was ergiebt sich aus dem Sprachgebrauch Xenophons in der* Anabasis *für die Behandlung der griechischen Syntax in der Schule?*, Berlin

Kagan, D., and G. Viggiano (eds.) 2013. *Men of bronze: hoplite warfare in ancient Greece*, Princeton

Kahn, C. H. 1973. *The verb 'be' in ancient Greek*, Dordrecht

Kaye, J. W. 1857. *History of the war in Afghanistan*, 3 vols., London

Kelly, A. 2012. 'The Cretan slinger at war: a weighty exchange', *ABSA* 107: 273–311

Kim, L. 2010. 'The literary heritage as language: Atticism and the Second Sophistic', in E. J. Bakker, ed. *A companion to the ancient Greek language* (Oxford) 468–82

Kinneir, J. M. 1818. *Journey through Asia Minor, Armenia, and Koordistan, in the years 1813 and 1814, with remarks on the marches of Alexander and retreat of the Ten Thousand*, London

Kowalzig, B. 2013. 'Dancing dolphins on the wine-dark sea: dithyramb and social change in the archaic Mediterranean', in B. Kowalzig and P. J. Wilson, eds. *Dithyramb in context* (Oxford) 31–58

Krentz, P. 1991. 'The *salpinx* in Greek battle', in V. D. Hanson, ed. *Hoplites: the classical Greek battle experience* (London) 105–20

Kuhrt, A. 2007. *The Persian empire: a corpus of sources from the Achaemenid period*, London

Kurtz, D., and J. Boardman. 1986. 'Booners', *Greek Vases in the J. Paul Getty Museum* 3: 35–70

Lacave, M. 2017. 'Anabases en France 1900–2015. Pour une étude de la réception de l'*Anabase* de Xénophon en France: doctrines, opérations militaires et stratégies', *Anabases* 25: 71–93

Lane Fox, R. (ed.) 2004a. *The long march: Xenophon and the Ten Thousand*, New Haven

2004b. 'Introduction', in Lane Fox 2004a: 1–46

2004c. 'Sex, gender and the Other in Xenophon's *Anabasis*', in Lane Fox 2004a: 184–214

Lang, M. L. 1984. *Herodotean narrative and discourse*, Cambridge, MA and London

Langslow, D. R. 2000. *Medical language in the Roman empire*, Oxford

Lateiner, D. 2005a. 'Telemakhos' one sneeze and Penelope's two laughs (*Odyssey* 17.541–50, 18.158–68)', in R. J. Rabel, ed. *Approaches to Homer: ancient and modern* (Swansea) 91–104

2005b. 'Signifying names and other ominous accidental utterances in classical historiography', *GRBS* 45: 35–57

Launey, M. 1987. *Recherches sur les armées hellénistiques*, Paris

Layard, A. H. 1853. *Discoveries in the ruins of Nineveh and Babylon, with travels in Armenia, Kurdistan and the desert*, London

Lazenby, J. F. 2012. *The Spartan army*, 2nd edn, Barnsley

Lee, J. W. I. 2004. 'For there were many *hetairai* in the army: women in Xenophon's *Anabasis*', *Ancient World* 35: 145–65

2005. 'Xenophon's *Anabasis* and the origins of military autobiography', in A. Vernon, ed. *Arms and the self: war, the military, and autobiographical writing* (Kent, OH) 41–60

2007. *A Greek army on the march: soldiers and survival in Xenophon's* Anabasis, Cambridge

2016. 'Cyrus the Younger and Artaxerxes II, 401 BC: an Achaemenid civil war reconsidered', in J. J. Collins and J. G. Manning, eds. *Revolt and resistance in the ancient classical world and the Near East* (Leiden and Boston) 103–21

Leimbach, R. 1985. *Militärische Musterrhetorik: eine Untersuchung zu den Feldherrnreden des Thukydides*, Stuttgart

Liddel, P. 2007. *Civic obligation and individual liberty in ancient Athens*, Oxford

Lillo, A. 2013. 'Ionic and Attic: on temporal constructions in Thucydides, Xenophon and Plato', *Glotta* 89: 146–69

Llewellyn-Jones, L. 2010. 'The big and beautiful women of Asia: picturing female sexuality in Greco-Persian seals', in S. Simpson and J. Curtis, eds. *The world of Achaemenid Persia* (London) 165–76

2013. *King and court in ancient Persia 559 to 331 BCE*, Edinburgh

Lloyd, G. E. R. 1987. *The revolutions of wisdom: studies in the claims and practice of ancient Greek science* (Sather Classical Lectures 52), Berkeley

Loraux, N. 2006. *The invention of Athens: the Funeral Oration in the classical city*, trans. A. Sheridan, New York

Lorimer, H. L. 1950. *Homer and the monuments*, London

Lossau, M. 1990. 'Xenophons *Odyssee*', *A&A* 36: 47–52

Luccioni, J. 1947. *Les idées politiques et sociales de Xénophon*, Paris

Luschnat, O. 1942. *Die Feldherrnreden im Geschichtswerk des Thukydides* (*Philologus* Supplement 42), Leipzig

Ma, J. 2004. 'You can't go home again: displacement and identity in Xenophon's *Anabasis*', in Lane Fox 2004a: 330–45

2010. 'A note on lead projectiles (*glandes, molybdides*) in support of sling bullets: a reply to T. Rihll', *JRA* 23: 427–8

Maclaren, M. 1934. 'Xenophon and Themistogenes', *TAPA* 65: 240–7

Macleod, C. W. 1978. 'Reason and necessity: Thucydides iii 9–14, 37–48', *JHS* 98: 64–78

Manfredi, V. 1986. *La Strada dei Diecimila: topografia e geografia dell'Oriente di Senofonte*, Milan

Mari, F. 2014. 'La main infidèle: le Grand Roi et la mutilation de Cyrus le Jeune', in A. Allély, ed. *Corps au supplice et violences de guerre* (Bordeaux) 79–94

Marincola, J. 1999. 'Genre, convention, and innovation in Greco-Roman historiography', in C. S. Kraus, ed. *The limits of historiography* (Leiden) 281–324

2007. 'The Persian Wars in fourth-century oratory and historiography', in E. Bridges, E. Hall and P. J. Rhodes, eds. *Cultural responses to the Persian Wars: antiquity to the third millennium* (Oxford) 105–25

Mark, S. 2005. *Homeric seafaring*, College Station, TX

Marsh, D. 1992. 'Xenophon', in V. Brown, P. O. Kristeller and F. E. Cranz, eds. *Catalogus translationum et commentariorum* VII (Washington, DC) 75–196

Millingen, F. 1870. *Wild life among the Koords*, London

Missiou, A. 1993. 'Δοῦλος τοῦ βασιλέως: the politics of translation', *CQ* 43: 377–91

Mitchell, L. G. 2007. *Panhellenism and the barbarian in archaic and classical Greece*, Swansea

Mommsen, T. 1895. *Beiträge zu der Lehre von den griechischen Präpositionen*, Berlin

Morier, J. J. 1818. *A second journey through Persia, Armenia, and Asia Minor, to Constantinople, between the years 1810 and 1816*, London

Morr, J. 1926–7. 'Xenophon und der Gedanke eines allgriechischen Eroberungszuges gegen Persien', *WS* 45: 186–201

Münscher, K. 1920. *Xenophon in der griechisch-römischen Literatur*, Leipzig

Mygind, B. 1999. 'Intellectuals in Rhodes', in V. Gabrielsen *et al.*, eds. *Hellenistic Rhodes: politics, culture, and society* (Aarhus) 247–93

Naveh, J., and S. Shaked (eds.) 2012. *Aramaic documents from ancient Bactria (fourth century BCE): from the Khalili collections*, London

Nicolai, R. 2014. 'At the boundary of genre', in G. Parmeggiani, ed. *Between Thucydides and Polybius: the golden age of Greek historiography* (Washington, DC) 63–87

Niehoff-Panagiotidis, J. 1994. *Koine und Diglossie*, Wiesbaden

Nielsen, T. H. 2004. 'The concept of *patris* in archaic and classical sources', in M. H. Hansen, ed. *Once again: studies in the ancient Greek polis. Papers from the Copenhagen Polis Centre* 7 (Stuttgart) 49–76

Norden, E. 1974 [1909[2]]. *Die antike Kunstprosa vom* VI. *Jahrhundert v. Chr. bis in die Zeit der Renaissance* I, Darmstadt

Nussbaum, G. B. 1967. *The Ten Thousand: a study in social organization and action in Xenophon's Anabasis*, Leiden

Ophuijsen, J. M. van. 1993. 'Οὖν, ἄρα, δή, τοίνυν: the linguistic articulation of arguments in Plato's *Phaedo*', in C. M. J. Sicking and J. M. van Ophuijsen, *Two studies in Attic particle usage: Lysias and Plato* (Leiden) 67–164

Osborne, M. J. 1973. 'Orontes', *Historia* 22: 515–51

Parke, H. W. 1933. *Greek mercenary soldiers: from the earliest times to the battle of Ipsus*, Oxford

Parker, R. C. T. 2004. 'One man's piety: the religious dimension of the *Anabasis*', in Lane Fox 2004a: 131–53

Parpola, S., and R. M. Whiting (eds.) 1997. *Assyria 1995: proceedings of the 10th anniversary symposium of the Neo-Assyrian Text Corpus Project, Helsinki, September 7–11, 1995*, Helsinki

Pelliccia, H. 1995. *Mind, body and speech in Homer and Pindar*, Göttingen

Pelling, C. B. R. 2013. 'Xenophon and Caesar's third-person narratives – or are they?', in A. Marmodoro and J. Hill, eds. *The author's voice in classical and late antiquity* (Oxford) 39–76

Pernot, L. 2014. 'La réception antique de Xénophon: quel modèle pour quels orateurs?', in Pontier 2014: 281–94

Perry, B. E. 1967. *The ancient romances: a literary-historical account of their origins*, Berkeley

Persson, A. W. 1915. *Zur Textgeschichte Xenophons*, Lund

Petit, T. 2004. 'Xénophon et la vassalité achéménide', in Tuplin 2004b: 175–99

Pontier, P. (ed.) 2014. *Xénophon et la rhétorique*, Paris

Porter, R. K. 1821–2. *Travels in Georgia, Persia, Armenia, Ancient Babylonia, &c. &c., during the years 1817, 1818, 1819, and 1820*, 2 vols., London

Postgate, J. N., and J. E. Reade. 1976–80. 'Kalḫu', *RLA* v.303–23

Probert, P. 2015. *Early Greek relative clauses*, Oxford

Purves, A. 2010. *Space and time in ancient Greek narrative*, Cambridge

Rahn, P. J. 1981. 'The date of Xenophon's exile', in G. S. Shrimpton and D. J. McCargor, eds. *Classical contributions: studies in honour of Malcolm Francis McGregor* (New York) 103–19

Rawlings, L. 2000. 'Alternative agonies', in H. van Wees, ed. *War and violence in ancient Greece* (London) 233–59

Rawlinson, H. C. 1850. 'On the inscriptions of Assyria and Babylonia', *JAS* 12: 401–83

Reade, J. E. 1998–2001. 'Ninive/Nineveh', *RLA* IX 388–433

2002. 'The ziggurrat and temples of Nimrud', *Iraq* 64: 135–216

2015. 'Xenophon's route through Babylonia and Assyria', *Iraq* 77: 173–202

Renault, M. 2015 [1956]. *The last of the wine*, London

Rennell, J. 1816. *Illustrations, (chiefly geographical,) of the history of the expedition of Cyrus, from Sardis to Babylonia, and the retreat of the Ten Thousand Greeks, from thence to Trebisonde and Lydia*, London

Rhodes, P. J. 1972. *The Athenian Boule*, Oxford

Richards, H. 1907. *Notes on Xenophon and others*, London

Rijksbaron, A. 1976. *Temporal and causal conjunctions in ancient Greek: with special reference to the use of ἐπεί and ὡς in Herodotus*, Amsterdam

1991. *Grammatical observations on Euripides'* Bacchae, Amsterdam

1997. 'Adverb or connector? The case of καί . . . δέ', in A. Rijksbaron, ed. *New approaches to Greek particles* (Amsterdam) 187–208

2002. 'The Xenophon factory: one hundred and fifty years of school editions of Xenophon's *Anabasis*', in R. Gibson and C. S. Kraus, eds. *The classical commentary* (Leiden) 235–67

2006a. 'The meaning and word class of πρότερον and τὸ πρότερον', in E. Crespo, J. de la Villa and A. R. Revuelta, eds. *Word classes and related topics in ancient Greek* (Louvain) 441–54

2006b. *The syntax and semantics of the verb in classical Greek: an introduction*, 3rd edn, Chicago

2011. 'Introduction', in J. Lallot, A. Rijksbaron, B. Jacquinod and M. Buijs, eds. *The historical present in Thucydides: semantics and narrative function* (Leiden) 1–18

2012. 'The imperfect as the tense of substitutionary perception', in P. da Cunha Corrêa *et al.*, eds. *Hyperboreans: essays in Greek and Latin poetry, philosophy, rhetoric and linguistics* (São Paulo) 331–75

Rinner, W. 1978. 'Zur Darstellungsweise bei Xenophon, *Anabasis* III 1–2', *Philologus* 122: 144–9

Robert, F. 1950. 'Les intentions de Xénophon dans l'*Anabase*', *Information littéraire* 2: 55–9

Roche, H. 2016. 'Xenophon and the Nazis: a case study in the politicization of Greek thought through educational propaganda', *Classical Receptions Journal* 8: 71–89

Rood, T. C. B. 1998a. *Thucydides: narrative and explanation*, Oxford

1998b. 'Thucydides and his predecessors', *Histos* 2: 230–67

2004a. 'Panhellenism and self-presentation: Xenophon's speeches', in Lane Fox 2004a: 305–29

2004b. *The sea! The sea! The shout of the Ten Thousand in the modern imagination*, London

2006. 'Advice and advisers in Xenophon's *Anabasis*', in D. J. Spencer and E. M. Theodorakopoulos, eds. *Advice and its rhetoric in Greece and Rome* (Bari) 47–61

2010a. *American anabasis: Xenophon and the idea of America from the Mexican War to Iraq*, London

2010b. 'Xenophon's parasangs', *JHS* 130: 51–66

2011. 'Black Sea variations: Arrian's *Periplus*', *Cambridge Classical Journal* 57: 135–61

2012. 'A delightful retreat: Xenophon and the picturesque', in Hobden and Tuplin 2012: 89–121

2013a. 'Xenophon and the Barberini: Pietro da Cortona's *Sacrifice to Diana*', *JWI* 76: 1–22

2013b. 'Redeeming Xenophon: historiographical reception and the transhistorical', *Classical Receptions Journal* 5: 199–211

2014. 'Space and landscape in Xenophon's *Anabasis*', in K. Gilhuly and N. Worman, eds. *Space, place, and landscape in ancient Greek literature and culture* (New York and Cambridge) 63–93

2015a. 'Political thought in Xenophon: Straussian readings of the *Anabasis*', *Polis* 32: 143–65

2015b. 'Self-characterization and political thought in Xenophon's *Anabasis*', in R. Ash, J. Mossman and F. B. Titchener, eds. *Fame and infamy: essays for Christopher Pelling on characterization in Greek and Roman biography and historiography* (Oxford) 97–109

2018. 'Cato the Elder, Livy, and Xenophon's *Anabasis*', *Mnemosyne* 71: 823–49

Root, M. C. 2007. 'Reading Persepolis in Greek: gifts of the Yauna', in Tuplin 2007: 177–224

Rostovtzeff, M. 1943. 'The Parthian shot', *AJA* 47: 174–87

Rougé, J. 1959. 'Utricularii', *CH* 4: 285–306

Roy, J. 1967. 'The mercenaries of Cyrus', *Historia* 16: 287–323

2004. 'The ambitions of a mercenary', in Lane Fox 2004a: 264–88

Rubinstein, L. 1998. 'The Athenian political perception of the *idiotes*', in P. A. Cartledge, P. C. Millett and S. von Reden, eds. *Kosmos: essays in order, conflict and community in classical Athens* (Cambridge) 125–43

Ruijgh, C. J. 2006. 'The use of the demonstratives ὅδε, οὗτος and (ἐ)κεῖνος in Sophocles', in I. J. F. de Jong and A. Rijksbaron, eds. *Sophocles and the Greek language: aspects of diction, syntax and pragmatics* (Leiden) 151–61

Russell, D. A. 1991. *An anthology of Greek prose,* Oxford

Russell, J. M. 1997. 'Sennacherib's palace without rival revisited: excavations at Nineveh and in the British Museum archives', in Parpola and Whiting 1997: 295–306

Rutherford, I. 1998. *Canons of style in the Antonine age: idea-theory in its literary context,* Oxford

Rutherford, W. G. 1881. *The new Phrynichus,* London

Salazar, C. F. 2000. *The treatment of war wounds in Graeco-Roman antiquity,* Leiden

Sandridge, N. B. 2012. *Loving humanity, learning and being honored: the foundations of leadership in Xenophon's* Education of Cyrus, Washington, DC

Sauppe, G. 1869. *Lexilogus Xenophonteus*, Leipzig

Schaefer, H. 1961. 'ΠΟΛΙΣ ΜΥΡΙΑΝΔΡΟΣ', *Historia* 10: 292–317

Schmitt, R. 2002. *Die iranischen und Iranier-Namen in den Schriften Xenophons*, Vienna

Sekunda, N. V. 2013. 'War and society in Greece', in J. B. Campbell and L. A. Tritle, eds. *The Oxford handbook of warfare in the classical world* (Oxford) 199–215

Sicking, C. M. J., and P. Stork. 1997. 'The grammar of the so-called historical present in ancient Greek', in Bakker 1997: 131–68

Slings, S. R. 1997. 'Figures of speech and their lookalikes: two further exercises in the pragmatics of the Greek sentence', in Bakker 1997: 169–214

Smith, D. L. 2012. *The rhetoric of interruption: speech-making, turn-taking, and rule-breaking in Luke-Acts and ancient Greek narrative*, Berlin and Boston

Snodgrass, A. 1964. *Early Greek armour and weapons from the end of the Bronze Age to 600 BC*, Edinburgh

1999. *Arms and armor of the Greeks*, 2nd edn, Baltimore

Soesbergen, P. G. van 1982–3. 'Colonisation as a solution to social-economic problems: a confrontation of Isocrates with Xenophon', *Anc. Soc.* 13–14: 131–45

Sommerstein, A. H., and A. J. Bayliss. 2013. *Oath and state in ancient Greece*, Berlin and Boston

Southgate, H. 1840. *Narrative of a tour through Armenia, Kurdistan, Persia, and Mesopotamia*, 2 vols., London

Spatharas, D. G. 2001. 'Patterns of argumentation in Gorgias', *Mnemosyne* 54: 393–408

Spence, I. G. 1993. *The cavalry of classical Greece: a social and military history with particular reference to Athens*, Oxford

Stein, M. H. 1984. 'Rational versus anagogic interpretation: Xenophon's dream and others', *Journal of the American Psychoanalytic Association* 32: 529–56

Sternberg, R. H. 2006. *Tragedy offstage: suffering and sympathy in ancient Athens*, Austin, TX

Stylianou, P. J. 2004. 'One *Anabasis* or two?', in Lane Fox 2004a: 68–96

Tamiolaki, M. 2010. *Liberté et esclavage chez les historiens grecs classiques. Le discours historique et politique d'Hérodote, Thucydide et Xénophon*, Paris.

Thesleff, H. 1954. *Studies on intensification in early and classical Greek*, Helsinki

Thirlwall, C. 1835–44. *A history of Greece*, 8 vols., London

Thumb, A. 1974. *Die griechische Sprache im Zeitalter des Hellenismus*, Berlin

Tritle, L. A. 1989. '*Epilektoi* at Athens', *AHB* 3: 54–9

Trundle, M. 2004. *Greek mercenaries: from the late archaic period to Alexander*, London

Tsagalis, C. C. 2002. 'Xenophon Homericus: an unnoticed loan from the *Iliad* in Xenophon's *Anabasis*', *C&M* 53: 101–21

2009. 'Names and narrative techniques in Xenophon's *Anabasis*', in J. Grethlein and A. Rengakos, eds. *Narratology and interpretation* (Berlin) 451–79

Tuplin, C. J. 1987a. 'Xenophon's exile again', in Michael Whitby, P. R. Hardie and Mary Whitby, eds. *Homo viator: classical essays for John Bramble* (Bristol and Oak Park, IL) 59–68

1987b. 'The administration of the Achaemenid empire', in I. Carradice, ed. *Coinage and administration in the Athenian and Persian empires* (London) 109–66

1991. 'Modern and ancient travellers in the Achaemenid empire: Byron's *Road to Oxiana* and Xenophon's *Anabasis*', in H. Sancisi-Weerdenburg and J. W. Drijvers, eds. *Achaemenid history* VII: *Through travellers' eyes: European travellers on the Iranian monuments* (Leiden) 37–57

1993. *The failings of empire: a reading of Xenophon* Hellenica *2.3.11–7.5.27*, Stuttgart

1997. 'Xenophon's *Cyropaedia*: education and fiction', in A. H. Sommerstein and C. Atherton, eds. *Education in Greek fiction* (Bari) 65–162

1998. 'The seasonal migration of Achaemenid kings: a report on old and new evidence', in M. Brosius and A. Kuhrt, eds. *Studies in Persian history: essays in memory of David M. Lewis* (Leiden) 63–114

2003a. 'Heroes in Xenophon's *Anabasis*', in A. Barzanò *et al.*, eds. *Modelli eroici dall'antichità alla cultura Europea* (Rome) 115–56

2003b. 'Xenophon in Media', in G. Lanfranchi, M. Roaf and R. Rollinger, eds. *Continuity of Empire (?): Assyria, Media, Persia* (Padua) 351–89

2004a. 'The Persian empire', in Lane Fox 2004a: 154–83

(ed.) 2004b. *Xenophon and his world: papers from a conference held in Liverpool in July 1999*, Stuttgart

2004c. 'Xenophon and his world: an introductory review', in Tuplin 2004b: 13–31

2004d. 'Herodotus and Xenophon's *Anabasis*', in V. Karageorghis and I. Taifacos, eds. *The world of Herodotus* (Nicosia) 351–63

(ed.) 2007. *Persian responses: political and cultural interaction with(in) the Achaemenid empire*, Swansea

2010. 'All the king's horse: in search of Achaemenid Persian cavalry', in M. Trundle and G. Fagan, eds. *New perspectives on ancient warfare* (Leiden) 101–82

2014. 'Le salut par la parole: les discours dans l'*Anabase* de Xénophon', in Pontier 2014: 69–120

Usher, S. (1969). *The historians of Greece and Rome*, London

Vivante, P. 1979. 'Rose-fingered dawn and the idea of time', *Ramus* 8: 125–36

Vlassopoulos, K. 2013. *Greeks and barbarians*, Cambridge

Wackernagel, J. 1907. *Hellenistica*, Göttingen

Wakker, G. C. 1994. *Conditions and conditionals: an investigation of ancient Greek* (Amsterdam)

Walker, A. D. 1993. '*Enargeia* and the spectator in Greek historiography', *TAPA* 123: 353–77

Walter, K. R. 1981. '"We fought alone at Marathon": historical falsification in the Attic Funeral Oration', *RhM* 184: 204–11

Waters, M. W. 2014. *Ancient Persia: a concise history of the Achaemenid empire, 550–330 BCE*, Cambridge

Wees, H. van. 2004. *Greek warfare: myths and realities*, London

Weiss, P., and N. Draskowski. 2010. 'Neue griechische Schleuderbleie: Tissaphernes und weitere Kommandeure', *Chiron* 40: 123–53

Wencis, L. 1977. '*Hypopsia* and the structure of Xenophon's *Anabasis*', *CJ* 73: 44–9

West, M. L. 1990. 'Colloquialism and naïve style in Aeschylus', in E. M. Craik, ed. *'Owls to Athens': Essays on classical subjects presented to Sir Kenneth Dover* (Oxford) 3–12

Westlake, H. D. 1987. 'Diodorus and the expedition of Cyrus', *Phoenix* 41: 241–55 (reprinted in his *Studies in Thucydides and Greek historiography*, Bristol, 1989)

Whitby, M. 2004. 'Xenophon's Ten Thousand as a fighting force', in Lane Fox 2004a: 215–42

Willi, A. 2003a. *The languages of Aristophanes: aspects of linguistic variation in classical Attic Greek*, Oxford

2003b. 'New language for a new comedy: a linguistic approach to Aristophanes' *Plutus*', *Cambridge Classical Journal* 49: 40–73

2010. 'Attic as the language of the Classics', in Caragounis 2010: 101–18

2012. '"We speak Peloponnesian": tradition and linguistic identity in post-classical Sicilian literature', in O. Tribulato, ed. *Language and linguistic contact in ancient Sicily* (Cambridge) 265–88

Wood, N. 1964. 'Xenophon's theory of leadership', *C&M* 25: 33–66

Wooten, C. W. 1987. *Hermogenes'* On types of style, Chapel Hill, NC

INDEXES

1 GENERAL INDEX

Numbers in italics are page references to the Introduction; other figures refer to the Commentary by chapter (of Book 3) and section. Bold numbers refer to a note with basic information about a character.

2 GREEK WORDS AND PHRASES